THE NEW BRITISH CONSTITUTION

The last decade has seen radical changes in the way we are governed. Reforms such as the Human Rights Act and devolution have led to the replacement of one constitutional order by another. This book is the first to describe and analyse Britain's new constitution, asking why it was that the old system, seemingly hallowed by time, came under challenge, and why it is being replaced.

The Human Rights Act and the devolution legislation have the character of fundamental law. They in practice limit the rights of Westminster as a sovereign parliament, and establish a constitution which is quasi-federal in nature. The old constitution emphasised the sovereignty of Parliament. The new constitution, by contrast, emphasises the separation of powers, both territorially and at the centre of government.

The aim of constitutional reformers has been to improve the quality of government. But the main weakness of the new constitution is that it does little to secure more popular involvement in politics. We are in the process of becoming a constitutional state, but not a popular constitutional state. The next phase of constitutional reform, therefore, is likely to involve the creation of new forms of democratic engagement, so that our constitutional forms come to be more congruent with the social and political forces of the age. The end-point of this piecemeal process might well be a fully codified or written constitution which declares that power stems not from the Queen-in Parliament, but, instead, as in so many constitutions, from 'We, the People'.

The old British constitution was analysed by Bagehot and Dicey. In this book Vernon Bogdanor charts the significance of what is coming to replace it.

The New British Constitution

Vernon Bogdanor

Professor of Government, Oxford University

·HART·
PUBLISHING

OXFORD AND PORTLAND, OREGON
2009

Published in North America (US and Canada) by
Hart Publishing
c/o International Specialized Book Services
920 NE 58th Avenue, Suite 300
Portland, OR 97213-3786
USA
Tel: +1 503 287 3093 or toll-free: (1) 800 944 6190
Fax: +1 503 280 8832
E-mail: orders@isbs.com
Website: http://www.isbs.com

Hart Publishing Ltd, 16C Worcester Place, Oxford, OX1 2JW
Telephone: +44 (0)1865 517530 Fax: +44 (0)1865 510710
E-mail: mail@hartpub.co.uk
Website: http://www.hartpub.co.uk

British Library Cataloguing in Publication Data
Data Available

ISBN: 978-1-84113-149-8 (Hardback)
978-1-84113-671-4 (Paperback)

Typeset by Hope Services, Abingdon
Printed and bound in Great Britain by
TJ International Ltd, Padstow, Cornwall

'When we mean to build,
We first survey the plot, then draw the model,
And, when we see the figure of the house,
Then must we rate the cost of the erection;
Which, if we find outweighs ability,
What do we then, but draw anew the model
In fewer offices, or, at least, desist
To build at all? Much more, in this great work
(Which is, almost, to pluck a kingdom down,
And set another up) should we survey
The plot of situation, and the model;
Consent upon a sure foundation;
Question surveyors, know our own estate,
How able such a work to undergo——'.

Shakespeare,
Henry IV, Part II

'I speak of those spiritual things that we call institutions'.

Maitland.

Contents

Acknowledgments

I have accumulated all too many debts of gratitude while working on this book. I owe particular thanks to the following for reading and commenting on either the whole or parts of the manuscript: Chris Ballinger, Denis Baranger, Nick Barber, Anthony Bradley, Nicola Brewer, Sir Brian Briscoe, Lord Butler of Brockwell, Anne Davies, Catherine Donnelly, Emma Douglas, David Feldman, Alicia Hinarejos, George Jones, Harry Judge, Guy Lodge, James Mitchell, Peter Riddell, Rabinder Singh QC, Michael Steed, Alex Stevenson, Wilf Stevenson, Andrew Stockley, Sandra Sullivan, Richard Thorpe, Stefan Vogenauer, Sir Michael Wheeler-Booth, Barry Winetrobe, and Derrick Wyatt, QC. These kind friends and colleagues have all improved the text to its very great benefit by exposing numerous confusions of thought and infelicities of style, but they are not to be implicated in my arguments, still less in my errors.

I am grateful to Alison Young for allowing me to see an advance copy of her fine book, *Parliamentary Sovereignty and the Human Rights Act*, which was published by Hart in 2008. Much of the material in this book was first delivered as lectures at Gresham College between 2004 and 2007. I am grateful to the College for electing me to its Chair of Law and to Barbara Anderson, the Acedemic Registrar, for her help and kindness.

Parts of chapters 3 and 4 of this book appeared, in different form, in an article entitled 'The New British Constitution' in *The Law Quarterly Review* (2004), and I am grateful to the editor, Francis Reynolds, for allowing me to use material from it. Parts of chapter 9 appeared in an article, written jointly with Stefan Vogenauer, entitled 'Enacting the British Constitution' in *Public Law* (2008). I am grateful to the editor, Andrew Le Sueur, and to Stefan Vogenauer, for allowing me to use some of the arguments from this article.

I would like to thank Pat Spight and Wendy Williams for their skilful secretarial help which went far beyond the call of duty.

But, above all, I would like to thank Sonia Robertson for her inspiration and encouragement. Without her support this book would never have been completed.

Vernon Bogdanor
January 2009.

---

* References to parliamentary debates are to Hansard 5th series until November 1981, and the 6th series for all debates after that.

Introduction

The New British Constitution has a large but limited theme—the creation of a new British constitution and the demise of the old, the replacement of one constitutional order by another. This shift comprises far more than a moving of the institutional furniture, something that would be of interest only to lawyers and students of government. For constitutions are concerned with the grandest and most important of issues—the relationship between the individual and the state, the conditions of political order, and the methods by which men and women are ruled. These matters are of particular importance to us in Britain. We have been living through an unprecedented period of constitutional change, an era of constitutional reform which began in 1997 and shows no sign of coming to an end. The aim of the constitutional reformers has been to improve the quality of democracy, and one of the questions which *The New British Constitution* seeks to answer is whether they have been successful in achieving this aim.

The main purpose, however, of *The New British Constitution* is not to evaluate but to describe. The central argument of the book is that the era of constitutional reform, together with Britain's entry in 1973 into the European Communities has had the effect of replacing one constitution, a constitution whose origins lie far in the past, with a new constitution. This new constitution is as yet incomplete and its final outlines are at present only partially discernible. The description, therefore, cannot be complete because the new constitution is not yet complete. The time is not yet ripe for a final analysis. But it is perhaps possible to chart the path that has been taken and to lay down guidelines which might help us understand the direction of future change.

Britain's traditional constitutional arrangements—'the old constitution'—were first analysed by two great nineteenth century thinkers. The first was a journalist of genius, Walter Bagehot, who lived from 1826 to 1877, and was editor of *The Economist* from 1860 until his death. The second was the constitutional lawyer, A V Dicey, who lived from 1835 to 1922, and was Vinerian Professor of English Law at Oxford University from 1882 to 1909. Bagehot published his most important book, *The English Constitution*, in 1867, the year of the second Reform Act, an Act which provided for male household suffrage. But the book had first been published in serial form between 1865 and 1867 in the *Fortnightly Review*. A second edition of *The English Constitution* appeared in 1872, with a long introduction seeking to analyse the consequences of the Reform Act. The title of Bagehot's book is of course curious. There had been no strictly **English** constitution since 1536, when England was joined with Wales. The new parliament so created was in turn superseded by a British Parliament after the Union with Scotland of 1707, which provided for a new constitution of Great Britain; but Bagehot's approach, like that of so many of his contemporaries, and indeed of most constitutional analysts before the rise of Irish and of Scottish nationalism, was distinctly Anglo-centric. There is hardly any mention of Ireland, Scotland or Wales in Bagehot's book.

Bagehot sought to analyse the nature of parliamentary government as it worked in the country which had been its home. 'No one else', so it has been said, 'has written with such insight about England's supreme invention of parliamentary government'.[1] Bagehot argued that the British system of government was characterised, not as John Stuart Mill had suggested in his book, *Considerations on Representative Government*, (1861) by a separation of powers, but by 'the close union, the nearly complete fusion of the executive and legislative powers'.[2] This fusion of powers of the Cabinet and Parliament was, for Bagehot, the essence of parliamentary government. Bagehot's analysis has proved enormously influential and has attained classic status. Yet it was in many respects misleading and, as we shall show in chapter 11, recent developments have underlined its irrelevance to the understanding of the modern constitution. Many have admired *The English Constitution*. Too few have analysed it critically.

Dicey's book, *An Introduction to the Study of Law of the Constitution*, first published in 1885, remains, like *The English Constitution*, a classic work. Like *The English Constitution*, it is a highly readable classic. But Dicey was trying to do something quite different from Bagehot. *The English Constitution* seeks to analyse the relationships between institutions. *An Introduction to the Study of the Law of the Constitution* analyses the legal principles underlying their working, the conceptual structure of the constitution. Dicey isolated three fundamental features— the sovereignty of Parliament, the rule of law, and the role of constitutional conventions. Of these, the most important was the sovereignty of Parliament, which was 'from a legal point of view the dominant characteristic of our political institutions'.[3] This principle meant that Parliament had 'the right to make or unmake any law whatever; and . . . no person or body is recognised by the law . . . as having a right to override or set aside the legislation of Parliament'. If this principle were to be taken seriously, there could clearly be no room in Britain for a written or codified constitution superior to the ordinary law of the land. If Parliament is sovereign, then the British constitution can be summed up in just eight words—what the Queen in Parliament enacts is law.

Dicey's work has been as at least as influential as Bagehot's. 'Dicey's word', it has been suggested 'almost served as a surrogate written constitution'.[4] Judges and constitutional lawyers still cite his principles, and, in particular, the sovereignty of Parliament, even if only sometimes to react against them. Over one hundred and

---

[1] Norman St. John-Stevas, 'Editor's Preface' in *The Collected Works of Walter Bagehot*, vol 5 (London, The Economist, 1974) 30.

[2] 'The English Constitution' in *Collected Works*, vol 5, 210.

[3] A V Dicey, *Introduction to the Study of the Law of the Constitution* (10th edn, London, Macmillan, 1959) 39.

[4] Preface to the sixth edition of J Jowell and D Oliver (eds) *The Changing Constitution* (Oxford, OUP, 2007) v.

twenty years after it was first published, *The Law of the Constitution* remains a living work. Frequently criticised, it has not yet been superseded.

The New British Constitution suggests, however, that Dicey's analysis, which perhaps offered a reasonably accurate account of Britain's constitutional arrangements in the past, has been made irrelevant by the constitutional reforms since 1997, and by Britain's entry into the European Communities in 1973. We are now in transition from a system based on parliamentary sovereignty to one based on the sovereignty of a constitution, albeit a constitution that is inchoate, indistinct and still in large part uncodified. But we are gradually becoming a constitutional state. And, perhaps, peering into the distance, we can perceive, in dim outline, the vision of a state based, not upon parliamentary sovereignty, but upon popular sovereignty, upon the sovereignty of the people. Britain would then have finally accepted the full implications of a commitment to democratic government.

The New British Constitution, then, seeks to analyse a changing constitution. The first part outlines the old constitution, the constitution of Bagehot and Dicey, and then considers why it came under strain. The central part of the book describes the main elements of the new constitution: the Human Rights Act, the cornerstone of the new constitution; the devolution legislation, which has turned Britain from a unitary into a quasi-federal state; the new arrangements for the executive and legislature which have been needed to accommodate government without a majority in Scotland; reform of the House of Lords, which has radically altered the role of the upper house; the new government of London, which has given Britain the first directly elected mayor in her history; and the referendum, which has been used to validate many of the constitutional reforms, but which, before 1975 when it was first employed, was regarded by many as unconstitutional. These reforms have strengthened the case for Britain to follow almost every other democracy by adopting a written or codified constitution. The final part of the book seeks to peer into the future—to the prospects of a new localism, to the nature of a constitutional state, and finally, to the new opportunities for democratic participation which could turn Britain into a popular constitutional state.

The conclusion emphasises that the constitution so brilliantly analysed by Bagehot and Dicey no longer exists. What, then, has replaced it? No definitive answer is, as yet, possible, since the construction of the new constitution is still far from complete. But there are hints and signposts pointing to the direction of change.

The New British Constitution, then, is not intended as a history of the future. But it is perhaps the essential prologue to such a history.

Part I

The Old Constitution

1

A Peculiar Constitution

I

'WE ENGLISHMEN', DECLARES Mr Podsnap in Charles Dickens's novel, *Our Mutual Friend*, 'are Very Proud of our Constitution . . . It was Bestowed Upon Us by providence. No other Country is so Favoured as this Country'.

What Dickens intended as satire seemed to many, until the second half of the twentieth century, no more than sober realism. Mr Podsnap's view was to be echoed not only in Britain but also by observers in other countries, who studied the British constitution to discover the secret of successful government, the secret of how to combine freedom with stability.

At the beginning of the twentieth century, in 1908, an American scholar, A Lawrence Lowell, professor of government at Harvard University, published a two-volume work entitled *The Government of England* (sic). In the preface, he declared that:

> 'The typical Englishman believes that his government is incomparably the best in the world. It is the thing above all others that he is proud of. He does not, of course, always agree with the course of policy pursued but he is certain that the general form of government is well-nigh perfect.'[1]

Forty-five years later, in 1953, a visiting American academic, attending a dinner party at a British university, was surprised to hear 'an eminent man of the left to say—in utter seriousness—that the British Constitution was "as nearly perfect as any human institution could be"'. He was rather more surprised that 'No one even thought it amusing'.[2] In 1965, another professor from Harvard University, Samuel Beer, concluded his book, *Modern British Politics*, with the following words:

> 'Happy the country in which consensus and conflict are ordered in a dialectic that makes of the political arena at once a market of interests and a forum for debate of fundamental moral concerns'.[3]

---

[1] A L Lowell, *The Government of England* vol 2 (London, Macmillan, 1908) 507.
[2] E Shils, 'British Intellectuals in the Mid-Twentieth Century', *Encounter*, April 1955, reprinted in Shils *The Intellectuals and the Powers* (Chicago, University of Chicago Press, 1972) 135.
[3] S H Beer, *Modern British Politics* (London, Faber, 1965) 390.

These American professors were Anglophiles. Yet, in April 1960, a similar tribute was paid by someone who had never been accused of being an Anglophile, the French president Charles de Gaulle, speaking in Westminster,

'Your outstanding role in the midst of the storm is owed not only to your profound national qualities, but also to the value of your institutions. At the worst of moments, who among you challenged the legitimacy and authority of the State . . . With self-assurance, almost without being aware of it, you operate in freedom a secure, stable political system. So strong are your traditions and loyalties in the political field that your government is quite naturally endowed with cohesion and permanence; that your parliament has, throughout each term of office, an assured majority; that this government and this majority are permanently in harmony; in short, that your executive and legislative powers are balanced and work together by definition as it were . . . Thus, lacking meticulously worked out constitutional texts, but by virtue of an unchallengeable general consent, you find the means, on each occasion, to ensure the efficient functioning of democracy without incurring the excessive criticism of the ambitious; or the punctilious blame of purists. Well! I can tell you that this England, which keeps itself in order while practising respect for the liberties of all, inspires trust in France'.[4]

Yet, during the 1960s, Mr Podsnap began to go out of favour. Britain's seemingly insoluble economic difficulties were giving rise to a debate about the adequacy of her institutions and even about her much-admired constitution. That debate was to increase in intensity during the following decades, and was not stilled even when the country moved into calmer economic waters in the 1990s. Indeed the great period of constitutional reform in Britain occurred after the election of Tony Blair's Labour government in 1997, at a time when the economy was buoyant. But the wide-ranging reforms of the Blair era would hardly have been introduced had the British people been as satisfied with their institutions as they seem to have been in Mr Podsnap's time. One of the central themes of British history during the second half of the twentieth century seems to be a striking loss of national self-confidence; and this was reflected in a loss of confidence in our institutions and in our constitutional arrangements. 'If you are always altering your house,' Bagehot points out, 'it is a sign either that you have a bad house, or that you have an excessively restless disposition—there is something wrong somewhere'.[5]

The alterations to the house have certainly been extensive. The years since 1997 have been marked by an unprecedented and, almost certainly, uncompleted series of constitutional changes. It is worth listing the main reforms.

1. The independence of the Bank of England from government in monetary policy.
2. Referendums, under the Referendum (Scotland and Wales) Act, 1997, on devolution to Scotland and Wales.
3. The Scotland Act, 1998, providing for a directly elected Scottish Parliament, and with a Scottish Executive responsible to it on devolved matters.

---

[4] Quoted in C de Gaulle, *Discours et Messages. Vol III: Avec le renouveau 1958–1962* (Plon, 1970) 179–81.
[5] W Bagehot, *Collected Works*, vol VII, 226.

4. The Government of Wales Act, 1998, providing for a directly elected National Assembly in Wales.
5. The Northern Ireland Act, 1998, providing for a referendum on a partnership form of government and devolution in Northern Ireland.
6. The establishment, under the Northern Ireland Act, 1998, following the successful outcome of the referendum, of a directly elected Assembly in Northern Ireland.
7. A referendum, under the Greater London Authority (Referendum) Act, 1998, on a directly elected mayor and assembly for London.
8. The introduction of proportional representation for the elections to the devolved bodies in Scotland, Wales, Northern Ireland and the London assembly.
9. The European Parliamentary Elections Act, 1998, providing for the introduction of proportional representation for elections to the European Parliament.
10. The Local Government Act, 2000, requiring local authorities to abandon the committee system and providing for the possibility of directly elected mayors, following referendums.
11. The Human Rights Act, 1998, requiring government and all other public bodies to comply with the provisions of the European Convention on Human Rights.
12. The House of Lords Act, 1999, providing for the removal of all but 92 of the hereditary peers from the House of Lords, intended as the first phase of a wider reform of the Lords.
13. The Freedom of Information Act, 2000, providing for a statutory right of access to government information.
14. The Political Parties, Elections and Referendums Act, 2000, requiring the registration of political parties, controlling donations to political parties and national campaign expenditure and providing for the establishment of an Electoral Commission to oversee elections and to advise on improvements in electoral procedure.
15. The Constitutional Reform Act, 2005, providing for the Lord Chief Justice, rather than the Lord Chancellor, to become head of the judiciary, depriving the Lord Chancellor of his role as presiding officer of the House of Lords, and establishing a new Supreme Court, whose members, unlike the law lords, will not be members of the House of Lords.

This is a formidable list. It is scarcely an exaggeration to suggest that a new constitution is in the process of being created before our eyes. But, because the reforms have been introduced in a piecemeal, unplanned and pragmatic way, rather than in one fell swoop, we have hardly noticed the extent of the change. It is much easier to notice change in the United States, or indeed in any country with a codified constitution than it is in Britain, with its peculiar, uncodified constitution. In a country with a codified constitution, the framework must be visibly and noticeably altered either by an amendment to the constitution or through a decision by judges which in effect re-interprets the constitution. In Britain, by contrast, the framework can be gradually adapted to create a wholly different constitution almost without anyone noticing.

We are as a nation notoriously uninterested in our constitution. The debate since the 1970s has been conducted primarily amongst the elite—politicians, academics, lawyers, judges and journalists. The people have, on the whole, been little interested, and perhaps even unaware of the wide-ranging nature of the constitutional changes that have been introduced, except of course in Northern Ireland, which remains the great exception to most generalizations about British government.

When, during the 1997 election campaign, the British people were asked, by the opinion research organisation, MORI, to rate the priority of various issues, they put constitutional issues 14th out of 14. Little had changed by the time of the 2001 general election despite the plethora of constitutional reforms in Blair's first term. Just 5% thought that the constitution was an important issue in determining their vote, as compared with, for example, 61% who thought that health care was the most important issue, 53% education and 24% asylum-seekers. Even in Scotland, where there had been some clamour for devolution, only 8% thought that either the constitution or devolution would 'be very important . . . in helping . . . decide which party to vote for'.[6] The Scots who favoured devolution did so for instrumental reasons—that it was likely to make Scotland richer, improve public services, etc.—rather than because they favoured self-government. They saw constitutional reform as a means rather than an end. In the words of two Scottish social scientists, 'Most have expectations that it will make a difference to their lives in terms of the services they want it to provide. Those are the grounds on which its effectiveness is likely to be judged, rather than as an affective expression of nationhood'.[7] From this point of view, the movement for Scottish devolution should be sharply distinguished from the Irish demand for Home Rule in the nineteenth century, or for the movement for colonial independence in the twentieth, for these were demands for self-government regardless of the economic cost. The people of India or of Kenya would not have been deterred from demanding independence by being told that it would make them poorer.

Turnout figures for the various referendums confirmed that, with the exception of Northern Ireland, devolution did not arouse massive enthusiasm. The turnout figures were:

Scottish devolution referendum 1997:	60.2%
Welsh devolution referendum 1997:	50.1%
Referendum on the Belfast Agreement 1998:	80.0%
Referendum on a directly elected London mayor and Authority 1998:	34.0%

[6] R Worcester and R Mortimore, *Explaining Labour's Landslide* (London, Politico's, 1999) 152; R Worcester and R Mortimore, *Explaining Labour's Second Landslide* (London, Politico's, 2001) 29, 228.

[7] P Surridge and D Crone, 'The 1997 Scottish referendum vote' in B Taylor and K Thomson (eds) *Scotland and Wales: Nations Again?* (Cardiff, University of Wales Press, 1999) 52.

In Wales, only half of those eligible could be bothered to vote. In London, despite apparently widespread criticism that the capital had been left without proper representation since 1986, when the Greater London Council had been abolished, just over one-third of those eligible voted.

The British people remain obstinately concerned with the substance of politics, not its procedures. That may perhaps be a sign of political maturity. What cannot be doubted is that constitutional issues do not lie very high on most people's list of priorities.

Many of the constitutional reforms have been validated by referendum. That is remarkable, for, until 1975, when Britain held her first, and so far her only, national referendum, this instrument was widely held to be unconstitutional. In 1964, a standard work on British government remarked, 'It has occasionally been proposed that a referendum might be held on a particular issue, but the proposals do not ever appear to have been taken seriously'.[8] Yet, there can be little doubt that the referendum has now become an accepted part of the constitution.

A second, hardly noticed but momentous feature of the reforms, is that it has now come to be accepted that elections to any body other than the House of Commons or a local authority should be by proportional representation. It was generally agreed that the devolved bodies in Scotland, Wales and Northern Ireland, and also regional bodies in England, if created, should be elected by proportional representation. This is a quite unexpected development. Until the 1970s, it was generally assumed that the plurality or 'first-past-the-post' electoral system was the natural one for Britain to use. Opposition to this system was confined almost wholly to the Liberal Party whose arguments could easily be dismissed as special pleading. But, by 2009, there were no fewer than four electoral systems in operation in Britain in addition to the first-past-the-post system. These systems are:

1. The single transferable vote method of proportional representation used for all elections in Northern Ireland, except elections to the House of Commons, and for elections to local authorities in Scotland.
2. A system of proportional representation based on the German method of voting, sometimes called the 'additional member' system, used for elections to the Scottish Parliament, the National Assembly of Wales and the Greater London Assembly.
3. The regional list method of proportional representation used for elections to the European Parliament.
4. The supplementary vote used in elections for all directly elected mayors, including the mayor of London.[9]

---

[8] A H Birch, *Representative and Responsible Government: An Essay on the British Constitution* (London, Allen and Unwin, 1964) 227.

[9] For short descriptions of these various systems, see chapter 3 of V Bogdanor, *Power and the People: A Guide to Constitutional Reform* (London, Victor Gollancz, 1997).

At the beginning of the twentieth century Britain enjoyed a uniform electoral system, the plurality or the first-past-the-post system, but a diversified franchise, there being no less than seven different ways in which a man could qualify for the vote.[10] By the end of the twentieth century, by contrast, the qualification for the franchise was uniform, but there were a wide variety of electoral systems. An elector in London would use four different electoral systems. In voting for a Member of Parliament she would use first-past-the-post; in voting for a mayor of London she would use the supplementary vote; in voting for the Greater London Assembly she would use a variant of the German system of proportional representation; and in voting for the European Parliament she would use regional list proportional representation.

II

We have, then, since 1997, been engaged in a process, by no means yet complete, of constitutional reform. But how, it may be asked, can we reform our constitution when, notoriously, we have no constitution? For the first feature that strikes even the most casual observer of British government is that Britain has no constitution. What can 'constitutional reform' mean in a country without a constitution?

To answer this conundrum we need to distinguish between two different meanings of the term 'constitution'. The **first** and most obvious meaning of the term refers to a selection of the most important legal rules regulating the government and embodied in a document promulgated at a particular moment of time, such as the American constitution of 1787 or the French Fifth Republic constitution of 1958. In this sense, of course, Britain has no constitution, and is one of just three democracies not to have such a constitution, the other two being New Zealand and Israel. Someone who wishes to discover the basic rules of the American system of government can easily obtain a copy of a document outlining these rules—the American constitution—and can, within less than half an hour, gain a reasonable idea of the basic principles of American government, and the rights which individuals living under its jurisdiction enjoy. The American constitution forms an excellent starting-point for civics lessons in the United States, and no doubt encourages Americans to think about their politics from a constitutional perspective. Americans, it is often suggested, think more about their rights and duties, and understand more about how their government works than we in Britain precisely because they have a codified constitution. In Britain, by contrast, we have no such document, and therefore no obvious framework within which to discuss the rules of government and the rights of the individual.

There is, however, a **second** sense of the term 'constitution'. In this second sense of the term, we in Britain, together with anyone living in an organised society,

---

[10] See J Curtice, 'The Electoral System' in V Bogdanor (ed) *The British Constitution in the Twentieth Century* (Oxford, OUP, 2003) esp 484–86.

most certainly possess a constitution. A society is distinguished from a mere conglomeration of individuals in that it comprises a group of people bound together by rules; and a constitution is nothing more than a collection of the most important rules prescribing the distribution of power between the institutions of government—legislature, executive and judiciary—and between the individual and the state. There is no inherent reason why these rules should be written down and brought together in one single document as they are in most modern democracies. But there must, in every society, by definition, be a constitution in this second sense of the term, whether that constitution is written down or not. When Mr Podsnap declared that our constitution was bestowed upon us by providence, it was this second sense of the term that he had in mind.

Britain is peculiar, then, not in lacking a constitution—for there is a sense in which every organised society has a constitution—but in lacking a written constitution. But that perhaps is a misleading way of putting the point. It is not as if in Britain the rules describing the distribution of governmental powers and the rights of the individual are passed down from generation to generation by word of mouth. Many, if not most, of our rules about the working of government are most certainly written down, in the form either of statutes, or judicial decisions. The Parliament Acts of 1911 and 1949, for example, regulating the powers of the House of Lords, and the Constitutional Reform Act of 2005, regulating the role of the Lord Chancellor, the judiciary and appointments to it, are certainly part of the British constitution; and they are of course written down.

The real difference between Britain and almost every other democracy is that in Britain the various constitutional rules have not been brought together in a single document. They are not codified, but scattered. Britain is distinctive, together with New Zealand and Israel, in that she has an uncodified rather than a codified constitution. Many would say that this arrangement is now anachronistic, and that it is time the British fell into line and produced a codified constitution. The Liberal Democrats have long held this view; and Gordon Brown, both as Chancellor of the Exchequer and as Prime Minister, has called for a debate on whether Britain should have a codified constitution. To produce a codified constitution, however, is no simple task, as we shall discover in chapter 9.

This book, however, is concerned not just with the arguments for and against producing a codified constitution, but with constitutional reform more generally. When we talk of constitutional reform, we are concerned, clearly, with the second meaning of the term 'constitution'—the rules regulating the system of government and the rules regulating the relationship between government and the individual. This second and broader sense of 'constitution' can be defined as 'the collection of rules regulating a country's system of government'. When we speak of the constitution of a country, it is often this second and broader meaning that we have in mind. When, for example, we say that the constitution of a country is democratic, we generally mean that its system of government is democratic. It is in this, broader sense, that we have been speaking, above, of 'constitutional matters' and 'the constitution' in Britain.

We have thus isolated two different meanings of the term 'constitution'. The first refers to a written instrument containing the basic and most important rules of government. The second refers to the rules, whether or not written down, which regulate government—and in this sense every society, by definition, has a constitution. It is this second sense of constitution which we shall be primarily discussing in this book.

III

It is worth beginning, however, by asking why it is that Britain remains almost unique amongst modern democracies in not having a codified constitution. We enjoy constitutional government, so we believe, but we enjoy it in the absence of a codified constitution. Perhaps part of the reason why we are so uninterested in constitutional matters, in our broader sense of the term, is because we do not have a codified constitution, a constitution in the first and narrower sense of the term.

There seems, at first sight, no obvious reason why we should not have a codified constitution, why our most important rules about government and the rights of the individual should not be brought together into a single document as they are in almost every other democracy. The exercise of drafting a British Constitution, of bringing together the scattered material into a single document, has become a staple of university seminars on constitutional matters; and, from time to time, interested experts produce draft constitutions. In 1993, for example, a think-tank sympathetic to the Labour Party, the Institute for Public Policy Research, published a highly detailed *Constitution for the United Kingdom*. The present writer remembers, many years ago, as an undergraduate, participating in an Oxford seminar whose purpose was precisely to draft a British constitution. The seminar was led by the doyen of constitutional scholars, K C Wheare, whose book, *Modern Constitutions*, published by Oxford University Press in 1951, has become a modern classic. In the autumn of 2006 the present writer decided to resurrect this seminar, together with a colleague, Stefan Vogenauer, Professor of Comparative Law at the University of Oxford. We held weekly meetings at which small groups of students, both graduates and undergraduates, each week prepared drafts of part of the constitution, eg the legislature, the judiciary, human rights, for discussion and amendment. The version which was eventually agreed can be found in a book edited by Christopher Bryant, MP, entitled *Towards a New Constitutional Settlement*, published by the Smith Institute in 2007, and also in the *Political Quarterly*, 2007, to accompany an article entitled 'Should Britain Have a Written Constitution?' by Vernon Bogdanor, Tarunabh Khaitan and Stefan Vogenauer.[11]

The reasons why we lack a codified constitution lie deep in British history. They relate both to our evolution as a society and to the way in which we understand government. The reasons are both historical and conceptual.

---

[11] See also V Bogdanor and S Vogenauer 'Enacting a British Constitution: Some Problems' (2008) *Public Law*.

Almost all codified constitutions are enacted to mark a new beginning. They are enacted when states attain their freedom, either from an external ruler, or from an old regime. The constitution marks the occasion on which the state is constituted. It signifies a fresh start, as, for example, with Italy in 1948 and Germany in 1949, which drew up new constitutions following defeat in war and the destruction of the previous Fascist and National Socialist regimes. This was also the case with India whose constitution was enacted in 1950 shortly after achieving independence from British rule. In Britain, however, there has seemed no such obvious break in our constitutional development since the seventeenth century. There is, admittedly, a sense in which Britain may be said to have begun in 1707 when the Acts of Union between England and Scotland created the new state of Great Britain. Then, in 1801, the Union with Ireland created the United Kingdom of Great Britain and Ireland. This in turn became in 1921, when all but six of the Irish counties seceded to form the Irish Free State, the United Kingdom of Great Britain and Northern Ireland, which remains the official title of the British state.

But these dates, 1707, 1801 and 1921, important though they are, hardly have the character of defining moments in the creation of a new state, as 1776 does in the history of the United States, or 1789 in the history of France. Admittedly, the Acts of Union of 1707 created a new Parliament, the Parliament of Great Britain. But this new Parliament was located in Westminster, as the old one had been, and, in practice it took on almost all of the characteristics of the old English parliament. In theory, no doubt, 1707, 1801 or 1921, could have been seen as 'constitutional moments', to be marked by the enactment of a constitution, and there are certainly those in Scotland who regard the Acts of Union as a constitutional document. In practice, however, the fundamental characteristics of the state remained unchanged and the English, at least, have felt little need for a codified constitution.[12]

The constitution has thus remained uncodified precisely because there has never appeared to be a genuine 'constitutional moment', and that is because there is a sense in which England, the core of the United Kingdom, never began. It is hardly possible to fix a date at which England began as a modern state. There has been no formal breach in the historical continuity of England since 1689, when James II was deposed. Even then, the breach was masked by the use of traditional forms since it was held that James, rather than being deposed, had voluntarily 'abdicated'. There has been no fundamental change in the nature of the English state since the time of Oliver Cromwell in the seventeenth century, and the brief period of republican rule which lasted from 1649 to 1660. In 1653 Cromwell drew up a codified constitution, an Agreement of the People, which can be regarded as the first codified constitution in modern European history. Yet, the brief republican interlude was followed by what was significantly called the Restoration, not a new beginning, but the return of a traditional institution, the monarchy. It is precisely because there has been no sharp break in our constitutional history since the

---

[12] These issues are discussed in more detail in the first chapter of my book, *Devolution in the United Kingdom* (Oxford, OUP, 1999).

seventeenth century that, unlike almost every other democracy, we have felt neither the desire nor the need to enact a constitution.

The emphasis on evolutionary adaptability was strengthened in the nineteenth century by the Great Reform Act of 1832. The Acts of Union with Scotland in 1707, with Ireland in 1801, and the Anglo-Irish treaty of 1921 defined the boundaries of the British state. The Great Reform Act went far to define its character. It was passed because the governing elite was prepared to respond in conciliatory fashion to a widespread popular demand. Perhaps 1832 is the nearest that Britain has ever come to a constitutional moment. The Great Reform Act seemed to show that the British constitution developed through a process of evolution, and the Act also served to reinforce the supremacy and centrality of Parliament in her political arrangements. It showed, as Macaulay stressed, 'that the means of effecting every improvement which the constitution requires may be found with the constitution itself'.[13] It is easy to understand how, in the later nineteenth century, both Bagehot and Dicey saw the supremacy of Parliament as lying at the heart of the evolutionary British constitution.

It was suggested above that we took so little interest in constitutional matters because we did not have an enacted constitution. But perhaps the truth is the other way round. One of the reasons why we have no enacted constitution is that we have had so little interest in constitutional matters, and perhaps that in turn is because our constitutional history has been on the whole, with the striking and significant exception of Northern Ireland, peaceful and evolutionary; we have felt little need, therefore, to interest ourselves in constitutional developments.

We have seen that the classical analysis of the legal principles of the British constitution was made by A V Dicey in his book, *An Introduction to the Study of the Law of the Constitution*. But, in addition to his published work, Dicey left unpublished lectures on comparative constitutions. In these unpublished lectures Dicey argued that the British Constitution was unique in being an 'historic' constitution. By this he meant not only that it was very old, but also that it was original and spontaneous, a product of historical development rather than deliberate design.[14] This is a view that has been echoed by many other writers on British government. In a book published in 1904 entitled *The Governance of England* (sic), the author, Sidney Low, wrote that 'Other constitutions have been built; that of England has been allowed to grow . . .'. Our constitution, Low declared, was based not on codified rules but on tacit understandings, although, as he ruefully remarked, 'the understandings are not always understood'.[15]

But, in addition to this historical reason why we do not have a codified constitution, there is also a conceptual reason. It is that the fundamental, perhaps the only principle at the basis of our system of government, has been the sovereignty

---

[13] T B Macaulay, *The History of England from the Accession of James the Second*, vol II (London, Longman, 1861) 669.

[14] Dicey's unpublished lectures on the Comparative Study of Constitutions are held in the Codrington Library, All Souls College, Oxford: MS 323 LR 6 b 13.

[15] S Low, *The Governance of England* (London, T Fisher Unwin, 1904) 12.

of Parliament, the idea that Parliament can legislate as it chooses and that there can be no superior authority to Parliament. But if Parliament is sovereign then there is no point in having a codified constitution. Part of the purpose of such a constitution is to limit the power of the legislature. Almost all constitutions demarcate provisions which are fundamental, and which are included in the constitution, from provisions which are not fundamental. The fundamental laws can usually be amended only through some special procedure, over and above that of a simple majority vote in the legislature. In the United States, for example, constitutional change requires the support of two-thirds of Congress and three-quarters of the states. In some constitutions, there are provisions which are regarded as so fundamental that they cannot be amended at all. Certain provisions of the German constitution—the basic principles of the federal system, and the basic rights laid down in Articles 1 to 20—cannot be amended at all. In countries with enacted constitutions, it is normally not Parliament, the legislature, which is supreme, but the constitution. Article VI, clause 2 of the American Constitution, for example, specifically provides that the constitution is 'the supreme Law of the Land'.

In Britain however there has, until recently at least, been no such thing as fundamental law. In the nineteenth century a distinguished French observer of Britain, the political theorist Alexis de Tocqueville, commented in his book *Democracy in America*, that, in Britain 'the Parliament has an acknowledged right to modify the constitution; as, therefore, the constitution may undergo perpetual changes, it does not in reality exist; the Parliament is at once a legislative and constituent assembly'.[16] It would, therefore, have been futile to attempt to demarcate any particular selection of provisions which should enjoy a special status as 'constitutional'. The British constitution was, in a sense, indeterminate. There was no clear-cut boundary between what was constitutional and what was not. Were the rules regulating the trade unions or race relations, for example, part of the constitution? The website of the House of Lords Constitution Committee declares that 'The Committee's remit is broad, because . . . Any public bill may have constitutional implications, whether these arise directly from new government policies or indirectly from other changes in the law'. There seems no obvious criterion for deciding what is constitutional and what is not, and no authoritative selection of provisions which could be called 'the constitution'. In chapter 27 of Anthony Trollope's novel, *The Prime Minister*, the Duchess of Omnium declares that 'Anything is constitutional or anything is unconstitutional just as you choose to look at it'. 'It was clear', Trollope continues, 'that the Duchess had really studied the subject carefully'.

The British Constitution could thus be summed up in just eight words: "What the Queen in Parliament enacts is law." It was because the sovereignty of Parliament has been seen as the central principle of the British Constitution that it appeared pointless to draw up a codified constitution. Thus the arduous activity of selecting those provisions thought to be of 'constitutional significance' seemed,

---

[16] A de Tocqueville, *De la Democratie en Amérique*, Pt 1, ch 6.

to most people, somewhat futile, a topic for university seminars rather than serious public debate; and it is primarily for this reason, because Parliament is sovereign, that the British Constitution has remained uncodified.

There is no point in having a constitution unless one is prepared to abandon the principle of the sovereignty of Parliament, for a codified constitution is incompatible with this principle. A constitution would have specifically to *limit* the sovereignty of Parliament. Most of those who favour an enacted constitution are not arguing that it should merely bring together in one document Britain's current arrangements; they believe instead that these arrangements should be improved and reformed, and, in particular, that they should limit parliamentary sovereignty. They want a constitution that reflects not what *is* but what they believe it *ought to be.*

In the past, however, we in Britain have not only seen no need for a codified constitution, but we have seen no virtue in one either. We did not believe that it would improve our system of government. Our 'historic' and uncodified constitution gave us, so we thought until recently, many advantages. It seemed to have the great virtue of flexibility, since its provisions could be changed with relative ease. Any of the rules regulating our institutions or regulating the relationships between the state and the individual, could be altered with the same ease as any other rule. There were no entrenched provisions, provisions which required some special procedure if they were to be changed. We were, therefore, saved from being bound by the preconceptions of our forebears; we were saved from ancestor worship, something which Bentham and his Utilitarian followers had warned us so strongly against. A codified constitution would merely reflect the dead hand of the past; precisely because we did not have a codified constitution, we did not have to subscribe to statements which would rapidly become redundant as a result of political change. A constitution drawn up in the year 1830, for example, would have made statements about voting rights and about the powers of the House of Lords, which would have become rapidly redundant after the Great Reform Act of 1832. A constitution drawn up in 1996 would, likewise, have become rapidly redundant following the reforms of the Blair government elected in 1997.

There was in much of the writing on the advantages of Britain's 'flexible' constitution, an implication that we were not as other countries, that we were made in a different and more durable way, that we had discovered, to adapt Samuel Beer's words (quoted above on p 3) the secret of how to order consensus and conflict in a manner that best reconciled freedom and stability. That no doubt was what Mr Podsnap meant in his eulogy of the constitution.

IV

The sovereignty of Parliament, our fundamental constitutional principle, is a legal doctrine. It means that Parliament can make or unmake any law, and that a court does not have the power, as, for example the American Supreme Court does, to declare a statute invalid. But this legal doctrine says nothing about where political power resides; it does not imply that Parliament is politically all-powerful. It says nothing at all about the relative power of Parliament and the executive. Today much is heard of 'the decline of Parliament', meaning that Parliament is now weaker than it was vis-à-vis government. Much of the debate on the powers of Parliament, as we shall see in chapter 11, is vitiated by a 'golden age' view of a time when Parliament, supposedly, really did rule. But not since the mid-nineteenth century has Parliament been **politically** supreme, in the sense that it was genuinely able to make and unmake governments, to control government. With the growth of organised and disciplined political parties, the position has come to be reversed so that today, by and large, it is government which controls Parliament rather than Parliament controlling government. The **legal** doctrine of the sovereignty of Parliament has thus come to legitimize a **political** doctrine, the doctrine that a government enjoying an overall majority in the House of Commons should enjoy virtually unlimited power. What the governing party enacts thus becomes, ipso facto, constitutional.

When Lenin sought to make revolution in Russia, his slogan was 'All power to the Soviets'. Critics of the British system of government might argue that the doctrine of parliamentary sovereignty had come to be transmuted into a slogan nearly as pernicious—'All power to the government'. One important consequence of the doctrine of parliamentary sovereignty is that there can be no formal legal or constitutional checks upon the power of government.

We have, in consequence, lacked those checks and balances on government which generally operate in countries with codified constitutions; nor did we have a Bill of Rights such as the Americans enjoy, a document laying out specific rights which the government cannot infringe. It was difficult for our system to accommodate positive rights against the government in the absence of a court which could strike down government legislation abridging rights. Instead, we had an unprotected constitution, a constitution that approached the condition famously identified by Lord Hailsham, Lord Chancellor in the Conservative governments of Edward Heath and Margaret Thatcher, in his Dimbleby Lecture of 1976 as an 'elective dictatorship'. The principle of the sovereignty of Parliament acted as a shield for that elective dictatorship. 'Since', Lord Hailsham complained, 'an election can nowadays be won on a small minority of votes . . . it follows that the majority in the House of Commons is then free to impose on the country a series of relatively unpopular measures, not related to current needs, using the whole powers of the elective dictatorship that carried them through. And in doing so, it is not effectively controlled'. He concluded that 'it is idle to pretend that such a system is rational, necessary or just'.[17]

This does not of course mean that governments in practice have been tyrannical or authoritarian. They have conceived themselves to be limited, not by formal checks and balances, but by informal checks, generally known as conventions.

---

[17] Lord Hailsham, 'Elective Dictatorship', *The Listener*, 21 October 1976, 497.

A convention is a non-legal rule which supplements legal rules, imposing non-legal rather than legal obligations. All modern systems of government contain conventions. In the United States, for example, the constitution prescribes that the president is to be elected not directly by the people but by an electoral college, a list of presidential electors in each state. By convention, however, these electors vote in each state for the candidate who has won a plurality of votes in that state. In Switzerland there is a convention that the executive, the Federal Council, contains members from all of the main parties, and that the minority French and Italian speaking areas should each be represented by at least two out of the seven members.

But, although conventions are present, to some degree or other, in all democratic systems, they are likely to play a more important role in a country without a codified constitution, such as Britain, than they do in countries with codified constitutions. One obvious example of a convention in Britain is that which provides that the Queen, on the advice of her ministers, assents to laws duly passed by Parliament. Legally, the Queen could refuse to give her assent to legislation, but no sovereign has done so since 1707, and, were the Queen now to refuse assent, there would be a constitutional crisis which might put in doubt the future of the monarchy. In this case the convention supplements and limits the legal rule that legislation requires the agreement of the Commons, the Lords and the monarch.

Not all conventions are as unproblematic as this one. The so-called Salisbury Convention regulating the House of Lords is a good example of a convention which has become highly problematic. This convention provides that the House of Lords should not defeat or wreck any item of legislation which has been foreshadowed in the government's election manifesto. The argument for the convention is that the governing party, in winning the election, has acquired a mandate for its policies, and that it is not for an unelected house to dispute this mandate.[18] The Salisbury Convention differs from the convention regulating the actions of the Queen in that it was enunciated at a specific moment of time by a person in a position of authority, Lord Cranborne, the Conservative Leader of the House of Lords (later to become Lord Salisbury), in 1945, and it was treated, from the time it was enunciated, as authoritative. The convention regulating the actions of the Queen, by contrast, seems to have grown gradually out of the political experience of the eighteenth and nineteenth centuries, and it was slow to develop. As late as 1914, George V still believed that he enjoyed the right to refuse assent to government legislation, and seriously considered exercising this right with regard to the Government of Ireland Bill of 1914, providing for Irish Home Rule.[19]

The Salisbury Convention, by contrast, arose in response to a specific set of circumstances. In 1945, the overwhelming Conservative majority in the Lords had to decide upon its response to the first majority government of the Left since passage of the Parliament Act of 1911 regulating relations between the Lords and the

---

[18] The correct interpretation of the Convention is by no means free from ambiguity: see I Richard and D Welfare, *Unfinished Business* (London, Vintage, 1999).

[19] See V Bogdanor, *The Monarchy and the Constitution* (Oxford, OUP, 1995) 130–2.

Commons. The Salisbury Convention is based upon the no-doubt dubious doctrine of the mandate according to which voters are deemed to have endorsed all of the various items in the governing party's manifesto. Should it still apply in the circumstances of today when, by contrast with 1945, no single party enjoys an overall majority in the House of Lords? Some argue that observance of the convention was appropriate only when the House of Lords was permanently dominated by one party, the Conservatives. Since the 1999 House of Lords Act, however, removing all but 92 of the hereditary peers from the House of Lords, no single party has enjoyed an overall majority in the Lords. Therefore, so it is argued, the basis for the convention has now disappeared. Lord Thomas of Gresford, an official Liberal Democrat spokesman in the Lords, has argued that 'The Salisbury Convention has run its day and should be abolished'[20]. Others, however, argue that the convention rests not on one-party domination of the upper house, but on the fact that the House of Lords remains a non-elected body. We shall consider the conflict between these two interpretations of the Salisbury Convention in greater detail in chapter 6.

These examples of conventions serve to illustrate how constitutional conflict characteristically arises in Britain. Conflict generally arises on the issue of whether or not a convention has been broken; and the conflict is resolved by political and electoral means. In the United States, by contrast, and in many other countries with codified constitutions, a constitutional conflict is a conflict about the interpretation of the law. There has, for example, been a conflict for many years in the United States as to the precise meaning of the clause in the fourteenth amendment to the constitution prescribing equal protection. Does this clause prohibit or allow affirmative action in entrance procedures of universities—that is, an admissions policy designed to secure an appropriate balance between different racial groups? Different judges give different answers to this question, but the conflict is resolved by the ultimate judicial body—the Supreme Court, and not, as in Britain, by political or electoral means. In the United States, it is the task of this Court to determine whether a particular statute or act is unconstitutional or not. 'Unconstitutional' in the American context generally means 'contrary to law'. In Britain, by contrast, 'unconstitutional' tends to have a quite different meaning. Were the Queen to veto legislation, or were the House of Lords to break the Salisbury convention and reject on second reading government legislation foreshadowed in its election manifesto, no one would suggest that this would be against the law. In Britain, to say that something is unconstitutional generally means not that it is contrary to law, but that it is contrary to convention, against what Sidney Low called the 'tacit understandings'.

But it is by no means easy to determine what the conventions are at any particular moment in time, nor how they should be interpreted. It is not only, as Low suggested, that the understandings are not always understood. The problem is that there is not always agreement on what they are or what they should be. Almost by

---

[20] House of Lords Debates, vol 672, col 275, 23 May 2005.

definition, when there is a constitutional conflict, there is unlikely to be agreement on the precise nature of a convention and on its proper meaning or interpretation. Constitutional conflicts tend to arise when one of the assumptions on which a convention has been based has disappeared, or is thought to have disappeared. Thus, one of the assumptions on which the Salisbury Convention was based was that of a permanent Conservative majority in the House of Lords. Once that assumption has been removed, the convention no longer provides unequivocal guidance, and some would argue that it should no longer apply. Others would dispute this, drawing attention to the fact that the House of Lords is still a non-elected chamber, and that therefore the convention should still be observed.

In the case of conventions, unlike laws, it is not normally possible to resolve problems by means of an impartial umpire such as a Supreme Court, since the rules in question are not legal rules. Conventions are non-legal rules, and different from, for example, the rules of football since their precise delineation and interpretation is not always clear and there is no neutral referee to enforce them. It is, therefore, not always easy to distinguish between the question 'what in fact is the convention', and the question 'what ought the convention to be'.

It might be suggested that one obvious test of whether a convention exists is whether or not a political penalty is exacted when it is broken. When the House of Lords in 1909 rejected the Lloyd George 'Peoples' budget, there was a political penalty in the form of the Parliament Act of 1911, limiting its power. Perhaps one test of the existence of a convention is whether the political concatenation of forces is such that the government of the day can get away with breaking it.

If that is so, then when the political circumstances change, so also might the conventions; and conventions depend upon broad agreement amongst opinion-formers, if not also in the wider society, as to what is constitutionally proper and what is not. They depend upon consensus, an agreement upon fundamentals. That agreement has certainly existed in Britain. It could perhaps be taken for granted in the immediate post-war years. There were of course widespread differences of view on political issues, but there was agreement on how the disagreements should be resolved. That consensus may no longer be present, especially, as we shall see in chapter 3, on matters connected with civil liberties and human rights.

V

The difficulty, then, with analyzing the role of conventions in the British constitution is that they seem to depend so much on political vicissitudes. They are in general clear and reasonably easy to formulate accurately during periods of constitutional stability. When the constitution is in ferment, however, or when we are living in a period of constitutional transition, as is the case today, then the interpretation of the conventions comes to be disputed. This lessens their value as restraints upon the power of government. As a recent government memorandum on conventions declared, 'For a convention to work properly . . . there must be a shared understanding of what it means. A contested convention is not a convention at all'.[21] Eventually, no doubt, the disputed convention will be clarified or it will be replaced with a new convention. But such a change is not likely to come about without a political struggle.

The old constitution, then, was a political constitution, in that its character was determined by events rather than pre-existing constitutional norms. One authority went so far as to claim that the old constitution was 'no more and no less than what happened. Everything that happens is constitutional'.[22] If something happened, then it was constitutional. The point may be put in another way by suggesting that, under an uncodified constitution, the constitutional limits upon government have tended to coincide with the political limits, the practical limits imposed by such factors as the state of public opinion, the attitudes of the governing party, and feeling in Parliament and the Cabinet. Thus an argument that appeared at first sight to be one about the interpretation of general principles and the significance of past precedents became in reality one about the balance of political power. On this view, the test for what was a convention seemed to be primarily a political one, and so what counted as constitutional tended to coincide with what was politically possible.

This had an important consequence. It meant that the existence of conventions did not, despite appearances, serve to provide real and permanent limits on the power of British government. Conventions tended to reflect the balance of political power and the balance of power in society. They helped to ensure responsible government, a government responsible to Parliament; and they helped perhaps to ensure that the will of the majority prevailed. But they could do little to help protect the rights of **minorities,** of those who did not form part of the ruling consensus. There can be no real and permanent limits on the power of the majority for so long as the doctrine of the sovereignty of Parliament holds sway.

VI

The fundamental peculiarity of the British constitution, as it has been traditionally conceived, is that it seems possible to analyse it only in descriptive terms, as a summation of past experience, rather than in genuinely constitutional terms as representing the recognition of certain normative principles. The constitution is what happens. This is in contrast to, for example, the American constitution which can be understood in terms of principles such as the separation of powers, federalism, and the protection of human rights through a Bill of Rights. These are all principles which serve to limit the power of the federal government. In Britain, by contrast, the principle of the sovereignty of parliament is an inductive generalization derived from the behaviour of Parliament and the courts over many years;

---

[21] Memorandum by HM Government, to the Joint Committee on Conventions, HC 1212-II, HL 265-II, para 19, 13 June 2006.

[22] J A G Griffith, 'The Political Constitution' (1979) *Modern Law Review* 19.

while the conventions of the constitution might be little more than reflections of the political or social balance of power at a particular point of time.

This criticism can be applied, not only to Dicey's analysis of the constitution, but to Bagehot's also. Bagehot took account, as Dicey did not, of political as well as legal factors. At the beginning of *The English Constitution*, he drew a basic distinction between the 'dignified' elements of the constitution and its 'efficient' elements. The 'dignified' elements, such as the monarchy and the House of Lords, were elements which played little part in the process of government, but whose purpose was to 'excite and preserve the reverence of the population'. By adding colour to the workings of government, they helped to secure allegiance to it. They conferred legitimacy on the 'efficient' elements of the constitution. These, such as the House of Commons and the Cabinet, were those which lay at the heart of the process of government. Bagehot searched for what he called the 'efficient secret' of the constitution, the key to its successful working. He found it in 'the close union, the nearly complete fusion, of the executive and legislative powers'.[23] The successful working of the British system, in his view, depended upon Cabinet government, upon the Cabinet being responsible to Parliament.

But this 'efficient secret' of the constitution was very far from being a 'principle' of the constitution as it might be understood in a country with a codified constitution. Bagehot's 'efficient secret', the idea of Cabinet government, like Dicey's parliamentary sovereignty, was not in any way a normative principle, a principle capable of limiting government. It was, rather, a principle of a sociological sort, an indication of how power was in practice distributed in the British state. What Bagehot was saying was that, in practice, the most powerful institution in Britain was not the monarchy or the House of Lords, as perhaps some had thought, but the Cabinet, and that the Cabinet was responsible to Parliament. That was an empirical statement, capable in principle of verification or refutation, a sociological generalization dressed up as a normative principle. The constitution was simply what worked. For Bagehot also, the British constitution was what happened.

What Bagehot did was in effect to merge the 'is' and the 'ought'. For him the principles of the constitution seemed no more than the summation of a pattern of behaviour, the rules of political practice writ large. So the constitution, as Bagehot understood it, could be used to legitimize almost anything. Bagehot seemed little interested in developing a conceptual logic of the constitution, a body of doctrine, of constitutional principle which would serve to limit government. For him the principles of the British constitution, unlike those of the codified constitutions of almost every other democracy, were peculiar precisely because they could be no more than a mere collection of empirical generalisations from past experience, a summation of Britain's historical experience; and most British constitutional analysts have followed Bagehot in this regard. In other democracies, by contrast, a constitution is understood as being something that is anterior to government, and as containing principles whose purpose is to limit the scope of government.

---

[23] Bagehot, 'The English Constitution', *Collected Works*, vol 5, 210.

The old British constitution, then, consists of a *process*, analysed by Bagehot—the evolutionary process—and a *doctrine*, analysed by Dicey—the sovereignty of Parliament. Both the process and the doctrine make it difficult to fashion instruments to limit the power of the state. They served, contrary to what both Bagehot and Dicey would have wished, to legitimize the omnicompetence of government. But one main purpose of a codified constitution is to sustain the doctrine of constitutionalism, the doctrine that government ought to be limited by certain fundamental principles. It is the reference to a pre-existing document laying down basic principles which forms the essence of constitutionalism; and those living under a constitution for any length of time and taking its provisions seriously may be expected to develop a constitutional sense, a sense of what it might be appropriate for governments to do. In Britain, by contrast, the old constitution seems to have been little more than a set of inductive generalizations. It was perhaps this absence of a codified constitution in Britain that prevented us from developing a constitutional sense, a real sense of the limitations of government. It is partly for this reason that what once seemed attractive peculiarities no longer seem quite so attractive. It is partly for this reason that the old constitution has come under strain in recent years. Political developments in post-war Britain have persuaded many that it has outlived its usefulness.

2

The Old Constitution Under Strain

IN THE IMMEDIATE post-war years, the constitution played little part in British politics. The political agenda was dominated largely by socio-economic issues. The division between the parties on domestic matters concerned such issues as the role of the state in society and the economy, the scope of redistributive taxation and the limits of public ownership. The two major parties, Labour and the Conservatives, saw little need to question the viability of British institutions, and the Liberals, who were committed to a belief in proportional representation and various other constitutional reforms, such as Scottish Home Rule, were, until the 1970s, a negligible force. British institutions, so it seemed, had been validated by victories in two world wars and the British system of government was widely admired as an exemplar of what a liberal polity should be. In the 1950s and 1960s, the so-called Westminster Model of government came to be exported to the ex-colonies of Africa and Asia, for whom it seemed the very touchstone of democracy. Proportional representation seemed discredited by inter-war experience in Germany and Italy, where, so it was argued, it had facilitated the rise of Fascism and National Socialism. During the immediate post-war years, the experience of France, where there were 15 governments between 1946 and 1958 under the Fourth Republic, further discredited it. West Germany, which recovered rapidly under a federal system and proportional representation, might have yielded a counter-example, but the connection, if there was one, between economic success and the German constitution, was not drawn until the 1970s. It was understandable perhaps if there was, during the immediate post-war years, a somewhat complacent acceptance of the constitutional status quo and little appetite for reform.

But, by the end of the century, the intellectual atmosphere had radically changed. In 1953, the American sociologist Edward Shils had been surprised to find 'an eminent man of the Left' deliver his encomium on the British constitution, and even more surprised that no one seemed prepared to disagree. By the end of the century, however, it would have been difficult, if not impossible, to find any similar 'eminent man of the Left' prepared to deliver a similar encomium on the British system of government. By the beginning of the twenty-first century, any defence of the old constitution tended to have a distinctly defensive air. The years of celebrating British political institutions had gone, never perhaps to return. They have been replaced by an anxious questioning and a search, sometimes desperate, for innovations to revive a seemingly outworn system. The British constitution was no longer the exemplar of modern democratic practice. Not one of the post-communist democracies of central and eastern Europe had so much as contemplated adopting the Westminster model, although they were still prepared to learn from British parliamentary procedures. In Britain itself, constitutional reform, which had hardly been an issue in politics since the 1920s, came, from the 1970s, to form part of the staple of political debate. During the 1970s, Labour joined the Liberals in supporting constitutional reform, and in particular devolution, although the Party continued to reject the favoured Liberal nostrum of proportional representation. In the 1980s, the SDP (Social Democratic Party), a short-lived breakaway party from Labour, which formed an alliance with the Liberals, and in 1988 merged with them, claimed that the British constitutional system was outworn and proposed a whole raft of constitutional reforms, including proportional representation, devolution to Scotland and Wales and the English regions, decentralization to local government, a bill of rights and freedom of information. The SDP put constitutional reform at the centre of its programme, a programme which prefigured many of the reforms of the Blair government after 1997.

Why did the constitution return to the political agenda in the 1970s? What were the causes of the renewed interest in constitutional reform after so long a period of quiescence?

The constitution first came back into British politics in what was, for most people, a far-away and remote part of the United Kingdom, Northern Ireland. Since 1920, when the Government of Ireland Act had provided for Home Rule or devolution in the province, with its own parliament, it had seemed insulated from the politics of the rest of the United Kingdom. One Labour MP, who became chairman in the 1960s of the Campaign for Democracy in Ulster, complained that it proved impossible to 'penetrate the blank wall of incomprehension and ignorance about Ulster. Members who knew about Saigon and Salisbury seemed to know nothing of Stormont'.[1] Whereas in the rest of the country the main political issues were socio-economic, in Northern Ireland, the divide lay between the majority, Unionist, community, predominantly Protestant, and the minority, Nationalist community, predominantly Catholic. In 1968, the activities of the civil rights movement in Northern Ireland, designed to secure rights for the Nationalist minority, led to violence between the two communities, and the problems of Northern Ireland forced themselves upon the attention of successive British governments.

Both Labour and Conservative administrations at Westminster came to the same conclusion about Northern Ireland, namely that the Westminster Model could not work there. This Model presupposed alternating or potentially alternating majorities. In Northern Ireland, however, where conflict was between two rigid and tribal

---

[1] P Rose, *Backbencher's Dilemma* (London, Frederick Muller, 1981) 179.

communities, rather than between fairly mobile social classes, alternation was not possible. The parties representing the Unionist majority remained permanently in power, and they had no incentive to cater for the needs of the Nationalist minority. Any Unionist government which appeared too friendly to that minority was in danger of being outflanked by more intransigent Unionists.

Therefore, successive British governments, whether Conservative or Labour, found themselves proposing constitutional innovations to meet the special conditions of Northern Ireland, innovations such as power-sharing, devolution, proportional representation, the referendum and a Bill of Rights, innovations which they strenuously resisted when it was suggested that they might be applied to the rest of the United Kingdom.

In 1972, Edward Heath's Conservative government abolished the Northern Ireland Parliament which had been a vehicle for majority rule by the Unionists, and Northern Ireland came to be ruled directly from Westminster. Direct rule, however, was seen as a temporary expedient, and new proposals for devolution were prepared. Any new devolved body, however, would have to allow for participation of the Nationalist minority in the government of Northern Ireland as well as the Unionist majority. In 1973, the Heath government proposed a new power-sharing executive for Northern Ireland with an assembly elected by proportional representation. The government also proposed a further constitutional innovation, a referendum or border poll designed to test whether the people of Northern Ireland wished to remain in the United Kingdom, or whether they preferred to join the Irish Republic.

The Northern Ireland border poll was held on 8 March 1973. The Unionists of course voted solidly to retain the link with the United Kingdom. But the nationalists boycotted it, regarding it as a propaganda exercise. They argued that the border between Northern Ireland and the rest of the island of Ireland had been deliberately drawn in 1920 so as to secure a permanent Protestant majority; and, so long as there was a Protestant majority, it was inconceivable that Northern Ireland would vote to join the republic. Thus the result of the border poll was, in their view, predetermined by the way in which the boundary had been drawn in 1920. For this reason, the poll did little to resolve the complex problems of Northern Ireland, nor did it answer the question of how Northern Ireland was to be governed were it to remain part of the United Kingdom. Nevertheless, it was an important innovation for two reasons. The first was that it introduced direct democracy into British politics. Until the border poll, it was widely held that the introduction of a referendum into British politics, except when used to decide local matters such as liquor licensing in Wales, was unconstitutional, since Parliament was sovereign. It was perhaps forgotten that, if Parliament is sovereign, if Parliament can do what it likes, then it can call a referendum.

The second was that the border poll implied that one part of the United Kingdom could, if it so wished, exercise the right of self-determination and secede. That was an implication whose significance would not be missed by the Scottish nationalists whose electoral support was rising rapidly in the early 1970s.

The new Northern Ireland Assembly, provided for in the Northern Ireland Constitution Act of 1973, departed significantly from the Westminster model of single-party majority government, since it was based upon the principle of power-sharing between the Unionist majority and the Nationalist minority. Whatever the outcome of elections to the Assembly, the minority Nationalists would be guaranteed places in the executive government of Northern Ireland. But the executive lasted just five months, since in May 1974 a strike of Unionist workers forced a return to direct rule from Westminster. Nevertheless, the principle of power-sharing remained a fundamental requirement for devolution in Northern Ireland, and it formed a central motif in the Belfast or Good Friday Agreement of 1998, which provided for a new and even more complex system of government than that proposed in 1973.

The third innovation in Northern Ireland was the introduction of proportional representation by the single transferable vote method both for district council elections and for elections to the Northern Ireland Assembly. This was the first experiment with proportional representation in Britain since the abolition of the university seats in 1950. It is hardly surprising that the Electoral Reform Society, which had been campaigning for this reform for nearly ninety years, labelled 1973, a 'red letter year', and declared:

> 'The reform this Society seeks is no longer an academic matter, capable of being dismissed as the concern of a few enthusiasts; it is now something actually operating within the United Kingdom ... The whole subject is topical as it has not been for half a century'.[2]

Since 1973, it has come to be accepted that all elections in Northern Ireland, except elections to the House of Commons, should be conducted by the single transferable vote. This showed that the first-past-the-post system, whatever its merits for Westminster, did not necessarily have to be applied to other bodies; and, in due course, when Scottish and Welsh devolved bodies were established in 1998, it was decided that they too would be elected by proportional representation, though by a different system from that used in Northern Ireland.

The Unionists were, for many years, suspicious of these reforms, for they feared that Northern Ireland was being singled out for special treatment differentiating it from the rest of the United Kingdom, and that the ties connecting it to the rest of the United Kingdom were being loosened. But the Blair government's proposals for devolution to Scotland and Wales helped reconcile Unionists to devolution in Northern Ireland since they could now argue that Northern Ireland was being treated like the other non-English parts of the United Kingdom, rather than as a special case.

---

[2] *Representation* (Journal of the Electoral Reform Society), October 1973, 54.

II

Developments in Northern Ireland had only a marginal impact upon opinion in the rest of the United Kingdom. But the 1960s and 1970s saw the introduction of a more momentous issue into British politics: British entry into the European Community. This issue had major constitutional implications, and seemed to threaten the fundamental principle of parliamentary sovereignty, since, if Britain were to join, then decisions which had been previously taken by Westminster would in future be taken by a body—the Council of Ministers of the European Community—which was not and could not be responsible to Parliament.

Joining the European Community, therefore, would be a decision quite unlike joining any other international organisation such as, for example, the United Nations, or NATO. The decisions made by these organisations could not bind Parliament unless Parliament wished so to be bound. The regulations and directives of the European Community, by contrast, would bind Parliament even against its wishes. The legal order of the European Community was superior to that of the Member States, and European legislation would therefore 'trump' any legislation of the Member States which was inconsistent with it. This doctrine of the supremacy of European law had been laid down by the European Court of Justice (ECJ) in the case *Costa v ENEL*, decided in 1964, nine years before Britain joined the Community.

'The transfer by the States from their domestic legal systems to the Community legal system of rights and obligations arising under the Treaty carries with it a permanent limitation of their sovereign rights, against which a subsequent unilateral act incompatible with the concept of the Community cannot prevail'.[3]

In addition, the supremacy of Community law could be enforced against national governments and legislatures by individuals before national courts. This doctrine, the doctrine of so-called 'direct effect', was first laid down in a case in 1962, *Van Gend en Loos*. In this case, the ECJ argued that the Treaty of Rome which had established the European Community was not just 'an agreement which merely creates mutual obligations between the contracting states' but 'a new legal order of international law for the benefit of which the states have limited their sovereign rights, and the subjects of which comprise not only the Member States but also their nationals'.[4] This doctrine meant that the approval of Parliament was no longer necessary for EU legislation, which would automatically become law in Britain.

These two doctrines—the doctrine of supremacy and the doctrine of direct effect—would obviously have important and momentous consequences for the doctrine of parliamentary sovereignty. In 1971, a leading constitutional lawyer, S A de Smith defined the European Community as 'an inchoate functional

---

[3] Case 6/64 [1964] ECR 585, at 593.
[4] Case 26/62 [1963] ECR 1, at 12.

federation', which would require 'the pooling of sovereignty'. It was for this reason that 'full recognition of the hierarchical superiority of Community law would entail a revolution in legal thought'.[5]

Edward Heath's Conservative government, which led Britain into the Community, faced the problem of how to give legislative effect to membership of a body which could overrule Parliament. The Heath government resolved this problem in the European Communities Act of 1972, which provided for the recognition of all directly enforceable Community law in preference to any Act of Parliament, past or future. Thus, until the Act were to be repealed, European Community law would trump existing or future legislation passed by Westminster. The radical consequences of this provision became apparent in 1991 in the second *Factortame* case.[6]

In 1988, Parliament had passed a Merchant Shipping Act, in effect restricting the right of foreign-owned vessels to fish in British waters. The ECJ ruled that this was contrary to Community law. Spanish fishing-boat companies adversely affected by this Act then secured an interim injunction preventing the Secretary of State from moving Spanish-owned ships from the register of British fishing vessels allowed to fish in British territorial waters. The Spanish companies brought an action in the British courts claiming that the Merchant Shipping Act was incompatible with the European Communities Act. The House of Lords accepted the case put by the Spanish company and declared that the courts would 'disapply' the relevant provisions of the Merchant Shipping Act. Lord Bridge declared that 'it was the duty of a United Kingdom court, when delivering final judgment, to override any rule of national law found to be in conflict with any directly enforceable rule of Community law'. The reason for this was that 'If the supremacy . . . of Community law over the national law of Member States was not always inherent in the EEC Treaty, it was certainly well established in the jurisprudence of the Court of Justice long before the UK joined the Community'.[7] Directly applicable European Community law therefore prevailed over national law, and the courts were prepared to give effect to that even where the national law consisted of an Act that was later than the relevant Community provision. It seemed, therefore, that in the European Communities Act, Parliament had parted with its sovereignty, in the sense that this particular Act, for so long as it was on the statute book, was supreme with regard to later legislation. In the words of Hoffmann J, admittedly obiter, and without reference to *Factortame*,

'The Treaty of Rome is the supreme law in this country, taking precedence over Acts of Parliament. Our entry to the Community meant that (subject to our undoubted but probably theoretical right to withdraw from the Community altogether) Parliament surrendered its sovereign right to legislate contrary to the provisions of the Treaty on the matters of social and economic policy which it regulated'.[8]

[5] S A de Smith, 'The Constitution and the Common Market: A Tentative Appraisal' (1971) *Modern Law Review*, 613.
[6] *R v Secretary of State for Transport, ex p. Factortame* (No 2) [1991] 1 All ER 70; [1991] 1 AC 603.
[7] [1991] 1 AC 658, 643.
[8] In the case, *Stoke on Trent City Council v B&Q* [1991] 4 All ER 223–4.

One commentator summed up the consequence of the *Factortame* decision by arguing that 'For the first time since 1688 a court suspended the operation of an Act of Parliament. Contrary to Dicey's oft-quoted assertion, it appeared that there was now a body with power to set aside the legislation of Parliament and that body was the House of Lords'.[9]

It seemed, then, that Parliament in 1972 had been able to do something which many had previously thought impossible, that is, to limit its sovereignty. European Community legislation was superior to statute and so could not be impliedly repealed by later legislation. One authoritative commentator, the leading constitutional lawyer, H W R Wade, declared that the effect of the *Factortame* decision was that 'Parliament can bind its successors. If that is not revolutionary, constitutional lawyers are Dutchmen'. Admittedly, if Parliament had succeeded in binding its successors, it had done so voluntarily, and presumably Parliament could withdraw from the European Union if it so wished. The abortive European constitution of 2003 and the Lisbon Treaty which superseded it, provided, for the first time, machinery by which a Member State could withdraw from the European Union if it so wished. Nevertheless, there can be little doubt that the European Communities Act produced a structural change in the British constitution.

The Act raised a further awkward question: if Parliament could voluntarily limit its sovereignty with respect to membership of the European Communities, why might it not also do so with respect to other statutes—the Human Rights Act, for example, or the devolution legislation? Wade indeed concluded that 'the new doctrine' adumbrated in *Factortame*, 'makes sovereignty a freely adjustable commodity whenever Parliament chooses to accept some limitation'.[10]

The doctrine that legislation of the European Communities is superior to that of Westminster has never really been accepted by the general public. It is sometimes said that the British public were deceived into joining the European Communities by politicians who told them that membership was solely a matter of economics and that it did not involve the pooling or the surrender of sovereignty. That charge, however, cannot be sustained. The Treaty of Rome had declared that its signatories were determined 'to lay the foundations of an ever closer union among the peoples of Europe', and the government's White Paper, *The United Kingdom and the European Communities*, stated unequivocally that,

'The six [i.e. the existing Member States of the Communities] have firmly and repeatedly made clear that they reject the concept that European unity should be limited to the formation of a free trade area'.[11]

The Member States had committed themselves to monetary union at the Paris summit in 1972, the first European Communities heads of government meeting to be attended by Britain; and on 10 June 1971, Edward Heath, as Prime Minister,

---

[9] E Wicks, *The Evolution of a Constitution: Eight Key Moments in British Constitutional History* (Oxford, Hart, 2006) 156.
[10] H W R Wade, 'Sovereignty—Revolution or Evolution?' (1996) *Law Quarterly Review*, 573.
[11] Cmnd 4715, July 1971.

told the Commons that 'we as members of the enlarged Community . . . should play our full part in the progress towards economic and monetary union'.[12] A Labour back-bencher, Ivor Richard argued:

'We who believe in the cause of Europe do ourselves and the cause of Europe itself a grave disservice if we pretend that entry into the Communities does not involve some loss of autonomy. Of course it involves some loss of autonomy—and of course it should, because it is in the nature of the organization that we are entering, and in the nature of the organization which, hopefully, will emerge in Europe, that out of it we will get a European political entity rather than a set of incidental national units'.[13]

The opponents of entry acknowledged that the issue of sovereignty had been central to the debate. Enoch Powell, for example, declared that

'those who are the keenest supporters of British entry are the most ready to confess—not to confess, but to assert—that of course this involves by its very nature a reduction of the sovereignty of the House'.[14]

There was, in addition, a referendum in 1975 on whether Britain should remain in the European Communities or withdraw, a referendum which gave the opponents of British membership every opportunity to make their case on the grounds that Parliament would lose its sovereignty. The vote in the referendum, however, was around two to one in favour of Britain remaining in the Communities.

Nevertheless, even though it cannot be argued that the politicians sought to deceive the public, it is doubtful if the message that Parliament was ceding sovereignty really reached many of the voters; and even if it did, it may have been seen as merely an abstract proposition without any real concrete policy consequences. It is noteworthy that, when the European constitution was produced in 2003, and when, after that constitution was rejected in France and the Netherlands, the Lisbon Treaty was produced as a substitute, many commentators attacked these documents on the ground that they would make British law subordinate to European law. They had not appreciated that British law had been subordinate to European Community law since 1973 when Britain joined. The consequence, however, is that this new doctrine lacks popular acceptance, and that is a serious problem from the point of view of constitutional legitimacy.

But entry into the European Community did not only raise the issue of sovereignty, fundamental as that issue has proved to be. It also raised, as Northern Ireland had done, the issue of proportional representation. Article 138 (iii) of the Treaty of Rome, committed the British government together with the governments of the other Member States, to direct elections to the European Parliament 'by direct universal suffrage in accordance with a uniform procedure in all Member States'. That uniform procedure would almost certainly prove to be a proportional one since, of the nine Member States of the European Community

---

[12]   House of Commons Debates, 10 June 1971, vol 818, col 1235.
[13]   House of Commons Debates, 28 October 1971, vol 823, col. 2150.
[14]   House of Commons Debates, 28 October 1971, vol 823, col. 2186.

after 1973, when Britain joined, only Britain and France did not use a proportional system to elect their national legislatures. The traditional arguments for the first-past-the-post system in Britain, that it provided for stable government and close links between MPs and their constituents, seemed irrelevant in the European context. It was not the function of the European Parliament, unlike the House of Commons, to sustain a government, and so the argument that proportional representation would lead to weak or unstable government was hardly relevant. Constituencies in the European Parliament elections would each contain around half a million electors, and it seemed, therefore, that close contact between legislators and constituents would be difficult to achieve whatever electoral system was adopted. British governments, nevertheless, resisted the arguments for proportional representation for elections to the European Parliament until 1999 when a proportional system was at last introduced.

III

Britain's entry into the European Community in 1973 thus proved to be a major constitutional innovation, and one which continues to put heavy strains upon the body politic. It was to lead, almost immediately, to a further constitutional innovation, in 1975, the country's first, and so far only, nationwide referendum.

The question of whether Britain ought to enter the European Community was an issue which transcended party loyalties. It was to split both of the major parties, Labour in the 1970s and 1980s and the Conservatives in the 1990s. During the period when the Conservative government under Edward Heath was negotiating entry in the early 1970s, a minority of Conservative MPs, led by Enoch Powell, were opposed precisely because they believed that it involved an unacceptable curtailment of national sovereignty. Many Labour MPs also were opposed, though for quite different reasons, because they believed that the European Community would prevent a Labour government from implementing necessary social reforms and from managing the economy. Opinion was divided in the country, also, and the divisions in popular opinion did not by any means follow party lines. With the parties and public opinion so divided, it was not easy to see how the parliamentary system could effectively resolve the issue of whether Britain should enter or not.

But there was a further problem. During the 1970 general election, all three of the major parties had supported British entry. There was no way, therefore, in which a voter opposed to entry could make her voice felt, and so it was argued that the Heath government could not claim a mandate for entry. During a press conference in the 1970 election campaign, on 2 June, Edward Heath had declared:

'I always said that you could not possibly take this country into the Common Market [as the European Community was then known in Britain] if the majority of the people were against it, but this is handled through the Parliamentary system'.

Heath did not explain, however, how 'the Parliamentary system' could reflect public opinion when all three parties had supported entry; and, since entry to the European Community seemed likely to prove irreversible, it would appear that the voter was being denied the right to express her opinion on the most important constitutional issue of the century, one involving in effect a permanent transfer of sovereignty from Westminster. It was perhaps for this reason that survey evidence indicated that, from February 1971, a large majority of the electorate favoured it being decided by referendum.[15]

The Labour government did not, however, propose a referendum in 1975 for any high-minded constitutional reasons. It did so to avoid a party split. In opposition, after 1970, Labour had moved away from its position of supporting entry, and its official position had become one of opposing entry to the Communities on the terms negotiated by Edward Heath. But a significant minority of Labour MPs, led by Roy Jenkins, deputy leader of the Party, supported entry. In October 1971, 69 Labour MPs voted for the government's motion to approve the decision of principle to join the Community. Other Labour MPs, mainly on the Left of the Party, were opposed to entry on any terms. Labour's leader, Harold Wilson, in a skilful balancing act, had been able to hold the party together by opposing the terms of entry, rather than the principle, and committed a Labour government to a renegotiation of the terms. He promised that the renegotiated terms would then be put to the people for approval, either by means of a general election or a referendum. The Labour Party was duly returned to power as a minority government in the general election of February 1974, but it had not completed its renegotiation until after a second election had been held, in October 1974, yielding Labour a minuscule overall majority of three seats. It would obviously be impracticable to hold a third general election after the renegotiation had been concluded in 1975. Therefore, the only way of consulting the people would be through a referendum. The commitment to the referendum could, so it seemed, reconcile most sections of the Labour Party—whether for or against Europe—so unifying the Party. Those hostile to Europe could hope to secure withdrawal, while those in favour of Britain remaining in Europe believed that they could secure popular endorsement for this project. The referendum, therefore, proved to be, as James Callaghan had predicted, 'a rubber life raft into which the party may one day have to climb', a device to avoid a party split.[16]

The referendum on whether Britain should stay in the European Community on the renegotiated terms took place in June 1975 and yielded a two-to-one majority for staying in. The referendum, however, was not seen as an instrument for regular use, but as an ad hoc response to what was seen as a unique issue. Yet, once the principle of the referendum had been conceded, it was bound to create a precedent, whatever the intentions of those who introduced it. Within just eighteen months of the referendum on Europe, the Labour government was forced, as a

---

[15] See the evidence cited in S Alderson, *Yea or Nay? The Referendum in the United Kingdom* (London, Cassell, 1975) 2.

[16] Quoted in D Butler and U Kitzinger, *The 1975 Referendum* (Houndmills, Macmillan, 1976) 12.

result of backbench pressure, to concede further referendums on devolution to Scotland and Wales. Backbench sceptics had refused to vote for devolution, unless they were assured that there was a real demand for it. These referendums led to the defeat of devolution in 1979, although eighteen years later, in 1997, another Labour government was to hold further referendums on devolution in Scotland, Wales and Northern Ireland, as well as a referendum in London on whether voters in the capital approved of a directly elected mayor and strategic authority, which all yielded 'yes' votes. The Blair government also promised that it would not enter the eurozone nor ratify the now defunct European constitution without popular approval in a referendum.

IV

Devolution proved to be another issue which placed a severe strain on the old constitution. Devolution, like Europe, seems to challenge the political implications of the sovereignty of Parliament. According to that doctrine, which derives in essence from Hobbes, sovereignty and also power, had to be concentrated in one particular place. It needed to be concentrated either at Westminster, Brussels or Edinburgh. The only genuine alternatives for Britain, therefore, were either a *Europe des patries*, with power remaining concentrated at Westminster, or a 'European super-state' with power concentrated at Brussels, or Scottish independence, with power in Scotland concentrated in Edinburgh. The idea of a division of powers between Westminster, Brussels and Edinburgh was a chimera. Dicey had argued in various polemical works that Home Rule or devolution were in a sense illusory concepts. There could be no middle way between the unitary state and independence other than federalism. But England, the majority nation in the United Kingdom, did not want federalism. How, then, could the old constitution accommodate the notion of a territorial division of power?

Devolution came onto the political agenda in the 1970s primarily as a result of the spectacular success of the SNP in the two general elections of 1974. In the first, held in February, the party won 22% of the Scottish vote and 7 of the 71 Scottish seats; in the second, held in October, it won 30% of the vote, and 11 seats, coming second to Labour in thirty five of Labour's forty one seats. The SNP had become the second strongest ethnic party in the whole of Western Europe. It threatened Labour's hegemony in Scotland, and therefore also its chances of forming the government of the United Kingdom. This was because, until that time, only the Labour governments of 1945 and 1966 had enjoyed majorities which did not depend upon MPs from Scotland. It is hardly surprising that the Labour government elected in February 1974 proceeded rapidly to produce and seek to implement proposals for devolution to Scotland. It also proposed devolution for Wales, even though Plaid Cymru, the Welsh nationalist party, had not succeeded in emulating the success of the SNP.

Many of the Labour ministers who pushed forward the ill-fated devolution legislation in the 1970s had been opposed to it until they came to fear electoral losses to the SNP. After the last draft of the White Paper, *Democracy and Devolution: Proposals for Scotland and Wales* (Cmnd 5732), had been agreed, Harold Wilson offered his benediction, 'And God help all who sail in her'. Barbara Castle, the Health Secretary, found that civil servants 'were deeply alarmed at the whole exercise', while the Home Secretary, Roy Jenkins, upset at the levity with which the issue was being treated, burst out, 'You cannot break up the United Kingdom in order to win a few seats at an election'.[17]

Devolution, like the issues of Northern Ireland and elections to the European Parliament, raised once again the issue of proportional representation. One main motive for devolution, after all, was to check the rise of the SNP in Scotland. Yet, in a four-party political system, the SNP might well have been able to win an overall majority in the Scottish Parliament on just 35% of the Scottish vote, and claim a mandate for independence. Since, in October 1974, the SNP had secured 30% of the Scottish vote, an overall majority for the SNP in the new Scottish parliament seemed far from a remote possibility. Proportional representation, therefore, might help to preserve the Union with Scotland. Nevertheless, in the 1970s, Labour governments insisted on preserving the first-past-the-post system for the devolved bodies. By the 1990s, however, Labour had changed its mind, and the elections to the Scottish Parliament and the National Assembly of Wales in 1999 were the first, outside Northern Ireland, to be held under proportional representation since the abolition of the university seats in 1950.

Devolution posed two fundamental constitutional problems. The first was whether there was a genuine half-way house between the unitary state on the one hand, and federalism or separation on the other. Could devolution really hope to settle the aspirations of the Scots and Welsh, or would it lead inevitably through a slippery slope to separation? Was it compatible with the doctrine of the sovereignty of Parliament, or would devolution turn Britain, almost unnoticed, into a federal state? Could the demands of the Scots and the Welsh be contained within the traditional parameters of the British constitution, or would devolution involve constitutional upheaval on a massive and unpredictable scale? Devolution, it rapidly became clear, was a new and untried policy, with the exception of the unhappy experiment in Northern Ireland between 1921 and 1972. It meant entering uncharted waters. No one could be clear what the final destination would be.

The second problem was that the demand for devolution was so unevenly distributed in the United Kingdom. There was, no doubt, a real demand for it in Scotland, and perhaps a lesser demand for devolution in Wales. But it seemed that few in England sought devolution. Certainly, there seemed a minuscule demand for it anywhere south of Birmingham. Therefore, devolution would inevitably be asymmetrical. Would this pattern not mean, however, that the distribution of benefits and burdens would become so skewed that it would provoke discontent amongst the English? Could an asymmetrical system survive or would it merely

---

[17] B Castle, *The Castle Diaries, 1974–76* (London, Weidenfeld and Nicolson, 1980) 179, 497; E Dell, *A Hard Pounding: Politics and Economic Crisis, 1974–76* (Oxford, OUP, 1991) 51.

lead to new discontents and prove a springboard for further grievances? We shall consider these questions in detail in chapter 4.

V

These issues—the government of Northern Ireland, Europe, and devolution—important though they were, were nevertheless probably peripheral to the perceptions of most people in England, and did not immediately impinge upon them. However, the outcome of the general election of February 1974, perhaps the crucial general election of the whole post-war period, served to bring the constitution back to the political agenda for the whole of the United Kingdom such that it became difficult for any elector to ignore it.

The general election had been called by Edward Heath, faced with a miners strike, to enable voters to answer the question 'Who governs?' The voters, however, failed to return an unequivocal answer. The outcome of the election was as follows:

	Seats	% Votes
Conservatives	297	37.9
Labour	301	37.1
Liberals	14	19.3
SNP	7	2.0
		(22% of Scottish vote)
Plaid Cymru	2	0.6
		(10.8% of Welsh vote)
Northern Irish parties	12	3.1
Others	2	0.4
Total	635	100.0

The election yielded an unexpected outcome—a hung parliament, Britain's first since 1929. The proliferation of minor parties meant that the two major parties—Conservatives and Labour—would each need the support of at least two of the minor parties to achieve an overall majority of 318 seats. The Liberals won just 14 out of the 635 seats despite gaining over 19% of the vote. In Northern Ireland, the United Ulster Unionist Council, formed to oppose the 1973 Sunningdale Agreement providing for a power-sharing executive in Northern Ireland, won 11 of the 12 Northern Ireland seats on just 51% of the vote in the province. This result effectively doomed the constitutional experiment, since it seemed to have been repudiated by the voters. In Scotland, the SNP won 22% of the Scottish vote but only 7 of the 71 Scottish seats. Most striking of all, perhaps, the 'wrong' side had won the general election, for the first time since 1951, Labour being the largest party despite winning fewer votes than the Conservatives. The outcome was a Labour minority government.

The election cast doubt on a number of assumptions which had hitherto governed thinking about the British constitution. The first was that Britain had a two-party system and was a geographically homogeneous country rather than a territorially diversified one. The second was that the first-past-the-post electoral system yielded 'strong government'. It was by no means obvious that a government resting on just 37% of the vote would enjoy the authority needed to resolve Britain's deep-seated social and economic problems.

The decline in support for the two major parties, Labour and the Conservatives, in the February 1974 general election, far from proving a unique event, seemed to be the harbinger of a major change in popular attitudes. The average share of the two party vote in the eight general elections between 1945 and 1970 had been 91%. But, in the nine general elections between February 1974 and 2005, it was to be just 73%, and in the general election of 2005, the two-party share fell to 69%. Between the general elections of 1945 and 1970, there were on average just 10 MPs from parties other than Labour and the Conservatives. Since 1970, the average has been 54. In the 2005 parliament, no fewer than 92 MPs came from parties other than Labour or the Conservatives, nearly 15% of the total membership. In the general election of 2005, nearly one-third of those voting—31%—had refused to support either of the major parties. Since February 1974 the share of third and other parties has never fallen below 20%. This trend of course made a hung parliament more likely in the future, an issue we shall consider in greater detail in chapter 5.

But the decline of two-party politics in the country was little noticed, since, for most of the years between 1974 and 2005, Britain was still ruled by single-party majority governments. The exceptions were: first, the period between the February and October 1974 general elections; second, the period between April 1976, by which time Labour had lost the small overall majority which it had won in October 1974, and the general election of May 1979; and, third, the period between November 1996, by which time the Conservative majority of 21, gained in the 1992 general election, had evaporated as a result of by-election losses and defections, and the general election of May 1997. Otherwise, however, the decline of the two party system amongst the electorate had seemingly little effect upon the politics of the House of Commons.

The continuation of single-party majority government, during a period when support for the two major parties was declining, was due more to the working of the electoral system, which manufactured a majority for a party with just over two-fifths of the votes, than to the choices of the voters. In 1983 and 1987, the Conservatives, under Margaret Thatcher, won landslide victories, with majorities of 144 and 100 respectively. Yet these victories were won on just over 42% of the vote. Nearly three-fifths of those voting had voted against the Conservatives. Remarkably, the Conservative percentage of the vote was around 2% lower in 1983 than in 1979, when the party had won a majority of just 43. For every 1% of the vote that the Conservatives lost between 1979 and 1983, they gained 50 seats!

From 1997, it was Labour's turn to become the beneficiaries of the electoral system. In 1997, it won a majority of 179, the largest in its history and the largest majority gained by any party since the war. Yet that majority was secured on just 43% of the vote, a lower percentage of the vote than Labour gained in the general elections of 1951 and 1955 which it had lost. In 2001, Labour's vote fell slightly to 42%, but it still won a hefty majority of 166. Of the seven general elections since October 1974, four—those in 1983, 1987, 1997 and 2001—yielded landslide majorities in the House of Commons, majorities of 100 or more, on just 42% or 43% of the vote

In 2005, Labour gained a comfortable working majority of 67, although its vote had slumped to just 36%, the lowest percentage vote ever recorded for a majority government with a secure majority. Labour was returned to office even though nearly two-thirds of those voting had voted against it. During the period since 1974, the two-party share of the vote never reached more than 80%, and the highest percentage of the vote gained by a winning party was 43.9% by the Conservatives in 1979. There was thus a disjuncture between a broadly two-party system at Westminster and the development of multi-party competition amongst the voters, between popular attitudes and their representation in the House of Commons.

It is hardly surprising that in 1974 the issue of proportional representation came, for the first time since the 1920s, to the forefront of the political agenda. Until then it had seemed a dead issue. As recently as 1964, a standard account of British government had accurately stated that 'the electoral system is no longer a bone of contention'.[18] That could no longer be said after 1974. Admittedly, the supporters of proportional representation did not succeed in securing change at Westminster. Nevertheless, it has now come to be accepted that first-past-the-post is not the best system for elections to bodies other than the House of Commons. We have already seen that all elections in Northern Ireland, other than elections to the House Commons, are conducted by the single transferable vote method of proportional representation. When, in 1998, provision was made for a Scottish Parliament and a National Assembly of Wales, and in 1999 for a directly elected London strategic authority, they too were to be elected by proportional representation, although not by the single transferable vote method, but by a variant of the additional member method employed in Germany. In 1999, Parliament also decided that elections to the European Parliament should be by yet another system of proportional representation, based on regional, multi-member constituencies and party lists. In 2004, the Labour government held a referendum in the north east of England, asking voters whether they wanted a regional assembly. That too would have been elected by proportional representation. Although regional devolution was rejected by voters in the north east, it is generally accepted that, if there are to be directly elected regional bodies in the future, they too should be elected by proportional representation. In 2007, the Scottish Parliament introduced the single transferable vote method of proportional representation for local government elections; and the National Assembly of Wales is currently considering whether the voting system for

[18] A H Birch, *Representative and Responsible Government* (London, Allen & Unwin, 1964) 227.

local government in Wales should be changed to a proportional one. Proportional representation, so it seems, is rather like the incoming tide, flowing into the estuaries and along the rivers. It is becoming difficult, if not impossible, to hold it back. Certainly it has now come to be broadly accepted that all directly elected bodies other than the Commons and local authorities ought to be elected by one of the various systems of proportional representation.

But the two general elections of 1974 and the coming to power of governments based on under 40% of the vote gave rise to a wider debate on the constitution which went much further than advocacy of proportional representation. In his 1976 Dimbleby lecture on 'Elective Dictatorship', Lord Hailsham declared himself profoundly concerned that a government, elected by just 37% of the vote—a little over one in three of those voting—could yet propose to implement radical reforms which, in his view, the public did not desire. He had come to the conclusion, so he stated in his lecture, that 'Our constitution is wearing out. Its central defects are gradually coming to outweigh its merits, and its central defects consist in the absolute powers we confer on our sovereign body, and the concentration of those powers in an executive government formed out of one party which may not fairly represent the popular will'.[19] Lord Hailsham remained an opponent of proportional representation for elections to the House of Commons, but in other respects his proposals were far-reaching. He advocated nothing less than a written constitution, to be drawn up by a constitutional convention, and validated by referendum. Lord Hailsham was in fact the first senior politician to propose that Britain adopt a written constitution. This constitution would make provision for limiting the powers of parliament through a bill of rights, based on the European Convention on Human Rights, a directly elected upper house, devolution to the English regions as well as the non-English parts of the United Kingdom, plus a special procedure to amend it involving a qualified majority in parliament and a referendum. Lord Hailsham's advocacy of reform proved highly influential and it now appeared that the old constitution was under attack by an elder statesman who had occupied the very heart of its citadel.

VI

One of the central themes of British politics in the early post-war years was an increase in the role of the state, which was to play a far greater part in the management of the economy and in social welfare than it had done hitherto. This increase in the role of the state was to be only partially reversed in the 1980s and 1990s by the Conservative governments of Margaret Thatcher and John Major. In consequence, the state plays a far larger role in our lives than it did in 1945. This has led to a renewed concern with whether there are sufficient checks on the power of government; and, in particular, whether such checks can be really effective in an

---

[19] *The Listener*, 21 October 1976, 500.

unprotected constitution, that is a constitution in which there are no legal limits to the power of Parliament.

The main check upon government in the immediate post-war years was widely believed to be the 'swing of the pendulum', the alternation of power between governments of opposing political colours. This was held to act as a constraint upon government, since if an administration of one political colour sought to acquire excessive power, it would become unpopular at the polls and its excesses would be countermanded by its opponents. After 1979, however, it seemed that the pendulum had ceased to swing. The Conservatives, under, first, Margaret Thatcher and then John Major, remained in office for 18 years, a longer period of single-party government than Britain had seen since the time of the Napoleonic wars. Opponents of the Conservatives alleged that, untrammelled by fear of opposition, they were straining Britain's uncodified constitution to its limits. They cited as one particularly flagrant example the abolition by Margaret Thatcher's government of the Greater London Council and the metropolitan councils, strongholds of the Left, in 1985. They also alleged that the Conservatives were undermining civil liberties. 'The major source of the problem in our view', two critics argued in 1990, 'is a political system which has allowed the concentration of power in the hands of the executive (and the Prime Minister in particular) and the absence of effective checks and balances. The position is all the more remarkable for the fact that power has been concentrated in the hands of an executive branch which by all accounts enjoys the support of less than half the voting public and certainly much less than half of the total adult population'[20] By the end of the Conservative period of office, in 1997, that had become a representative view among many liberal-minded commentators.

Fears of overweening government were, perhaps, felt particularly strongly in Scotland and Wales, where the Conservatives remained a weak minority party during the whole of their period of government from 1979 to 1997. By 1987, the Conservatives retained just 10 of the 72 Scottish seats, with just under one quarter of the Scottish vote; and 8 of the 38 Welsh seats with just under 30% of the vote. This minority position did not, however, inhibit the Conservatives from applying their full programme in Scotland and Wales. The Scots and Welsh argued that they were being governed by a party for which they had not voted, and resentment in Scotland grew when the community charge—the so-called poll tax—was first tried out there in 1987. This fuelled arguments for devolution which, by 1997, had become a firm Labour commitment.

It was perhaps in reaction to the increase in state power that, from 1997, constitutional reforms were instituted to transfer power away from the government of the day, whether to politicians outside Westminster—in Northern Ireland, Scotland, Wales and London—to judges, as in the Human Rights Act, or to the people—as with the use of the referendum to validate some of the reforms.

---

[20] K D Ewing and CA Gearty, *Freedom Under Thatcher: Civil Liberties in Modern Britain* (Oxford, Clarendon Press, 1990) 255–26.

Formally, the doctrine of the sovereignty of Parliament has been maintained, and no explicit attack has been made upon it; but, nevertheless, all of the reforms have served to limit the power of what had hitherto been an omnicompetent government.

VII

The era of constitutional reform took place under the aegis of a Labour government, a government of the Left whose main professed aims traditionally had little to do with the constitution. The main purpose of the Labour Party had been to transform society, not alter the constitution. The founding fathers of the party at the beginning of the twentieth century had, admittedly, sought to reform the constitution by securing universal suffrage, for, at that time, only around 60% of adult males had the vote. But, otherwise, Labour seemed content with the constitution. They sought to capture the state not to transform it. Keir Hardie, one of Labour's founders, wrote in 1907, that 'The workman will use the political freedom which his fathers won for him to win industrial freedom for his children. That is the real inward meaning of the Labour Party'.[21] In the years immediately after 1945, the climax of the collectivist era, many on the Left tended to see British democracy as having evolved in a linear fashion from constitutional and political democracy in the nineteenth century to social and economic democracy in the mid-twentieth century, a point of view well-expressed by the sociologist, T H Marshall, in his book, *Citizenship and Social Class*, published in 1950. The Labour Party had inherited a political democracy. Its task now was to transform it into a social democracy. Constitutional reform would be a distraction from the aims of the Left, not a contribution towards them. An unprotected and uncodified constitution was actually an advantage to the Left, since it enabled radicals to implement major social and economic reforms without hindrance. 'I think', said the nineteenth century radical, Joseph Chamberlain, 'a democratic government should be the strongest government from a military and imperial point of view in the world, for it has the people behind it. Our misfortune is that we live under a system originally contrived to check the excesses of Kings and Ministers, and which meddles far too much in the Executive of the country'.[22] This view was echoed by twentieth century radicals. 'The absence of a written constitution', wrote Aneurin Bevan in 1952,

> 'gives British politics a flexibility enjoyed by few nations. No courts can construe the power of the British Parliament. It interprets its own authority, and from it there is no appeal. This gives it a revolutionary quality, and enables us to entertain the hope of bringing about social transformations, without the agony and prolonged crises experienced by less fortunate nations. The British constitution, with its adult suffrage, exposes all rights and privileges, properties and powers, to the popular will'.[23]

---

[21] K Hardie, *From Serfdom to Socialism* [1907] (reprinted, Brighton, Harvester Press, 1974) 77.

[22] A J Balfour, *Chapters of Autobiography* (London, Cassell 1930) 220–21.

[23] A Bevan, *In Place of Fear* (London, Heinemann, 1952) 100.

More recently, a leading constitutional lawyer has referred to the doctrine that 'legal sovereignty continues to rest with Parliament' as 'the first constitutional principle of democratic socialism'.[24]

The leaders of the Labour Party were more inclined than their counterparts in Continental social democratic parties to accept the constitution of the country in which they lived since, by contrast with most Continental countries, they had not been faced with the irredeemable hostility of the capitalist state. At the beginning of the twentieth century, Labour had actually been helped by one of the 'capitalist' parties, the Liberals, through an electoral pact. Thus, Labour did not see itself, as so many of the Continental social democratic parties had done, as being locked into a 'socialist' ghetto against its 'capitalist' opponents. The Labour Party would, most of its members believed, receive fair play from the British state, a feeling reinforced in 1924 when the first minority Labour government was formed. George V refused to listen to entreaties by Labour's opponents to engineer a coalition to keep Labour out; and he offered the Labour government exactly the same facilities that he had previously offered to its Conservative and Liberal opponents. It was 'essential', the king told a confidant of the defeated Conservative Prime Minister, Stanley Baldwin, 'that their rights under the Constitution should in no way be impaired'.[25]

It was partly for this reason that Labour, almost alone amongst social democratic parties in Europe, was hostile to proportional representation. The informal alliance with the Liberals in the early years of the twentieth century offered the infant party hope that it could prosper even under the first-past-the-post electoral system. The more far-sighted Labour leaders, such as Ramsay MacDonald, looked forward to the day when Labour would become one of the major parties in the state and would then come itself to benefit from the distortions of the first-past-the-post system, with its well known tendency to exaggerate the support of large parties. 'Speaking quite personally', George Lansbury was to tell the Labour Party Conference in 1926, 'he thought that the majority of the decisions under the present system had worked for the other people; but if they were wise they could now make it work for themselves'.[26] And so it proved to be.

Labour, therefore, came to identify strongly with the first-past-the-post electoral system and was deeply hostile to electoral reform. In February 1974, Labour was returned to office as a minority government on just 37% of the vote. The Home Secretary, Roy Jenkins, perhaps prefiguring his defection to the SDP in 1981, sought to persuade his Cabinet colleagues of the virtues of proportional representation, but found himself roundly rebuked by the Scottish Secretary, Willie Ross, who declared that 'If we were not too careful we could see the end of any possibility of a Labour Government'.[27] In 1976, Ron Hayward, the general secretary of the Labour Party, insisted that, 'Proportional representation means coalition

[24] K D Ewing, 'The Human Rights Act and Parliamentary Democracy' (1999) *Modern Law Review*, 99.

[25] R Rhodes James, *Memoirs of a Conservative* (London, Weidenfeld and Nicolson, 1969) 191.

[26] Report of the 26th Annual Conference of the Labour Party, 1926, p 273.

[27] B Castle, *The Castle Diaries 1974–1976* (London, Weidenfeld and Nicolson, 1980) 70.

government at Westminster, on the lines of our European partners, and it is good-bye then to any dreams or aspirations for a democratic socialist Britain'.[28]

But, by 1997, a Labour government was ready to institute proportional representation for elections to the European Parliament and to the various devolved bodies. Admittedly, it remained opposed to changing the system for Westminster elections, but it established an 'Independent Commission on the Voting System', chaired by Lord Jenkins, as Roy Jenkins had now become, to consider alternative methods of election to the House of Commons. The report, published in 1998 as Cm 4090, advocated a mild form of proportional representation, but was shelved by the government which contented itself with declaring that it would publish a review of voting systems, and that the system for Westminster could not be changed without a referendum. The review was published in January 2008 as Cm 7304, as a contribution to the debate, but made no proposals for change.

Many constitutional reforms have been validated by referendum. Before 1975, however, Labour had been bitterly opposed to use of the referendum, and on this it was at one with its social democratic colleagues on the Continent. In 1945, when Winston Churchill proposed that the wartime coalition be allowed to continue until Japan had been defeated, which, it was thought, might take some time, he had proposed to Attlee, the Labour leader, that the continuation of the coalition be put to referendum. Attlee, however, rejected this proposal, saying that the referendum was 'a device . . . alien to all our traditions', and adding that it 'has only too often been the instrument of Nazism and Fascism. Hitler's practices in the field of referenda and plebiscites can hardly have endeared these expedients to the British heart'.[29]

The basis of the opposition of Labour and social democratic parties to the referendum was the fear that it was an essentially reactionary device, since the people would probably prove wary of change. In 1948, Sweden's Social Democrat Prime Minister, Tage Erlander, declared

> 'It is obvious that referendums are a strongly conservative force. It seems much harder to pursue an effective reform policy if reactionaries are offered the opportunity to appeal to people's natural conservatism and natural resistance to change . . . The referendum system . . . provides an instrument for blocking radical progressive policy'.[30]

The Labour government elected in 1997 has, however, ignored these strictures. It initiated referendums before establishing devolution in Scotland, Wales and Northern Ireland, and before establishing a directly elected mayor and authority in London; and has promised further referendums. It seems, then, to have been accepted by Labour that constitutional change should depend upon a vote of the people as well as a vote by Parliament.

---

[28] Quoted in V Bogdanor, *The People and the Party System: The Referendum and Electoral Reform in British Politics* (Cambridge, CUP, 1981) 55.

[29] Bogdanor, *The People and the Party System*, above n 28, at 35

[30] Quoted in L Lewin, *Ideology and Change: A Century of Swedish Politics* (Cambridge, CUP, 1988) 235.

In two somewhat unnoticed pieces of legislation, Labour has gone even further, allowing voters themselves to trigger referendums. Under the School Standards and Framework Act of 1998, provision was made for parental ballots on grammar schools. The Labour government was opposed to the retention of grammar schools, but believed that there should be local ballots before they were abolished. Under the regulations, a ballot must be held if a petition is signed by 20% of the relevant eligible parents. At the time of writing, however, only one such ballot has been held. More important is the Local Government Act, 2000, which provided that 5% of registered local electors in a local authority could require that authority to hold a referendum on whether to introduce a directly elected mayor. This provision is discussed in greater detail in chapter 10.

These two Acts—the School Standards and Framework Act of 1998 and the Local Government Act of 2000—provide for the use of the petition or initiative, a mechanism that is new to Britain, although its use is fairly common in Switzerland, and in many of the western states of the United States. The initiative is an instrument that is pregnant with possibility. If local electors can petition their authority to hold a referendum on whether to elect a mayor, why not also, it might be argued, on other matters such as, for example, the organisation of the schools or the size of the local authority budget? Perhaps, in the fullness of time, the initiative might even come to be introduced at national level, and that could have very far-reaching consequences. What is clear, however, is that Labour is no longer hostile to the instruments of direct democracy, and that use of the referendum has proved an important supplement to the machinery of representative democracy in implementing constitutional change.

The Labour government also passed a Human Rights Act in 1998. One likely consequence of this Act will be that judges come to play a much more important role in determining the scope of our rights than they have done hitherto. In addition, the judges are likely, in the long run, to gain greater influence as a result of the devolution legislation. This is because it is for the judges to determine whether legislation from the Scottish Parliament or Northern Ireland Assembly lies within the powers of those bodies. If it does not, the judges can declare it unlawful; and, since 1973, when Britain entered the European Community, judges have been required to interpret Westminster statutes so that they are in accordance with European Community law, since Parliament, in the European Communities Act of 1972, declared that it would be bound by the law of the Community.

To anyone interested in the history of the labour movement, it is remarkable and striking that the Labour government elected in 1997 has chosen to increase the influence of the judges. The growth of the early Labour Party was in large part due to the resentment of the trade unions at what they regarded as interference by judges, in the *Taff Vale* judgment of 1901 declaring the liability of the unions to damages in tort following a strike, and the *Osborne* judgment of 1909, forbidding trade unions from contributing money to a political party. Both of these judgments were in effect repealed by legislation introduced by the 1905 Liberal government, in 1908 and 1913 respectively, in part as a result of pressure by the infant

Labour Party. The *Taff Vale* judgment, in particular, had led many trade unions to the view that their interests were not satisfactorily represented at Westminster by the existing political parties, and therefore that a new party, independent of the Liberal and Conservative parties, was needed to defend their interests. Many trade unions decided, in consequence, to affiliate to the infant Labour Party.

The early Labour Party, therefore, was distinctly hostile to the judges, who seemed to be drawn from a class which was generally opposed to the aspirations of the Labour movement. When Aneurin Bevan was setting up the National Health Service, he declared himself fearful of 'judicial sabotage of socialist legislation'.[31] This hostility towards the judges was strengthened after 1971, when Edward Heath's Conservative government established an Industrial Relations Court in an attempt to bring the trade unions within the framework of the law. In 1973, 180 Labour MPs signed a motion calling for the removal of Sir John Donaldson who presided over the Court. In 1977, Michael Foot, Labour's Deputy Prime Minister, speaking to a conference of the Union of Post Office Workers, declared that

> 'If the freedom of the people of this country and especially the rights of trade unionists— if these precious things of the past had been left to the good sense and fair-mindedness of the judges, we would have few freedoms in this country at all'.[32]

But, in the 1980s, the Left, faced with Margaret Thatcher's determination to use the power of the state to the full, came to be much more favourably disposed to the idea of constitutional limits on government, limits which would be determined, in part at least, by the judges. They were encouraged by the fact that the judges themselves seemed more liberal than their counterparts in earlier years. By the 1980s, the judiciary had come to be regarded by many on the Left as a possible counterbalance to the depredations of a reactionary government.

Reform of the House of Lords was another issue on which Labour had been, perhaps surprisingly, somewhat indifferent. In theory, the Labour Party had always been hostile to a chamber composed primarily of hereditary peers; and logically, no doubt, Labour should have called for the abolition of the Lords, as in fact the party did in its early days. Labour came to appreciate, however, that to propose a unicameral system of government might not prove electorally popular; yet it has never been able to reach any settled conclusion as to the appropriate composition of any alternatively constituted upper house.

Therefore, until the 1960s, Labour concentrated less on rationalizing the composition of the House of Lords than on reducing its powers. The Attlee government had, in the 1949 Parliament Act, reduced the delaying power of the Lords on non-money bills from three sessions to two. But the government did not want to rationalize the composition of the Lords since that might strengthen the legitimacy of the upper house and make it more of a threat to the Labour government's legislation. In his book, *Government and Parliament*, published in 1954, Herbert

---

[31] House of Commons Debates, vol 425, col 1983, 23 July 1946.
[32] Quoted in V Bogdanor, *Politics and the Constitution: Essays on British Government* (Aldershot, Dartmouth Press, 1996) 189.

Morrison, who had been Leader of the House of Commons in the Attlee government, declared that this government had not been

> 'anxious for the rational reform or democratization of the Second Chamber, for this would have added to its authority and would have strengthened its position as against that of the House of Commons. Changes which gave the House of Lords a democratic and representative character would have been undemocratic in outcome, for they would have tended to make the Lords the equals of the Commons. . . . The very irrationality of the composition of the House of Lords and its quaintness are safeguards for our modern British democracy'.[33]

In 1963, Richard Crossman, who would later become Leader of the House of Commons in Harold Wilson's Labour government in 1966, was able pithily to summarise Labour's standpoint on the Lords as being that 'an indefensible anachronism is preferable to a second Chamber with any real authority', a position which he found 'logical, but rather reactionary'.[34]

In 1968, however, Harold Wilson's government departed from the previous Labour consensus and produced a bill, proposing a highly complex reform of the composition as well as the powers of the Lords. This bill fell foul both of Tory traditionalists such as Enoch Powell who were opposed to change, and Labour left-wingers such as Michael Foot, who argued that the House of Lords should be abolished not reformed. MPs who belonged to neither of these two extremes were disturbed at the increase in Prime Ministerial patronage which would have been one of the consequences of the reform. The bill was made subject to a filibuster in committee and eventually abandoned by the government.

Once again, eighteen years of opposition, from 1979 to 1997, served to alter Labour attitudes and many in the Party came to be convinced that a stronger upper house was needed to act as a check upon government. Labour entered the 1997 election campaign proposing a two-stage reform of the Lords. The first stage would involve removal of all of the hereditary peers, so also removing the Conservative majority in the Lords. The second stage would involve elections for some or all of the members of the new upper house, to put it on a more democratic basis.

The final issue on which the Blair government departed from an earlier Labour consensus was devolution. Admittedly, the Labour Party in its early years was a Home Rule party, favouring Home Rule for Scotland and Wales as well as Ireland. But, in the 1920s, Labour dropped its commitment to devolution, regarding it as irrelevant during a time of economic and social dislocation. Aneurin Bevan, when he established the National Health Service, pointedly declined to establish a separate Scottish or Welsh Health Service, even though he himself was Welsh and

---

[33] H Morrison, *Government and Parliament: A Survey From the Inside*, [1954] (3rd edition, Oxford, OUP, 1964) 205.

[34] Quoted in M Taylor, 'Labour and the Constitution' in D Tanner, P Thane and N Tiratsoo (eds) *Labour's First Century* (Cambridge, CUP, 2000) 169. Taylor's chapter is a valuable one, but I find his attempt to argue that constitutional reform has always lain at the centre of Labour's programme singularly unconvincing.

represented a Welsh constituency, Ebbw Vale. 'Is it not rather cruel', Bevan asked, 'to give the impression to the 50,000 unemployed men and women in Wales that their plight would be relieved and their distress removed by this constitutional change? It is not socialism. It is escapism'.[35] As a young man working in a South Wales colliery, Bevan declared that he was concerned with just one practical question, 'Where does power lie in this particular state of Great Britain and how can it be attained by the workers?' The answer, he believed, was that 'power meant the use of collective action designed to transform society and so lift all of us together'.[36] Such collective action could best be undertaken by central government. The needs of the South Wales working class were no different from those of the Scottish working class and the English working class. They could be met only by a strong Labour government, representing the interests of the working class in the United Kingdom as a whole, at Westminster. 'My colleagues', Bevan insisted, 'have no special solution for the Welsh coal industry which is not a solution for the whole of the mining industry of Great Britain. There is no Welsh problem'.[37] Devolution, by fragmenting the state would merely weaken the socialist response to the depredations of capitalism.

Bevan, like most socialists of his day, insisted that the welfare state required that benefits and burdens be distributed according to need and not according to geography. It would be wrong for a sick person in Ebbw Vale to receive a different standard of care from that offered to a sick person in the north of England, just because Wales had a devolved body that could press for higher standards while the north did not. Bevan's aspiration has not of course been achieved, and there remain widely different standards of care today in different parts of the country. But the aim of a Labour government, he believed, was to help remove such inequalities, not perpetuate them through devolution.

In the 1970s, Labour adopted a policy of devolution, somewhat unwillingly, in response to the Scottish nationalist threat. Many Labour MPs, however, remained unreconciled to it, because it seemed to threaten the traditional socialist aim of territorial equity. 'If comprehensive education is right in Glasgow,' one MP declared during the devolution debates, 'it is right in the South of England'.[38] It was because it threatened the principle of territorial equity that, in the 1970s, Bevan's disciple, Neil Kinnock, declared that devolution could be 'an obituary notice for this movement'.[39] He came to change his mind later.

The Conservative argument against devolution had been that, by undermining the sovereignty of Parliament, it would lead to the break-up of the kingdom. The Labour argument against it was somewhat different. It was that devolution would deprive Westminster, not so much of sovereignty, as of power, the power to correct territorial disparities. Only a strong Labour government at Westminster could

---

[35] House of Commons Debates, vol 428, col 405, 28 October 1946.
[36] *In Place of Fear*, above n 23, 1–2.
[37] House of Commons Debates, vol 403, col 2312, 10 October 1944.
[38] House of Commons Debates, vol 922, col 1396, 13 December 1976.
[39] Labour Party Conference, 1976, cited in M Taylor, 'Labour and the Constitution', above n 34, 180.

secure the socialist values of equity and territorial justice. But, faced with nationalist pressures, Labour came to regard devolution as essential if the United
Kingdom was to be held together.

The radical programme of constitutional reform upon which the Labour government embarked from 1997 was, then, in many respects a programme contrary
to its traditional instincts. When Bagehot had said that a happy man is not con-
tinually worrying about repairs to his house, he was implying that a country which
is self-confident and sure of itself does not use its energies to reform its constitution. By analogy, so one might suggest, a political party which is confident of its
ultimate aims, does not spend its time on reforming the constitution. The Liberal
Party, at the beginning of the last century, did not propose reform of the Lords,
until the peers forced it to do so by rejecting Lloyd George's 'People's Budget' in
1909. At the time, the Liberal Party was perfectly happy with the first-past-the-
post-electoral system which had given it a landslide majority of 130 in the 1906
general election on just 49% of the vote. The Party did not come to espouse proportional representation until the general election of 1922, by which time it was
already the third party in the system.

The Labour Party, similarly, did not expend its energies on constitutional
reform in 1945 when it was confident of its socialist aims. The Attlee government
was constitutionally conservative, using inherited institutions to achieve radical
social and economic reform. It is hard to avoid the conclusion that Labour's
espousal of constitutional reform was in some measure a response to the vacuum
created by a decline in the belief in socialism and social democracy. The commitment to constitutional reform, therefore, was in part the outcome of frustration at
domestic political failure and exclusion from office, but it arose also from a loss of
confidence in the ultimate aims of the Labour movement. Those who founded and
fought for the Labour Party when socialism appeared to be the wave of the future
were concerned less with changing the rules regulating the exercise of power than
with changing society. A party which is concerned more with procedures than
with substance has lost faith, so it might be argued, in its ultimate aims. If one
joined a cricket club, one would feel that there was something wrong if the club
spent much of its time on rewriting its rules. From this point of view, therefore,
Labour's commitment to constitutional reform may be seen as the Party's
response to a post-social democratic age.

But it is possible to look at the evolution of the Left towards a policy of constitutional reform in a more positive light. During the 1980s and 1990s, the Left came
to be more sympathetic to the pluralist and decentralist elements of the socialist
tradition, elements which had been submerged during the immediate post-war
years when the Attlee government had been constructing the welfare state, but
which had always been part of the Party's heritage. The Left has always been concerned to expand opportunity and freedom. Such expansion, the Left came to
argue, was no doubt best achieved in the conditions of 1945 by an increase in the
power of the state. Today, by contrast, it may be better achieved through a
programme of constitutional reform which includes restrictions on the scope of

government and the decentralization of power. Those taking this view regard the constitutional reform programme of the Blair government from 1997 as a natural consequence of a process of rethinking on the Left.

For, by 1997, it had become clear that the old certainties of ideology and class were breaking down. Tony Blair's New Labour Party was based upon a recognition that the familiar landmarks of twentieth century politics were rapidly disappearing. Tribal allegiances were dissolving and society had become both more diverse and more complex than had been foreseen by earlier prophets of the Left, a process summed up by the term 'political dealignment'. Political identities were now more fluid than they had been during the immediate post-war years. For some on the Left, therefore, constitutional reform came to fill what might otherwise have proved an ideological vacuum. The collapse of the old certainties was leading, not to the end of history, but to the emergence of new themes, or rather the re-emergence of old themes, motifs powerfully present in political debate before 1914, but eclipsed during the trench warfare politics of ideology and class which had characterised so much of the twentieth century, a type of politics which the critic, Ferdinand Mount, has labelled 'rage and fear politics'.[40]

One central aim of constitutional reform has been to limit the power of the state. But there was also a second theme, subordinate perhaps in the years immediately following 1997, but likely to increase in importance in the future. This second theme is the introduction of popular participation in decision-making. The referendum was obviously one way of attempting to secure this objective, even though few of the referendums so far held have aroused much popular enthusiasm. Nevertheless, the referendum seems one way in which constitutional reform can come to terms with the realities of social change at the end of the twentieth century. With the decline of deference and an increase in the percentage of those staying on for higher education, people seem much less willing to rely upon ministers and members of Parliament to make decisions on their behalf. They feel perfectly well qualified to make decisions for themselves. There is at the same time a growing scepticism towards the pretensions of political parties as vehicles of the popular will, and, more generally, towards the political process as a whole. This is shown, both in low turnout rates in general elections—58% in 2001 and 62% in 2005, the lowest since universal suffrage was introduced in 1918—and in the declining membership of political parties.

These are themes that we shall return to in the final chapter of *The New British Constitution*. What seems already clear, however, is that changes in voting behaviour since 1974 have reflected more profound social changes. This had been predicted by the political scientist S E Finer as early as 1980, when he pointed to 'a prodigious change in the public perception of the nature of political parties and the way they have carried out their functions. That change is part of the more subtle and half-concealed changes detectable once the façade of the parliamentary duopoly has been penetrated'.[41] These wider social changes have undermined

---

[40] 'What is Labour Doing to the Constitution', *Prospect*, May 2004.
[41] S E Finer, *The British Party System 1945–1979* (Washington, American Enterprise Institute, 1980) xiv.

support for the traditional 'Westminster Model' of government and the old constitution. Perhaps acceptance of the old constitution had depended upon specific features of British society which have now passed away. The post-war era has been a period of massive socio-economic change, and it seemed that the existing institutions of government had been slow to respond to these changes. That perhaps is why constitutional issues have returned to the political agenda, why the old constitution has found itself under strain. But before asking how well the constitutional reforms have served to cure these deficiencies of the political system, we need to examine the reforms in more detail. We begin with the Human Rights Act, cornerstone of the new constitution.

Part II

The New Constitution

3

The Human Rights Act:
Cornerstone of the New Constitution

CONSTITUTIONS HAVE THREE main aims. The first is to provide a sense of purpose, a rallying-cry. The American Constitution, for example, declares its purpose to be to 'form a more perfect Union, insure domestic Tranquility, provide for the common defence, promote the general Welfare, and secure the Blessings of Liberty to ourselves and our Posterity'. This statement of aims is generally put in the preamble of a constitution rather than in the main text. Some argue that an important part of the argument for Britain following almost all other democracies and adopting a codified constitution lies in the statement of values that would be part of it. A constitution, so it is held, would codify the values of citizenship and make it easier both for the young and for those coming to Britain from abroad, to understand what our basic values are. Ideally, perhaps, a constitution would be kept in the pockets of those studying civics in schools, and those seeking citizenship would be required to understand and swear allegiance to it. There is, so it is coming increasingly to be argued, need for an authoritative statement of values, of what it means to be a member of our society.

The second aim of a constitution is to provide, as it were, an organisation chart of government, to clarify the functions of the organs of government, the legislature, the executive and the judiciary, and the inter-relationships between them. That has been the traditional function of constitutions. The first codified constitutions of which we have knowledge, those of the Greek city-states, were little more than organisation charts delineating functions. Just as any game, if it is to be effectively played, requires an authoritative set of rules and authoritative interpreters of these rules, any society, except perhaps for the most primitive, needs an authoritative guide to the way in which its institutions work. That guide is provided by the constitution.

With the advent of the American constitution in 1787, however, a third element enters. The constitutions of the Greek city states and later constitutions may provide for limited government, but the American constitution was the first to provide for limitations on what the citizens themselves could do to each other. Earlier constitutions had provided rights against government, the American constitution provided rights against the citizen, or rather against the majority. The Founding Fathers in the United States were anxious to resist what came to be called 'the tyranny of the majority', a tyranny exercised by the majority against minorities. The theme of the tyranny of the majority was to become, in the nineteenth century, a staple theme of liberal thought, emphasised by political philosophers such as Benjamin Constant, Alexis de Tocqueville, and John Stuart Mill; in our own times, it has been re-emphasised with equal eloquence, by such liberal philosophers as Isaiah Berlin and H L A Hart.

The Americans sought to guard against the tyranny of the majority through a Bill of Rights, the name generally given to the first ten amendments of the American constitution, ratified shortly after the constitution. Without the Bill of Rights, it is very likely that the constitution would not have been ratified at all since the states regarded it as conceding too much to the federal power. The American Bill of Rights is quite unlike the English Bill of Rights of 1689 and the Scottish Claim of Right. The English Bill of Rights was a statute guaranteeing the rights of Parliament against the King. No limitations were placed upon the King-in–Parliament, whose powers remained unlimited, but the balance of power was altered, in favour of Parliament and against arbitrary rule by the King. The sovereignty of Parliament remained unlimited. The American Bill of Rights, by contrast, served to entrench fundamental rights against the majority as represented in Congress. The first amendment to the American constitution, for example, prevents Congress from making any law restricting the freedom of speech or religion. Thus, even if the majority in the United States wanted to pass such a law, it is not empowered to do so; and were Congress to seek to pass such a law, the Supreme Court would declare it invalid.

The Bill of Rights cannot be altered simply by passing a law through Congress with a simple majority. Instead, a special procedure is needed to amend the constitution, and this is typical of the workings of bills of rights. If rights could be altered by majority vote, what would be the point of having a bill of rights at all? In the United States, the consent of two-thirds of Congress and also three-quarters of the American states is required to amend the constitution. That, of course, is very difficult to achieve, and it is not perhaps surprising that, in addition to the first ten amendments, there have been only 17 further amendments to the American constitution in over two hundred years.

The American constitution, then, aims to secure not only rights against government, but also rights against the people themselves, rights against the majority. Most modern constitutions follow the American example and contain bills of rights. This, then, is the third purpose of a constitution, to secure the rights of individuals, not only against government, but also against the majority. Until the Human Rights Act of 1998, however, Britain did not have a bill of rights in the American sense of the term, provisions designed to protect the individual against the tyranny of the majority. This is not of course to say that minorities had no rights against the state. They did enjoy such rights, but their rights were derived not from the constitution, but from Parliament and the judges. Parliament, many believed, took good care not to infringe human rights, which were protected, so it was argued, in the last resort by public opinion. The premise was that the electorate was sensitive to human rights and would punish any government which sought to infringe them. It could be argued that rights in Britain, with the significant exception of Northern Ireland, were better protected than in many countries with codified constitutions. There is little doubt that, during the first half of the twentieth century, the condition of ethnic minorities in Britain was far better than, for example, that of Afro-Americans in the southern states of the United States, subject as they were to segregation and lynch law. In most democracies, however, it has come to be believed that minorities need stronger institutional protection and that this is best provided by a bill of rights. Britain remained one of the few advanced democracies to rely so heavily upon the legislature to defend human rights.

Deference towards Parliament came to be eroded during the post-war years which saw rising levels of education and greater insistence upon the protection of individual rights. People came to be more aware of what their rights were and more determined to defend them. It is largely for this reason that administrative law, the branch of law concerned with the powers of ministers, executive bodies and local authorities, a subject hardly known before the 1960s, became such a flourishing discipline in the latter half of the twentieth century. A further reason for a bill of rights is that there is now much less of a moral consensus in society than there used to be. There is a much greater divergence of lifestyles and more disagreement about how individuals should live their lives. In addition, Britain has become a multicultural and multidenominational society, and that too has served to dissolve consensus as well as making it more necessary to ensure that the rights of minorities—whether ethnic, religious or cultural—are protected. While some of these minorities might be able to secure their rights through the electoral process, not all of them can. Very unpopular minorities such as, for example, asylum seekers and suspected terrorists, would be unlikely to receive much sympathy from the public or from the public's representatives in Parliament.

Britain, then, is no longer as homogeneous a society as it was in the 1950s, and no longer a society in which there is general agreement on the proper limits of government or on how government ought to be organised. These changes in public opinion were bound to have an effect upon the constitution. The two have always been interconnected. Dicey followed his classic work on the constitution, *An Introduction to the Study of the Law of the Constitution* (1885), with a volume in 1905 entitled, *Lectures on the Relation Between Law and Public Opinion in England During the 19th Century*. It was the force of public opinion, or rather perhaps of elite opinion, since of course public opinion accounted for less in the nineteenth century than it does today, which gave vitality to the constitution, and to the conventions which underpinned it. Today, however, public opinion is no longer merely elite opinion, and it is far less unified than it was at the time when Dicey wrote.

New threats, and, in particular, the growth of terrorism, mean that neither public opinion nor Parliament can any longer necessarily be relied upon to protect the rights of unpopular minorities. The progress through Parliament of the 2001 Anti-Terrorism, Crime and Security Act and of the 2005 Prevention of Terrorism Act shows that parliamentary scrutiny of legislation bearing on human rights can be somewhat perfunctory during a period of moral panic. The Anti-Terrorism, Crime and Security Act provided for the indefinite detention of suspected terrorists, who were not British citizens, if the Home Secretary had reasonable grounds to suspect that they were a threat to national security. The bill was debated for just 16 hours in the House of Commons, and for an even shorter time in the House of Lords. It received the Royal Assent in December 2001, just one month after being introduced into the Commons, insufficient time surely for the proper scrutiny of legislation bearing so closely on human rights and personal liberties. Those detained under the Act appealed to the courts, and in the case *A v Secretary of State for the Home Department* [2005] 2 AC 68 (known as the *Belmarsh Prison* case), the House of Lords ruled that the relevant part of the 2001 Act was incompatible with the European Convention prohibition on discrimination in respect of the right to liberty. The government then repealed the legislation and replaced it with a Prevention of Terrorism Act, providing for control orders to be issued restricting the freedom of suspected terrorists. This legislation, too, was rushed rapidly through Parliament. There was no proper Second Reading debate in the House of Lords at all. The peers did not like the bill, but allowed it to go through after the government gave an undertaking that it would be brought back early in the next session. Following the London bombings in July 2005, however, this undertaking became inoperative.

During the last quarter of the twentieth century, there had arisen a growing belief that some extra protection of human rights was needed over and above that provided by parliamentary scrutiny. This belief was to be strengthened by experience of IRA terrorism in the 1970s and Al Qaeda terrorism at the beginning of the twenty first century. It became apparent that the courts might well view the issue of the appropriate balance between freedom and security quite differently from Parliament. It would be natural for Parliament, responsible as it is to a frightened electorate seeking strong measures against terrorism, to give greater emphasis to security and less perhaps to the rights of suspects. Therefore, so it was argued, some extra form of protection for human rights was needed. During an earlier IRA bombing campaign in 1974, Lord Scarman, a future law lord, had declared, in his Hamlyn lectures of that year.

> 'When times are normal and fear is not stalking the land, English law sturdily protects the freedom of the individual and respects human personality. But when times are abnormally alive with fear and prejudice, the common law is at a disadvantage: it cannot resist the will, however, frightened and prejudiced, it may be, of Parliament'.[1]

It was for this reason that Lord Scarman became the first prominent judge to advocate a bill of rights for Britain.

---

[1] L Scarman, *English Law—The New Dimension* (London, Stevens, 1974) 15.

Entry into the European Community in 1973 was a further factor encouraging support for the stronger protection of human rights. It exposed Britain to other legal systems, none of which relied upon the doctrine of parliamentary sovereignty. Most of them offered stronger protection of human rights than Britain did; and, although the European Community lacked a bill of rights, its court, the European Court of Justice began, from the 1970s, to develop the idea that there were certain fundamental rights that limited the power of Community institutions and of Member States when operating to give effect to Community law. European Union law has now become an increasingly potent channel for bringing the recognition of human rights into the British constitution. But, of more immediate importance, entry into the European Community opened up the possibility that Parliament could be bound by the decisions of a higher legal order. In the *Factortame* decisions, the House of Lords, the ultimate court of appeal in Britain, decided to 'disapply' part of an Act of Parliament. When, in 1994, the House of Lords declared that legislation, relating this time to part-time employees, violated a directive of the European Union, as the Community had by then become, *The Times* commented that 'Britain may now have, for the first time in its history, a constitutional court'.[2] If Acts of Parliament could be 'disapplied', in effect ruled invalid by the courts, there would seem no objection in principle to allowing them also to be 'disapplied' if they offended against the provisions of a bill of rights.

Thus, although, in Britain, it had been Parliament and the decisions of judges rather than a constitution, which had traditionally determined the rights of individuals against the state, the country could not remain immune from the general feeling in Europe that stronger protection of human rights was needed. After WWII Britain had played the lead in encouraging the trend towards stronger protection of human rights on the Continent, where the reaction to Fascism and National Socialism meant that there was some scepticism as to whether the legislature and the force of public opinion alone were sufficient protection against the threat of dictatorship. Most Continental countries believed, therefore, that they should strengthen the role of the courts so as to guard against new outbreaks of popular intolerance. British lawyers, including Sir David Maxwell-Fyfe, later to be Home Secretary and Lord Chancellor in the Conservative government elected in 1951, played a major role in drafting for Europe a Convention on Human Rights, a bill of rights for Europe, designed to ensure that the Continent was never again disfigured by the horrors of Fascism and National Socialism, drawn up and signed in Rome in 1950. Britain was among the first countries to ratify the Convention in 1951, and, unlike some Continental countries, provided that the Convention should apply to the colonies as well as to Britain itself. The Convention was, ironically in the light of current political alignments, supported more strongly by lawyers of a Conservative bent than by lawyers from the left. It had particularly strong support from the Conservative leader, Winston Churchill, who believed that it could help to unify Europe on the basis of the rule of law.

---

[2] *R v Secretary of State for Employment ex parte EOC* [1995] 1 AC 1 (HL); *The Times*, 5 March 1994.

The European Convention on Human Rights is not a product of the European Communities or the European Union, neither of which existed in 1950. It emanates instead from the Council of Europe, a wholly different body, and one which, unlike the European Union, is purely intergovernmental and consultative, with no power to bind individual Member States. The Council of Europe is open to all European democracies, and at present has 47 members including nearly every country on the continent. The institutions of the Council of Europe include the European Court of Human Rights which adjudicates on claims against Member States over breaches of Convention Rights and a Parliamentary Assembly which makes recommendations to the Member States. The European Court of Human Rights is based in Strasbourg. The Court of Justice of the European Union, on the other hand, sits in Luxembourg. The European Convention, unlike the European Communities, is not for Britain, a superior legal order, and it is binding only as a treaty obligation in international law, rather than in domestic law. It is, therefore, not directly enforceable in British Courts.

Every Member State of the Council of Europe, except the two common law members, Britain and Ireland, did, however, decide to incorporate the provisions of the Convention into their domestic law. This meant that the Convention became part of their legal system. Britain chose initially and for many years, not to incorporate the Convention, largely because this would conflict with the doctrine of the sovereignty of Parliament. According to this doctrine Parliament could enact whatever legislation it pleased, and it could not, therefore, be bound by any bill of rights. There could be no higher law over and above Parliament. On 18th January 1951, when the Labour Cabinet considered whether to accede to the European Convention, the Cabinet Secretary's notes, recently released, show that Chuter Ede, the Home Secretary, believed it to be 'inconsistent with our conception of unwritten constitution'. Herbert Morrison, Leader of the House of Commons, asked whether a 'subsequent Government' could 'then contract out', and was assured by the Foreign Secretary, Ernest Bevin that it could 'on 6 months notice'. Even so, Morrison declared that he had 'always been against this Convention—all of it. Humbug', while Lord Addison, Lord President of the Council, said that he would 'Prefer a frontal attack on this nonsense. Don't express any sympathy'. The Lord Chancellor, Lord Jowitt had previously referred to 'a half-baked scheme to be administered by some unknown court'.[3] Nevertheless Britain was the first Member State of the Council of Europe to ratify the Convention, in 1951. In 1966, the government accepted the right of individual petition to the European Court.

But the consequence of Britain not incorporating the European Convention into her domestic law, was that while, for example, a German litigant who felt that her rights had been infringed could seek redress in a German court, since Germany had incorporated the European Convention, a British litigant who felt that her

---

[3] CAB 195/8, 317–18; A Lester, 'Fundamental Rights: The United Kingdom Isolated?' (1984) Public *Law*, 52.

rights had been infringed could not obtain redress in a British court, but would have to seek it in the Strasbourg court. But one could only seek such a remedy when all national remedies had been exhausted. The process, therefore, involved much extra expense and a longer wait for redress, since the Strasbourg court was always clogged up with cases. It seemed illogical that the British government had accepted that it was bound by certain rights, but that it would not allow them to be secured in British courts.

The Human Rights Act of 1998 was an attempt to resolve this illogicality without formally undermining the doctrine of the sovereignty of Parliament. The Act did not, as is sometimes alleged, create new rights. What it did was to allow the rights guaranteed under the European Convention, to which the British government had long since committed itself, to be secured in British courts. If a litigant failed to secure redress in British courts, it would still be open to her to seek redress in the Strasbourg court. The purpose of the Human Rights Act, therefore, was well stated in the title of the White Paper issued by the Labour government in 1998 published alongside the Human Rights Bill—*Rights Brought Home;* or, to use more technical language, the Act had the effect of patriating rights rather than creating new ones.

The Human Rights Act has three elements. The first is that ministers are now required, when introducing legislation into Parliament, to certify whether, in their belief, it complies with the European Convention; and Parliament has established a Joint Select Committee, composed of MPs and peers, to scrutinise the human rights aspects of legislation and to make recommendations.

The second element places an obligation upon the courts. They are required to interpret *all* legislation, whether passed before or after the Human Rights Act, so that it is compatible with the European Convention so far as it is possible to do so. The Convention thus becomes a standard of interpretation for the courts.

Thirdly, however, if legislation cannot be so construed as to be made compatible with Convention rights, then the courts may issue a declaration of incompatibility. But judges have not been given the power which judges enjoy in the United States to invalidate legislation incompatible with the bill of rights. The offending statute or part of a statute remains part of the law unless and until Parliament decides to alter the law, and has to be applied to the individual in the particular case at stake. In this way, the Human Rights Act sought to reconcile the idea of a bill of rights with the doctrine of parliamentary sovereignty.

The Act does, all the same, impose some restriction on the sovereignty of Parliament. Article 3 of the Act provides that the courts read legislation so as to give effect to Convention rights 'whenever enacted'. The Act thus applies to both existing and future legislation. The doctrine of implied repeal does not apply with respect to such legislation. This doctrine states that when two statutes conflict, the later statute prevails even if the later statute does not explicitly repeal the former. Implied repeal had been a standard principle of construction since two cases in the 1930s, *Vauxhall Estates v Liverpool Corporation* [1932] 1 KB 723; and *Ellen Street Estates Ltd v Minister of Health* [1934] 1 KB 590. Some jurists went so far as to suggest that the doctrine of implied repeal was a logical consequence of the principle of the sovereignty of Parliament; since, if an earlier statute could override a later statute, it would be possible for one Parliament to limit what a later Parliament could do. But, if Parliament wishes to contravene the Human Rights Act, it must do so explicitly. A later statute cannot 'trump' the Human Rights Act. To this extent, therefore, the Human Rights Act modifies the strict doctrine of parliamentary sovereignty. There is now at least one thing that Parliament cannot do. It cannot impliedly repeal the Human Rights Act.

Rights, nevertheless, still depend upon the discretion of Parliament. There is no legal obligation upon either Parliament or government to amend a legislative provision which has been found by a court to be incompatible with the Convention. When they believe that rights are infringed by primary legislation, the judges can do no more than issue a declaration of incompatibility. They can do nothing to remedy the infringement. All that they can do is to make a statement. It is then for Parliament, led by ministers, to decide how to react to that statement. Parliament, however, is given, under the Act, the power to repeal or amend the offending statute or part of a statute by a special fast-track procedure. The Human Rights Act does not, then, remove the protection of human rights from Parliament to the courts. It does not make the judiciary the exclusive arbiter of human rights. Instead, it enables the judges to participate in a debate about the appropriate balance between human rights and executive power. Final resolution of the debate remains, formally at least, with Parliament.

The Human Rights Act, therefore, does not provide for a judicial remedy. It does not include Article 13 of the European Convention which provides that:

'Everyone whose rights and freedoms as set forth in this Convention are violated shall have an effective remedy before a national authority . . .'.

It is thus incorrect to say that the European Convention has been incorporated into law. The remedy depends upon Parliament. It is not automatic. For this reason, many would argue that the term 'Human Rights Act' is a misnomer, since the courts cannot **guarantee** the rights of the individual. All that the courts can do is to say that a statute or part of a statute is incompatible with rights. They can do nothing to assist the wronged defendant in securing her rights. Or, alternatively, one might say that the courts in judging legislation incompatible with the Convention cannot claim that, strictly speaking, it infringes rights, since, under the doctrine of the sovereignty of Parliament, rights cannot be superior to Parliament. Yet, the whole purpose of asserting legal rights is to assert that there are some measures which a legislature ought not to be able to enact by simple majority, if at all.

If, however, government and Parliament were to decide *not* to take remedial action following a declaration of incompatibility, a litigant would still be able to take her case to the European Court of Human Rights at Strasbourg, and would be well placed, armed as she would be with a favourable decision from a British court. The British government is committed by treaty to accept a decision made by the European Court of Human Rights, and failure to do so would be a breach of the government's obligations under international law. There are, however, some areas, such as national security and public morals (for example abortion), where the European Court allows a wide margin of appreciation for domestic authorities; and in such cases, a declaration of incompatibility would not necessarily lead to a change in the law in a situation where the government and Parliament were to take a different view from that of the domestic courts. Even more fundamentally, the idea of a declaration of incompatibility assumes that rights are given and taken away by Parliament rather than being inherent in the individual, as most advocates of human rights believe. It implies that human rights are not for the courts alone but also for politicians, that they are the outcome of an inter-institutional dynamic, between Parliament and the courts. Individuals, then, have rights so long as government and the legislature agree that they do.

In a case, *Burden and Burden v The United Kingdom* (Application no. 13378/05), heard by the European Court of Human Rights in December 2006, the Court declared that the Human Rights Act did *not* provide an effective remedy, since the remedy 'is dependent on the discretion of the executive and [one] which the Court has previously found to be ineffective on that ground', (para 40). But the Court also declared it to be

> 'possible that at some future date evidence of a long-standing and established practice of ministers giving effect to the courts' declarations of incompatibility might be sufficient to persuade the Court [of Human Rights] of the effectiveness of the procedure. At the present time, however, there is insufficient material on which to base such a finding'.

What the European Court is saying, presumably, is that, if ministers and Parliament regularly give effect to declarations of incompatibility by the courts, this practice would, at some time in the future, harden into a convention, though it has not yet done so. If or when that occurs, the European Court would be prepared to regard such a convention, since it imposes an obligation upon the government, albeit a non-statutory one, as a remedy. But that is not yet the position.

At the time of writing ministers and Parliament have in fact altered every one of those statutes or parts of statutes against which declarations of incompatibility have been issued, though they have generally done so either by pushing through special legislation, as with the Prevention of Terrorism Act 2005, or by inserting provisions into a bill that is before Parliament at the relevant time, rather than by using the fast track procedure. Between the year 2000, when the Human Rights Act came into force, and January 2009, there were 17 declarations of incompatibility; 14 have been remedied, one is the subject of public consultation and two are under consultation as to how to remedy the incompatibility. Of the 17 cases, only 3 arose from statutes which had come into force since the passage of the Human Rights Act. Even so, the legislation so far enacted to remove incompatibilities has not operated retrospectively so as to provide a recompense for those whose human rights have been breached. A declaration of incompatibility, therefore, does not necessarily help a litigant whose rights have been violated, precisely because it is Parliament that has the last word.

It is only with regard to Westminster legislation, and not to the legislation of the devolved bodies, that there is no domestic remedy. The devolution legislation specifies that the devolved bodies cannot act in a manner that is incompatible with European Convention rights. The Human Rights Act reinforced the devolution legislation. Thus judges *can* set aside legislation of the devolved bodies which is contrary to the Human Rights Act. That is because the devolved bodies are, unlike Westminster, non-sovereign legislatures, and so giving judges the right of judicial review of legislation of the devolved bodies does not undermine the doctrine of the sovereignty of Parliament. The devolved bodies cannot legislate incompatibly with Convention rights. The National Assembly of Wales does not at present have primary legislative powers, its powers being confined to the passage of secondary legislation—statutory instruments, regulations, orders and the like. Nevertheless, human rights are written into the Government of Wales Act of 1998 so that the Assembly cannot act in any way that is incompatible with the European Convention. Under the Government of Wales Act 2006, the National Assembly was given the power to pass 'measures' that have the force of primary legislation; but here too, they have no power to pass any measure which is incompatible with the Convention. The European Convention is thus fundamental law for the devolved bodies, but not for England. In the non-English parts of the United Kingdom, the Convention has in effect been incorporated as regards those domestic matters which lie under the jurisdiction of the devolved bodies. It may be that, in consequence of, for example, Scottish legislation being found to be in breach of the Convention by the courts in Scotland, similar United Kingdom legislation comes to be amended so that the validity of legislation does not depend upon where an individual lives. For the moment, however, rights are not yet standardised across the United Kingdom, and the protection of rights rests on different foundations in different parts of the kingdom.

II

The Human Rights Act is the cornerstone of the new British constitution, 'a defining moment in the life of our constitution', in the words of the Shadow Lord Chancellor, Lord Kingsland, when the bill was introduced into the House of Lords.[4] It gives us something very near to a bill of rights. In fact, it revolutionises our understanding of rights. It is likely in the long run, to transform both our understanding of human rights and the relationship between government and the judiciary. It has also increased the power of the judiciary. It is noteworthy that classic texts on the British Constitution, such as those of Bagehot or Sidney Low's *The Governance of England*, contain no chapter on the judiciary; and, until perhaps the 1960s, one could teach British government without giving much attention to the judiciary or knowing very much law. That would hardly be possible today.

---

[4] House of Lords Debates, vol 582, col 1234, 3 November 1997.

Our traditional understanding of these matters owes much to Dicey. For Dicey, the common law protected liberties by providing remedies rather than by enforcing rights. The principles on which our liberties were based were generalisations drawn from the circumstances in which judges provided remedies. In his book, *Introduction to the Study of the Law of the Constitution*, Dicey declared that 'There is in the English constitution an absence of those declarations or definitions of rights so dear to foreign constitutionalists'. Instead, he argues, the principles defining our civil liberties are 'like all maxims established by judicial legislation, mere generalisations drawn either from the decisions or dicta of judges, or from statutes'. By contrast, 'most foreign constitution-makers have begun with declarations of rights. For this', he adds, and he is not being ironic, 'they have often been in no wise to blame'.

The consequence, however, of this contrasting approach to the protection of human rights was that

'the relation of the rights of individuals to the principles of the constitution is not quite the same in countries like Belgium, where the constitution is the result of a legislative act, as in England, where the constitution itself is based on legal decisions—the difference in this matter between the constitutions of Belgium and the English constitution may be described by the statement that in Belgium individual rights are deductions drawn from the principles of the constitution, whilst in England the so-called principles of the constitution are inductions or generalisations based upon particular decisions pronounced by the courts as to the rights of given individuals'.[5]

Dicey was a strong believer in the rule of law. But for him it was seen primarily as a check upon the executive. It meant that no claim to authority would be recognised unless there were some legal backing for it; and only Parliament could confer that backing. Dicey hardly considered the possibility of a conflict between parliamentary sovereignty and the rule of law. He did not, in his great classic, *Introduction to the Study of the Law of the Constitution*, directly confront the possibility that Parliament itself might pass legislation infringing human rights. Rights, therefore, were dependent upon Parliament. In our own times, however, the term 'rule of law' has a broader interpretation than that given to it by Dicey. It implies recognition of those basic human rights which ought to be acknowledged in any liberal society; and in this sense of course there could well be a conflict between parliamentary sovereignty and the rule of law.

It is clear that one consequence of the Human Rights Act is that our rights will gradually come to be derived from 'principles of the constitution', rather than, as in Dicey's day, being mere inductions or generalizations from decisions made by the courts. The principles of the constitution will be the provisions of the European Convention. Issues which were in the past decided by ministers accountable to Parliament will come to be the responsibility of the courts. For Parliament is no longer trusted to the extent that perhaps it once was as an

---

[5] A V Dicey, *Introduction to the Study of the Law of the Constitution* (10th edn, London, Macmillan, 1959) 144.

effective guardian of human rights. The Human Rights Act now provides judges with a weapon. No one can predict how they will use it.

Following the passage of the Human Rights Act, judges are now entrusted with interpreting legislation in the light of a higher law, the provisions enshrined in the European Convention on Human Rights. Dicey, however, had declared that there can be no such higher law in the British Constitution. 'There is no law which Parliament cannot change. There is no fundamental or so-called constitutional law', and there is no person or body 'which can pronounce void any enactment passed by the British Parliament on the ground of such enactment being opposed to the constitution'.[6] Formally of course these propositions remain true. Judges can do no more than issue a declaration of incompatibility if they believe that a particular statute cannot be reconciled with the European Convention. They cannot declare that statute void, and Parliament can still refrain from amending or repealing the offending statute. Nevertheless, the Human Rights Act makes the European Convention in effect part of the fundamental law of the land. It brings the modalities of legal argument into the politics of the British state.[7] In a lecture in 2005, Lord Steyn, a former law lord, declared that,

> 'In the development of our country towards becoming a true constitutional state the coming into force of the Human Rights Act 1998 . . . was a landmark. . . . By the Human Rights Act Parliament transformed our country into a rights-based democracy. By the 1998 Act Parliament made the judiciary the guardians of the ethical values of our bill of rights.'

He defined 'a true constitutional state' as one which has 'a wholly separate and independent Supreme Court which is the ultimate guardian of the *fundamental law* of the community'.[8] (Emphasis added). The idea of fundamental law is of course something new in our constitutional experience, and its being cited by Lord Steyn is a good indication that the Human Rights Act is a first step on what may prove a long and tortuous journey to a codified constitution.

We may remember Tocqueville's famous remark, quoted in chapter 1, that 'In England the Parliament has an acknowledged right to modify the constitution; as, therefore, the constitution may undergo perpetual change, it does not in reality exist; the Parliament is at once a legislative and constituent assembly'.[9] Parliament, however, insofar as human rights are concerned, is a constituent assembly no longer, although of course it retains the right of refusing to amend or alter a statute which the judges have challenged; and of repealing the Human Rights Act.

---

[6] *Law of the Constitution*, above n 5, 88, 91.

[7] Compare P Bobbitt, *Constitutional Interpretation* (Oxford, Blackwell, 1991).

[8] Lord Steyn, '2000–2005: Laying the Foundations of Human Rights Law in the United Kingdom': Lecture to The British Institute of International and Comparative Law, 10 June 2005.

[9] A de Tocqueville, *De la Democratie en Amérique*, Part 1, chapter 6.

III

The Human Rights Act is likely to strengthen the role of the judiciary, which now has the responsibility of interpreting legislation to determine whether it is in accordance with the rights outlined in the Act. Judges, therefore, will increasingly be making decisions which MPs and others will regard as 'political' since they will encroach upon and perhaps limit the freedom of action of government and Parliament on matters of civil liberties. The new duty placed upon the judges to interpret legislation in accordance with the Convention, together with the possibility of issuing a declaration of incompatibility, in the words of one authority, 'take the courts into the examination of questions that, apart from the Human Rights Act, would have been regarded as political questions'.[10] There is likely, therefore, to be a much greater focus on who the judges are and on how they are appointed. In the United States, where Supreme Court judges have the right to invalidate federal legislation which contravenes the constitution, considerable attention is paid to the issue of whether particular judges are 'liberal' or 'conservative'. One of the issues in the presidential election of 2008 was that Barack Obama, if elected, would appoint liberal judges to the court who would take a more sympathetic line towards civil liberties than the judges appointed by previous Republican presidents. There can be little doubt that judicial decisions in the United States are greatly affected by the appointments process. Between 1933 and 1969, the Democrats held the White House for all but eight years, and it is hardly surprising that the Supreme Court in these years moved strongly in a liberal direction. Between 1969 and 1993, by contrast, all Supreme Court appointments were made by presidents belonging to the Republican Party, since, by chance, no vacancy arose during the presidency of the one Democrat to occupy the White House during that period, Jimmy Carter. It is hardly a coincidence that the Supreme Court moved in a conservative direction during these years.

In the United States, the president, elected by the people, is charged with appointing Supreme Court justices, subject to confirmation by the Senate. The American people, in 1787, gave themselves a constitution; and it is, therefore, for the people, under that constitution, through their popularly elected representative, the president, to appoint those who are to interpret that constitution. In Britain, by contrast, it is held that the appointment of judges, although made by politicians, should be unaffected by the political process, and that judges should be appointed regardless of whether their stance is 'liberal' or 'conservative'. Nevertheless, even before the Human Rights Act came into force, newspapers were beginning to profile judges. During the period of the *Pinochet* case, *The Times* described the judicial style of some of the law lords. Lord Browne-Wilkinson was,

---

[10] A W Bradley, 'The New Constitutional Relationship Between the Judiciary, Government and Parliament', in House of Lords: Select Committee on the Constitution: *Relations Between the Executive, Judiciary and Parliament*, 6th Report, 2006–7, HL 151, para 27.

apparently, 'a humane liberal and charming'; Lord Hope of Craighead was 'quiet, with a meticulous style and middle of the road politics'; Lord Hutton was 'the most right leaning of the panel'; Lord Saville was 'friendly, affable and sporty'; Lord Millett was 'the highest rating Freemason in the judiciary'; Lord Phillips was 'liberal'; while Lord Goff was 'known for intelligence and moderation'.[11]

The implication of these profiles is that the predilections of judges will affect the decisions which they make. As long ago as 1972, a distinguished judge, Lord Reid declared, in a lecture entitled 'The Judge as Lawmaker', that,

> 'There was a time when it was thought almost indecent to suggest that judges make law, they only declare it. Those with a taste for fairy tales seem to have thought that in some Aladdin's cave, there is hidden the Common Law in all its splendour, and on a judge's appointment there descends on him a knowledge of the magic words, 'Open Sesame'. Bad decisions are given when the judge has muddled the password, and the wrong door opens. But we do not believe in fairy tales any more, so we must accept the fact that for better or worse, judges do make law and tackle the question how do they approach their task and how should they approach it'.[12]

The more that judges are asked to provide the answers to complex moral and political questions, which are the subject of debate in society, the greater will be the pressure to make them politically accountable. Therefore, it becomes even more important than it was in the past to isolate the judges from political pressures.

Until the Constitutional Reform Act of 2005, judges were appointed by the Lord Chancellor. The Lord Chancellor was head of the judiciary but also a member of the Cabinet, and Speaker of the House of Lords. The department of the Lord Chancellor was responsible not only for the appointment of judges and QCs, but also for the administration of justice, constitutional reform and the protection of human rights. This arrangement was of course a spectacular denial of the doctrine of the separation of powers. There was clearly some danger that appointments to the judiciary might be influenced by the political standpoint of the Cabinet to which the Lord Chancellor belonged. Some Lord Chancellors, for example, Lord Hailsham, Lord Chancellor from 1970 to 1974, and again from 1979–87, remained robust party politicians, and participated vigorously in political debate. Lord Mackay, Lord Chancellor from 1987 to 1997 spoke out strongly against Scottish devolution. Lord Irvine, Lord Chancellor from 1997 to 2003, took on special responsibility for law reform and constitutional reform. He was thus active, as a Cabinet minister, in discussions on the very laws which he and his judicial colleagues would have to interpret. Admittedly, in recent years, the Lord Chancellor had rarely sat as a judge. Lord Irvine, for example, sat around 9 times in the years 2001–3—and never on matters affecting the government. Lord Mackay, however, did sit in the leading case *Pepper v Hart*, [1993] AC 593, on which he offered a dissenting judgment.

---

[11] *The Times*, 25 March 1999.
[12] (1972–3) *Journal of the Society of Public Teachers of Law*, 22.

Despite these interconnections, it has never been suggested, in recent years at any rate, that judicial decisions or judicial appointments have been influenced by political considerations. Nevertheless, the removal of political influence over the appointment of judges is a more recent development than many think. At the end of the nineteenth century, Lord Salisbury, the Conservative Prime Minister, referred to what he called 'the unwritten law of our party system'. 'There is', he went on,

> 'no clearer statute in that unwritten law than the rule that party claims should always weigh very heavily in the disposal of the highest legal appointments. In dealing with them you cannot ignore the party system as you do in the choice of a general or an archbishop. It would be a breach of the tacit convention on which politicians and lawyers have worked the British Constitution together for the last 200 years. Perhaps it is not an ideal system—some day no doubt the Master of the Rolls will be appointed by competitive examination in law reports, but it is our system for the present; and we should give our party arrangements a wrench if we threw it aside'.[13]

Lord Salisbury also took the view, if his daughter, Lady Gwendolen Cecil is to be believed, that it would in general be best if the judges were Conservatives, since 'within certain limits of intelligence, honesty and knowledge of the law, one man would make as good a judge as another, and a Tory mentality was *ipso facto* more trustworthy than a Liberal one'.[14] Until the 1950s it was generally accepted that, when there was a vacancy in the position of Lord Chief Justice, it should first be offered to the Attorney General, a law officer of the government, and therefore a political appointee.

With the passage of the Human Rights Act, the process by which judges were appointed was bound to come under the spotlight; and it was to meet concerns that the process was insufficiently transparent that the Constitutional Reform Act was passed in 2005. Under the provisions of this Act, the Lord Chief Justice, rather than the Lord Chancellor, becomes the head of the judiciary in England and Wales, and the Lord Chancellor can no longer sit as a judge. There is no requirement that the Lord Chancellor be a member of the House of Lords, and in 2007 Jack Straw was appointed Lord Chancellor, and continued to sit in the Commons; nor is there any requirement that the Lord Chancellor be a qualified lawyer. Currently, the office of Lord Chancellor is combined with that of Secretary of State for Justice, though the two offices remain distinct in law.

The Constitutional Reform Act reforms the procedure for judicial appointments in England and Wales. The Lord Chancellor continues to enjoy a minimal power over judicial appointments, but the new arrangements for the appointment of judges give him a much reduced role in the process, almost a purely formal one.

---

[13] Cited in R F V Heuston, *Lives of the Lord Chancellors 1885–1940* (Oxford, Clarendon Press, 1964) 52 and 36–37. I owe this reference and much stimulating discussion on the relationship between politicians and judges to Professor Robert Stevens.

[14] Lady Gwendolen Cecil, *Life of Robert, Marquess of Salisbury*, vol iii, (London, Hodder and Stoughton, 1931) 192–3.

There is to be, from 2009, a new Supreme Court, situated in Middlesex Guildhall rather than in the House of Lords, and new judges of this Supreme Court will not be members of the House of Lords.

Vacancies in the new Supreme Court will be filled by an ad hoc selection commission, formed when a vacancy arises. The commission, convened by the Lord Chancellor, will normally comprise the President and Deputy President of the new Supreme Court, and members of the appointments bodies for England and Wales, Scotland and Northern Ireland. The role of the Lord Chancellor will be confined to notifying to the Prime Minister the name of the person selected. The Prime Minister will then advise the sovereign to appoint that person. Other senior judges are now selected by a permanent non-political Judicial Appointments Commission, chaired by a lay person and with a majority of lay members. The Commission nominates a candidate to the Lord Chancellor, who then recommends the person chosen for appointment. The Judicial Appointments Commission is statutorily required to make its recommendation on the basis of merit; but it is also required to have regard to the need to make the bench more representative by appointing more women and more members of ethnic minorities. The Lord Chancellor can recommend only the nomination of the person named by the selection committee or commission. He may reject a nomination only if there is evidence that the person selected is not suitable for the office or is not the best candidate on merit. The Lord Chancellor must give reasons for rejection. The appointments procedure then begins all over again and the committee or Commission will again recommend just one person to fill the vacancy. The presumption, however, is that the Lord Chancellor will normally accept the Commission's nominee, and it is probable that a constitutional convention will develop that he will do so. The Lord Chancellor's role in the appointments process would then become purely formal, and appointments will be determined by two wholly non-political bodies, the ad hoc selection committee and the Judicial Appointments Commission. The appointments procedure, therefore, has become insulated from political interference.

IV

The Human Rights Act, then, preserves the sovereignty of Parliament, but provides for Parliament, ministers and the courts, to play a much more important role in the protection of human rights than hitherto. Since ministers have to declare, when introducing legislation, whether it conforms, in their opinion, to the European Convention, they are required to scrutinize it for its human rights implications more carefully than in the past. The Joint Select Committee is likely also to encourage greater awareness of human rights.

The Human Rights Act proposes a compromise between the doctrines of Parliamentary sovereignty and that of the rule of law. It seeks in a sense to muffle the conflict by proposing a dialogue between the judiciary, Parliament and government, all of whom are required to observe human rights. It seeks to avoid the question, 'What happens if there is a conflict between parliamentary sovereignty and the rule of law?' When I put that very question to a senior judge—what happens if there is such a conflict—he replied, 'That is a question that ought not to be asked!' Lord Justice Laws has argued that the middle way between parliamentary sovereignty and a written constitution, is but an 'intermediate stage' 'between parliamentary supremacy and constitutional supremacy'.[15] However, the effectiveness of the compromise depends upon a sense of restraint on the part both of judges and of Parliament. Were the judges to seek to invade the political sphere and to make the judiciary supreme over Parliament, there would be great resentment on the part of ministers and MPs. The judges would be accused of transforming judicial review into judicial supremacy. Conversely, were Parliament to ignore a declaration of incompatibility on the part of judges, and refuse to repeal or amend the offending statute or part of a statute, the Human Rights Act could prove of little value. Thus, the Human Rights Act, as well as giving judges a more important role over human rights matters, seeks to secure a democratic engagement with rights by the representatives of the people in Parliament with the objective of securing a human rights culture.

Nevertheless, the compromise between the two potentially conflicting principles of parliamentary sovereignty and the rule of law could easily prove tenuous. When the European Convention was originally drawn up, the main concern was to prevent any resurgence of Fascism or National Socialism. That was a cause which united parliamentarians and people. Today, by contrast, in Britain at least, most human rights cases concern the rights of very small minorities, minorities too small to be able to use the democratic machinery of party politics and pressure groups very effectively, and sometimes highly unpopular minorities—suspected terrorists, asylum-seekers, prisoners, even perhaps suspected paedophiles. Victims of injustice may not always prove to be attractive characters or particularly nice people. Perhaps life would be much simpler if they were. What is clear is that there is little consensus between government and the judges when it comes to the rights of unpopular minorities. They approach the issue from different perspectives.

If the compromise proves to be unsustainable there is likely to be a clash between the government and the judiciary. The judges could find themselves on a collision course with the government. In fact the danger of a clash has become clear much more rapidly than anyone could have predicted, and, by 2006, just six years after the Human Rights Act came into force, both the Prime Minister and the Leader of the Opposition were arguing that it should be amended.

Two issues in particular—asylum and terrorism—have come to the fore since passage of the Human Rights Act, and it is worth looking in some detail at the problems to which they have given rise, since they show how enactment of the Human Rights Act has increased the likelihood of conflict between government and the judiciary.

[15] In *International Transport Roth GmbH v Secretary of State for the Home Department* [2003] QB 759.

Problems associated with asylum, of course, long predated the Act, but they have grown in significance since the year 2000. Immigration, with which asylum is often confused, is now a major political issue and a highly emotive one, and both government and opposition are agreed that it should be more tightly controlled. Worries about immigration have burgeoned with the increase in immigration from new members of the European Union, such as Poland, Bulgaria and Romania, who, unlike the citizens of non-EU countries, usually have the legal right to come to Britain to seek work. Immigration and asylum, so most politicians believe, are issues capable of influencing votes in a general election, and politicians do not want to lose control of these issues to the judges.

In December 2003, the government introduced an Asylum and Immigration (Treatment of Claimaints etc.) bill into the House of Commons. Clause 10 of this bill entitled, euphemistically, 'Unification of appeal system', would have had the effect of excluding the courts from jurisdiction over decisions made by the Asylum and Immigration Tribunal. A failed asylum-seeker or an immigrant would have no redress against the Tribunal even if she believed that its decision had been capricious or unreasonable, or that there had been an error of law or a breach of natural justice. Nor would a court have been able to review the decision to deport a failed asylum seeker. Review would have been possible only when the President of the Tribunal, who need not be a judge, believed that an important or complex point of law was involved. The President was thus invited to decide whether review was needed. She was invited to be a judge in her own cause.

Clause 10 flouted a basic principle of English law that the High Court exercises supervisory jurisdiction through judicial review over administrative decisions and the work of tribunals, so that there would be a remedy where unfair decisions were made or when mistakes of law occurred. It could be argued that observation of this principle was of particular importance for highly vulnerable people facing deportation to countries where they might fear oppression or torture. For such people, the ability to appeal against a decision on asylum might prove, literally, a matter of life or death.

But clause 10 also had important implications for the working of the Human Rights Act. If governments were able to exclude the jurisdiction of the courts, then the protection given by the Human Rights Act becomes illusory. If access to the courts is denied, the Human Rights Act cannot be invoked. The protection of the law would have been removed from an unpopular minority. In a speech at Cambridge University in March 2004, Lord Woolf, the then Lord Chief Justice declared, 'I am not over-dramatising the position if I indicate that, if this clause were to become law, it would be so inconsistent with the spirit of mutual respect between the different arms of government that it could be the catalyst for a campaign for a written constitution'.[16] Fortunately, however, the offending clause was amended before the report stage in the House of Lords after two former Lord Chancellors, Lords Mackay and Irvine, objected to it.

---

[16] 'The Rule of Law and a Change in the Constitution' (2004) *Cambridge Law Journal*, 328.

A number of other recent asylum cases have raised human rights concerns. A case in 2006, *R (S) v Secretary of State for the Home Department* EWHC 1111 (Admin), concerned a group of Afghans who, in the year 2000, had hijacked a plane on an internal flight in Afghanistan to flee from the Taliban regime. They were then condemned to death by the Taliban as enemies of Islam. They landed in Britain and claimed asylum. In 2003, they were convicted of hijacking but their conviction was quashed on appeal, on grounds of duress, and no retrial was ordered. The Home Secretary did not wish the hijackers to be granted discretionary leave to stay in Britain. But the High Court issued a mandatory order requiring the Home Secretary to give the Afghans discretionary leave to stay in Britain for a renewable period of six months. This judgment was not based primarily on human rights considerations, but the judge found that the government's policy on discretionary leave had nevertheless failed to meet the requirement of 'lawfulness' as laid down in Article 8 of the European Convention, since it was not a clear and publicly accessible rule of law, but gave the minister an open-ended discretion. In fact, the Home Secretary had issued a revised set of rules relating to discretionary leave **after** a panel of three independent adjudicators had allowed an appeal against his decision not to allow the hijackers to be granted discretionary leave. These revised rules had not been put before Parliament. Under the revised rules, the hijackers could be denied discretionary leave, and it was these revised rules that the judge had in mind when he found that the policy did not meet human rights standards.

The judgment was greeted with much distortion, some of it wilful, in the press. The *Sun* denounced what it called 'the European Union Human Rights Act', even though the European Convention is a distinct system of law and separate from European Union law. The European Union and the Council of Europe are quite distinct bodies—although no country has ever joined the European Union without first joining the Council of Europe. But Britain would remain bound by the European Convention even if she left the European Union, unless she chose to repudiate it, an option that we shall discuss later. Little of the press discussion of the case pointed out that the alternative to granting the Afghans discretionary leave was not deportation, and the Home Secretary had not argued for deportation. The alternative was to grant the Afghans merely temporary admission, which would mean that they would have to report to the police regularly and would not be allowed to work. If granted discretionary leave, on the other hand, they would be allowed to work. Contrary to what was frequently suggested in the press, the judge was not deciding that the Secretary of State should grant the Afghans permanent residence in Britain, merely discretionary leave which was subject to renewal every six months.

The decision did not, therefore, mean, as many press commentators suggested, that the hijackers could not in principle be deported, nor that action could not be taken to discourage hijacking. It meant only that deportation would have to be by due process of law. It is, however, certainly true that, under Article 3 of the European Convention, which declares that 'No one shall be subjected to torture or to inhuman or degrading treatment or punishment', no one can be deported to a territory where they may face torture or worse; and that was the reason why the

Home Secretary was not proposing that they be deported to Afghanistan. Few, surely, would wish to argue against this provision as a principle, though of course there can be dispute in specific cases as to how it should be applied. But there are not many who would wish to have supported the deportation of a Jew to Nazi Germany or a dissident to the Soviet Union. The case did, however, show how the protection of asylum-seekers by the courts could give rise to populist distortion, and how difficult it can be to preserve the compromise between the sovereignty of Parliament and the rule of law.

Terrorism is the second issue which has given rise to conflict between government and the judiciary. That is largely because it has taken on a different form since the horrific atrocity of the 9/11 attacks in the United States, in 2001, less than one year after the Human Rights Act came into force. The form of terrorism to which Britain had become accustomed, that of the IRA, was in a sense, an old-fashioned and limited form of terrorism which was easier to contain. The IRA saw itself as a volunteer army, and claimed to be seeking only military targets. It had a single specific and concrete aim, the reunification of the island of Ireland. The new form of terrorism, global terrorism, as championed by Al-Qaeda, is quite different. It is a far more ruthless form of terrorism with wide if not unlimited aims, amongst which are the establishment of a new, Islamic empire, and the elimination of the state of Israel. Al-Qaeda attacks not a country, as did the IRA, but a civilisation, seeing anyone belonging to an opposing civilisation as a target, and inculcating an ethos of martyrdom. It apparently has terrorist cells in around 60 countries. To deal with this new form of terrorism, so governments argue, new methods are needed and these new methods may well infringe human rights. The judges, however, retort that there should be no compromise with traditional principles—habeas corpus and the presumption of innocence—principles which have been tried and tested over many centuries and which have served Britain well in the past. During the 1970s, measures to combat the IRA were, broadly, the responsibility of Parliament and not the judges. Following the enactment of the Human Rights Act, however, the response to terrorism has become a matter for the judges as well as Parliament.

The 2001 Anti-Terrorism, Crime and Security Act provided for indefinite detention without trial for those who were, in the Home Secretary's view, a threat to national security. In the Belmarsh prison case, *A v Secretary of State for the Home Department* [2005] 2 AC 68, the House of Lords, by an 8 to 1 majority, declared that, while it was not for the judges to dispute the government's view that there was an emergency, the provisions for detention in the 2001 Act went beyond what was required to meet that emergency. This judgment was very much in accord with the words of Winston Churchill on preventive detention in 1943 at the height of the Second World War, when he said that 'The power of the executive to cast a man into prison without formulating any charge known to the law, and particularly to deny him the judgment of his peers, is in the highest degree odious, and the foundation of all totalitarian government whether Nazi or Communist'.[17]

---

[17] Cited in A W B Simpson, *In the Highest Degree Odious: Detention without trial in Wartime Britain* (Oxford, Clarendon Press, 1992) 391.

The government responded to the decisions of the judges in the *A* case with new legislation, the Prevention of Terrorism Act, 2005, replacing detention with a system of control orders. These control orders restrict the freedom of suspected terrorists by requiring them, for example, to report to a police station at regular intervals, to remain in their place of residence, to surrender their passport, and to admit police officers to their home at any time to search their premises. It is worth emphasizing that the control orders are issued by the executive and not by the courts, and that no charge is brought against the suspects; and because most of the evidence is based on intelligence sources, neither the suspect nor her lawyers are able to see all of the evidence and in some cases not even a summary of it. In one case, *Secretary of State for the Home Department v JJ and others* [2007] UKHL 45, it was held that a group of control orders requiring those affected to remain in their place of residence for 18 hours of the day, amounting almost to house arrest, fell foul of Article 5 of the European Convention and amounted to a deprivation of liberty. Here, too, the compromise between the principles of the sovereignty of Parliament and the rule of law came under severe strain.

V

There is, then, a serious difference of view between government and the judges on issues relating to asylum and to counter-terrorism. But the effectiveness of the compromise embodied in the Human Rights Act depends essentially upon consensus between government and the judges. Perhaps an implication of the Act was that breaches of human rights would generally be inadvertent and that, when judges pointed out such a breach, the government would normally be happy to put things right. Clearly that consensus does not exist in the case of asylum seekers and suspected terrorists and perhaps other unpopular minorities also, such as prisoners. Nor is there a consensus between the general public, over-influenced perhaps by the tabloid press, and the judges.

The judges might claim that they have a special role to play in protecting the rights of unpopular minorities, and that, in undertaking this task, they are doing no more than applying the Human Rights Act as Parliament has asked them to do. The government, however, and most MPs, together with much of the press and public, would disagree. The government and MPs might argue that it is for them, as elected representatives, to weigh the precise balance between the rights of the individual and the needs of society. They are elected and accountable to the people, but the judges are not. There is thus coming to develop a profound difference of view as to how issues involving human rights should be resolved. Many politicians believe that they should continue to be resolved by Parliament. The judges, however, believe that they should be resolved by the courts.

There is, it has been suggested,[18] in every legal system, an ultimate norm, a rule of recognition, a basic criterion for determining how the law is to be recognised.

---

[18] By H L A Hart in his classic work, *The Concept of Law* (Oxford, Clarendon Press, 1961).

In the past, this rule of recognition in Britain was undoubtedly the sovereignty of Parliament. The Human Rights Act formally leaves the sovereignty of Parliament intact; in practice, however, it puts some pressure upon it. In practice, the principle of the rule of law, as embodied in the Human Rights Act, may be coming to supersede the doctrine of the sovereignty of Parliament. This has led to two contrasting reactions. Politicians, led, in 2005 and 2006, by the then Prime Minister, Tony Blair, and the Leader of the Opposition, David Cameron, have come to believe that the Human Rights Act should be amended; while some senior judges, fearful perhaps that Parliament may come to ignore the rule of law, are hinting that the judges might at some time in the future come to disapply legislation which flagrantly breaches human rights.

In 2005, the then Prime Minister Tony Blair, angered by decisions of the High Court over the rights of suspected terrorists, argued that there should be legislation limiting the role of the courts in human rights cases. This proposal presumably meant amending the Human Rights Act. In 2006, David Cameron, for his part, renewed the pledge in the Conservative Party's 2005 election manifesto, to 'reform, or failing that, scrap' the Human Rights Act. He argued that the Act should be replaced by a British Bill of Rights, a 'home-grown, hard-nosed' measure that would help to restore parliamentary supremacy.

Gordon Brown, by contrast, did not attack the Human Rights Act, but argued that a British Bill of Rights was needed to supplement it, perhaps as a possible precursor to a codified constitution. This proposal, for a British Bill of Rights, is now supported by all three of the major parties. In August 2008, the parliamentary Joint Committee on Human Rights published a report, *A Bill of Rights for the UK?* HL165, HC 150, 2007–8. It recommended that Britain adopt a Bill of Rights and Freedoms since this would provide 'a moment when society can define itself.' Such a Bill should 'set out a shared vision of a desirable future society: it should be aspirational in nature as well a protecting those human rights which already exist'.[19] Such a Bill would, in the Joint Committee's view, have to build upon the Human Rights Act without weakening it in any way, and it would have to supplement the protections in the European Convention.

A Bill of Rights and Freedoms would not, however, allow Britain to opt out of the decisions of the European Court of Human Rights at Strasbourg since Article 46 of the European Convention obliges member states to comply with its rulings; nor could a home-grown Bill of Rights prevent judges, whether in London or Strasbourg, coming to decisions which politicians did not like.

Were a Bill of Rights and Freedoms merely to replicate the European Convention, it would clearly be superfluous; while, if it were to conflict with the Convention, the judges would have to resolve the conflict. That would increase the power of the judiciary, not reduce it. The only rationale for a home-grown Bill of Rights would be if it either yielded more rights than the Convention, and/or offered stronger protection than the Human Rights Act by, for example, entrench-

---

[19] *A Bill of Rights for the UK?*, 5.

ing rights more firmly. But if it did either of these things then, again, the power of the judiciary would be increased, not reduced, and there would be a greater likelihood of a clash between the judges and Parliament.

A Bill of Rights and Freedoms could hardly offer a lower standard of protection than the Convention. If it did, the only consequence would be that more cases would come to be decided by the European Court of Human Rights in Strasbourg, something that the Human Rights Act was designed to avoid. The position would be similar to what it was before the Human Rights Act was passed when litigants had to seek redress at Strasbourg, at the cost of considerable time and money, because it was not available in British courts. It would defeat the stated purpose of the Human Rights Act—'An Act to give further effect to the rights and freedoms guaranteed under the European Convention on Human Rights'. David Cameron suggested that if Britain had a home-grown Bill of Rights that was more restrictive than the European Convention, the Strasbourg court might take account of this so as to interpret laws more favourably from the point of view of the British government. There would then be a British balance of rights and responsibilities which would be different from that offered by the European Court. But the Court has to apply common, Continent-wide standards of human rights, and these cannot vary according to a country's particular constitutional arrangements. A Bill of Rights and Freedoms, therefore, could not be used to dilute Convention rights, nor to provide a narrower interpretation of well-established Convention case law on fundamental rights.

Lord Tebbit, an elder statesman of the Conservative Party, criticised David Cameron for what he saw as an illogical compromise. It was inconsistent, Tebbit believed, to seek amendment or repeal of the Human Rights Act, while Britain remained a member of the European Convention. The logic of Cameron's argument required, so Lord Tebbit believed, withdrawal from the Convention. It would certainly be illogical to revert to the position as it was before the Human Rights Act when individuals could secure recognition of their rights only through an international court. Withdrawal from the Convention, however, while, in a sense, it follows the logic of David Cameron's approach, would have the consequence of isolating Britain from every other democracy in Europe. Britain would then become the only democracy in Europe publicly to declare that she could not conform to standards of human rights accepted by the rest of the Continent.

Although there is nothing in any of the European Union treaties which obliges Britain to be a party to the European Convention, the 1992 Maastricht treaty declares that one of the foundations of the European Union is respect for human rights, and that the Union should therefore respect fundamental rights as guaranteed by the Convention. Were a Member State seriously to breach human rights, or were it to withdraw from the European Convention, its voting rights in the Council of Ministers could be suspended. In addition, Member States must respect European Union fundamental rights standards when implementing European Union law, and these rights standards were inspired by the Convention, although they are not exactly the same.

The only rationale for a Bill of Rights and Freedoms, then, is that it would increase the number of rights which the courts protect and/or strengthen this protection by some form of entrenchment. The European Convention of Human Rights was regarded by its signatories in 1950 not as a ceiling, the maximum protection which Member States should grant, but as a floor, the very minimum which any state claiming to be governed by the rule of law, should support.

In Northern Ireland there is already broad agreement that greater protection of rights is needed than is offered by the Human Rights Act. The 1998 Belfast Agreement recognised that there ought to be

> 'rights supplementary to those in the European Convention on Human Rights to reflect the particular circumstances of Northern Ireland . . . These additional rights to reflect the principles of mutual respect for the identity and ethos of both communities and parity of esteem and—taken together with the ECHR—to constitute a Bill of Rights for Northern Ireland'.

The Agreement provided for the establishment of a Northern Ireland Human Rights Commission providing for the identity and ethos of both communities in the province to be respected, and also a general right to non-discrimination. It also envisaged that the Human Rights Commission in the Republic would join with that of Northern Ireland to produce a charter endorsing agreed measures to protect the fundamental rights of all those living in the island of Ireland. As yet, however, no Bill of Rights for Northern Ireland has been enacted.

Many have proposed rights additional to those in the ECHR which ought to be recognised in the United Kingdom as a whole—a general right to equality, for example; a right to privacy; a right to a healthy environment, something guaranteed in the 1996 post-apartheid South African constitution; a right to freedom of information; a specific right to anti-discrimination on grounds of sexual orientation; recognition of the rights of children, as recognised in the United Nations Convention on the Rights of the Child—these are all examples of rights which, so it has been suggested, ought to be protected in addition to those protected by the Convention. There is also the large but contentious area of social and economic rights. The Convention recognizes a right to education but not a right to health care.[20] Many of these rights are recognised in international treaties which the British government has signed. Nevertheless, additional rights would have to be formulated very carefully were they to be embodied in a Bill of Rights and Freedoms. It would be difficult to make economic and social rights, for example, justiciable; and the law cannot become a mechanism for resolving complex social or economic problems. In a case in 1995, Lord Bingham commented that:

> 'It is common knowledge that health authorities of all kinds are constantly pressed to make ends meet. They cannot pay their nurses as much as they would like; they cannot provide all the treatments they would like; they cannot purchase all the extremely expensive medical equipment they would like, they cannot carry out all the research they would

---

[20] Interestingly, the students in the exercise discussed on p 10, believed by a very large majority that a right to health care ought to be recognised.

like; they cannot build all the hospitals and specialist units they would like. Difficult and agonizing judgments have to be made as to how a limited budget is best allocated to the maximum advantage of the maximum number of patients. This is not a judgment which the court can make'.[21]

The courts must remain a last resort, not a path taken by those who cannot secure the reforms they wish to enact through the ballot box and Parliament.

In its report, *A Bill of Rights for the UK*, however, the Joint Committee on Human Rights proposed five types of rights for inclusion.

1. Civil and political rights and freedoms, such as the right to life, freedom from torture, the right to family life and freedom of expression and association. It also proposed a new right to equality.
2. Fair process rights such as the right to a fair trial and the right of access to a court. The Committee also proposed a right to fair and just administrative action.
3. Economic and social rights, including the right to a healthy and sustainable environment. The Joint Committee accepted that such rights could not easily be made justiciable, and declared that they would impose a duty on the part of government and other public bodies, of 'progressive realisation', the principle adopted in the South African constitution. This principle would require the government to take reasonable measures within available resources to achieve these rights and report annually to Parliament on progress. But individuals would not be able to enforce them against the government or any other public body.
4. Democratic rights, such as the right to free and fair elections, the right to participate in public life and the right to citizenship.
5. The rights of particular groups such as children, minorities, people with disabilities and victims of crime.[22]

One argument for adding such rights to those already recognised in the Convention is that it would make it easier for the British people to feel that they, as it were, 'owned' the Bill of Rights, that the Bill of Rights was indigenous. At present, many feel that the Human Rights Act is an elite project, designed only to protect highly unpopular minorities, such as suspected terrorists and asylum seekers. The Act, therefore, is not grounded in strong popular support. Rights that might be generally used by all would give human rights legislation greater popular salience, and might thus, paradoxically, make it easier to protect the rights of unpopular minorities.

In March 2009, the Ministry of Justice published a Green Paper, *Rights and Responsibilities: Developing our Constitutional Framework*, Cm 7577, as a basis for consultation. The document recommended a number of areas for potential inclusion in any future Bill of Rights—for example, welfare entitlements, rights related

[21] *R v Cambridgeshire Health Authority, ex parte B* [1995] 1 WLR 898.
[22] HL165, HC 150, 2007–8

to the environment and to the wellbeing of children, and the rights of victims in the criminal justice system. It also emphasised various responsibilities that we all owe as members of society. These rights and responsibilities would not necessarily be directly enforceable in the courts. Indeed, the government preferred a Bill of Rights and Responsibilities in the form either of a declaratory or symbolic statement, or perhaps a statement of principles, endorsed by Parliament, to inform future legislation.

One difficulty, which the government recognised, however, is that some at least of the rights which might be embodied in a Bill of Rights and Responsibilities would seem to encroach upon the powers of the devolved bodies—the Scottish Parliament, the National Assembly of Wales and the Northern Ireland Assembly. From a legal point of view, the protection of rights is a reserved matter. Nevertheless, the devolved bodies have responsibility for such matters as health care, and would undoubtedly see a Bill of Rights and Responsibilities providing for the right to health as a form of creeping centralisation, depriving them surreptitiously of powers which had been transferred to them by the devolution legislation. The devolved bodies might well wish to decide for themselves whether or not to provide for additional rights to those in the European Convention. There is some tension, then, between the principle of devolution and that of the entrenchment of rights UK-wide; and, insofar as a Bill of Rights and Responsibilities was based on the idea of rights that were fundamental to British citizenship, it could serve to unpick the delicate settlement reached in the Belfast Agreement which served to reconcile the unionists of Northern Ireland, who wished to remain British citizens, and the nationalists, who did not, and who do not see themselves as British at all. It would be necessary, then, to secure the consent of the devolved bodies, as well as MPs at Westminster, to a Bill of Rights and Responsibilities. That would not be easy since neither the SNP nor Sinn Fein would want to agree to something that they saw as 'British'. They would prefer rights for Scotland and Northern Ireland that were, as it were, self-generated. But, if the devolved bodies were not involved in the negotiations, they might not accept a Bill of Rights and Responsibilities as legitimate. In 1980, when Pierre Trudeau sought to patriate the Canadian constitution, he did not consult the Canadian provinces until required to do so by the Supreme Court of Canada. Quebec, which already had its own provincial Bill of Rights, refused to accept the patriated constitution since this would have deprived it of autonomy in relation to French language and education rights.[23] The issue remained a running sore, poisoning relations between Canada and Quebec for many years. A Bill of Rights and Responsibilities, therefore, could prove a highly divisive issue both in Scotland and in Northern Ireland.

If the British government preferred not to involve itself in difficult disputes with the devolved bodies, the alternative would be to propose a Bill of Rights applying only to England. There would then be an English, rather than British, Bill of

---

[23] See G Marshall, 'Canada's New Constitution (1982): Some Lessons in Constitutional Engineering', in V Bogdanor (ed) *Constitutions in Democratic Politics* (Aldershot, Gower 1988).

Rights, and the devolved bodies could be left to adopt whatever arrangements they wished if they sought to add to the rights already recognised in the Human Rights Act. An English Bill of Rights, however, could hardly be expected to strengthen the sense of Britishness. It might, on the contrary, weaken it.

Even apart from this problem, a Bill of Rights and Responsibilities might prove of very limited value in strengthening the sense of citizenship. It could delineate only the very minimum requirements of citizenship. For many, if not most of the duties of good citizenship—eg the duty to be a good neighbour, the duty to contribute to one's community—are not such as can be ensured by law. They are problems for society, not for the legal system. It is a mistake to overburden the legal system by giving judges the duty to resolve complex social problems, problems that they are ill-equipped by training to resolve. Nor could the rights of the individual become dependent upon the extent to which she performed her social duties. The right to freedom of speech, and to the other rights enshrined in the Human Rights Act, are not dependent upon the satisfactory performance of social duties. They are granted to everyone living in Britain, regardless of whether or not they are good citizens. Some of the most contentious issues relating to rights concern the rights of prisoners, people who, by definition, have shown that they are not good citizens.

In addition to adding to the rights listed in the Convention, the Human Rights Act could be strengthened in another way, by providing stronger protection for existing rights than is provided in the Act. There are two ways in which this can be done, by legislative entrenchment and by judicial entrenchment.

When calling for a home-grown British Bill of Rights, David Cameron suggested that it might be made exempt from the Parliament Act, which allows the Commons in the last resort to override the Lords. At present the only legislative provision that is exempt from the Parliament Act is that requiring a general election to be held at least once every five years. The reason for this, of course, is to ensure that an unscrupulous government with a majority in the Commons cannot postpone the date of a general election beyond five years to keep itself in power. Similarly, the effect of exempting a Bill of Rights from the Parliament Act would be to ensure that a government could not alter its provisions without securing the agreement of the Lords. An alternative might be to provide that the Act could be amended only by a special majority in the House of Commons, for example, two-thirds of those voting. Such provisions are common in relation to Bills of Rights. The American Bill of Rights can only be amended by a special majority of Congress and a special majority of the states; the same is true of the protection of rights in the South African constitution. The Canadian Charter of Rights and Freedoms of 1982 can be amended only by two-thirds majorities in both houses. New Zealand and Israel, which, like Britain lack a codified constitution, both give special legislative protection to certain rights. The 1993 Electoral Act in New Zealand contains an entrenched provision which can be amended only by 75% of the MPs in the single-chamber parliament or by referendum. Israel has a set of Basic Laws protecting rights which can be amended only by an **absolute** majority in the single-chamber parliament, the Knesset.

The second way of strengthening the protection offered by the Human Rights Act is by giving judges power to do more than simply issue a declaration of incompatibility when, in their view, legislation infringes the European Convention. In most countries with a Bill of Rights, such as the United States, South Africa and Germany, judges can invalidate legislation which conflicts with the Act. In Canada, the government can over-ride the judges by introducing legislation, accepting explicitly that it is not in accordance with the Charter of Fundamental Freedoms of 1982, but declaring that 'notwithstanding', this, it ought to be enacted. All legislation of this 'notwithstanding' type needs to be renewed every five years; but the political stigma attached to introducing legislation with such a clause is so great that the Federal government has never employed it—although it has been employed at provincial level by provincial governments. The Canadian government and parliament can thus, like the British government and parliament, decide to ignore the decision of a judge in a human rights case. It is, however, more difficult to take this course in Canada than it is in Britain, since if Parliament in Britain disagrees with a declaration of incompatibility, it merely does nothing but maintain the status quo; whereas, the Canadian Parliament has to act positively to override the Charter.

Judicial entrenchment in Britain would entail explicit recognition that the Human Rights Act was fundamental constitutional legislation. It already has a certain status as fundamental law precisely because it is not subject to the doctrine of implied repeal. But to allow judges to invalidate legislation would be to go considerably further in undermining the doctrine of parliamentary sovereignty. It might be argued, however, that if we can modify this doctrine by subscribing to a superior legal order, the European Union, and providing for judges to 'disapply' legislation which is contrary to European legislation, then we can also modify it by giving judges the power to disapply other legislation. In gradually coming to distinguish between 'fundamental' and 'non-fundamental', we are moving in a tortuous and crab-like way towards establishing real constitutional principles, towards becoming a constitutional state.

VI

In the White Paper, *Rights Brought Home*, accompanying the introduction of the Human Rights bill into Parliament, the government declared of the proposal that judges be given the power to set aside Acts of Parliament that it 'would be likely on occasions to draw the judiciary into serious conflict with Parliament. There is no evidence to suggest they desire this power, nor that the public wish them to have it'.[24] Yet, some senior judges are coming to believe that they may need the power to disapply legislation if protection of human rights is to be effective. A natural

---

[24] *Rights Brought Home: The Human Rights Bill* Cm 3782, 1997, para 2:13.

consequence, so it may seem, of the Human Rights Act, is an erosion of the principle of the sovereignty of Parliament. Some judges are coming to argue that this principle is but a judicial construct, a creation of the common law. If the judges could create it, they could now, equally justifiably, supersede it, and the time is coming when they should consider doing so. In a case, *Jackson and others v Attorney-General* in 2005, concerning the validity of the 1949 Parliament Act, law lords for the first time declared, obiter, that Parliament's ability to pass primary legislation might be limited in substance. Lord Steyn declared that the principle of the sovereignty of Parliament, while still being the '*general* principle of our constitution' was:

'a construct of the common law. The judges created this principle. If that is so, it is not unthinkable that circumstances could arise where the courts may have to qualify a principle established on a different hypothesis of constitutionalism'.

He then went on to say in words which were to be much quoted:

'In exceptional circumstances involving an attempt to abolish judicial review of the ordinary role of the courts, the Appellate Committee of the House of Lords or a new Supreme Court may have to consider whether this is a constitutional fundamental which even a sovereign Parliament acting at the behest of a complaisant House of Commons cannot abolish'.[25]

Lord Steyn has since elaborated by saying that,

'For my part the dicta in *Jackson* are likely to prevail if the government tried to tamper with the fundamental principles of our constitutional democracy, such as five year Parliaments, the role of the ordinary courts, the rule of law, and other such fundamentals. In such exceptional cases the rule of law may trump parliamentary supremacy'.[26]

He was perhaps influenced in these comments by the government's attempt in the Asylum and Immigration bill to deprive asylum seekers of access to the courts.

In another obiter dictum in *Jackson*, Lady Hale of Richmond said,

'The courts will treat with particular suspicion (and might even reject) any attempt to subvert the rule of law by removing governmental action affecting the rights of the individual from all judicial powers'.[27]

In a further obiter dictum in the same case, another law lord, Lord Hope of Craighead, declared:

'Parliamentary sovereignty is no longer, if it ever was, absolute. It is not uncontrolled ... It is no longer right to say that its freedom to legislate admits of no qualification whatever. Step-by-step, gradually but surely, the English principle of the absolute legislative sovereignty of Parliament ... is being qualified'.

---

[25] [2005] UKHL 56. Para 102.
[26] The Attlee Foundation Lecture: 11 April 2006: 'Democracy, The Rule of Law and the Role of Judges' 20.
[27] Para 159.

He then said: 'The rule of law enforced by the courts is the ultimate controlling factor on which our constitution is based'.[28]

It is a fundamental implication of the doctrine of the sovereignty of Parliament that Acts of Parliament are not subject to judicial review. But, in the last resort, that depends upon the acceptance of this situation by the judges. Until the European Communities Act, it appeared unthinkable that judges would seek to alter the balance of the constitution by seeking to challenge provisions in an Act of Parliament. The *Factortame* decision may be thought to cast some doubt on that view; the obiter dictum of the three law lords casts further doubt upon it, although the judges have not as yet, outside the field of European law, declined to give effect to any statutory provision. Nevertheless, the basic implication of the obiter remarks by the three law lords is that the sovereignty of Parliament is a doctrine created by the judges which can also be superseded by the judges. It seems that some senior judges would like to see the sovereignty of Parliament supplanted by an alternative rule of recognition, the rule of law. In the mid-1990s, even before the Human Rights Act was enacted, Mr Justice Sedley declared that parliamentary sovereignty was already coming to be replaced by 'a new and still emerging constitutional paradigm' comprising 'a bi-polar sovereignty of the Crown in Parliament and the Crown in the courts'.[29] The difficulty with such a paradigm, of course, is that the two poles of the new bi-polar sovereignty, far from collaborating in the sharing of authority, can all too easily come into conflict.

The question raised by the arguments of the senior judges is whether it is for them alone to determine what the rule of recognition ought to be. Are they right in arguing that the sovereignty of Parliament is but a judicial construct? Dicey, for one, would have thought that they were wrong. He believed that the doctrine was a fundamental part of our constitutional history. The roots of parliamentary sovereignty, he argued, 'lie deep in the history of the English people and in the peculiar development of the English Constitution' (*sic*).[30] They derive perhaps from the political settlement following the civil war and the Glorious Revolution in the seventeenth century. If this view is correct, then the judges alone cannot supersede the principle of parliamentary sovereignty, unless Parliament itself, and perhaps the people, as well, through referendum, agree with them. They cannot supersede parliamentary sovereignty until there has been a

---

[28] Paras 107 and 120; Compare Jowell and Oliver, *The Changing Constitution* (6th edn, Oxford, OUP, 2007) vi. 'It may now be that the rule of law has supplanted parliamentary sovereignty as our prime constitutional principle'. It may be significant that Lord Hope is a Scottish law lord, for the Scots have always been somewhat more sceptical than the English of the doctrine of the absolute sovereignty of Parliament which they find difficult to reconcile with the Acts of Union of 1707. In these Acts, uniting the Scottish and English parliaments, the Scottish negotiators sought and believed that they had succeeded in preserving the Scottish legal system and the system of Presbyterian church government in Scotland from alteration by the English. It was difficult to reconcile such a viewpoint with the doctrine of the sovereignty of Parliament.

[29] Cited in J Goldsworthy, *The Sovereignty of Parliament: History and Philosophy* (Oxford, Clarendon Press, 1999) 2.

[30] A V Dicey, *Introduction to the Study of the Constitution*, 69fn.

new political settlement. There is, so far, little sign of any willingness to reach such a settlement.

There is, then, some danger of a conflict between two constitutional principles, the sovereignty of Parliament and the rule of law. There is some danger that the compromise embodied in the Human Rights Act will break down. If that happens, the Act could generate a constitutional crisis. A constitutional crisis does not occur simply because there are differences of view between the government and the judges on constitutional matters. That, perhaps, is to be expected in any healthy democracy. A constitutional crisis occurs when there comes to develop a difference of view as to how such differences should be settled, the method by which they should be settled. A constitutional crisis occurs when there comes to develop a difference of view as to what the rule of recognition is or ought to be.

The government and most MPs believe that issues involving human rights should continue to be resolved by Parliament. The judges, however, are required by the Human Rights Act to decide human rights issues, and no doubt believe that it is their decision, not that of Parliament or government, which should be final. Because they are coming to disagree about the rule of recognition, both government and the judges are beginning to believe that the other has broken the constitution. Ministers and MPs say that judges are usurping power and seeking to thwart the will of Parliament; they are, on this view, misusing the power of judicial review so that it becomes a power of judicial supremacy over the nation's elected representatives. The judges say that ministers are proposing legislation which infringes human rights and then attacking the judiciary when it does its job of reviewing legislation for its compatibility with the Human Rights Act. The British Constitution, then, is coming to mean different things to different people. It is coming to mean something different to the judges from what it means to government, Parliament and people. The argument from parliamentary sovereignty points in one direction, the argument from the rule of law in another. It is too early to tell how the constitutional conflict will be resolved and what the shape of the final constitutional settlement is likely to be.

What is remarkable, perhaps, is the speed with which the Human Rights Act has led to a conflict between government and the judges. In the United States, it was 16 years from the drawing-up of the constitution in 1787 before the Supreme Court invalidated an Act of Congress in the landmark case of *Marbury v Madison*, 1803. After that, no further Act of Congress was invalidated until the famous *Dred Scott* case in 1857, a case which unleashed the Civil War. Not until after the Civil War of 1861–65 did the Supreme Court really come into its own as a court which would review federal legislation. In France, the 5th Republic established a new body, the *Conseil Constitutionnel*, in 1958, empowered to delimit the respective roles of parliament and government. Yet the *Conseil* did not really assume an active role until the 1970s. It is only since 1971, when the *Conseil* started to strike out acts of parliament contrary to the rights guaranteed in the preamble of the 1946 constitution, and also in the 1789 Declaration of the Rights of Man and the

Citizen, that its role as a constitutional court developed. The impact of the Human Rights Act has been far more rapid.

VII

We have seen that the Human Rights Act is leading to conflict between government and the judiciary. Is there any way in which the tension that has come to characterize the relationship can be lessened? One way of reducing the tension, surely, is to institute a better dialogue between the judges and Parliament.

The Constitutional Reform Act of 2005 provides for judges to be more independent of the political process. The Lord Chancellor is no longer head of the judiciary, and there is to be a new supreme court, separate from Parliament, replacing the House of Lords in its judicial capacity, as the final court of appeal. Judges in the Supreme Court will no longer sit in the House of Lords. The Act recognizes that the judiciary is a third branch of the constitution, separate from Parliament and the executive, and it acknowledges the vital importance of the separation of powers in buttressing the independence of the judiciary. All ministers are placed under a statutory duty to 'uphold' the independence of the judiciary. The Lord Chancellor has in addition a specific statutory duty also to 'defend' that independence.

But one consequence of the Act is that there is likely to be less dialogue between Parliament and the judiciary. That could be harmful at a time when there is some danger of conflict between them. It is important, therefore, to consider means by which the judges might once again be brought into contact with Parliament without compromising either the principle of the separation of powers or that of the independence of the judiciary.

It would be a great misunderstanding of the doctrine of the separation of powers to interpret it as meaning that judges should be entirely walled off from the other branches of government. James Madison, one of the Founding Fathers of the United States constitution, in the *Federalist Papers*, written to obtain support for it, declared 'Unless these departments be so far connected and blended, as to give each a constitutional control over the others, the degree of separation . . . essential to a free government can never in practice be duly maintained'.[31] Madison believed that, as well as insisting upon the *independence* of the various branches of government, it was essential also to recognize their essential *interdependence*. The institutions were to be separate but the powers were to be to some extent shared or interdependent. The American system of government has sometimes been described as a government of separate institutions sharing powers. Perhaps the same is now also becoming true of Britain as we shall argue in chapter 11. How might this interdependence of powers be institutionally acknowledged in the British context?

Clearly, if the independence of the judiciary is to be maintained, judges cannot be accountable to Parliament in the same way that ministers are accountable to

---

[31] *The Federalist Papers*, No 48.

Parliament. Judges must be independent. This means, however, that the judiciary is the only one of the three branches of government to hold unchecked and unaccountable power. The decisions of the Supreme Court are absolutely final. Judges are, therefore, an exception to the constitutional principle that those holding power in a democracy should be accountable to the people through their elected representatives. The Human Rights Act increases the power of the judiciary. It therefore emphasises the requirement that they should use their power with restraint. 'We are not final', the United States Supreme Court Justice Jackson once declared, 'because we are infallible, but we are infallible only because we are final'.[32] When, in the 1930s, the United States Supreme Court was using its power of judicial review to cripple President Roosevelt's economic and social programme, Justice Stone reminded his colleagues that 'While an unconstitutional exercise of power by the executive and legislative branches of the government is subject to judicial restraint, the only check on our own exercise of power is our own sense of self-restraint'.[33] This was a salutary reminder.

The fact that judges cannot be accountable to Parliament need not, however, mean that they should have no relationship with Parliament at all. It is worth distinguishing between two different meanings of accountability. The first meaning is what one might call sacrificial accountability. This dictates that ministers take the credit for what goes right in their department, and the blame for what goes wrong, to the extent of being required to resign if something goes seriously wrong. Clearly, judges cannot be held accountable to Parliament in this sense or it would make nonsense of the principle of the independence of the judiciary; and under the Constitutional Reform Act of 2005, Parliament will have no role in the appointment of judges. There will not be, as there are in the United States, confirmation hearings before one or the other Houses of Parliament before judges are appointed. In its consultation paper on the Act, the government specifically declared that this would be inconsistent with its policy of removing the Supreme Court from the political arena.

Ministers, however, are accountable to Parliament in a second, explanatory, sense, quite different from the first, sacrificial sense. They are accountable in that they are required to give an account of their stewardship to Parliament. In the first, sacrificial, sense, they are **answerable** to Parliament, in this second sense they **answer** to Parliament. There is no reason why senior judges should not answer to Parliament on a restricted range of issues and hence be accountable in this second, explanatory, sense of the term. There is no reason why judges should not regularly appear before Parliament, or rather before a Select Committee of Parliament, perhaps a Joint Select Committee, **after** they have been appointed, to be questioned on their judicial approach. In recent years, senior members of the judiciary, such as the Lord Chief Justice and the Master of the Rolls, have regularly appeared before Select Committees to answer questions on issues related to the machinery

---

[32] *Brown v Allen* 344 US (1953) 540.
[33] *United States v Butler* 297 US (1936) 79.

of government as it affects the judges; and the Lord Chief Justice now appears annually with the Lord Chancellor before the House of Lords Select Committee on the Constitution. The House of Commons Constitutional Affairs Committee has argued that:

> 'the views of judges on the role of the Supreme Court approaches to broad questions of law, especially constitutional law and human rights law and law reform are all matters of legitimate public interest. A constructive dialogue between Parliament and the UK's most senior judiciary need in no way undermine judicial independence. The Supreme Court itself has much to gain from such dialogue, especially if senior members of the judiciary cease to sit as peers in the House of Lords—we recognise the potential benefits to public understanding of the role of the new Supreme Court if a practice were to be adopted of inviting judges, including recently appointed ones, to appear before an appropriate Committee from time to time (including this Committee)'.[34]

Members of the judiciary cannot of course be expected to discuss particular judgments, nor matters which are likely to prove justiciable; nor is it for Parliament to consider the conduct of individual judges, nor to hold judges to account for their judgments, nor to examine the merits of particular appointments to the bench. Such matters would have to be expressly excluded from the terms of reference of the relevant Select Committee.

Some judges might be resistant to this proposal, arguing that their judicial outlook should not be any concern of Parliament. Yet senior judges often do communicate their views to the informed public, through lectures and articles in law journals. There is no reason why these views should not also be communicated to the representatives of the people in Parliament through a Select Committee, nor any reason why judges should not be questioned upon them. If a clash between government and the judiciary is to be avoided, it is vital to renew a dialogue between the judges and Parliament. It is vital that the role of the judges is better understood. The Constitutional Reform Act has many merits, but it makes dialogue more difficult to achieve by withdrawing senior judges from the House of Lords. The Constitution Committee of the House of Lords has argued that since judges views on various 'broad legal questions' 'are already in the public domain in the form of articles, it would be odd if Parliament was denied the opportunity to probe such opinions in more detail . . . However, it would be inappropriate for committees to question judges on the pros and cons of particular judgments'.[35]

There is a precedent for such a dialogue in the scrutiny hearings conducted by the Treasury Select Committee with newly appointed members of the Monetary Reform Committee of the Bank of England, following their appointment. The Committee has only once reported that a candidate was unsuitable, but the appointment was not reversed by the Treasury. The Select Committee cannot, therefore, undo the appointment of members, but it can discuss the views of

---

[34] House of Commons Constitutional Affairs Committee, HC 48-I, 2003–4, paras 86, 87.

[35] House of Lords Constitution Committee: *Relations between the Executive, the Judiciary and Parliament*, HL 151, 2006–7, para 125.

appointees on economic and monetary policy generally. Initially, the Treasury was uncomfortable about the scrutiny hearings, just as the judiciary may feel uncomfortable about a dialogue with a Select Committee. But the Treasury has come to accept that the hearings can perform an importance service in underpinning the legitimacy of the Monetary Policy Committee. That could well be a model for a dialogue with the judges.

Such a dialogue would benefit the judges and Parliament as well as the people. Democracy, it has often been said, is government by explanation. If the judges can explain their role in the defence of civil liberties and the rights of minorities, Parliament will be better able to understand why it is that judges so often make judgments that seem to go against the tide of public opinion. That is of some importance since, under the Human Rights Act, judges have to rely upon Parliament to correct abuses; the judges cannot do it themselves.

A dialogue would also be of benefit to Parliament, since it is important for Parliament to understand the philosophy of senior judges and trends in their thinking. Parliament, as well as the judges, needs to understand the nature of human rights and civil liberties and be willing to defend them. 'It must be remembered', the great American judge, Oliver Wendell Holmes, once said 'that legislators are the ultimate guardians of the liberties and welfare of the people in quite as great a degree as the courts'.[36] The effectiveness of the Human Rights Act depends upon the compliance of ministers and MPs with decisions made by the judges. It depends upon how well the three branches of government are able to work together. They are more likely to work together if their interdependence is institutionally recognised.

But the dialogue would also benefit us, the people. The Human Rights Act offers stronger protection for human rights, but it would be dangerous to believe that the protection of human rights can be delegated to the judges alone. One of the aims of the Human Rights Act was to create a human rights culture, a culture that permeates society as well as the courts. There is some danger that liberals, feeling themselves to be a beleaguered minority in society, will alone turn to the courts to achieve what they are unable to achieve by means of the ballot box.

In the last resort, the preservation of our rights depends upon popular support at least as much as it depends upon institutional mechanisms or legislation, however enlightened. Edmund Burke is supposed to have said that 'all that is necessary for evil to triumph is for good men to do nothing'. No one has ever been able to find the source for this quotation in Burke, but, whether he said it or not, the history of Fascism and National Socialism in Europe in the first half of the twentieth century provides eloquent testimony to its message. We err, therefore, if we believe that human rights legislation and independent institutions will alone be sufficient to preserve our freedoms.

In a book published in 1925 on *The Usages of the American Constitution,* H W Horwill, tells the story of the Holy Trinity Church in Guildford. On the site of this church, apparently, was an earlier building which was destroyed in 1740,

---

[36] *Missouri, Kansas and Texas Railway Company v May* 194 US (1904) 270.

when the steeple fell and carried the roof with it. One of the first to be informed of the disaster was the verger. 'It is impossible', he exclaimed, 'for I have the key in my pocket'![37]

The key to our liberties is the Human Rights Act, cornerstone of the new constitution. But the Act will not of itself prevent the fall of the steeple. Only a vigilant public opinion can ensure that it remains upright and that civil liberties are preserved. The success of the Human Rights Act depends upon that popular vigilance.

[37] H W Horwill, *The Usages of the American Constitution* (Oxford, OUP, 1925) 243.

4

Devolution

I

EVOLUTION, THE CREATION of subordinate legislatures and assemblies in Scotland, Wales and Northern Ireland, the non-English parts of the United Kingdom, forms a key element of the new constitution. It has transformed Britain from a unitary state to a quasi-federal state. It is also transforming our understanding of the United Kingdom itself. Previously most English people, at least, regarded the United Kingdom as the home of a single nation, the British nation. Now, we are coming to see it as a multinational state, holding together people belonging to a number of different nations.

Although devolution is a modern policy, implemented in 1998 by a Labour government, it reflects themes of very long ago, from a period even before the Labour Party was founded. In his Midlothian campaign of 1879, Gladstone declared, "If we can make arrangements under which Ireland, Scotland, Wales, portions of England can deal with questions of local and special interest to themselves more efficiently than Parliament now can, that, I say, will be the attainment of a great national good".[1] It took nearly 120 years for a government of the Left to begin the fulfillment of this Gladstonian vision of a 'great national good'. But Northern Ireland, Scotland and Wales now enjoy institutions through which they can 'deal with questions of local and special interest to themselves', although it seems unlikely that the 'portions of England' will, in the near future, at any rate, come to enjoy similar 'arrangements' by which they too would be able to deal with such questions.

Devolution may be defined as the transfer of powers from ministers and Parliament to a subordinate elected body. Its purpose is to provide some degree of self-government on a territorial basis, falling short of independence or of a federal system of government, and also to secure decentralisation and the dispersal of power. Until the 1920s, however, devolution, as we now understand it, was generally called Home Rule.

Devolution has been the firm policy of the Liberal Democrats, and the Party's predecessor, the Liberal Party, since, in 1886, Gladstone first proposed Home Rule for Ireland. Between 1886 and 1914, the Liberals introduced no fewer than three Irish Home Rule bills into Parliament. The first was defeated in the Commons in 1886, while the second was defeated in the Lords in 1893. The third reached the

---

[1] M R D Foot, *Midlothian Speeches* (1879, Leicester, Leicester University Press, 1971) 181. It will be noted that Gladstone spoke of devolution not to an English Parliament but to 'portions of England'.

statute book in 1914, but was suspended until the conclusion of the First World War. By then, however, the majority in Ireland sought national independence, and, after the Anglo-Irish Treaty of 1921, Ireland, with the exception of the six counties of Northern Ireland, became an independent country. Home Rule was, however, given to Northern Ireland by the Government of Ireland Act of 1920, despite the fact that the representatives of Northern Ireland would have preferred complete integration with the rest of the United Kingdom. Between 1921 and 1972, there was a devolved Parliament, known as Stormont, sitting in Belfast and responsible for the domestic affairs of Northern Ireland. In this Northern Ireland Parliament, the Unionists, predominantly Protestant, enjoyed a permanent majority, while the Nationalists, predominantly Catholic, felt themselves to be second-class citizens. Following the civil rights movement of the late 1960s, communal violence broke out in Northern Ireland, and in 1972, the Parliament was first prorogued and then abolished. It remained, however, the policy of successive British governments to restore devolution to Northern Ireland, but in a form that allowed for participation by the minority, Nationalist, community, as well as the majority, Unionists. Various attempts to secure such an outcome failed until the Belfast or Good Friday Agreement of 1998, which finally came into force in 2007.[2] The problems of devolution in Northern Ireland are, however, somewhat different from those elsewhere in the United Kingdom, precisely because of the division between the two communities. Devolution in Scotland and Wales did not arrive on to the modern political agenda until the 1970s, when the Scottish nationalists seemed about to make an electoral breakthrough.

Labour, in its early days, under the leadership of men such as Keir Hardie and Ramsay MacDonald, both Scots, had, like the Liberals, been a Home Rule party. In the 1920s, however, with most of Ireland now independent, Labour abandoned its support for Home Rule, believing it to be irrelevant in an era of slump and unemployment. But, in the 1970s, faced with the threat of Scottish nationalism Labour, at first somewhat unwillingly, resurrected its commitment to Home Rule, or devolution as it was now called, and produced proposals for devolution in Scotland and Wales. These proposals were, however, massively rejected in 1979 in a referendum in Wales by a majority of four to one; and, while there was a small majority for devolution in Scotland, this majority fell far short of the 40% 'Yes' vote from the electorate that Parliament had required for devolution to proceed. Shortly after the devolution referendums, there was a general election in which the Conservatives were returned to power, and the new Prime Minister, Margaret Thatcher, who had always been unsympathetic to devolution, proceeded to repeal the devolution legislation. For the time being, at least, devolution seemed quite dead.

During the 18 years of Conservative government, however, pressure for devolution in Scotland and Wales revived. That was because the Conservatives, although enjoying a majority in the United Kingdom as a whole, were now very much in a minority in both Scotland and Wales, as is shown in the tables below.

---

[2] *The Belfast Agreement: An Agreement Reached at the Multi-Party Talks on Northern Ireland,* Cm 3883, 1998.

Scotland

	1979	1983	1987	1992
Conservatives	22	21	10	11
Labour	44	41	50	49
Liberals (Alliance in 1983 and 1987, Liberal Democrats in 1992)	3	8	9	9
Scottish Nationalist Party	2	2	3	3
Total	71	72	72	72

Wales

	1979	1983	1987	1992
Conservatives	11	14	8	6
Labour	22	20	24	27
Liberals (Alliance in 1983 and 1987, Liberal Democrats in 1992)	1	2	3	1
Plaid Cymru	2	2	3	4
Total	36	38	38	38

From 1987 to 1997, Conservative strength in Wales was so weak that they were forced to choose as Secretary of State for Wales an MP representing an English constituency—Peter Walker, MP for Worcester, from 1987 to 1990, David Hunt, MP for the Wirral from 1990 to 1993, John Redwood, MP for Wokingham from 1993 to 1995 and William Hague, MP for Richmond, Yorkshire, from 1995 to 1997.

Conservative unpopularity in Scotland and Wales was strengthened during the 18 years of Conservative rule by policies which appeared, to many, to be unsympathetic to the special needs of the non-English parts of the United Kingdom. The Thatcher government's policies of competitive individualism and the free market seemed inappropriate to the more communally orientated societies of Scotland and Wales. Conservative rule seemed, to many Scots, to be alien rule. Particularly resented in Scotland was the community charge, popularly known as the poll tax, which was implemented in Scotland before it was tried in England, even though the vast majority of Scottish MPs had voted against it in the House of Commons. In both Scotland and Wales, therefore, support for devolution revived in the years before 1997.

Tony Blair, while sympathetic to devolution, remembered the fiasco of the 1970s when the Labour government had spent a great deal of time on devolution only to find its proposals rejected by the Scots and the Welsh in referendums. To avoid a similar outcome, he proposed that referendums be held **before** the legislation was presented to Parliament, rather than **after** it had been enacted, as had been the case in 1979. These referendums yielded majorities for devolution, following which the government proceeded to legislate for it. The Scotland Act, 1998, established a Scottish Parliament, and the Government of Wales Act, 1998, established a National Assembly of Wales. The government also legislated in 1998 for the establishment of a Northern Ireland Assembly.

The devolution legislation, however, did not provide for a similar structure of government in the three non-English parts of the United Kingdom. The Scottish Parliament was given legislative powers over a wide range of matters connected with Scottish domestic affairs. The National Assembly of Wales, by contrast, was given powers only over secondary legislation in Wales, that is statutory instruments, orders, regulations and the like. It was not given powers over primary legislation. Its powers, therefore, were, in 1998, restricted to the implementation of legislation drawn up at Westminster. Power to pass all laws for Wales still remained with Westminster. In 2006, a further Government of Wales Act greatly extended the powers of the National Assembly, but it still lacks primary powers. The Act provided that a two-thirds majority of all votes in the Assembly, not simply of those voting, and a majority in both chambers at Westminster as well as approval in a referendum would be needed before primary powers would be granted.

The Northern Ireland Assembly, like the Scottish Parliament, was given full legislative powers, but the provisions of the Northern Ireland Act of 1998 require the Northern Ireland executive to contain representatives of both of the two opposing communities—Unionists and Nationalists—in the province. The executive in Northern Ireland is composed in a very different way from that at Westminster. The First and Deputy First Minister must be elected jointly by the Assembly on the basis of cross-community support, with the votes of a majority of members of the Assembly present and voting, and also a majority of Unionists and of Nationalists present and voting. The First Minister and Deputy First Minister hold office jointly as a dyarchy, and, if one resigns, the other also loses office. Other ministers are appointed from the Assembly members, proportionally, on the basis of party strengths, thus ensuring a cross-community government. In addition, all key legislative decisions, including the budget, require cross-community support. It is as if legislation required that the Cabinet in London needed the support of a majority of MPs, a majority of Labour MPs and a majority of Conservative MPs.

Devolution is but one of three strands in the settlement reached in the Belfast Agreement of 1998. The other two comprise a North-South agreement, linking Northern Ireland with the Republic through a consultative North-South Ministerial Council, which gives the Irish government in effect access to devolved matters in Northern Ireland; and an East-West agreement, linking the governments of Britain and Ireland, the devolved administrations, the Channel Islands and the Isle of Man, in a consultative British-Irish Council. There is also a British-Irish Intergovernmental Conference by means of which the two governments can discuss matters of common interest in Northern Ireland. This in effect gives the

Irish government access to policy formulation on non-devolved matters relating to Northern Ireland.

The settlement in Northern Ireland thus comprises far more than devolution. It is indeed primarily from the Unionist perspective that the Belfast Agreement is a devolution settlement, and one of the reasons which persuaded the Unionists to accept it was that the Agreement coincided with devolution to Scotland and Wales, so seeming to reinforce Northern Ireland's continued membership of the United Kingdom. But, from the Nationalist perspective, the devolution aspect of the settlement is part of a wider peace process which leaves open the question of whether Northern Ireland should remain part of the United Kingdom. The Agreement providing for devolution in Northern Ireland was signed between two sovereign states, the United Kingdom and Ireland, and, significantly, the referendum held in Northern Ireland on the Agreement in May 1998 was paralleled by a referendum held on the same day in the Irish Republic, the first all-island vote since the Westminster parliamentary elections of 1918. Nevertheless, the Belfast Agreement confirms the **right** of Northern Ireland to remain within the United Kingdom for as long as its people wish to do so, while also recognising the **aspiration** of the minority community to Irish unity. The right is given institutional recognition in the British-Irish Council, the aspiration in the North-South Ministerial Council. Thus, while in Scotland, the purpose of devolution was to preserve the Union, in Northern Ireland, the purpose of the settlement in which devolution was embodied was to allow for a peaceful dialogue between those who wished to preserve the Union and those who did not.

England, the largest part of the United Kingdom, containing around 85% of its population, has no devolved body, and, while there are calls for an English Parliament to be established, they have so far proved weak. The Blair government was, however, sympathetic to regional devolution in England, provided that there was sufficient demand for it. In 2003, a Regional Assemblies (Referendums) Act was passed, providing for referendums in the regions on the creation of regional authorities. One referendum has so far been held, in November 2004, in the north-east region, thought to be the region most sympathetic to devolution. The outcome, however, was a heavy defeat for devolution. It is unlikely, therefore, that there will be any further regional devolution referendums in the immediate future, and so devolution in England is, for the time being at least, dead.

The outcome, however, is a system of asymmetric devolution in which the four component parts of the United Kingdom are governed in four quite different ways. These variations can be defended as a justifiable response to dissimilar conditions in different parts of the country. Scotland, it is argued, both seeks and requires a greater degree of devolution than Wales on account of her separate legal system; and the demand for devolution was clearly stronger in Scotland than in Wales. Northern Ireland requires special arrangements, since any majority government composed solely of Unionists would be unacceptable to the minority, Nationalist, community. It is, nevertheless, difficult to deny that, in the words of a former Conservative minister, Douglas Hurd, devolution has led to 'a system of amazing untidiness . . . a Kingdom of four parts, of three Secretaries of State, each with different powers, of two Assemblies and one Parliament, each different in composition and powers from the others'.[3]

II

Devolution poses two fundamental and inter-related constitutional questions. The first is whether it is likely, as its supporters hope, to yield a stable solution to the problems posed by Scottish nationalism, strengthening the United Kingdom through respecting and acknowledging the differences between its component parts; or whether, by contrast, it is likely to prove a mere springboard for further demands, leading eventually to the break-up of the United Kingdom. The second question is whether asymmetrical devolution, that is, devolution for just some parts of the United Kingdom and not others is viable.

The central aim of devolution was to avoid the break-up of the United Kingdom by containing the centrifugal forces of nationalism in Scotland and Wales, and, in Northern Ireland, by providing a guaranteed role in government for the minority, nationalist, community. In Scotland, however, the nationalists welcomed devolution because they believed that it would encourage separatism rather than avert it; while, in Northern Ireland, Sinn Fein welcomed devolution as a step towards detaching the province from the rest of the United Kingdom. By 2008, nationalists were in power in all of the devolved bodies, as coalition partners in Wales and Northern Ireland, and as a minority government in Scotland. The SNP government in Scotland proposed to hold a referendum on independence in 2010. Opponents of devolution, therefore, maintained that it was a policy which, far from holding the kingdom together, would disrupt it by creating friction between London and Edinburgh, and a deadlocked form of government in Northern Ireland which, unable to operate effectively, would encourage the men of violence, and loosen the ties binding the province with the rest of the United Kingdom. Is devolution, then, likely to succeed in its main aim of preserving the United Kingdom?

Many journalists rushed immediately to judgment on these matters, and most of these judgments were pessimistic. Some commentators diagnosed Britain, immediately after devolution, as in a state of terminal decline. A Scottish commentator, Tom Nairn, wrote a book called *After Britain*, in which he 'outlined a prospect of four nations and a funeral', believing that 'Britain has already broken up in spirit and the fact will soon follow'.[4] Andrew Marr, the television journalist, entitled his book about devolution *The Day Britain Died*;[5] while

---

[3] Douglas Hurd, 'On From the Elective Dictatorship', First Hailsham Lecture to the Society of Conservative Lawyers, 2001.

[4] Tom Nairn, *After Britain: New Labour and the Return of Scotland* (London, Granta, 2000); Arthur Aughey, *Nationalism Devolution and the Challenge to the United Kingdom State* (London, Pluto Press 2001) 112, vii.

[5] Andrew Marr, *The Day Britain Died* (London, Profile Books, 2000).

another journalist, Peter Hitchens, wrote a book entitled *The Abolition of Britain*.[6] The Conservative MP, John Redwood, wrote a book with a similar title, *The End of Britain?* But, with the scholarly caution appropriate to a Fellow of All Souls, he dignified this somewhat lurid title with a question-mark.[7] Nine years after these books were written, however, the United Kingdom does not seem within sight of dissolution or break-up.

Those who fear the break-up of Britain are afraid of an imbalance between a Scotland straining to burst the bounds of the devolution settlement and an England unable to express her Englishness for fear of disrupting the kingdom. Those on the Left tend to emphasise the strength of Scottish nationalism; those on the Right tend to emphasise the frustrations of the English. It may be that the fears of both are exaggerated. The short answer to the first question has to be, in the words of the famous Chinese proverb, that it is far too early to tell.

In the second edition of The *English Constitution*, published in 1872, Bagehot wisely remarked that it was

'too soon as yet to attempt to estimate the effect of the Reform Act in 1867. The people enfranchised under it do not yet know their own power. . . . A new constitution does not produce its full effect as long as all its subjects were reared under an old constitution, as long as its statesmen were trained by that old constitution. It is not really tested till it comes to be worked by statesmen and among a people neither of whom are guided by a different experience'.

It is perhaps natural to seek a verdict on whether devolution has 'worked' or not, just ten years after the first Scottish Parliament and the first National Assembly of Wales were elected. Yet, any judgment on the effectiveness or success of devolution must surely be very tentative. It would be dangerous to make rash generalisations about the workings of a new constitutional settlement, based on just ten years experience. New institutions and organisational structures take some years to settle down— a generation perhaps—and establish their distinctive patterns. Constitutional reforms take time to percolate and for their full effects to be understood.

What is already clear, however, is that devolution is more than a mere institutional or organisational change. It is a very radical constitutional reform, creating a form of government hitherto unknown in the United Kingdom, except for the experience of Northern Ireland between 1921 and 1972. This experience, however, is of little use in helping to predict the likely course of devolution in Scotland and Wales. This is because devolution in Northern Ireland was not conceded, as it was in Scotland, to meet a separatist claim, but imposed by the British government partly to loosen the ties between the province and the rest of the United Kingdom. It was imposed upon Northern Ireland although not sought by the majority, Unionist, community, and against its wishes. The experience of devolution in Northern Ireland was of course deeply influenced by the religious-cum-tribal

---

[6] Peter Hitchens, *The Abolition of Britain* (London, Quartet Books, 1999).

[7] John Redwood, *The Death of Britain? The United Kingdom's Constitutional Crisis* (Basingstoke, Macmillan 1999).

conflict in the province and by the first-past-the-post electoral system, which allowed for the permanent dominance of one political party, the Unionists, who enjoyed an overall majority in the Parliament throughout its existence. This experience, fortunately, has no relevance to Scotland or Wales.

The experience of devolution in Scotland and Wales is likely to depend upon the evolution of party politics not only in Edinburgh and in Cardiff, but also at Westminster. From this point of view, the relationship between Westminster and the devolved bodies between 1999 and 2007 was, in a sense artificial, in that a Labour government in London was complemented by Labour or Labour/Liberal Democrat administrations in Edinburgh and in Cardiff. In 2007, this pattern was broken in Scotland and in part in Wales. In Scotland, the SNP became the leading party in the Scottish Parliament and proceeded to form a minority administration. In Wales, in 2007, Labour formed a coalition with Plaid Cymru. So, after 2007, nationalist parties were in power in all three of the devolved executives—the SNP in Scotland, Plaid Cymru in Wales, and Sinn Fein in Northern Ireland. It is possible that the result in 2007 heralds a period of conflicting majorities in which relationships between London and Edinburgh will be put under greater strain than before. Nevertheless, at the time of writing, the fact that nationalist parties are in power in all three devolved bodies does not seem to have threatened the unity of the kingdom.

A second circumstance favouring devolution between 1999 and 2007 was the expanding economy. The years after 1999 saw a considerable expansion of the public services, so that Edinburgh and Cardiff could not say that they were starved of financial resources by a mean government in London. Most political arrangements can be guaranteed to work when the economic circumstances are favourable. But the rate of increase of public expenditure has now begun to slow down, and this process is likely to accelerate with the recession, putting a serious strain upon relationships between London and the devolved administrations. It is during a time of economic retrenchment, when the administrations in Edinburgh and Cardiff, financed by block grants from London, are forced to curtail their expenditure, that the true test of devolution will come. Until then, any conclusions as to whether devolution is likely to succeed in its aims can be only speculative.

It is, nevertheless, worth suggesting that there has perhaps been too much emphasis upon the factors tending towards the break-up of the United Kingdom. Even if the SNP were to secure a majority for independence in a referendum, that would be the first rather than the last step in the process of separation. It could not be the springboard for a unilateral declaration of independence. There would be many complex matters to be settled before independence could become a reality, such as, for example, the division of the National Debt between England and Scotland, the allocation of revenues from North Sea oil, and the future of United Kingdom defence bases on the Clyde. These matters could prove highly contentious. The 'velvet' divorce between the Czech Republic and Slovakia in 1993 was preceded by no fewer than 31 treaties and over 2,000 separate agreements. The 2010 referendum, therefore, could do no more than authorise the SNP government to enter into negotiations with the British government on the terms of independence. Assuming that agreement could be reached on these terms, a second referendum would then be needed for the Scottish people to confirm their agreement to them. The process of separation, therefore, could easily prove a long and highly tortuous one. It could not be settled by a single 'Yes' vote in a referendum.[8]

At the time of writing, however, it seems reasonable to be sceptical as to whether there would in fact be a majority for independence in such a referendum. It should be remembered that the Scottish National Party achieved its highest vote in a general election—30%—35 years ago, in October 1974. Its vote in the most recent general election, in 2005, was around 20%. This means that 80% of Scottish voters voted for unionist parties and that the SNP has lost one-third of its vote over the last 35 years; and survey evidence suggests that by no means everyone who votes for the SNP is a separatist. In parts of Scotland the SNP is seen as a Left-wing opposition to Labour, the 'establishment' party in Scotland. Elsewhere, a vote for the SNP is a vote against remote and over-centralised government and a vote for further devolution rather than for separatism.

Much is heard of the artificiality of Britain. It is said that Britain is an 'imagined community', an artificial construct, a conglomerate state, put together in the eighteenth century on a basis of anti-Catholicism in order to build an imperial nation. Now that the empire has disappeared, and that religion is of little importance in British public life, the artificial props of Britishness are, so it is suggested, disappearing, and the forces holding the country together are loosening.[9] There is much current agonizing about the nature of Britishness, and its true meaning in a multinational and multidenominational society. Yet, from one point of view, the criterion for Britishness is simple. It consists in wishing to be represented in the United Kingdom Parliament at Westminster and voting for parties which favour such continued representation. From this point of view, a substantial majority of the population in Scotland and Wales as well as in Northern Ireland remain firmly British and unionist. The brute facts of electoral behaviour seem to refute the view that Britishness is merely a constructed identity or that Britain is no more than an 'imagined community'. If to be British is to wish to continue to be represented at Westminster, then there can be little doubt that there is a majority in each of the component parts of the United Kingdom for remaining British, more of a majority than there was 35 years ago. Perhaps then, Britain is less of an artificial or imagined construct and British loyalty is more organic and primordial than many commentators have suggested.

Perhaps there has been too little analysis of the factors which hold the United Kingdom together. Perhaps too much has been written explaining what has not happened, the break-up of the United Kingdom, and too little on the factors which hold Britain together. Britain is still held together by common economic and

---

[8] See Robert Hazell, 'Rites of Secession', *Guardian*, 29 July 2008.

[9] See, for example, Benedict Anderson, *Imagined Communities* (London, Verso 1983), and Linda Colley, *Britons: Forging the Nation 1707–1837* (New Haven, Yale University Press 1992).

social concerns. Survey evidence in Scotland seems to show that support for devolution is based primarily on a belief that a Scottish Parliament would improve the quality of public welfare, especially health and education. By contrast with the Irish demand after 1886, the Scots seemed to regard constitutional change as a means rather than an end in itself. They hope that devolution will make a difference to their lives in terms of the services provided by government. Those are the grounds on which its effectiveness is likely to be judged, rather than as an expression of nationalism.

III

The second question posed by the devolution legislation of 1998 is whether asymmetrical devolution can provide a stable settlement. Asymmetrical devolution breaches the principle of equal rights for all citizens of the United Kingdom. Those in the non-English parts of the United Kingdom enjoy devolution, while the English do not. Scotland receives, as it did before devolution, around 20% more per head in public spending than England. Wales is over-represented at Westminster, returning 40 MPs, whereas on a comparable basis to England, she should return only 33 MPs. Scotland, Wales and Northern Ireland still have Secretaries of State, admittedly part-time incumbents, to represent their interests in the Cabinet, while England does not. But perhaps the most important institutional expression of the inequality of rights is that MPs from the non-English parts of the United Kingdom can vote on all English matters, while English MPs cannot vote on Scottish or Northern Irish matters, or on Welsh secondary legislation. These matters are decided not at Westminster, but in Edinburgh, Cardiff and Belfast.

This imbalance in representation has given rise to the 'West Lothian Question', named after Tam Dalyell, a Scottish Labour MP hostile to devolution, who, from 1962 to 1983 represented the constituency of West Lothian, and from then to 2005, when he retired from the Commons, that of Linlithgow. The West Lothian Question asks whether it is right that Scottish MPs should be able to vote at Westminster on English domestic legislation, such as, for example, city academies and foundation hospitals, legislation which does not apply in Scotland, where domestic affairs are devolved and have become the responsibility of the Scottish Parliament. Bills on such matters as education and health are, it is argued, mainly English bills or English and Welsh bills; yet Scottish MPs are entitled to vote upon them. This Question is likely to be asked with considerable insistence when, as in 1964 or 1974, the government—Labour in both cases—is dependent upon MPs from Scottish constituencies. In 1995, the Scottish Secretary in John Major's Conservative government, Michael Forsyth, declared that the Question would be the 'Bermuda triangle' of devolution.[10]

---

[10] Cited in V Bogdanor, *Devolution in the United Kingdom* (Oxford, OUP, 1999) 228.

The West Lothian Question draws attention to the supposed disadvantage which England suffers as a result of devolution. England is by far the largest and most populous part of the United Kingdom, yet it is the only part of the United Kingdom without a Parliament or assembly of her own. It is therefore the anomaly in the devolution settlement. England has always resisted federalism, but she has also resisted, in the twentieth century at least, the integration of the non-English parts of the United Kingdom, preferring a system of indirect rule, which allowed the indigenous institutions of the non-English parts of the United Kingdom to be preserved. Nor has English nationalism been a particularly strong force for much of the twentieth century. Part of the reason for this no doubt is that, with a characteristic lack of logic, many in England have failed to recognise the distinction between being English and being British, treating the two as interchangeable. In 1924, Stanley Baldwin, speaking at the annual dinner of the Royal Society of St George, was able to confess to 'a feeling of satisfaction and profound thankfulness that I may use the word "England" without some fellow at the back of the room shouting out "Britain" '.[11] Because so many use 'English' and 'British' as interchangeable terms, English nationalism has found itself without any obviously recognisable patriotic symbols of its own. Devolution perhaps raises the dilemma of Englishness first noticed by Henry James in his novel, *The Tragic Muse*, which describes an Englishman, Nick Dormer, surveying a landed estate which he will never inherit, and feeling 'the sense of England—a sort of apprehended revelation of his country' which 'laid on him a hand that was too ghostly to press, and yet somehow too urgent to be light'.

Can Englishness remain as ghostly as it was for Nick Dormer, or has it now become a matter of urgency to discover an institutional basis for it? Devolution was a solution to the perceived lack of legitimacy of British government in the non-English parts of the United Kingdom, and particularly Scotland. Has it now transferred the legitimacy question away from Scotland to England, so that it will, in the future, be England that questions the legitimacy of British government, particularly when that government is dependent upon the votes of Scottish MPs, as was the case with the Labour governments of 1964–66 and 1974–79.

Devolution seems to raise, in a highly acute form, the question of Englishness and how it should be expressed. How should England be governed? Some have argued that devolution to the non-English parts of the United Kingdom should be complemented by devolution in England so as to make the settlement more nearly symmetrical, and a nearer approximation to territorial equality of rights. There are two methods by which there could be devolution to England. The first is through an English Parliament, with powers perhaps similar to those of the Scottish Parliament. The second is through breaking up England into regions and establishing regional devolved bodies. These two methods correspond, however, to two different and perhaps inconsistent diagnoses of the problem of English

---

[11] Cited in A Aughey, *Nationalism, Devolution and the Challenge to the United Kingdom State* (London, Pluto Press, 2001) 65.

government. The first answers the questions—what should England's place be in the United Kingdom, how can England's position be made more secure, how can England's voice be properly heard now that the Scots and Welsh are speaking with a louder voice? The second answers the questions—how can England resolve the problem of over-centralised government which the Scots and the Welsh have answered through devolution? How can England come to be better governed so that the regions furthest from London, and especially perhaps, the north of England, secure more attention to their needs? The two proposals, the creation of an English Parliament and the creation of English regional assemblies, offer answers to different questions. Those who favour an English Parliament are not, in general, sympathetic to dividing England into regions, since they believe that such a division would fragment the voice of England just at a time when that voice needs to be heard loud and clear if it is to compete with the voices from Scotland and Wales. Supporters of English regional government, by contrast, find little merit in proposals for an English Parliament, which, legislating as it would, for around 50 million people, would do nothing to solve the problems of over-centralisation and overloaded government which, in their view, currently bedevil Westminster.

An English Parliament with legislative powers could, in theory, provide an answer to the West Lothian question. But there seems little demand for such a Parliament. When William Hague, as Conservative leader, proposed such a solution in the 1997–2001 Parliament, he found few supporters, and rapidly abandoned the idea. It would seem pointless to answer the West Lothian Question by making such a massive upheaval in governmental arrangements unless this would make for more effective government. Part of the dynamic for devolution, after all, was to secure decentralization and increase accountability. An English Parliament, however, situated in Winchester and York, could do little to help achieve this aim. It would appear as remote and over-centralised as Westminster. Further, and perhaps even more important, an English Parliament could hardly help appearing a rival to Westminster. There is no federal system in the world in which one of the units represents over 80% of the population—the nearest equivalent is Canada where 35% of the population live in Ontario; but that is not a very near equivalent. Federal systems in which the largest unit dominates do not in general survive. That is the lesson of the USSR which was dominated by Russia, Czechoslovakia which was dominated by the Czechs, and Yugoslavia which was dominated by the Serbs.

As long ago as 1973, the Royal Commission on the Constitution, the Kilbrandon Commission, summed up the case against an English Parliament in trenchant terms.

'A federation consisting of four units—England, Scotland, Wales and Northern Ireland—would be so unbalanced as to be unworkable. It would be dominated by the overwhelming political importance and wealth of England. The English Parliament would rival the United Kingdom federal Parliament; and in the federal Parliament itself the representation of England could hardly be scaled down in such a way as to enable it to be outvoted by Scotland, Wales and Northern Ireland, together representing less than one-fifth of the population. A United Kingdom federation of four countries, with a federal Parliament and provincial Parliaments in the four national capitals, is therefore not a realistic proposition'.[12]

It is difficult to improve upon this verdict.

An alternative answer to the West Lothian Question is to be found in the slogan 'English votes on English laws'. This proposal, unlike that for an English Parliament, does have considerable popular resonance both in England and in Scotland. It has been supported by the Conservatives and by the Scottish National Party. The Conservatives first embraced it under William Hague's leadership in 1999, and it formed part of the Party's election manifestoes in 2001 and 2005. The SNP has a settled policy of not voting on English legislation, which it defines as legislation that has no 'direct or indirect legislative or financial impact on Scotland, Wales or Northern Ireland'.[13] Tam Dalyell, who first posed the West Lothian Question, and who was the only Scottish Labour MP to have opposed devolution, followed the same self-denying ordinance, until retiring from the Commons in 2005.

In 2006, Lord Baker of Dorking, formerly Kenneth Baker, Education and Environment Secretary in the government of Margaret Thatcher, put forward a private members bill in the Lords providing that House of Commons procedure be altered so that only English MPs should be able to vote on English legislation. This proposal was sympathetically received not only by Conservatives, but also by some leading Liberal Democrats, including Sir Menzies Campbell and by Simon Hughes, hoping perhaps that it might prove a step towards the federal Britain which the Party favours.

In 2007, a variant on this proposal was produced by Sir Malcolm Rifkind, a former Conservative Foreign Secretary, who had been MP until 1997 for a Scottish constituency, Edinburgh Pentlands, but was now MP for an English constituency, Kensington and Chelsea. Sir Malcolm proposed that an English Grand Committee be established, the membership of which would be proportional to the strength of the parties in England. All English legislation would be sent to this committee, and although the whole House of Commons would retain the right to overrule the English Grand Committee, by convention it would not do so. Thus, MPs representing non-English constituencies would retain the right to vote on all matters, but they would not normally exercise that right, just as the Commons, dominated by English MPs does not normally override the Scottish Parliament on devolved matters, since that would be incompatible with the principle of devolution. Sir Malcolm sees his own proposal as one that extends the principle of devolution to England without the need for an English parliament and without the need to restrict the voting rights of MP representing non-English constituencies. This proposal was adopted in modified form by a Democracy Taskforce established by

---

[12] Royal Commission on the Constitution, HMSO 1973, Cmnd 5460, para 531.
[13] Cited in M Russell and G Lodge, 'The government of England by Westminster', in R Hazell (ed) *The English Question* (Manchester, Manchester University Press, 2006) 86. This book provides an admirable account of proposed solutions to the West Lothian Question.

the Conservatives, and chaired by Kenneth Clarke, a former Chancellor of the Exchequer. This Committee did not accept the idea of an English Grand Committee, but proposed that 'English' bills be voted on only by English MPs at the committee and report stages. That proposal has now been accepted as official Conservative policy. But it does little to overcome the difficulties of principle faced by all proposals for 'English votes for English laws', difficulties that make them unworkable in the British constitutional context.

The effect of proposals for 'English votes for English laws' would be that, whenever a government depended upon Scottish MPs for its majority, as in 1964 and 1974, the Commons becomes bifurcated. There would be in such circumstances, a United Kingdom majority—Labour—for foreign affairs, defence, economic policy and social security; but an alternative majority, without the Scots, for health, education and other matters devolved to Scotland. Ministers would have to switch rapidly to the opposition front bench when an English matter was under discussion, while the opposition front benchers would come to take their places on the ministerial benches. These proposals would therefore undermine the principle of collective responsibility according to which a government must stand or fall as a whole, commanding a majority on all of the issues that come before Parliament, not just a selection of them. While suspensions of the principle can perhaps be defended on unusual occasions such as the European Communities referendum of 1975, it would be difficult to see how Britain could be effectively governed when a government could not be held responsible to parliament for a very wide range of issues. Nor is it clear how the opposition frontbenchers making their transition to the government side of the House would relate to civil servants or to government departments. In short the proposal for 'English votes for English laws', disturbs not only the logic of parliamentary arrangements, but also of the whole governmental process.

It may be objected that the position of a government in those circumstances would be no worse than that faced by a minority government such as the Wilson government of 1974 or the Callaghan government of 1976–1979. In such cases, so it is suggested, the government could not be assured of getting its proposals through the Commons. It might have to negotiate with other parties, and on occasion withdraw its proposals, or refrain from making proposals because it knew that there would be no chance of carrying them.

The position with 'English votes for English laws' or an English Grand Committee would be quite different. Minority governments survive because there is not, in the House of Commons, a determined majority against them. The other parties being, for one reason or another, opposed to a rapid general election, tolerate the continued existence of a minority government. In consequence, it is true, minority governments fail to secure all of their legislative proposals, but they have been able to achieve a good deal of their programme. In the case of the Rifkind proposal, by contrast, a government with a majority at Westminster would be unable to secure whole swathes of its legislation—it would be able to secure none of its legislation on education, health, transport, nor any of the other subjects devolved to Scotland. That would mean a bifurcated government.

One of the subjects reserved to Westminster is taxation, Scotland having only the very minor power of varying income tax by 3p in the pound. This means that, under the Rifkind proposal, the English Grand Committee would be making decisions on education, health etc. which might have revenue-raising implications, without having control over taxation. So the United Kingdom government might be forced to raise taxes to promote policies with which it disagreed. Thus, the government could no longer retain collective responsibility for its policies but only for a selection of them. Electors, whether in Scotland or England, would not be very happy to elect a government which cannot secure the bulk of its programme, and which, when legislating on health, education etc. would run the risk of legislative gridlock leading to paralysis.

Both the proposal for 'English votes for English laws' and the Rifkind proposal would yield in practice an English Parliament, a parliament for English domestic affairs, within the United Kingdom Parliament at Westminster. Its logic would seem to require the creation of a separate English Parliament, but there is neither the political will to create such a Parliament, nor would it be easy to govern such an unbalanced quasi-federation as the United Kingdom would then have become.

It would not be at all easy for the Speaker to determine precisely which bills were 'English'. Some bills contain clauses which provide for changes in one area of the United Kingdom only, but other clauses which provide for changes in other areas also. For example, most of the 2004 Higher Education bill providing for top-up fees in universities applied just to England and Wales. But, with respect to Wales, the bill provided that the National Assembly for Wales could decide for itself whether to introduce top-up fees in Wales; and, in the event, the National Assembly decided not to do so. It is, therefore, unclear whether Welsh MPs would or would not be allowed to vote in divisions on the Higher Education bill. In addition, part 1 of the bill as well as clauses 42, 43, 44, 47, 48 and 50, extended to Scotland and Northern Ireland as well as to England and Wales. Would MPs from Scotland and Northern Ireland, therefore, be brought back in what a Scottish Labour MP, George Foulkes, called a kind of 'legislative hokey-cokey' to vote just on these particular clauses.[14] Significantly, both the SNP and Tam Dalyell decided to vote on the bill, and they voted against it, because of its implications for higher education in Scotland.

But there is an even more fundamental objection to the idea of 'English votes for English laws'. It was made by the Kilbrandon Commission on the Constitution when it pointed out that

'Ability to vote could not depend simply on whether the matter at issue related to a reserved or transferred subject. Any issue in Westminster involving expenditure of public money is of concern to all parts of the United Kingdom since it may directly affect the level of taxation and indirectly influence the level of a region's own expenditure'.[15]

---

[14] In an opposition day debate on the idea of English votes for English laws, House of Commons debates, 21 January 2004, vol 416, col 1394.
[15] Royal Commission on the Constitution, para 813.

Scotland, Wales and Northern Ireland are financed through a block fund, the size of which depends, through the Barnett formula, on expenditure in England. The block fund for Scotland, Wales and Northern Ireland is calculated as a fraction of total United Kingdom spending, of which of course English spending forms the preponderant part. Suppose that a radical government at Westminster were to decide to cut expenditure on education by introducing a voucher scheme, or to cut expenditure on health, by introducing a social insurance system. The Scottish Parliament, dominated by Labour, would probably be opposed to such schemes, and not wish to introduce them for Scotland. Public expenditure on education and health in Scotland, therefore, would be significantly greater than in England. The block fund for Scotland would, however, have been reduced. There would thus be a knock-on effect on Scotland, making it more difficult for her to maintain expenditure on her public services. The Scottish Parliament has only very limited tax-raising powers; it can raise income tax up to 3p in the pound. Thus, if the Scottish Parliament was not prepared to reduce public expenditure, it would have to raise income tax, or use an indirect tax-raising power by withholding money from Scottish local authorities. But this would mean that Scottish local authorities would, in turn, have either to reduce expenditure or cut services.

It is fundamentally for this reason that MPs from the devolved areas need the right to continue voting on what might seem to be merely English domestic affairs. The level of public spending in the devolved areas will continue to depend upon England, the dominant nation in the United Kingdom. In fact, any issue at Westminster involving the expenditure of public money must be of concern to all parts of the United Kingdom since it will directly affect the size of the block fund going to a devolved body.

This argument does not apply to an issue not involving public expenditure such as, for example, the abolition of hunting, where there might be a case for MPs from the devolved areas following a policy of abstention. But, with issues involving, public expenditure, it is difficult to isolate a purely 'English' issue, having no consequential effects in Scotland and Wales.

The West Lothian Question derives from asymmetrical devolution. There seem, at first sight, to be three ways of making devolution symmetrical. The first is by establishing an English Parliament, and the second is by securing 'English votes for English laws'. But the second proposal in practice collapses into the first. It implies the creation of a separate English Parliament, even if that parliament remains, for the time being, inside Westminster, rather than being separately located in, eg Winchester or York. Such a policy would encourage separatism which is why the SNP supports 'English votes for English laws'. The implication is that the English no longer want the Scots at Westminster. But the proposal for 'English votes for English laws' also poses a problem for the Conservative Party. The Conservative Party has always been the Party of the Union. It was against devolution to Scotland in the twentieth century just as it was against Home Rule to Ireland in the nineteenth. In terms of representation, however, it is now almost a purely English Party, with all but four of its MPs representing English constituencies. A United

Kingdom without Scotland would nearly always have a Conservative majority. The Conservatives, therefore, have to choose whether to remain a Unionist party or to become an English nationalist party. The future of the United Kingdom could depend upon their choice.

There would seem to be a third method of securing symmetry, by establishing English regional parliaments. That, however, is illusory. Proposals for an English regional assembly in the north-east were heavily defeated in a referendum in November 2004, so that the establishment of directly elected regional bodies seems unlikely in the foreseeable future. But, even if the regional proposals had been accepted, they would not have helped to resolve the West Lothian Question unless the regional assemblies had been given legislative powers roughly similar to those of the Scottish Parliament. No one, however, would seriously propose that England be broken up into regional legislative bodies so that there would be different laws in Manchester from those in Newcastle or Birmingham, as there are in New York, Connecticut and New Jersey. Regional devolution, therefore, whatever its merits, cannot make any contribution to answering the West Lothian Question.

It seems, therefore, that none of the three responses to the West Lothian Question—an English Parliament, 'English votes for English laws' and English regional assemblies—can provide a satisfactory answer. For the time being, therefore, the West Lothian Question will have to remain unanswered. Need this matter?

It may be argued that asymmetrical devolution yields a constitutional imbalance between a Scotland straining to extend the devolution settlement, and perhaps to burst its bounds, and an England unable to express its nationalism for fear of disrupting the kingdom. Some bolder spirits on the Right go so far as to argue that devolution imposes so much injustice upon the English that they should no longer be expected to make the effort to hold the kingdom together by submerging their identity. Therefore, it would be better from the point of view of the English were the United Kingdom to break up. The English, on this view, can remain English only if they burst the bounds of union. Such is the argument of the Conservative commentator, Simon Heffer, biographer of Enoch Powell, in his book, *Nor Shall My Sword*.[16] The English, Heffer argues, should come home from Britain and break up the Union so that they can at last become truly English.

The response on the Left has been somewhat different. It has been to search for some essence of Britishness, some statement of values which can help to hold a post-devolution Britain together. Some look longingly to the United States or to France, where, so it is suggested, there is, as well as a constitution, a narrative, such as the Declaration of Independence in the United States, or the Declaration of the Rights of Man and the Citizen in France, which helps to forge national cohesion.

This viewpoint, however, suggests a somewhat idealised view of foreign experience. The American narrative, however valuable it has been, did not serve to

---

[16] S Heffer, *Nor Shall My Sword: The Reinvention of England* (London, Weidenfeld and Nicolson, 1999).

prevent slavery nor the deprivation of civil rights for the Afro-American minority until the 1960s; nor did it prevent a ruinous civil war which almost tore the nation apart. The French narrative did not prevent a long-running dispute about the appropriate form of constitutional arrangements, a dispute which perhaps only the Fifth Republic, founded in 1958, has been able to bring to a close.

A narrative is not something that can be imposed artificially. If it does not exist it cannot be invented. Nor is it clear how a conclusion to an essentially philosophical debate—on the nature of Britishness—can serve to resolve what are essentially practical problems. There is in fact no need to ascend into the realms of philosophy to discover the essence of Britishness. If, as we have argued, Britishness can be understood, in a far more practical fashion, as the willingness to be represented and to continue to be represented in Parliament, then to be British is to seek to be represented in Parliament. From this point of view, the sense of Britishness remains very strong in Scotland and Wales, and remains the majority sentiment in Northern Ireland; while in England, there is no English nationalist party seeking to break up the United Kingdom. From the practical point of view, therefore, there seems little need to worry about Britishness, and perhaps those who have suggested that Britishness is an artificial entity that was in the past buttressed by empire, have underestimated the deep organic ties that hold the country together. These organic ties are symbolised by the predominance of nation-wide, unionist parties, the Labour, Conservative and Liberal Democrat parties, whose policies assume that members of the United Kingdom share a common functional interest in the protection and improvement of the public services. These organic ties are likely to be strengthened during a period of recession when separatism comes to seem an expensive luxury. The Union continues to rest, therefore, on strong common interests and common institutions. And perhaps, even though there may not be a common narrative, a common story, there is an inchoate understanding of a common destiny.

Survey evidence seems to indicate that a majority of the English now accept devolution in Scotland and Wales. There is no English backlash in the sense that the English believe devolution should be rescinded, as many believe that membership of the European Union should be rescinded. The English have adjusted to the new status quo, but are uninterested in further constitutional change. It was for this reason that when, during the 1997–2001 Parliament, the Conservative leader William Hague sought to put himself at the head of an English army by proposing an English parliament, he found himself bereft of followers. The worry, such as it is, is not about the fact of devolution, but the consequences in terms of inequity for England. The English do not appear to wish to remedy this inequity by seeking devolution for themselves. Support for devolution either to an English Parliament or to English regional assemblies has rarely exceeded 25% in recent years. The English, unlike the Scots and the Welsh, do not appear to feel the need to have their identity legitimised by institutions. It is difficult to resist the conclusion of John Curtice, a leading authority on the interpretation of survey data, that 'devolution in Scotland and Wales is thought neither to have been so successful that it demands to be emulated nor to have done so much harm that the damage needs to be repaired'[17]

Are there other ways in which the feeling of inequity in England might be resolved? The inequity would be felt less if there were less of an imbalance between the political parties in Scotland. This imbalance is comparatively recent. From 1945 to 1964 the largest gap between the two parties in Scotland was just 8 seats, when, in 1945, Labour won 37 Scottish seats and the Conservatives 29. In 1955, the Conservatives won not only a majority of seats in Scotland, but also a majority of the Scottish vote, the only time that a party has achieved such a success in Scotland since the war. In 1964, however, the gap between the parties was 21 seats and, after the general election of 2005, it was 39 seats, Labour winning 40 seats and the Conservatives just 1. If the Conservatives were able to recover their position in Scotland, the West Lothian Question would be less of a problem. Were proportional representation to be introduced for elections to the House of Commons, then also the West Lothian Question would be less of a problem. Under the first-past-the-post system, minorities, including the Conservative minority in Scotland, find themselves drastically under-represented. The Conservatives won just one seat in Scotland in 2005, but around 17.5%—over one-sixth—of the Scottish vote. The first-past-the-post system exaggerates the support of a dominant party in a region and makes it appear as if hardly anyone votes for the Conservatives in Scotland, which of course is far from being the case.

Whether or not a better political balance is achieved in Scotland, however, there is no doubt that improvements could be made in the way that England is governed. That does not require the creation of an English parliament. English alienation stems, not from the lack of a secure sense of identity but from a feeling that government is too remote, too far away from the people. An English parliament would of course be equally remote. The remedy then would seem to lie in renewed attention to localism. If, therefore, it is believed that England suffers from over-centralised and remote government, the cure is likely to be found, not in the creation of regional assemblies, but in a strengthening of local government, perhaps through directly elected mayors as suggested in chapters 8 and 10. It is a weakness of the devolution settlement that it did not accompany reforms to the government of Scotland and Wales with some consideration of what was needed for government in England. Devolution should have been accompanied by a radical policy designed to strengthen local government in England.

One crucial reason, however, for the relative indifference displayed by the English towards devolution is that the English remain by far the dominant nation in the United Kingdom, and this dominance has hardly been affected by the establishment of devolved bodies in Scotland and Wales. It is sometimes suggested that Britain has come to be dominated by the Scots. Yet, 528 of the 646 MPs in the Commons represent English constituencies. The English have no need to beat the

---

[17] J Curtice, 'What the people say—if anything' in Hazell (ed) *The English Question*, above n 13, 130, 132.

drum or blow the bugle. If they do, they will strain the devolution settlement, which rests fundamentally on restraint by the English, to breaking point. So far the English have certainly shown restraint. They accept devolution in Scotland and Wales, but do not seek it for themselves. Thus, the West Lothian Question is misconceived. Persisting with it could give rise to grave dangers. If the English were to seek to express their Englishness to the full, they could easily, as the dominant nation in the United Kingdom, threaten the unity of the country. In his valuable book *Nationalism, Devolution and the Challenge to the United Kingdom State*, Arthur Aughey draws an analogy between post-devolution Britain and the Austro-Hungarian empire depicted by Joseph Roth in his short story, 'The Bust of the Emperor'.[18] Roth suggests in the story that the empire declined not through the arguments of those who wished to destroy it, but because of the ironic disbelief of those who should have believed in it and supported it. And yet, one cannot but think that the Union is more likely to survive if its inhabitants continue to concentrate upon the substantive issues of politics and forget about the logical conundrums which devolution poses, and the philosophical arguments of English Gaullists whose conception of England can be a somewhat dogmatic one. Too much self-consciousness, after all, is as bad for a nation as it is for an individual.

England, the political scientist, Richard Rose, once suggested, 'is a state of mind, not a consciously organized political institution',[19] the sense of which has been better captured by her musicians, her painters and her writers, than by her politicians. England does not at present feel the need to have her identity legitimised by institutions. That perhaps is fortunate. If English nationalism were to move from culture to politics, it could seriously undermine the United Kingdom. The English, however, maintain their studied disavowal of nationalism and remain delightfully reluctant to reflect on their character as a nation. Exhorted by both multiculturalists and Powellites to become lions, they prefer to remain ostriches. While the polemicists insist upon an answer, the English simply refuse to acknowledge that there is a question, remaining content to repeat Disraeli's aphorism that England is governed not by logic but by Parliament.

There seems no reason, then, why asymmetrical devolution, despite its failures of logic, should not provide a stable solution to the problems raised by Scottish nationalism and over-centralised government. Britain has never been a wholly symmetrical state. In the nineteenth century Ireland was governed by a Viceroy and a Chief Secretary, while in 1885, the position of Scottish Secretary was created, 'to redress', as Lord Salisbury put it, 'the wounded dignities of the Scotch (*sic*) people—or a section of them—who think that enough is not made of Scotland'.[20] The post was, Gladstone believed, 'a little mouthful of Home Rule', and from 1892 its holder was always in the Cabinet except in time of war.[21] In 1921, Northern

---

[18] A Aughey, *Nationalism, Devolution and the Challenge to the United Kingdom State*, above n 11, 182.

[19] R Rose, *Understanding the United Kingdom* (Harlow, Longman, 1982) 29.

[20] Quoted in A Midwinter, M Keating and J Mitchell, *Politics and Public Policy in Scotland* (Houndmills, Macmillan 1991) 52.

[21] House of Commons Debates, 3rd series, vol 304, col 252, 13 April 1886.

Ireland had its own devolved Parliament, while in 1964, the Welsh Office was established. There is thus a tradition that the different parts of the United Kingdom should be governed in different ways according to their own particular practical needs.

Britain, it has been argued, was, even before devolution, not a *unitary* state but a *union* state. The distinction, which derives from a Norwegian social scientist, Stein Rokkan, is that a unitary state is a Jacobin state 'built up around one unambiguous political centre which . . . pursues a more or less undeviating policy of administrative standardization. All areas of the state are treated alike, and all institutions are directly under the control of the centre'.[22] There was no such requirement in the case of union states, and these, by contrast with unitary states, could remain asymmetrical. They were 'common in Europe prior to the nineteenth century, but were swept away in the wave of nation- and state-building after the French Revolution', a wave which Britain avoided. The theory of the unitary or Jacobin state is that, 'Once political legitimacy came to rest on the principle of popular sovereignty, it was assumed that there must be an undifferentiated populace or demos on which it could rest'.[23] That theory has never made much headway in Britain. Instead, as one commentator has perceptively remarked:

'The British constitution has been criticized by reformers for over 100 years for its unmodern features, its untidiness and the lack of a principle of popular sovereignty. Yet these archaic features might give it a distinct advantage over other European polities in the transition to a new era of differentiated and complex government, in which nations are embedded in different ways in states, which in turn are embedded in a broader European political order, since it has few Jacobin prejudices to overcome. . . . It is this continuing union tradition, among other things, that explains why the English appear so relaxed about Scottish devolution and why the debate on English constitutional reform has been divorced from the issue of Home Rule for the peripheral nations'.[24]

It is, fundamentally, for this reason that 'The English Question does not have to be answered. It is not an examination question which the English are required to answer. It can remain unresolved for as long as the English want. Ultimately only the English can decide if they want to seek an answer to the English Question'.[25]

It is often assumed that the provisions for asymmetrical devolution are inherently unstable, and that this instability threatens the continued existence of the United Kingdom. These propositions, however, need to be argued for rather than merely asserted. There have, after all, always been asymmetrical elements in British government, even before devolution in a United Kingdom with three different

---

[22] S Rokkan and D Urwin, 'Introduction: Centres and Peripheries in Western Europe' in Rokkan and Urwin (eds) *The Politics of Territorial Identity: Studies in European Regionalism* (London, Sage 1982) 11.

[23] M Keating, 'From Functional to Political Regionalism: England in Comparative Perspective', in Hazell, *The English Question*, above n 13, 143.

[24] Ibid.

[25] R Hazell, 'Conclusion: What are the Answers to the English Question' in Hazell, *The English Question*, above n 13, 240.

legal systems, Secretaries of State for the non-English parts of the kingdom, but not for England, and two established churches. Before devolution, an anomaly similar to that of which the English now complain, occurred with Scottish legislation, when the Conservatives were in power at Westminster. The Scottish legislative committees had to be filled with English MPs, and there were many occasions on which the Scottish political will was overridden by English votes, the most notorious being the poll tax, which was opposed by the vast majority of Scottish MPs. Current arrangements may differ in degree, but it is not clear that they differ in kind; and it is perhaps easier for the English to correct anomalies than it was for the Scots, since the English remain by far the dominant nation in the United Kingdom.

IV

Asymmetrical devolution, then, need not of itself threaten the continued existence of the United Kingdom; and it may well succeed in its aim of containing Scottish nationalism. Devolution, however, does threaten one fundamental principle which has lain at the basis of British social policy from the time of the Attlee government, if not from the era of Lloyd George. It is that the benefits which the individual derives from the state, and the burdens imposed upon her should depend, not upon geography, but upon need. It was for this reason that so many in the Labour Party, and especially on the Left of the Labour Party, were opposed to devolution until the threat from Scottish nationalism made it seemingly unavoidable. In 1946, Aneurin Bevan had strongly resisted the creation of separate Scottish, Welsh or Northern Irish health services. He created instead a *National* Health Service, in which treatment would depend upon need and not upon the accident of where one lived. This social democratic philosophy persisted into the 1970s. Social and economic problems were best resolved, not through devolution, but through a strong government of the Left at Westminster. Only a strong central government could determine a fair distribution of benefits and burdens between different regions of the country. Labour's scepticism towards devolution, therefore, was based less upon the idea that it would lead to the break-up of the United Kingdom, that it would undermine sovereignty, than that it would undermine the power of Westminster to correct territorial disparities. The divergences that have appeared in a number of the central planks of the Welfare State between Scotland and the rest of the United Kingdom since devolution, tend to show that such fears were not misplaced.

> 'You can't have Scotland doing something different from the rest of Britain', Blair complained to the Liberal Democrat leader, Paddy Ashdown in 1999 when the Scottish Liberal Democrats were pressing for a more generous policy on student support than was being implemented in England.
>
> 'Then you shouldn't have given the Scots devolution', Ashdown retorted, 'specifically, the power to be different on this issue. You put yourself in a ridiculous position if,

having produced the legislation to give power to the Scottish Parliament, you then say it is a matter of principle they can't use it'.

'Tony Blair (laughing), 'Yes, that is a problem. I am beginning to see the defects in all this devolution stuff'. [26]

Devolution allows the non-English parts of the kingdom to develop their own distinctive priorities in public policy. But the Welfare State was founded on the principle that the needs of citizens should be determined not locally but by central government, which alone could balance the requirements of different parts of the kingdom, and the needs of those living in different parts of the kingdom. Otherwise, the distribution of benefits would depend upon what is now contemptuously called a postcode lottery. Thus, while devolution may not threaten the unity of the United Kingdom, it does undermine the power of central government to correct territorial disparities.

Already, after only ten years, important divergences have appeared in welfare benefits between Scotland and the rest of the United Kingdom. The Scottish Parliament has decided to provide for the finance of university students, the salaries of teachers, and the needs of those in residential care, in a more generous way than has been provided by Westminster for England. Some of these differences, eg in the salaries of teachers and in residential care, were apparent before devolution, but were little noticed. As devolution progresses, it is likely that the non-English parts of the United Kingdom will continue to establish priorities of their own, distinct from those of Westminster. There would be little point in devolution were the devolved bodies merely to replicate the decisions of Westminster. It is not clear how far this process can go within a single state. Perhaps what is needed is a new definition of which social and economic rights are fundamental to citizenship, and should therefore remain uniform throughout the kingdom. Such rights might perhaps be embodied in a United Kingdom Bill of Rights and Freedoms. What cannot be denied is that devolution threatens the power of the government of the United Kingdom to secure equal social rights for all of its citizens. It is difficult to see how the state can secure these equal rights if it has been fragmented and cut into pieces by devolution.

V

Devolution, although it may not threaten the continued existence of the United Kingdom, does establish new constitutional relationships between the different parts of the United Kingdom, relationships not wholly dissimilar from those familiar in federal states, such as the United States and Germany, but wholly new in Britain, with the very limited exception of the 1921–1972 Northern Ireland experience of devolution.

[26] *The Ashdown Diaries*, vol 2, 1997–1999 (London, Allen Lane, The Penguin Press, 2001) 446: entry for 7 May 1999.

Devolution is of course not the same as federalism. Federalism involves dividing the powers of government between a central government and various states or provinces, between a federal government in Washington or Berlin and state governments in, for example, California or Bavaria. In a federal state, the legislature, Congress in the United States and the Bundestag in Germany, is not sovereign but subordinate to the constitution. It is the constitution not the legislature which is sovereign, and in most federal states, the courts can declare federal legislation which is contrary to the constitution, void.

Devolution, by contrast, preserves, in principle, the sovereignty of Parliament. Parliament can, in theory, continue to legislate for Scotland, Wales or Northern Ireland even on devolved matters; and it can, if it wishes, simply abolish the devolved bodies by a simple Act of Parliament, as it did with the Northern Ireland Parliament in 1972. The government was particularly insistent in emphasizing that devolution preserved the sovereignty of Parliament. The White Paper, *Scotland's Parliament*, which preceded devolution and was published in 1997, declared that 'The United Kingdom Parliament is and will remain sovereign in all matters'.[27] The Scotland Act, 1998, section 28 (7) repeated this claim, declaring that, 'This section', which provided for the Scottish Parliament to make laws, 'does not affect the power of the Parliament of the United Kingdom to make laws for Scotland'.

In practice, however, devolution imposes a severe limitation upon the sovereignty of Parliament. In Northern Ireland, there is a limitation imposed by the Belfast Agreement, a treaty between two states, Britain and Ireland. This requires the British government not to exercise power in Northern Ireland except in a manner that is consistent with the Agreement. In relation to Scotland, Parliament accepts, by the Sewel convention, that it will not normally legislate on devolved matters, without the consent of the Scottish Parliament. Thus, in practice, it is the Scottish Parliament which legislates on matters devolved to Scotland. The Scottish ministers at Westminster—the Secretary of State and his team—no longer accept questions on Scottish domestic affairs, since they are no longer responsible for them.

Even on Welsh matters, despite the fact that powers over only secondary and not primary legislation have been devolved to the National Assembly of Wales, ministers now refuse to accept questions on Welsh domestic affairs. In October 1999, the standing orders of the House of Commons resolved that questions may not normally be tabled on matters for which responsibility had been devolved by legislation to both Scotland and Wales. Thus whole swathes of policy-making have been removed from the purview of Westminster; nor would it be easy unilaterally to alter the devolution settlement. There is much talk of revising the financial terms of the settlement, since, under it, Scotland gains around 20% more per head in terms of public expenditure than England. But substantial revision would require full consultation with the Scottish Parliament and this might, in practice, allow the Scottish Parliament to veto change.

[27] Cm 3658, para 42.

It may be objected that ministers do not normally answer questions on matters which are the responsibility of local authorities, and yet of course Parliament remains sovereign over local authorities. This objection, however, is misconceived. The Scottish Parliament and the National Assembly of Wales are not local authorities but bodies with powers to legislate over a wide range of domestic activity and which represent national feeling in Scotland and Wales. While it is normally a fairly easy matter for Parliament to assert its will over local authorities and even, as in 1985, to abolish a whole tier of local government—the GLC and the metropolitan county councils—that will hardly be the case with the devolved bodies. The Northern Ireland Parliament precedent of 1972 is not really relevant, since that Parliament was not set up to placate a centrifugal nationalism, but, on the contrary, to make it easier for ministers to cede authority over a part of the United Kingdom for which many ministers had no particular love, and which, insofar as the minority, nationalist, community in Northern Ireland was concerned, lacked legitimacy. It would be far less easy for Parliament to abolish strong devolved institutions in Scotland and Wales which did enjoy widespread popular legitimacy.

It is therefore difficult to resist the conclusion that Westminster is in practice no longer sovereign over the domestic affairs of Scotland and Wales; or that, at the very least, the sovereignty of Parliament means something very different in Scotland, and to some extent in Wales, from what it means in England. In England, the sovereignty of Parliament still corresponds to a genuine supremacy over 'all persons, matters and things'. Parliament can legislate on all matters as it wishes, subject to the European Communities Act and the Human Rights Act. In Scotland, by contrast, the sovereignty of Parliament with regard to the domestic affairs of Scotland, which have largely been devolved, seems to mean little more than a vague right of supervision over the Scottish Parliament, with a perhaps somewhat theoretical right of abolishing the Scottish Parliament. In Scotland, however, by contrast with the Northern Ireland Parliament set up in 1920, the Parliament was set up following a referendum. If it were to be abolished by the United Kingdom government in London against the wishes of opinion in Scotland, there would be a real danger of Scotland separating from the United Kingdom. It would not be easy to abolish the Scottish Parliament without the approval of the Scottish people expressed in a referendum.

It is clear, then, that Parliament's sovereignty over England still corresponds to a real power to make laws affecting every aspect of England's domestic affairs. In Scotland, by contrast, it no longer corresponds to such a real power, but to a power—fairly nebulous in practice, one may suspect—to supervise another legislative body which enjoys the real power to make laws over a wide area of public policy. If this interpretation is correct, then devolution may prove in practice to be closer to federalism than might at first sight appear.

In one of his polemical works, Dicey wrote that,

'Under all the formality, the antiquarianism, the shams of the British Constitution, there lies latent an element of power which has been the true course of its life and growth. This secret source of strength is the absolute omnipotence, the sovereignty of Parliament . . .

Here constitutional theory and constitutional practice are for once at one. . . . It is like all sovereignty at bottom, nothing less but unlimited power.'[28]

Parliament's sovereignty over Scotland now amounts to something far less than 'unlimited power'.

But devolution has also introduced radical changes into Westminster. Excepting only the Northern Ireland experience between 1921 and 1972, Westminster has always been characterised by the principle that every Member of Parliament enjoys similar rights and duties. There have been no territorial differences in the responsibilities of MPs from different parts of the country, since every Member of Parliament was equally responsible for scrutinizing both the domestic and non-domestic affairs of every part of the United Kingdom. Since 1999, however, Members of Parliament have not been able to play any part in legislating for the domestic affairs of Scotland or Northern Ireland, nor any part in drawing up secondary legislation for the domestic affairs of Wales. Only with regard to England do Members of Parliament continue to enjoy the power which hitherto they enjoyed for the whole of the United Kingdom, of scrutinizing both primary and secondary legislation.

Thus, Westminster is no longer a Parliament for the domestic and non-domestic affairs of the whole of the United Kingdom. It has been transformed into a parliament for England, a federal parliament for Scotland and Northern Ireland, and a parliament for primary legislation for Wales. Westminster has become, it might be suggested, a quasi-federal parliament.

There is a further consequence, namely that Members of Parliament for Scotland and Northern Ireland have been deprived of most of their constituency duties. Most of the matters on which constituents contact their Member of Parliament, matters such as housing and education, are now in the hands of the devolved bodies in those parts of the United Kingdom. Members of Parliament for Scotland and Northern Ireland are responsible primarily for foreign affairs, defence and macro-economic policy. Thus, while MPs from England retain their constituency responsibilities, MPs from Scotland and Northern Ireland have hardly any constituency responsibilities, and MPs from Wales have much reduced constituency responsibilities.

In 1999, in the House of Commons, a Conservative MP proposed that the allowances for MPs representing Scottish and Northern Ireland constituencies be reduced since they had few if any constituency duties. In reply, the Leader of the House, Margaret Beckett said, 'I strongly hold the view . . . that there is not and should not be such a thing as two different kinds of Members of Parliament'.[29] But perhaps Mrs Beckett was turning a Nelsonian blind eye to a real problem. Her answer had no basis in logic. For the first time in its history, with the exception of the Northern Irish MPs between 1921 and 1972, there were indeed two kinds of

---

[28] A V Dicey, *England's Case Against Home Rule*, [1886] (reprinted, Richmond Publishing Company, 1973) 168–9.

[29] House of Commons Debates, vol 332, col 795, 10 June 1999.

Members of Parliament at Westminster—or three if the unique position of Welsh MPs were also to be taken into account.

Thus, the general elections of 2001 and 2005 did not decide domestic policy for Scotland, Wales or Northern Ireland, but only the political colour of the government that would be responsible for foreign affairs, defence and macro-economic policy in that part of the United Kingdom. During the 1997 general election campaign, Tony Blair had produced five specific policy pledges. Two of these pledges—reducing class sizes and reducing NHS hospital waiting lists—would lie beyond the Prime Minister's control after devolution. They would be the responsibility of the devolved bodies. The Scottish Parliament could, if it so wished, abolish the National Health Service entirely. Thus, in England, voters still elect a Parliament which is responsible for their domestic affairs. In Scotland, Wales and Northern Ireland, by contrast, voters elect the Parliament of a quasi-federal state. Westminster is thus both a quasi-federal Parliament and also an English parliament. The British government, similarly, has a dual role. It remains a government for the whole of the UK, part of whose responsibility is to arbitrate between the different parts of the United Kingdom, and also a government for England.

It may seem, however, as if there is a further difference between a federal system and legislative devolution, such as that established by the Scotland Act. In a federal system, disputes over the distribution of powers are determined by a court; with devolution, by contrast, the new Supreme Court will be able to pronounce upon the constitutionality of Scottish legislation, but not upon Westminster legislation. Westminster can at any time legislate for Scottish domestic affairs, on functions which have been devolved to Scotland; and it can, if it wishes, unilaterally alter the distribution of powers in its favour. Nevertheless, this clear juridical difference between federalism and devolution may not be so clear in practice. Were the Supreme Court to rule, in a particular dispute, that the Scottish Parliament was acting *intra vires*, it would be difficult, in practice, for Westminster to override it either by using its sovereignty to legislate for Scottish domestic affairs, or by altering the distribution of powers. If it did, Parliament would appear to be flouting the judgment of a court on an issue on which Scottish national sentiment might well be engaged. If this view is correct, then Westminster might in practice come to lose yet another of the characteristics of a sovereign parliament, the power to make laws from which there is no appeal; and the powers, not only of the Scottish parliament, but also of Westminster over Scotland will have come to depend upon the decisions of a court, a condition characteristic of a federal system of government.

'Devolution' is a delegation of power from Westminster to another body. In practice, however, the consequences of the Scotland Act and the Government of Wales Act go much further than a mere delegation of power. The Scotland Act, in particular, in practice divides the power to legislate for Scotland between Westminster and Edinburgh, thus creating a quasi-federal relationship between Westminster and the Scottish Parliament.

In his *Introduction to the Study of the Law of the Constitution*, Dicey detected "three leading characteristics of completely developed federalism—the supremacy of the constitution—the distribution among bodies with limited and co-ordinate authority of the different powers of government - the authority of the courts to act as interpreters of the constitution".[30] Were it to come to be recognised that devolution implies in practice an abdication of Westminster's ability to alter the settlement at will, then it will finally have been recognised that the logic of devolution points to the development of a codified constitution, and a constitution that bears strong resemblances to that of a federal state.

The Human Rights Act, then, is the cornerstone of the new British constitution. Devolution renders that constitution quasi-federal in nature.

There is a sense, however, in which devolution points even beyond a quasi-federal system of government. The legislation providing for devolution to Scotland, Wales and Northern Ireland, establishes a new constitutional settlement amongst the nations comprising the United Kingdom. The United Kingdom is, as a result of devolution, in the process of becoming a new union of nations, each with its own identity and institutions—a multi-national state rather than, as the English have traditionally seen it, a homogeneous British nation containing a variety of people. It seems to have become implicitly accepted, in consequence, that the various nations comprising the United Kingdom enjoy the right of self-determination, and that this includes the right of secession, a right denied in many federal constitutions. The United States in the nineteenth century fought a civil war to confirm the proposition that the states comprising it were part of an indissoluble union.

In Northern Ireland, by contrast, when Ireland left the Commonwealth in 1949, the Ireland Act provided that Northern Ireland would not cease to be a part of the United Kingdom without the consent of the Northern Ireland Parliament. The implication, although it was not specifically spelt out, was that, if the Northern Ireland Parliament ceased to favour continued membership of the United Kingdom, the British government would not stand in the way of allowing Northern Ireland to secede. Following the abolition of the Northern Ireland Parliament in 1972, the Northern Ireland Constitution Act was passed in 1973, and provided for a pledge in a different form, that Northern Ireland would not cease to remain a part of the United Kingdom without the consent of its citizens. This consent was to be asserted, according to the then Prime Minister, Edward Heath, by 'a system of regular plebiscites'.[31] So far, however, just one such plebiscite has been held, the Northern Ireland border poll, in March 1973.

It has come to be accepted, then, that the constitutional status of Northern Ireland cannot be changed without the consent of the people of Northern Ireland; if, however, a majority in Northern Ireland seeks to leave the United Kingdom and join with the Republic of Ireland, that wish will be accepted by the British government. The provisions of the Belfast Agreement of 1998 impose an express statutory duty upon the British government to facilitate such a transfer. The people of Northern Ireland, therefore, have been given an explicit right of self-determination.

---

[30] *Law of the Constitution*, 144.
[31] House of Commons Debates, vol 833, col 1862, 24 March 1972.

The Scots too have come to argue that they enjoy a right to self-determination, and it may be that this argument has been accepted by the British government. In 1989, a Scottish Constitutional Convention was established to draw up plans for a Scottish Parliament. This Convention comprised representatives of the Scottish Labour Party, the Scottish Liberal Democrats, representatives of the great majority of Scottish local authorities, and other bodies in Scottish life, including the Scottish TUC, the churches, ethnic minority groups, womens' movements and representatives of the business community. The Conservatives and the SNP did not participate in the Convention, the former because it was opposed to devolution, fearing that devolution would lead to independence, the latter because it feared that it would prove a barrier to independence. The Convention issued a Claim of Right, signed by 58 of Scotland's 72 MPs. It declared that 'We, gathered as the Scottish Constitutional Convention, do hereby acknowledge the sovereign right of the Scottish people to determine the form of Government suited to their needs'. On this view, sovereignty lay with the people of Scotland, not with Westminster, a claim that was implicitly accepted by the Blair government when it formulated the devolution proposals. The government closely followed the ideas of the Convention, and resisted departures from them, suggested by MPs in the House of Commons, on the grounds that they did not represent the wishes of the Scottish people. Significantly the Claim of Right was ceremonially handed over to the Presiding Officer of the new Scottish Parliament just before its inauguration on 1 July 1999.

The constitutional significance of the Claim of Right has been noticed by one authority, who has commented that 'The legal doctrine of Westminster's sovereignty meets its limits in the assertion of popular sovereignty. Crucially, the source of the Scottish constitution becomes rooted in the people as well as in the Westminster Parliament' Brigid Hadfield labels the Scottish constitution as established in the Scotland Act, "quasi-autochthonous" i.e. self-generated, a constitution rooted as it were, in Scottish soil, rather than, as the term 'devolution' implies, one handed down by Westminster. She speculates that 'devolution may lead to the emergence not of a federal United Kingdom but a (partially) confederal one, where the component nation states play a much more central role in the allocation of legislative responsibilities'.[32]

There is of course a potential conflict between the idea of the sovereignty of Parliament and the idea of the sovereignty of the Northern Irish or Scottish people. Yet, there can be little doubt that if, at some time in the future, it became the 'settled will' of the Scottish people, as shown in a referendum, to break the link with Westminster, the British government of the day would respect that wish, rather than, as it did in the nineteenth century over Ireland, resist it. Thus, in both Northern Ireland and Scotland, it has come to be accepted that their constitutional status depends not only upon the decisions of a supposedly sovereign Parliament

---

[32] B Hadfield, 'The United Kingdom as a Territorial State', in V Bogdanor (ed) *The British Constitution in the Twentieth Century* 623, 626.

at Westminster but also upon the wishes of their people. The Unions with Scotland and Northern Ireland rest on the consent of the people of Scotland and Northern Ireland. Westminster's role is to insist that this consent be clearly displayed before accepting the break-up of the kingdom.

In the nineteenth century, British statesmen resisted Home Rule for Ireland with the argument that the Irish were not themselves a nation, but part of a larger British nation, just as, for example, the Bavarians are not themselves a nation, but part of a larger German nation. The unitary British state was thus the expression of a belief that the non-English sections of the United Kingdom formed part of a single British nation. Devolution, by contrast, is a new constitutional settlement which expresses the belief that the non-English parts represent separate nations which, nevertheless, choose to remain within the larger multi-national framework of the United Kingdom. Devolution, therefore, transforms not only the state but also the nation.

There is, however, a further complexity so far as Northern Ireland is concerned. It is that neither of the two communities in Northern Ireland—neither the Unionists nor the Nationalists—regard themselves as belonging to a separate Northern Ireland nation. The Unionists regard themselves as part of the British nation, and seek to preserve their position of equal citizenship within the United Kingdom. The Nationalists regard themselves as part of the Irish nation from which they were illegitimately sundered when Ireland was partitioned in the Government of Ireland Act of 1920. Therefore, as well as providing for a new constitutional settlement amongst the nations comprising the United Kingdom, it was necessary for the Belfast Agreement to establish a constitutional settlement between the nations comprising the United Kingdom, and the other nation sharing these islands, namely the independent Irish nation. It was for this reason that the international treaty which gave legislative expression to the Belfast Agreement, signed on Good Friday, 1998, created a British-Irish Council, whose role would be, in the words of the Agreement, 'to promote the harmonious and mutually beneficial development of the totality of relationships among the people of these islands'. The members of this Council are Britain and Ireland, the devolved bodies in Scotland, Wales and Northern Ireland, and also representatives of three British Crown dependencies which are not part of the United Kingdom—the Isle of Man, Guernsey and Jersey. The Council meets at summit level, two or three times a year: it is primarily consultative and considers such issues as the misuse of drugs, the environment, social inclusion and transport links. It can agree upon common policies, but has no power to bind individual members, who can choose to opt out or not to participate in particular policies.[33]

The creation of devolved bodies in Scotland, Wales and Northern Ireland, together with the British-Irish Council, not only transform a unitary state into a quasi-federal one; they also provide for a confederal link between the United

---

[33] The British-Irish Council was modelled on the Nordic Council. For a fuller discussion, see V Bogdanor, 'The British-Irish Council and Devolution', *Government and Opposition*, vol 34, 1999, 287.

Kingdom as a multinational state and the Irish Republic. These arrangements constitute an attempt to recognize the various and distinctive national identities of the peoples living in these islands, and also of the close and complex links between them. It took almost the whole of the twentieth century for British politicians painfully to discover the essential truth of the Gladstonian proposition that neither the unionist state nor separatism could yield solutions to the complex problems posed by the multinational nature of the United Kingdom. The devolution legislation and the British-Irish Council propose a solution which both recognizes and yet seeks to transcend nationalism through institutions which express not only the separate national identities of the components making up the United Kingdom and the Republic of Ireland, but also their underlying inter-connections. To give effect to and yet to seek to transcend nationalism may seem contradictory aims. Yet that, after all, is the logic of federalism, and also the logic of the peculiar quasi-federal system with confederal elements that makes up the new British constitution. The sociologist, Karl Mannheim once said that the British had 'a peculiar genius for working out in practice the correlation of principles which seem to be logically opposed to each other'. That genius will certainly be needed if the devolution settlement is to prove a success. The Russian painter, Wassily Kandinsky, predicted that the twentieth century would see the triumph of 'and' over 'either/or'.[34] The tragic and blood-soaked history of the twentieth century refuted this prediction. It is just possible, however, that the evolution of the British state in the twenty-first century could prove him to have been in advance of his time.

---

[34] Cited in Aughey, *Nationalism, Devolution and the Challenge to the United Kingdom State*, 152, 156.

5

Hung Parliaments: Governing Without a Majority

I

S
O FAR, OUR discussion of the new British constitution has concentrated upon those major legislative enactments, such as the Human Rights Act and the devolution legislation, which have so fundamentally altered the constitution. They have done so by altering the balance of power between the three branches of government—legislature, executive and judiciary—and by altering the balance of power between the component parts of the United Kingdom. But the working of a constitution is influenced as much by the working of political factors, and, in particular, by the party system and by the electoral system, as it is by these legislative changes. The constitution would certainly work very differently were the first-past-the-post electoral system to be replaced by a proportional one. Some, including the present writer, have attempted to speculate as to how the introduction of proportional representation might affect the constitution.[1] But there is now less need to speculate since, in Scotland, Wales and Northern Ireland, the devolved bodies are elected by proportional representation, and it is possible to compare the operation of government there with its operation at Westminster. Proportional representation offers a challenge to two powerful elements of Britain's traditional political system—constituency representation and the two-party system. In the devolved administrations single-party majority government has everywhere been replaced by coalition and minority governments; and new conventions are coming to be developed to accommodate these new models of government.

Single-party majority government is generally regarded as the essence of the Westminster model. In a book published over thirty years ago, in 1978, entitled *Coalitions in British Politics*, the editor—the electoral analyst, David Butler—summed up the conventional wisdom when he wrote,

> 'Single-party government in the British system is the norm. Politicians and writers on politics assume that, in all but exceptional circumstances, one party will have a Parliamentary majority and will conduct the nation's affairs'.

---

[1] V Bogdanor, *Multi-Party Politics and the Constitution* (Cambridge, CUP, 1983).

In the next sentence, however, he showed that there were mythical elements to this conventional wisdom. He then went on to say,

'In fact, clear-cut single party government has been much less prevalent than many would suppose. The years from 1945 to 1974 have coloured contemporary thinking but, even with their inclusion, governments relying on a majority drawn from a single party have held office for less than half the twentieth century'.[2]

Between 1900 and 1945, the dominant form was coalition or minority government. There were single-party majority governments for just ten years during this period, from 1906 to 1910, from 1922 to 1923 and from 1924 to 1929.

The years since 1979 would, however, seem to suggest that there is rather more to the conventional view than Butler was prepared to allow. That is because these years have been marked by single-party majority government at Westminster, apart from a brief period in 1996–7 when John Major's government had lost its majority and was forced to rely upon the Ulster Unionists for support. Yet the working of the system has been very different since 1979 from what it was before 1974. Governments since 1979 have secured a much smaller percentage of the vote than they did before 1974. The 1980s are commonly seen as an era in which Margaret Thatcher commanded all before her. Yet, in her two landslide victories of 144 seats in 1983 and 100 in 1987, she secured just 42% of the vote, 2% less than in 1979 when her majority had been 43. Thus, at the height of her power nearly three-fifths of the voters were hostile to Thatcherism. Similarly, Tony Blair's two landslides of 1997 and 2001 were gained on just 42% of the vote. He too was opposed by nearly three-fifths of the voters, and in 2005 by nearly two-thirds, Labour's vote being just 36%.

It is clear, then, that the electoral system has worked very differently since 1979 from the way it worked in the 1950s when governments regularly gained between 46% and 49% of the vote. In the first ten post-war elections until October 1974, the lead for the winning party was usually small, the average lead being around 3.5%. Three general elections, those of 1950, 1964, and February 1974, produced short parliaments. From 1979 to 2009, by contrast, there has been a period of one-party dominance, first Conservative and then Labour. The average lead for the winning party at the seven general elections since 1979 has been around 9.2%, larger than the greatest lead during the earlier period. There have been no short parliaments. But, because the geography of the two-party vote has altered so fundamentally, there are many fewer marginal seats, and a working majority therefore depends upon a party having a large lead amongst the electorate. A hung parliament is therefore much more likely when the two parties are fairly evenly balanced, as they were during much of the 1950s and 1960s. At that time the system worked so that a small lead in votes was exaggerated into a large lead in seats. That is no longer the case. In 1992, John Major's Conservatives gained a lead of around

---

[2] D Butler (ed) *Coalitions in British Politics* (Houndmills, Macmillan, 1978) 112.

8.5% over Labour, a lead larger than that achieved by any government before 1979, except for Attlee's in 1945, but it yielded a majority of just 21, insufficient to retain a working majority for a full parliament. The presence of a substantial number of MPs not owing allegiance to the Labour or Conservative parties obviously adds to the likelihood of a hung parliament. The two party system continues to exist in the House of Commons, but it is much weaker in the country.

The electoral system, which maintains an artificial duopoly in the House of Commons, masks the erosion of the system in the country. It buttresses a party system which looks reasonably similar to that of the 1950s and 1960s but is in fact profoundly different. That, of course, is one reason why the electoral system remains a matter of political contention, and why the issue of proportional representation returned to the political agenda in the 1970s.

In addition, the Westminster system now faces competitors in the devolved bodies. The experience of the devolved bodies has shown that a different kind of politics can be perfectly viable without challenging the basic parliamentary assumptions of the Westminster model. At Westminster, the first-past-the-post electoral system allows an incipient multi-party system to be transmuted in the House of Commons into a two-party system. In the devolved bodies, by contrast, proportional representation allows a multi-party system to be reflected in the various legislatures and assemblies.

The electoral systems used for the devolved bodies allow opinion to be directly reflected in the legislature in accordance with their strength in the electorate. Neither in Scotland nor in Wales has any single party been able to win a comfortable overall majority of the seats in elections to the devolved bodies. No election in Scotland or Wales has delivered a secure single-party majority. This means that, except for the period May 2003 to May 2005 when Labour in Wales was able to govern as a single party enjoying a majority of one, both Scotland and Wales have been governed by coalition or minority administrations. In Northern Ireland, the legislation providing for the Assembly requires there to be a coalition government representing the two communities even when a single party is able to secure a majority.

Between 1999 and 2007, Scotland was governed by a Labour/Liberal Democrat coalition, the two parties between them enjoying a majority in the Scottish Parliament. In the election of 2007, however, Labour was replaced as leading party by the SNP. The outcome was as follows.

SNP	47 seats
Labour	46 seats
Conservatives	17 seats
Liberal Democrats	16 seats
Green	2 seats
Others	1 seat
Total	129 seats

It will be seen that, unless the SNP formed an administration with Labour, an unlikely prospect, no majority coalition was possible unless three parties combined together. In the event, the SNP formed a single-party minority government, and secured a 'co-operation agreement' with the Greens. The meaning and significance of this co-operation agreement are discussed later in the chapter.

Wales has seen considerable changes in its form of government since devolution. In the first elections, in May 1999, Labour, which had unexpectedly failed to win a majority of the seats, formed a single-party minority administration, controlling 28 of the 60 seats in the National Assembly. In October 2000, however, Labour formed a majority coalition with the Liberal Democrats, which lasted until the second round of Assembly elections in May 2003. In these elections, Labour won 30 out of the 60 seats, but the Presiding Officer—roughly equivalent to the Speaker in the Commons—was an opposition member. This enabled Labour to govern as a single-party majority administration until May 2005 when one Labour member defected, and Wales was governed by a single-party minority administration. In the third round of elections in May 2007, Labour won just 26 seats, making it more difficult for the Party to form a single-partly minority administration. The outcome left open the possibility of a number of alternative combinations.

Labour	26 seats
Plaid Cymru	15 seats
Conservatives	12 seats
Liberal Democrats	6 seats
Others	1 seat
Total	60 seats

Labour continued to govern as a minority administration, but, in July 2007, it achieved a coalition agreement with Plaid Cymru, committing it, among other matters, to the achievement of a Welsh Parliament with full legislative powers. Before that, however, there had been serious negotiations between the three non-Labour parties—Plaid Cymru, the Conservatives and the Liberal Democrats—with a view to forming a 'rainbow' coalition. But these negotiations foundered, in part because the Conservatives would not countenance the introduction of proportional representation for local government elections. The Welsh Conservatives were, apparently, prepared to consider this proposal, and David Cameron, the Conservative leader at Westminster, was prepared to allow them to do so, but the Shadow Cabinet would not hear of it.[3] After these negotiations broke down, Labour formed a coalition, not with the Liberal Democrats, but with Plaid Cymru. By contrast with Scotland, Labour, the Conservatives and the Liberal Democrats did not regard Plaid Cymru as separatist, and were therefore prepared to form a coalition with them. Whereas in Scotland, the SNP proposed a referen-

---

[3] Private information.

dum in 2010 on independence, in Wales the Labour/Plaid Cymru coalition proposed a referendum in 2011 on primary legislative power for the National Assembly.

The pattern of Welsh Assembly administrations, therefore, has been as shown below.

Date	Type of government.
July 1999–October 2000	Labour, single-party minority administration
October 2000–April 2003	Labour—Liberal Democrat coalition
May 2003–May 2005	Labour, single-party majority administration
May 2005–April 2007	Labour, single-party minority administration
July 2007–	Labour—Plaid Cymru coalition.

By July 2007 nationalists were in power in all three of the devolved bodies. But even where, as in Scotland, the nationalist party, the SNP, was the largest party in the Parliament, it had to work with other parties, all of whom with the exception of the Scottish Greens, were unionist parties, if it was to carry its legislation. The SNP leader, Alex Salmond, recognised after the Scottish elections in 2007 that his party was in a minority position when he declared that 'This Parliament is a proportional Parliament. It is a Parliament of minorities where no one party rules without compromise or concession. The SNP believes that we have the moral authority to govern, but we have no authority over this Parliament. The Parliament will be one in which the Scottish government relies on the merits of its legislation, not the might of a parliamentary majority'.[4] Under a first-past-the-post system, the SNP might have secured a majority of the seats in the Scottish Parliament on 33% of the vote. Labour, it will be remembered, secured a comfortable majority at Westminster in 2005 on just 36% of the vote. Had the SNP been able to win a majority of the seats under the first-past-the-post system, then, no matter how small its percentage of the vote, it might have claimed that it had a mandate for independence. But, in a proportional system, the SNP had to co-operate with other, unionist, parties. The separatists—the SNP and the Greens—currently have 49 seats in the Scottish Parliament. The Unionists currently have 79. A main plank of the SNP's programme is a referendum on independence for Scotland. It cannot, however, secure passage of this proposal through the Scottish Parliament unless it can obtain the support of at least one of the unionist parties. Proportional representation, then, has become a mainstay of the Union between England and Scotland. It makes it difficult for the SNP to win a majority in the Scottish parliament unless it is supported by a majority of Scottish voters. Proportional representation prevents the Union from being put into question but makes life difficult for a party, such as the SNP, whose *raison d'etre* is a policy which is opposed by every other party, except the Greens, in the Scottish Parliament. Such a party has to decide whether to adopt a

---

[4] Official Report, Scottish Parliament, 16 May 2007, col 24.

fundamentalist position, or whether it should seek to co-operate with unionist parties, in which case it might have to dilute its separatist policies and risk a split within its ranks. Proportional representation makes a split in the SNP more likely than a split in the United Kingdom.

The SNP, then, can govern only if it is prepared to co-operate with unionist parties. A party which refuses to co-operate condemns itself to impotence. That was the stance of the Scottish Conservatives before the 2007 elections to the Scottish Parliament. The leader of the Party, Annabel Goldie, declared that the Conservatives would not enter into any coalition or agreement with any other party. Had the Conservatives followed such a policy, it would have been equivalent to saying that they would never play any part in the government of Scotland. They would seem to be asking electors to vote for a party which would be permanently in opposition. That would have been a counter-productive stance, but, in practice, in the 2007 parliament, the Conservatives were skilful in winning policy concessions from the SNP without entering into any formal coalition or agreement with them. Like their Welsh counterparts, the Scottish Conservatives have proved themselves perfectly capable of adapting to the new system.

II

Experience of the first elections to the devolved bodies in Scotland and Wales has shown that, under the particular form of proportional representation used, the government may be chosen not by the voters but by party negotiations after the votes have been counted. In Scotland, a Labour/Liberal Democrat coalition in 1999 and 2003 might, admittedly, have seemed in accordance with the natural preferences of the voters since the two parties had collaborated together in the Scottish Constitutional Convention which had prepared the ground for devolution and from which both the Conservatives and the SNP had been absent. But there is no way of telling from voting patterns in the 1999 and 2003 elections whether Labour supporters would have preferred a single-party minority Labour government to a coalition with the Liberal Democrats; there is no way of telling from the voting patterns whether Liberal Democrat supporters were happy with the coalition with Labour or whether they would have preferred their party to remain in opposition; or whether, both in 2003 and 2007 Liberal Democrat voters would have preferred a 'rainbow' anti-Labour coalition of SNP, Conservatives and Liberal Democrats, to a Labour/Liberal Democrat coalition.

The outcome in 2007 left open other possibilities. Labour could in theory have formed a 'Defend the Union' coalition with the Conservatives and the Liberal Democrats, or a minority coalition with the Liberal Democrats. Admittedly such an arrangement would have looked as if Labour were refusing to accept the fact of having been relegated to the position of second-largest party. Nevertheless, the large majority of Scottish voters were opposed to the SNP, which had become the largest party on just 33% of the vote. This meant that two-thirds of the voters were opposed to the nationalists. So an SNP minority government was by no means the only possibility.

In Wales, too, the 2007 election left open the possibility of a 'rainbow' anti-Labour coalition, a Labour minority government, a Labour-Liberal Democrat majority coalition, or the Labour-Plaid Cymru coalition which eventually occurred. There is no way of telling from the voting patterns which of these alternatives was favoured by the voters. Thus, in Scotland and Wales, it seems that the voters have lost their chance directly to choose their government. The make-up of the government is determined, within the context of the election results, by the political parties and by the vicissitudes of the negotiations.

Coalition governments, where they have occurred, have been based on published inter-party agreements between the parties comprising the government, and it is not easy for the leader of the government, as it would be at Westminster, to escape from the agreement by dissolving Parliament, since the devolved bodies can only be dissolved by a two-thirds majority.[5] The coalition partners have, however, by agreement chosen to accept collective responsibility just as in a Westminster single-party government. But, in 2007, the co-operation agreement between the SNP and the Scottish Greens introduced a new element into government, one that could become more important as new political habits arrive with the realization that coalition and minority governments are likely to prove permanent features of the Scottish political scene. Following the election result in 2007, the SNP held talks with the Scottish Greens, who, like the SNP, favour Scottish independence. The two parties originally hoped that they would be joined by the Liberal Democrats and that a three-party majority coalition might be formed. But the Liberal Democrats, a unionist party, refused to join a separatist government, and, in particular objected to the SNP proposal of a referendum on Scottish independence, a proposal which, so they believed, would create uncertainty in Scotland by damaging prospects for investment there. The failure to secure Liberal Democrat support seemed to make a coalition with the Greens pointless since such a coalition could not command a majority in the Parliament.

The next option would have been a 'confidence and supply' agreement. The Lib-Lab pact of 1977–78 at Westminster, designed to sustain James Callaghan's Labour minority government, was an agreement of this sort. A 'confidence and supply' agreement is an arrangement whereby a party not in the government agrees to support the governments on votes of confidence and votes on the budget, so that the government can ensure its financial arrangements. In return, the party outside the government may receive certain policy concessions, but on all other issues it decides how it will vote on an issue-by-issue basis. It cannot, of course, be bound by collective responsibility since it is not part of the government. Such an arrangement allows for a joint working between two or more parties where there is some common ground, and allows the party not in the government to preserve both a certain

---

[5] Before the Government of Wales Act, 2006, the National Assembly of Wales was a fixed-term body, which could not be dissolved before the end of its term.

distance from the government and also its policy distinctiveness.[6] Since the ending of the Lib/Lab pact in 1978, there have been no similar agreements at Westminster, but they have become familiar in another country whose system of government is based on the Westminster Model, namely, New Zealand, which adopted proportional representation in 1996.

Attempts were apparently made by the SNP to secure such a 'confidence and supply' agreement with the Greens, but these too failed, partly, it seems, because there were considerable disagreements between the two parties on transport policy. The two parties therefore concluded a co-operation agreement which contained four main planks. First, the Greens agreed to vote for the SNP nominee as First Minister and for the SNP's other ministerial appointments. In exchange, the SNP agreed to consult Scottish Green party MSPs in advance on the broad shape of each year's legislative and policy programme, and also on key measures announced during each year. Second, the SNP agreed that it would nominate one of the Green MSPs as a Convenor, i.e. chair, for one of the Parliament's subject committees. Third, the two parties agreed that they would seek to extend the powers of the Scottish Parliament with a view to the eventual attainment of independence; and fourth, the SNP agreed to produce early legislation to reduce climate-change pollution, and to oppose the building of new nuclear power stations.

Coalition agreements, confidence and supply agreements and co-operation agreements are designed to make Cabinet government work when voters' preferences have been reflected in a plurality of parties, none of which has an overall majority, something which is a normal occurrence under proportional representation. Agreements of this type may also be seen as reactions against the methods of adversarial politics, often thought to be characteristic of Westminster. Yet, new methods of operating Cabinet government seem to have penetrated even into the heart of Westminster. Gordon Brown, when he came to form his government in 2007, apparently offered places in his government, including a Cabinet place, to Liberal Democrats. When that proposal was rejected, he apparently offered Lord Ashdown (the former Liberal Democrat leader, Paddy Ashdown) a Cabinet post.[7] Ashdown would, it seems, have been able to accept this post while remaining a member of the Liberal Democrat party. He decided, however, to decline. Had he accepted, it is not clear whether the rule of collective responsibility would have applied to him or whether he would have been allowed to differ publicly with the government on matters of importance to Liberal Democrats, for example, civil liberties. It is not clear, in other words, whether the convention of collective responsibility would have been suspended to accommodate Ashdown. In New Zealand, collective responsibility was suspended after an inconclusive general

[6] For the Lib/Lab pact, see D Steel, *A House Divided: The Lib-Lab Pact and the Future of British Politics* (London, Weidenfeld and Nicolson, 1980) and Bogdanor, *Multi-Party Politics and the Constitution*, 151–9.

[7] See the interview with Sir Menzies Campbell, the then Liberal Democrat leader in *The New Statesman*, 16 July 2007, 14–15.

election held under proportional representation in 2005. The Labour Prime Minister, Helen Clark, concluded agreements with two minor parties, New Zealand First and United Future. The leaders of these parties were given ministerial posts outside the Cabinet, but relieved of collective responsibility beyond their portfolio areas. The ministers concerned held the posts of Foreign Affairs, and Revenue. Thus the Foreign Minister would speak for New Zealand on the world stage, but would not be a member of the Cabinet nor would he be bound by collective responsibility.

Gordon Brown did appoint, as junior ministers in the House of Lords, people from outside the Labour Party. Sir Mark Malloch Brown became a minister in the Foreign Office, Sir Digby Jones, a former President of the CBI, became a minister in the Department for Business Enterprise and Regulatory Reform and the Foreign Office, and Sir Alan West, a former First Sea Lord, became a minister in the Home Office dealing with security matters. These three men were created peers but they were not, apparently, required to join the Labour Party, although they were of course required to take the Labour whip and to vote with the party in the House of Lords; they were also required to accept collective responsibility. In addition, Gordon Brown appointed advisers from the Liberal Democrat party—Lord Lester, a prominent QC, to advise on constitutional matters and Lady Neuberger, an expert on the National Health Service, to advise on the voluntary sector. These advisers both remained members of the Liberal Democrat party in the House of Lords, continuing to receive the Liberal Democrat whip, and were under no commitment to support the government in whipped votes.

These developments show that the new forms of government being developed in the devolved bodies in Scotland and Wales, to resolve the problem of governing without a majority, are not without their influence upon Westminster. The fascinating question that arises when comparing the political culture of Westminster with the newer political culture of the devolved bodies is—for how long can the two styles of politics co-exist together? For how long can a multi-party system in these bodies co-exist with a two-party system at Westminster which, in effect, hides the state of electoral opinion? Can the two political cultures continue to co-exist in tandem? It is unlikely that the Westminster culture will, as it were, infect the culture of the new bodies. There is certainly no significant pressure in Scotland or in Wales for a return to the first-past-the-post electoral system. What is more likely is that the culture of the new bodies will come to infect Westminster.

That is because the Westminster culture and the electoral system which sustains it are, in essence, a product of tribal politics. The Westminster culture was at its strongest and most unquestioned when tribal politics was at its height in the years 1945 to 1974, now misleadingly seen as a 'norm' from which politics has since deviated. At the height of this period, in 1951, the two major parties, Labour and the Conservatives, gained between them 97% of the vote, while winning parties in the 1950s gained at least 46% of the vote. There seemed no serious dissatisfaction with the British political system. The electoral system used in Scotland and Wales and the forms of government to which it has given rise may be seen as practical responses to the decline of tribal politics allowing, and indeed requiring, opposing parties to co-operate together. It may be argued, then, that the forms of government in Scotland and Wales are more suited to the modern age than those at Westminster, which still remain mired in the culture of tribal politics.

The strains which the erosion of tribal politics impose upon the Westminster culture will, of course, increase if there is a hung parliament and even more so if hung parliaments become the norm. A hung parliament is now much more likely than it was in the past since, even under the first-past-the-post system, parties other than Labour and the Conservatives are succeeding in gaining substantial representation. The larger the representation of parties other than Labour and the Conservatives, the more likely a hung parliament becomes. If there were no minor parties, then, obviously, a hung parliament could occur only if the two major parties received exactly the same number of seats—an unlikely outcome. At Westminster, and in local government, minority parties are becoming increasingly successful at gaining representation despite the hurdle imposed by the first-past-the-post system. Since 1983, the Liberal Democrats have gained around 20% of the vote in every general election. In the general election of 2005 they gained 22% of the vote, though only 10% of the seats in the House of Commons. In addition, there has developed, since 1974, when the Ulster Unionists ceased to take the Conservative whip, an entirely separate party system in Northern Ireland; while the nationalist parties in Scotland and Wales have also been able to secure regular representation at Westminster. In the 2005 general election, third parties, parties other than Labour and the Conservatives, gained just over 30% of the vote but only around 14% of the seats. So, although there have been only three hung parliaments since 1918—in 1924, 1929 and February 1974,—and although it is impossible to predict a future hung parliament, it is reasonable to suggest that the current party configuration, a configuration which shows no sign of being fundamentally changed, is likely at some time in the future to produce a hung parliament.

A hung parliament, were it to occur, would almost certainly put the reform of the first-past-the-post electoral system at the centre of the political agenda. This does not by any means imply that reform is assured. In the hung parliaments of 1922 and 1974 the Liberals, although in each case a pivotal party, were unable to secure any such concessions from the two major parties; nor did they succeed in securing such a concession during the period of the Lib-Lab pact in 1977–78, when the Labour government depended upon Liberal support on a confidence and supply basis; in the 1929–31 parliament, they did, eventually, secure a major concession from Labour, the alternative vote, but the Labour government collapsed before it could be implemented. The main reason for the Liberals' lack of success was that the minority governments following the 1923, 1929 and February 1974 general elections—Labour in each case—did not particularly want to accommodate the Liberals. They hoped, instead, by choosing a favourable moment for a dissolution, to increase their electoral strength, and move to a position where they could form a majority government. Under the Westminster system a minority government can generally be confident that it will be able to obtain a dissolution at a time of its choosing. If, however, a second general election were to result in a hung parliament, as nearly occurred in October 1974, when the Labour government was returned with an overall majority of just three, then electoral reform would become much more likely, since it would no longer appear possible to secure a majority government by a further dissolution.

The main Liberal aim in hung parliaments has been to secure electoral reform. After the inconclusive outcome of the February 1974 general election, Edward Heath, the Prime Minister, offered the Liberals a coalition with full participation in government and Cabinet posts. Jeremy Thorpe, the Liberal leader, declared that such an arrangement would be possible only if the Conservatives were prepared to make a serious commitment to proportional representation. Heath replied that the most he could offer was a Speaker's Conference to discuss the issue and report. Even had he personally been prepared to go further, his Cabinet colleagues would not have allowed him to do so. A Speaker's Conference was, however, quite inadequate for the Liberals since it offered no commitment to reform. The Liberals were prepared to offer general support from outside the government, a 'confidence and supply' agreement of the type that later formed the basis of the 1977–78 Lib-Lab pact, but Heath declined and resigned after a weekend of futile negotiation.

The hung parliament of 1974 differed fundamentally from the two earlier hung parliaments of 1923/4 and 1929. In the hung parliaments of the 1920s there were just three parties, and so the Liberals could decide to put either the Conservatives or Labour in office. In the hung parliament of 1974, by contrast, there were minor parties, in addition to the Liberals. The Liberals, whether they chose to support Labour or the Conservatives, would be insufficient to give Labour or the Conservatives a majority. The support of at least one minor party would also be necessary. The minor parties are likely to continue to be able to secure representation at Westminster. Therefore future hung parliaments are more likely to resemble that of 1974 than those of the 1920s. One possible pattern is that, as in 1974, a major party would need the support of both the Liberal Democrats and a minor party to secure a majority. Another, and perhaps more likely possibility, is that the Liberal Democrats would be able to secure a majority for one of the major parties, but not the other. Their leverage, then, would be less than it was in the 1920s, unless they were able to act together with at least one of the minor parties. In addition, the existence of minor parties as well as the Liberal Democrats might make it easier for a minority single-party government to survive, since the various small parties would find it difficult to get together to vote it out of office.

But the Liberal Democrats would otherwise be in a stronger position in the case of a future hung parliament than the Liberals were in 1974, since in 1974 the referendum was not at that time an acceptable constitutional mechanism. In a future hung parliament, the Liberal Democrats, if they could not obtain electoral reform, could at least press for a referendum on electoral reform, something that it would be much easier for the other parties to concede. Labour or the Conservatives could concede a referendum on electoral reform while campaigning against reform, or leaving it as an open question.[8] Since Labour has declared on a number of occasions, most notably in its 2005 election manifesto, that a referendum would be required before the electoral system were to be reformed, it would be difficult in any case for the Party to reject such a proposal. The commitment to a referendum serves to prevent a government from altering the electoral system in its own partisan interest as President Mitterrand did in France, when he altered the two-ballot system to one of proportional representation before the 1986 legislative elections so as to damage the chances of his right-wing opponents. When the Right, despite the change in the electoral system, did in fact secure a small majority in the National Assembly, the new Prime Minister, Jacques Chirac, promptly reverted back to the two ballot system. Use of the referendum would prevent the electoral system being similarly manipulated in Britain. The fact that the referendum has now become an accepted part of the British constitution makes it easier, therefore, for a pivot party such as the Liberal Democrats to make progress towards its goal of electoral reform in a future hung parliament.

A second constitutional reform could also improve the position of the Liberal Democrats in a hung parliament. In 2007, in the Green Paper, *The Governance of Britain*, the Brown government proposed, as part of its programme of constitutional renewal, to make dissolution the outcome of a vote in Parliament rather than a prerogative of the sovereign, but in reality of the Prime Minister. This reform would alter little during periods of single-party majority government. Presumably a Prime Minister with a majority could always persuade that majority to vote for a dissolution. But it would alter the political dynamics in the event of a hung parliament. The Prime Minister of a minority government would not be able any longer to rely upon securing a dissolution at a time of his own choosing. He would have to convince the members of at least one other party to support him. That would give much greater influence to a pivot party such as the Liberal Democrats. It would allow the Liberal Democrats to bargain hard for electoral reform in return for agreeing to a dissolution. If, therefore, the reform proposed in the Green Paper comes to be enacted, one consequence might be that it would need only one rather than two parliaments for proportional representation to enjoy a serious chance of implementation.

Another possibility in a hung parliament is, of course, a coalition government. That has not so far been the outcome of any of the previous inconclusive general elections, but were dissolution to become the prerogative of Parliament rather than of the sovereign, it might become a more attractive option. Since it would be impossible to make a rapid tactical escape from the hung parliament with the hope of securing a majority, it might be better instead to construct a coalition on the Scottish or Welsh models so as to secure some degree of long-term stability. A

---

[8] Before the 1997 election, Paddy Ashdown, the Liberal Democrat leader, put to Tony Blair as his price for active co-operation with Labour, a referendum on proportional representation at which Blair would campaign for reform. P Ashdown, *The Ashdown Diaries, Vol 1, 1998–1997* (London, Allen Lane/ the Penguin Press, 2000) 313, 387.

coalition agreement would, no doubt, contain a time-limit, which could be the length of a parliament, so as to avoid tactical manoeuvring.

III

If, however, coalition proves impossible, a confidence and supply agreement or a co-operation agreement might prove to be attractive alternative options. The looser kind of governmental arrangements in Scotland, and the precedent set by Gordon Brown in seeking support outside his party when forming his government, suggest that any future coalition government might be formed on a looser basis than in the past. One way in which a looser coalition, either in Scotland or in the United Kingdom as a whole, might be formed is to allow that coalition itself to exist on something like a 'confidence and supply' basis, that is to allow the convention of collective responsibility to be suspended for key matters on which the parties to the coalition disagree. Before 1914, when the age of tribal politics began, it was quite common to allow, even with single-party governments, 'open questions' where ministers could take different standpoints on policies which did not engage the confidence of the government. Female suffrage was one such issue in the 1905 Liberal government. Different ministers held different views on this issue and they were allowed to express these different views in public until, in 1912, the government produced legislation—abortive as it happened—on the suffrage. Perhaps the Blair government came near to such a doctrine, with the issue of whether or not Britain ought to join the eurozone being in the nature of an 'open question'.

One coded means of indicating dissent without formally abjuring collective Cabinet responsibility, very infrequently used, is the refusal of a key minister to sign a particular bill. A striking example of this occurred in 1988 with the bill imposing the community charge, the so-called poll tax, from which the name of the Chancellor, Nigel Lawson, was absent. 'It is virtually unheard of', Lawson writes in his memoirs,

> 'for the Chancellor not to be the backer of a major financial Bill presented by a colleague . . . I was of course asked to be one but declined. Nor could I bring myself to make a speech in support of the Poll tax; although collective responsibility obviously prevented me from speaking in public against it'.[9]

The suspension of collective Cabinet responsibility through an agreement to differ can be distinguished from an open question, since in the former case there is a policy laid down by the government, and supported by a majority in the Cabinet, with a whip being imposed in support of that policy, while dissenting ministers are allowed to speak and vote against the policy of the government. The government thus remains accountable to Parliament. With an open question, by contrast, the

---

[9] N Lawson, *The View from No 11: Memoirs of a Tory Radical* (London, Bantam Press, 1992) 584.

Cabinet has not, as yet, made any decision, and so there can be no question of a whip being imposed.

The convention of collective responsibility has been suspended on three occasions in modern British politics. The first occasion was in 1932 when the National government, an inter-party coalition, suspended it so as to allow the free-trade Liberals to oppose its tariff proposals. The other two occasions were in 1975, when Harold Wilson allowed Labour ministers to oppose Britain's continued membership of the European Communities in the referendum, although the majority in the Cabinet favoured a 'Yes' vote; and in 1977, when James Callaghan allowed Cabinet ministers to dissent on the issue of direct elections to the European Parliament. These last two occasions, unlike the precedent of 1932, involved single-party governments; although it might be argued that, in the 1970s, the Labour Party was, within itself, a coalition of pro and anti-Europeans. In 1975, dissenting ministers, however, were allowed only to argue for a 'No' vote in the country, not, as in 1932, in Parliament.[10] In 1932, by contrast, ministers were allowed to speak on different sides of the tariff issue in the House of Commons. This led to the incongruous spectacle of the Conservative Chancellor, Neville Chamberlain, insisting that the tariff was an essential instrument to achieve economic recovery, while the Liberal Home Secretary, Sir Herbert Samuel, declared that it would prove the road to ruin. The suspension of collective responsibility was defended by a former Deputy Secretary to the Cabinet, Thomas Jones, in a conversation with Stanley Baldwin, leader of the Conservative Party and Lord President of the Council in the National coalition government. 'What the Ministers have done is really to carry the expression of their dissent a step further than the practice of placing it on record in the Cabinet Minutes. And just as you drop your dissent once you record it, so they should drop it after stating it to the House'. 'Quite so', Baldwin replied.[11]

The 'agreement to differ' of 1932 was the subject of a censure motion in the House of Commons. But it was defended by Baldwin on two grounds. The first was that collective responsibility was a doctrine that had developed with the growth of political parties to ensure that they did not succumb to attack in the House of Commons. The National Government, however, was not a party government, but a coalition. 'The fate of no party is at stake', Baldwin told the House of Commons, 'in making a fresh precedent for a National Government. Had the precedent been made for a party Government, it would have been quite new, and it would have been absolutely dangerous for that party'.[12] The agreement to differ had been foreshadowed in the general election of 1931. In that election, each of the parties comprising the National Government—the Conservatives, the Liberals, the Liberal Nationals and National Labour—had issued its own party manifesto,

---

[10] A junior minister, Eric Heffer, who broke the rule and spoke in the Commons against Britain remaining in the European Community, was summarily dismissed without even being allowed the luxury of resignation.

[11] T Jones, *A Diary with Letters, 1931–1950* (London, OUP, 1954) 26.

[12] House of Commons Debates, vol 261, cols 534–5, 8 February 1932.

in which it stated its own individual positions on the tariff (the Conservatives in favour, the Liberals sceptical) while the manifesto of the National Government as a whole had sought merely 'a doctor's mandate', without committing itself to a specific view on the tariff. Baldwin's second argument was much simpler and did not depend on the particular circumstances of a coalition government. The argument was, simply, that the agreement to differ was a collective decision of the Cabinet. There had been, Baldwin declared, 'collective responsibility for the departure from collective action'.

The 'agreement to differ' did not, admittedly, last long; nor did it succeed in holding the coalition government together. In September 1932, just eight months after the suspension of collective responsibility, the Liberal ministers, and Lord Snowden, the Labour free trade minister, resigned from the government because they could not accept the Ottawa Agreements which buttressed the tariff with a scheme of Imperial Preference. The 'agreement to differ', therefore, failed to maintain the unity of the Cabinet for long. But the reason often given as to why it failed is somewhat wide of the mark. It did not fail simply because it breached the doctrine of collective Cabinet responsibility, but because it did so on what had become an issue of central importance for the government. The purpose of the 'agreement to differ' in January 1932, as with the separate manifestos in the 1931 general election, had been to prevent a subordinate issue from breaking up a coalition government of national recovery. The central purpose for which this government had been formed was the need to prevent a financial crisis by the use of emergency measures, not to impose a tariff. As long as the danger of a financial crisis lasted, the tariff was a subordinate issue. Once the danger was over, however, the tariff, in the view of the Conservative majority in the National Government, was no longer a subordinate issue, but the main policy aim of the government; while, with the danger of a financial crisis having passed, the Liberal free traders were no longer willing to subordinate a deeply held point of party doctrine to appease their colleagues. By September 1932, when the Liberal ministers resigned, the economy was far more stable than it had been when the government was formed, and the government was no longer in danger of collapse as it might have been a few months earlier. Thus the Conservatives were no longer willing to make concessions to keep the Liberals in the government, while the Liberals were unwilling any longer to sacrifice their beliefs to maintain the coalition. In the words of one of the Liberal leaders, the Liberals 'felt that the essential emergency of 1931 was over, that the parliamentary position of the Government would not be weakened . . .'.[13]

The 'agreement to differ' failed, then, to secure the maintenance of coalition for very long, not because it was intrinsically unsound, but because an instrument which can properly be used to resolve differences on subordinate issues was being employed to resolve an issue which many were coming to regard as central rather than subordinate.

---

[13] Lord Lothian to Thomas Jones, 9 September 1932 in Jones, *A Diary with Letters*, above n 11, 53.

In all three cases when collective responsibility was suspended, the Cabinet agreed to it in order to hold a warring government together. The implication would seem to be that collective responsibility is as much a maxim of political prudence as it is a convention of the constitution. It is in general sensible for a government to observe it, just as it is sensible for any collective executive, such as, for example, the board of a company, to maintain a united front, so as not to weaken its position by publicly displaying differences of opinion. On certain occasions, however, when there are deep-seated differences of opinion which cannot easily be reconciled, it may be the lesser evil to suspend the principle.

Such occasions, when it seems the path of prudence to suspend collective responsibility, are likely to occur with increasing frequency in Scotland and Wales. But they could occur also at Westminster whether or not the electoral system is changed. For the principle of collective responsibility is more appropriate to an era of collective duopoly and tribal politics than to a period of multi-party politics, when governments are less likely to be unified ideologically than they once were.

IV

The devolved bodies diverge from the Westminster model not only in the way in which their executives are formed and operate, but also in their legislative procedures. The National Assembly of Wales began as a body corporate, like an old-style local authority in which there was no legal distinction between the executive, that is, the Welsh Assembly Government, and the legislature, the Assembly. This made it difficult for the Assembly to hold the Executive to account. The 2006 Government of Wales Act, however, created a separate Welsh Assembly Government, and as a result the Assembly is now in a better position to hold ministers to account. The Assembly has established a Finance Committee to scrutinise budget proposals from the Assembly Government. This is perhaps an advance on Westminster where financial scrutiny is dispersed amongst the various departmentally-related Select Committees. It is, however, too early to analyse how well these new arrangements are working.

The structure of the Scottish Parliament has remained unaltered since 1999, and there have been considerable divergences from procedures at Westminster. The White Paper which preceded the establishment of the Parliament had, admittedly, declared that 'The relationship between the Scottish Executive and the Scottish parliament will be similar to the relationship between the United Kingdom Government and the United Kingdom parliament'.[14] Many Scots, however, were determined that different relationships would prevail. The Scottish tradition, so it was argued, was one of democracy from below, civic democracy not parliamentary sovereignty, democracy imposed, as it were, from above. The Scottish Claim of Right, drawn up by the Scottish Constitutional Convention, had referred to 'the

---

[14] *Scotland's Parliament*, Cm 3658, p 7, para 2.6

sovereign right of the Scottish people to determine the form of Government suited to their needs'. A parliament founded on the idea of the sovereignty of the people might prove to be a very different sort of animal from one, such as Westminster, founded on the idea of the sovereignty of Parliament. The first doctrine held that sovereignty, and therefore, presumably also power, flowed upwards from the people to the legislature; the second would seem committed to the view that it flowed downwards from the legislature to the people.

The final report of the Scottish Constitutional Convention, published in 1995, emphasised that the Scottish Parliament would be quite unlike Westminster, which it saw as a 'negative template', 'a case-study in worst practice'. 'The coming of a Scottish parliament', it argued,

> 'will usher in a new way of politics that is radically different from the rituals of Westminster; more participation, more creative, less confrontational—a culture of openness which will enable the people to see how decisions are being taken in their name and why . . . The Parliament we propose is much more than a mere institutional adjustment. It is a means to an end'.[15]

The aim was to escape from the executive-dominated, adversarial structure which characterised Westminster politics, by adopting a more accountable model in which power was shared between the executive, parliament and the people. Inevitably, perhaps, the final outcome has proved to be a compromise between the Westminster model and the idealistic schema put forward by the Convention.

Certainly, the Scottish Parliament is physically different from Westminster. It is a single-chamber parliament and semi-circular in shape rather than, as with the House of Commons, rectangular. In place of the Westminster custom of trooping through the lobbies to vote, voting is electronic. Members are addressed by name rather than, as at Westminster, by the names of their constituencies— Ms. Macdonald rather than the Right Honourable Member for Puddletown. The Scottish Parliament, like the National Assembly of Wales, is bilingual, although unlike Wales, where a substantial minority of the population—around 20%— speaks Welsh, in Scotland only around 50,000 out of a population of around five million can speak Gaelic.

The Scottish Parliament, unlike Westminster, is elected by proportional representation. This, so it was hoped, would allow for members to be elected from a wider range of parties and so a greater variety of political opinion would be represented in the Scottish Parliament than at Westminster. 'So many of the Westminster procedures, formal and informal', argued Sir Bernard Crick, a leading professor of political science, and David Millar, a former Clerk at Westminster and at Strasbourg, in a paper prepared for submission to the Scottish Constitutional Convention, 'not merely reflect the English (*sic*) two-party system, but seek artificially to reinforce it'.[16] Coalition governments might allow for a

---

[15] Cited in J Mitchell, 'New Parliament: New Politics in Scotland' (2000) *Parliamentary Affairs*, 608.

[16] B Crick and D Millar, 'Making Scotland's Parliament Work', John Wheatley Centre, Paper 1, 1991, 1.

more participative, consultative form of government in place of the Westminster Model in which, so it seemed, policies were imposed by a government enjoying a large majority in parliament. The First Minister would be appointed through parliamentary vote, not appointed by the Queen, as at Westminster, and other ministers would be chosen by the Parliament on a motion of the First Minister. The statutory involvement of the Parliament in the choice of minister would, it was hoped, strengthen its position in relation to the executive.

Westminster is a maximum-term parliament, not a fixed term parliament, and it can, under normal conditions, be dissolved by the Prime Minister at a time of his or her choosing. The Scottish Parliament, by contrast, is a four-year, fixed-term parliament. There can be an early dissolution only if the Parliament has failed, twenty-eight days after an election, to choose a First Minister; or, alternatively, if a two-thirds majority in the Parliament votes for a dissolution. But an early dissolution, unless it occurs within six months of the general election, does not obviate the need for the regular general election taking place at the end of the four-year cycle. There is thus little tactical advantage to be gained from dissolution. It is, therefore, the Scottish Parliament and not the executive, as at Westminster, which determines whether there should be a dissolution, and this is signified by the fact that, by contrast with Westminster, it is not the First Minister who asks the Queen for a dissolution, but the Presiding Officer of the Parliament. Decisions on the timing of the election are thus removed from the control of the leader of the Scottish government, and the Presiding Officer is able to seek a dissolution only as a servant of the Parliament. He has no independent discretion of his own.

But the divergences between Westminster and the Scottish Parliament comprise more than these obvious differences. They are apparent also in the way in which the Parliament actually operates. These differences can be summed up in the statement that, while at Westminster the chamber is the dominant institution and its committees subordinate, in Edinburgh the attempt has been made to create a committee-based parliament. At Westminster, the legislative committees—until 2007 standing committees, but now renamed as public bill or general committees—are ad hoc and set up to scrutinise particular bills, dissolving themselves once the committee stage of scrutiny has been concluded. The public bill committees, established in 2007, enjoy, by contrast with their predecessors the standing committees, a limited power to call and examine witnesses, and this has strengthened the role of the legislative committees at Westminster. In essence, however, Westminster's legislative committees remain adversarial bodies, while the Select Committees, whose method of working, by contrast to the legislative committees, is forensic and inquisitorial, enjoy a completely separate existence.

The Scottish Parliament was intended to be, like most Continental parliaments and like the European Parliament, a committee-based parliament. This meant that in place of the separate machinery of legislative and Select committees, there are specialised committees combining the functions of both. The all-purpose departmental committees would, according to Crick and Millar, enable members to 'acquire specialised knowledge, an advantage deliberately denied to members of the ad hoc legislative committees of the House of Commons.'[17] These committees scrutinise legislation, examine witnesses and conduct inquiries into both policy and administration. Crick and Millar argued that this arrangement was very much in accord with Scottish tradition. From 1689 to the time of its abolition in 1707 the Scottish Parliament, which preceded the Union with England, was based on a committee system, and it was the committees which drafted bills for the parliament to accept after two readings.[18] At Westminster, bills are first considered in a plenary session in the chamber at Second Reading, and then sent to legislative committees for the work of detailed scrutiny. But in the Scottish Parliament bills are scrutinised by the relevant committee and evidence taken from interested bodies before they reach the chamber. This procedure was intended to emphasise the forensic procedures of the committee stage by contrast with the more confrontational aspects of the plenary.

The specialised committees in the Scottish Parliament, unlike their Westminster counterparts, are empowered to initiate legislation and occasionally do so. 'Bills from standing committees', declared Crick and Millar, 'should be a regular feature of a more democratic and less government-dominated parliamentary ethos. We follow the [Scottish Constitutional] Convention in deliberately seeking to change the Westminster balance of power'.[19] By contrast with Westminster, where government bills always have priority and bills not sponsored by the government have little chance of reaching the statute book, private members bills in the Scottish Parliament are given equal priority in committee to bills from the executive. Non-executive bills and private members bills thus have a real chance of reaching the statute book.

In addition, the consultative process is far broader than at Westminster. In 2000, for example, policy development on the homelessness sections of the Housing (Scotland) bill was opened up by the creation of a 'Homelessness Task Force' which included individuals and representatives from organisations outside government. The recommendations of this task force provided the basis for the section on homelessness in the bill. In this way, representatives of civic society and 'stakeholders' could be represented and participate in the processes of government at the point at which policy was actually developed.[20]

The Scottish Parliament, however, was designed not only to ensure that the Scottish Executive was more accountable than Westminster, and that power was shared between the Executive and the Parliament. It was also intended to ensure that both the Parliament and the Executive were more accountable to the **people** than the Westminster Parliament, and that power was shared between these institutions and the people. The intention of the Scottish Constitutional Convention

[17] Above n 16 at 19.
[18] Ibid.
[19] Above, n 16 at 25.
[20] Scottish Parliament Procedures Committee, meeting 18 20002, 10 December 2002, Consideration of Draft Report of Consultative Steering Group Inquiry, PR/02/18/A, paras 300–304.

was to supplement the system of representative democracy which it had inherited
from Westminster with a system of participative democracy. The main instrument
for achieving this was by recognizing a right of petition, a right recognised in
Article 19 of the German constitution, and also in the European Union, which,
after the Maastricht Treaty of 1992, established a European Union Petitions
Committee. In addition, a number of the new democracies of Central and Eastern
Europe have a petitions system. At Westminster there is a system for presenting
petitions, but no way of ensuring that they are taken any notice of by the government; and action taken by the House of Commons is usually minimal. Reform is,
however, currently under consideration.

The Scottish Parliament established a Public Petitions Committee, empowered
to receive petitions from members of the public. These can then be passed on to
the relevant subject committee, with the Public Petitions Committee having the
task of monitoring what happens to them. But the Public Petitions Committee is
not just a postbox, feeding petitions to the subject committees. More often it takes
an active initial role itself, looking critically at the petitions it receives.

The petition, so the Procedures Committee of the Scottish Parliament believed,
'has the capacity to be a main driver in expanding and deepening participative
democracy in Scotland'.[21] But, unlike the referendum or initiative, a petition cannot be expected to override a decision made by Parliament, nor can it be expected
to interfere with or overturn a decision either of the Scottish Executive or of any
other public body in Scotland, such as for example a local authority, which of
course enjoys its own democratic mandate, or a health board. Nevertheless the
intention is that the Scottish Parliament might initiate legislation based on
demands from outside parliament. A petition, therefore, even though it cannot
override a decision by Parliament, should be able to influence the agenda of
Parliament by bringing the subject-matter of the petition to the attention of its
members. Thus the petitions process would, so it was hoped, enable the Scottish
Parliament to form a bridge with the people, enabling it to link the legislative
process with popular demands.

An example of how the petition process might work in influencing public policy was given in a 2002 report sponsored by the Procedures Committee of the
Scottish Parliament.[22] In 2001 the Blairingone and Saline Action Group submitted a petition requesting the Parliament to revise its legislation so as to ensure that
public health and the environment were not placed at risk from the practice of
spreading sewage, sludge and non-agricultural waste on land. The chair of the
Action Group gave evidence to the Public Petitions Committee, and the issue was
then sent on to the Transport and Environment Committee. This Committee
asked one of its members to carry out an investigation, including site visits and to
produce a report. The Transport and Environment Committee in turn produced
a report recommending action by the Scottish Executive and other public bodies

---

[21] Scottish Parliament Procedures Committee, loc cit, para 289.
[22] Above n 21, paras 210–13.

to amend the regulatory framework. This report was then debated in the Parliament and the appropriate legislation was passed.

In 2006 the Public Petitions Committee of the Parliament commissioned Dr Christopher Carman of Glasgow University to carry out an assessment of the petitions system. Dr Carman discovered that the petitioners, as might perhaps have been expected, did not by any means form a representative sample of Scottish public opinion. They

> 'do not represent a broad cross-section of Scottish society. Petitioners are disproportionately male, older, middle-class and better educated. While petitioners tend to be less attached to established political parties, they are, conversely more engaged in community affairs than the average person residing in Scotland. Finally, the evidence indicates that we are less likely to find petitioners coming from areas with a greater proportion of housing owned by local councils'.[23]

In short, the petitions process attracts those who already enjoy more than their fair share of political resources. It does not attract the socially excluded or underprivileged, but as one member of the Scottish Parliament characterised them, 'grey men in suits'. Thus, the petitions process has not really succeeded in engaging those traditionally excluded from the political process. That, of course, is a problem with all forms of advocacy democracy and, even more perhaps, with methods of direct participatory democracy.

Inevitably perhaps, the actual working of the petitions system has not met all of the hopes and inspirations of those who drew up the plans for the Scottish Parliament. In the survey carried out by Dr Carman few of those responding—just 30%—thought that their petition had been a 'success', while 54% thought that it had not been a success, and 55% were not satisfied with the outcome of the petitioning process. Nevertheless, 55% felt that the system had helped to develop stronger links between the people of Scotland and their Parliament, while around 28% disagreed.[24] Dr Carman concluded that the public petitions system is, 'a valuable component of the parliamentary system and clearly provides a vital link between the public and the Parliament'.[25] It has enabled the public themselves to put issues on to the political agenda which the politicians might wish to ignore. Perhaps Westminster has something to learn from it.

The Presiding Officer of the Scottish Parliament, George Reid, has argued that the petitions system was 'getting close to popular initiative'.[26] But this is a misconception. The Public Petitions Committee and the other committees of the Scottish Parliament act as gatekeepers to the petitions process, deciding whether or not to recommend action on the petition. Whether any action is in fact taken is for Parliament, not the people, to decide; if the Committee decides to take no

---

[23] Scottish Parliament; Public Petitions Committee Report: Sp Paper 654, *The Assessment of the Scottish Parliament's Public Petitions System 1999–2005* by Dr Christopher J. Carman, chapter 8, para 4.
[24] Ibid, ch 8, paras 31, 32 and 29.
[25] Ibid, ch 8, para 11.
[26] Ibid, ch 8, para 9.

action the petitioner has no further recourse within the petitions system. It is thus the Scottish Parliament and not the petitioner which is ultimately responsible for the decision on a petition. The Public Petitions Committee has, therefore, defined the petition system in Scotland, which it regards as 'firmly entrenched', as 'a form of advocacy democracy where the public is given a point of access to the Parliament but not a role in the decision-making process'. This distinguishes it from the initiative by means of which the people themselves can **require** action to be taken, and therefore become part of the decision-making process. The Public Petitions Committee therefore summarised the system as 'a valuable mechanism that affords Scots access to their Parliament, but not any capacity to determine outcomes or take decisions'.[27] So far, despite all the protestations of Scots that they seek more participative mechanisms, they have not given the people any direct say either in the formation of the Scottish Executive, which is chosen by post-election negotiations, or in the legislative programme of the Parliament, or in the determination of priorities of the Executive. The SNP minority administration, formed after the elections of 2007, is committed to a referendum on Scottish independence in 2010; but there have been no serious proposals from the major parties for referendums or initiatives in Scotland as part of the regular process of government. The people, therefore, are kept almost as much at arm's length from Holyrood as they are from Westminster.

In broader terms, although there have certainly been departures from the Westminster model of government in Scotland, they have not been as radical as some predicted. Proportional representation and the coalition structure of government have by no means ended adversarial politics. But they have given a real voice in policy formulation and review to those whose voices might not otherwise have been heard. Some hoped that one consequence of proportional representation, making one-party government less likely, would be that it would do away with the Westminster model of 'strong' and 'stable' governments with clear, overall majorities. But, where proportional representation has led to coalition governments, these governments have in general insisted upon collective responsibility and upon party discipline, just as governments have done at Westminster. The coalitions have been tightly-bound, have enjoyed clear working majorities, and have operated by using their majority in the Parliament rather than through processes of negotiation and consensus. That majority controls the legislative agenda and also enjoys a majority on the legislative committees. Although there is greater scope for backbench and committee bills in the Scottish Parliament than at Westminster, most legislation is still executive-inspired. There is still, both in Scotland and in Wales, a defined governing coalition faced with an opposition; and party discipline and cohesion remain strong, stronger perhaps than at Westminster, with few free votes and few party rebellions. The additional member proportional system puts a high premium on party discipline. Any member of the Scottish Parliament party who dissents from the party line can be disciplined by

[27] Ibid.

being denied a high place on the party list at the next election. Under first-past-the-post, by contrast, a dissenter enjoys immunity from the central machine provided that she can retain the support of her constituency. Some supporters of proportional representation no doubt hoped that it would serve to break down tribal politics. But there is no sign of that either in Scotland or in Wales.

There have been, then, real deviations from the Westminster model, even if these have not been as radical as some would have liked; and there has been a genuine attempt to renew the terms of engagement between the institutions of government and the citizen, particularly in Scotland. Perhaps the new system of minority government established in 2007 will alter relationships between the Scottish Executive and the Parliament, although of course it is, as yet, too early to tell. What is clear is that there is, in Scotland, a considerable tension between two models of government: the top-down model inherited from Westminster and treated as an example to be followed in the White Paper, *Scotland's Parliament*; and the drive to ensure wider participation both from parliamentarians and from the public. Only the future can show how this tension is to be resolved.

It has perhaps been insufficiently noticed that, despite deviations from Westminster practice, the new forms of government in Scotland and Wales have been able to work successfully while retaining most of the existing conventions of parliamentary government, and in particular the key principle that a government must be responsible to parliament. Some, including at one time the present writer, have taken the view that governing without a majority at Westminster could yield considerable discretion to the sovereign and run the risk of bringing her into party politics.[28] Tony Benn once coined the aphorism that first-past-the-post would come to be replaced by 'first-past-the-palace'. But there seems, upon reflection, no reason why this should be so. In a parliament without a majority the key vote will be the vote on the Address, in effect a vote of confidence in the government. Under first-past-the-post, this is generally a formality, although it was not so after the February 1974 general election, nor after the December 1923 general election, when Stanley Baldwin, the Prime Minister and leader of the largest party, the Conservatives, meeting Parliament six weeks after the general election in January 1924, was defeated on the Address by the combined vote of the Labour and Liberal parties. With proportional representation the vote on the Address might attain greater significance, since it would probably follow post-election negotiations. It is the vote on the Address which would give the Prime Minister in such a situation a constitutional mandate to hold or retain office. Thus, while the principle of collective Cabinet responsibility might be loosened and while parliamentary votes might come to take on a new significance, the essential structural features of the Westminster system would remain. In New Zealand, in a political system bearing striking resemblances to the Westminster model, after 12 years of government under proportional representation, a former Prime Minister, Sir Geoffrey Palmer, has commented that what is remarkable is 'not how much it has changed but how

---

[28] See Bogdanor, *Multi-Party Politics and the Constitution*, part 2.

little'. New Zealand's leading authority on the constitution has summed up the position by stating that 'Retaining the confidence of the House remains the axis around which the entire system revolves. This imperative facilitates the democratic ideal and is the bedrock of the Westminster system.'[29] Whether the electoral system is changed or not, retaining the confidence of the House of Commons will still remain the bedrock of the Westminster system. That will be no different under the new constitution from what it was under the old. Both the old and the new constitution can cope with hung parliaments precisely because of the crucial principle that a government is responsible to the Commons and must retain the confidence of the Commons. Under the new constitution, however, pressure for further constitutional reforms, in particular reform of the electoral system, is likely to prove greater than it was in the past.

[29] P A Joseph, 'Constitutional Law' in (2006) *New Zealand Law Review*, 130.

6

A Reformed House of Lords?

I

THE HUMAN RIGHTS ACT and the devolution settlement can be seen as fundamental building-blocks of a new constitutional settlement. This is not to say that they may not be subject to further development or amendment. Nevertheless, neither the principle of devolution nor the statutory recognition of human rights are likely to be repudiated. They form the foundation-stones of the new British constitution.

The precise role and composition of the upper house, by contrast, have yet to be ascertained. Reform of the House of Lords is in a state of flux. Although all three of the major parties seem committed to either a wholly or predominantly elected upper house, no specific scheme has yet been agreed; nor is there agreement on what the precise powers of a reformed upper house should be. The role of the upper house in the new British constitution is, therefore, somewhat unclear.

There was a major reform of the Lords in 1999, when the House of Lords Act provided for the removal of all but 92 of the hereditary peers from the upper house; and so, at the time of writing, the House of Lords is a predominantly appointed body. Yet the Labour government regarded the 1999 Act as merely the first stage of a two-stage reform. The Party's 1997 election manifesto had promised that 'the right of hereditary peers to sit and vote in the House of Lords will be ended by statute', but that this would be just 'the first stage in a process of reform to make the House of Lords more democratic and representative'.

This second stage has not yet been achieved, but in March 2007 the House of Commons voted for either a wholly elected upper house, or an upper house which would be 80% elected, and in 2008 a White Paper was published with proposals intended to realise this aim. The current, predominantly appointed, House of Lords thus lives in a curious kind of limbo, stigmatised as an interim institution and threatened with imminent extinction, yet continuing to perform the functions of a second chamber, with genuine, if limited, legislative powers.

Further reform of the Lords is unlikely to prove a rapid process. Making the House of Lords 'more democratic and representative', gives rise to a fundamental problem, which is to discover a principle of representation upon which a directly elected Lords can be based; a principle different from that of the representation of individuals, which is the basis of elections to the House of Commons. It is a problem which hardly any democracy, with the notable and untypical exception of the United States, has been able to resolve.

The House of Lords, as it has evolved since the 1970s, has succeeded in evading this problem since it does not claim to embody any principle of democratic representation at all. In theory, therefore, the non-elected House of Lords would seem to provide a means of avoiding the many problems which arise when there are two elected chambers representing alternative conceptions of democratic legitimacy. The difficulty is, however, that the very virtue of the House of Lords, from this point of view—its lack of democratic legitimacy—is increasingly seen as a disabling defect. Only an elected chamber, so it is increasingly coming to be argued, can provide an upper house fit for the conditions of the twenty-first century.

The problem of House of Lords reform is particularly acute for a government of the Left, which feels itself strongly committed to radical change. That requires efficient and speedy legislation. Yet, a strong and legitimate second chamber might well stand in the way of speedy legislative action. In the first half of the twentieth century the two majority governments of the Left, the Liberal government of 1905 and the Labour government of 1945, both emphasised the importance of securing the rapid passage of legislation. They had little patience with what they regarded as obstruction from a hereditary or appointed upper house. The main problem of democracy, according to this view, was not that of securing effective checks and balances so that power was constrained, but, on the contrary, that of ensuring that the cumbrous machinery of government did not frustrate the speedy translation of the peoples wishes into law. The task of a government of the Left, therefore, was to remove obstacles to the peoples will, and that meant reducing the powers of the Lords.

Modern-day critics, however, including critics on the Left, take a very different view of democracy. For them, the danger arises from too few checks on government, not from too many. These critics believe that government in Britain, with its unprotected constitution and unelected upper house, is always in danger of succumbing to the condition identified by Lord Hailsham as one of elective dictatorship. Such critics argue that an elected upper house would provide one means of checking that dictatorship.

II

Reform of the House of Lords involves two issues: reform of the powers of the Lords, and reform of its composition. The two are interconnected, but composition is more fundamental, since the composition of the Lords, or, to be more precise, its perceived degree of democratic legitimacy, largely determines the extent to which it can exercise its powers. However, in the first half of the twentieth century, the two majority governments of the Left which reformed the Lords—the Liberal government led by Asquith in 1911 and the Labour government led by Attlee in 1949—understood reform of the Lords to mean reform of its powers by reducing them, rather than reform of its composition, which would have had the effect of legitimizing and strengthening the role of the upper house.

The powers of the House of Lords were first put down in statute by the Liberals in the Parliament Act of 1911, following the rejection by the Conservative-dominated House of Lords of Lloyd George's 'Peoples Budget' of 1909. The Parliament Act removed the absolute veto over legislation which the Lords had hitherto enjoyed. It entirely deprived the Lords of its powers over any bill certified by the Speaker as a money bill. For non-money bills, the Act provided for a suspensory veto, an idea that had first been put forward by the utilitarian, James Mill, in 1836. Under the provision of the suspensory veto, any bill passed by the Commons in three successive sessions would be presented for Royal Assent, even if the Lords rejected it. This delaying power was reduced from three sessions to two by the Attlee government in a second Parliament Act in 1949.

The House of Lords retained just one absolute power under the Parliament Acts. It would continue to enjoy the absolute power to reject a bill proposing to extend the life of Parliament beyond the statutory five years. The purpose of this provision was of course to exclude the possibility of a government extending its own life, as it was to do during the two world wars, but for purely partisan purposes. In addition, the consent of the Lords is required for the dismissal of a High Court judge, Appeal Court judge or judge of the new Supreme Court. The Lords thus offers some protection against a government seeking to subvert either the electoral or the judicial process. It thus retains, in these very limited areas, the function of constitutional protection. This constitutional function, although limited, is nevertheless of great importance, since Britain lacks a codified constitution guaranteeing regular elections and the independence of the judiciary. Without the House of Lords, therefore, there would be a dangerous gap in the political system. The House of Lords is the only body which can prevent a transient majority in the House of Commons from extending its own life or dismissing a judge whom the government finds inconvenient.

When the 1911 Parliament bill was being debated, the Conservative MP Sir Philip Magnus proposed an amendment giving the House of Lords a further power of absolute veto over any measure modifying the Parliament Act itself, such as was to be passed by the Attlee government in 1949. Asquith, the Prime Minister, argued against this amendment on the grounds that there should be a single uniform rule for all legislation. There was, he claimed, no way, under a system in which Parliament was sovereign, of drawing a distinction between constitutional and other legislation. The amendment was defeated.[1] Asquith's argument ignored the fact that the 1911 Parliament bill did precisely what he suggested was impossible, namely draw a distinction between different types of legislation. Under it, three different types of measure could be distinguished: money bills, on which the Lords was to have no legislative role at all; non-money bills, on which it was to enjoy a suspensory veto; and a 'constitutional' bill providing for extending the life

---

[1] House of Commons Debates, vol 24, col 1473, 24 April 1911.

of Parliament beyond the statutory five years, on which it was to retain an absolute veto.

There is a sense, therefore, in which the Parliament Act of 1911 may be seen as a first very tentative step towards an enacted British constitution. It displayed some, though not of course all, of the signs of such a constitution. It distinguished between different categories of legislation—money bills and non-money bills—and it also provided for one category of legislation which was fundamental, namely legislation, which sought to extend the life of Parliament. Before 1911 there had been just one category of legislation, and the Lords had an absolute veto over all legislation. There had thus been a uniform rule for all legislation. After 1911 there was no longer any single such uniform rule.

The provision in the Parliament Act preventing the Commons from unilaterally extending the life of parliament gave a potential handle to the judges. If a bill passed under the Parliament Act procedure purported to extend the life of Parliament, the judges would, presumably, pronounce it invalid. This meant that the courts would be in a position to review primary legislation. The validity of legislation passed under the Parliament Act procedure would not, then, be inherent, as it had been for all legislation before 1911. Rather, the validity of legislation passed under the Parliament Act procedure would be dependent upon its compliance with the terms of that Act; and it might be for the courts to ensure that legislation did so comply. The courts in such cases would become constitutional courts. Of course, it is highly unlikely that any such case would arise, and there has in fact never been a case in which the courts were asked to pronounce on purported legislation passed under the Parliament Act procedure seeking to extend the life of parliament. In 2005, however, in the *Jackson* case, the courts were asked to pronounce on the validity of the 1949 Parliament Act by those who claimed that it was an invalid use of delegated power by the Commons. Although this contention was rejected, nevertheless the courts were, for the first time, being asked to pronounce on the validity of primary legislation from Westminster. That would not have been possible before the 1911 Parliament Act.

The rejection of Sir Philip Magnus's amendment to the Parliament bill was of crucial importance. It emphasised that the Parliament Act would yield, for most practical purposes, single chamber government. It would be open to any future government, following the precedent of the 1949 Parliament Act, to reduce the delaying power still further—to six months, perhaps even to one month, to one week, to one day, to 30 minutes. During the parliamentary proceedings on the Parliament bill in 1947, Emrys Hughes, a left-wing backbencher, suggested that the delaying power be reduced to just one month, a proposal which Herbert Morrison, the Leader of the House, characterised as 'Bolshevism gone mad'.[2]

The 1911 Parliament Act, by providing, for the first time, a statutory restriction on the powers of the Lords created, in effect, a constitutional limitation upon its powers. It might have been supposed to be a logical first stage in the production of

---

[2] House of Commons Debates, vol 445, col 634, 4 December 1947.

an enacted constitution, in that it prescribed by statute the respective powers of the two houses. Yet, the prime advantage of a constitution, so it might be held, is that it cannot be altered by a single chamber. The 1911 settlement could, however, be altered by a single chamber, as Sir Philip Magnus had pointed out, and it was to be so altered by the Attlee government in 1949. Before 1911 the constituent assembly in Britain was in effect both houses; the House of Commons could not change a fundamental law, nor indeed any law on its own, since the Lords enjoyed an absolute veto over all legislation. After 1911, by contrast, the constituent assembly was the House of Commons alone, which in practice meant the government of the day.

The 1911 Parliament Act thus marked a fundamental change in the British constitution. If Britain were to enjoy, for most practical purposes, single-chamber government, then the House of Commons which in practice means the governing party, could now unilaterally alter any part of the constitution, with the single exception that it could not extend the five year maximum interval between general elections without the consent of the Lords. Under the post-1911 constitution, the governing party which controlled the House of Commons became the sole and supreme judge of the extent of its power. The Parliament Act made possible, the 'elective dictatorship' to which Lord Hailsham was to draw attention in the 1970s. It was for this reason that Dicey declared in 1915 that the Parliament Act marked 'the last and greatest triumph of party government'. For it showed that party was 'not the accident or corruption, but so to speak, the very foundation of our constitutional system'.[3] Dicey believed that the Act left a gap in the constitution, a gap which he believed should be filled by the referendum. Perhaps, however, the gap is now being filled by the judges.

It is a striking paradox that the first step taken in Britain towards an enacted constitution replaced a customary constitution which was, nevertheless, a protected constitution, with a partly enacted constitution which was yet an almost wholly unprotected one. Yet, one main purpose of an enacted constitution is to make fundamental change more difficult. The Parliament Acts make it easier. Perhaps it is for this reason that, in 2000, the report of the Royal Commission on the House of Lords—the Wakeham Commission—proposed that any amendment of the Parliament Act should require the consent of both houses. They were recommending that the amendment proposed by Sir Philip Magnus in 1911 be implemented nearly 90 years after it had first been proposed. It has also been suggested that the Human Rights Act be entrenched by being put beyond the reach of the Parliament Acts, and giving the Lords an absolute veto over amendment or repeal of the Act.

[3] A V Dicey, 'Introduction' in the 8th edition of *Law of the Constitution* (8th edn, London, Macmillan, 1915) ci.

III

The House of Commons has not often had to use the statutory powers given to it in the Parliament Acts to overcome the opposition of the Lords. Just three non-money bills were passed under the 1911 Parliament Act procedure between 1911 and 1949. They were:

1. The Government of Ireland bill, 1914, providing for Home Rule for Ireland.
2. The Welsh Church bill, 1914, disestablishing the Church of Wales.

and

3. The Parliament bill, 1949, reducing the delaying power of the Lords from three sessions to two.

Just four non-money bills have been passed under the 1949 Parliament Act procedure since then. They were:

1. The War Crimes bill, 1999, providing for the prosecution of war criminals. This bill had been passed by the House of Commons in two successive sessions on free votes.
2. The European Parliamentary Elections bill, 1999, providing for closed rather than open lists in the proportional representation elections to the European Parliament.
3. The Sexual Offences (Amendment) bill, 2000, lowering the age of consent for homosexual activity to 16, the same as the age of consent for heterosexual activity.
4. The Hunting bill, 2004, outlawing hunting with dogs in England and Wales. (Hunting had already been outlawed in Scotland by the single-chamber Scottish Parliament.) Like the War Crimes bill, the Hunting bill had been passed in two successive sessions on free votes in the House of Commons.

Of course, the effects of the Parliament Acts cannot be measured solely by the number of times they have been used. It is possible that the House of Lords was deterred from carrying its opposition to a government measure to the limit precisely because it knew that it could be over-ruled. But it is clear, nevertheless, that, for most practical purposes, one main consequence of the Parliament Acts has been to produce single-chamber legislation on Britain, in that the Lords is no longer able to resist the legislation of a determined House of Commons. The 1911 Parliament Act ensured that Britain did not develop a strong bicameral legislature. Britain, so it seemed, might enjoy the inestimable advantages of what was in effect a unicameral system but with two chambers. Today, however, many believe that this is no longer an advantage.

Even in 1911, when the Parliament Act was passed, there were some on the Left who believed that it would not be an advantage. The Foreign Secretary in the Liberal government, Sir Edward Grey, was unhappy with the idea of reducing the power of the House of Lords to that of a mere delaying power, the so-called suspensory veto, for precisely this reason, claiming that it was 'open to the charge of being in effect a Single Chamber plan and from a Single Chamber, I believe the country would recoil'.[4] The country does not, however, at least until recent times, seem to have recoiled from it.

It has not been, however, only or even primarily the statutory restriction which has produced, in effect, single-chamber government. The 1911 Parliament Act still left the Lords with considerable powers should they choose to use them. Even after 1949, it would have been possible for the Lords to wreak havoc on a government's programme by delaying all legislation for a year; they could thus render the last year in office of a government of the Left completely futile. In addition, the Parliament Acts do not apply to secondary legislation—regulations, statutory instruments, orders and the like—over which the Lords retain an absolute veto. Since secondary legislation cannot be amended, the Lords face the straight choice of either passing or rejecting it. Secondary legislation was of little importance in 1911, and so it probably did not occur to the Liberals to include it in the Parliament bill. In modern times, however, no government can hope to operate successfully if it cannot secure its secondary legislation.

Yet, until 1999 at least, the Lords used the very considerable statutory powers which remain to them very sparingly. They adopted a policy of self-restraint, and only four government bills have had to be passed since 1949 against the wishes of the Lords. With regard to secondary legislation, the Lords rejected just one government Order before 1999—the Southern Rhodesia (United Nations Sanctions) Order in 1968. But a month later the Lords, agreed to a No 2 Order. The earlier position with regard to secondary legislation was well summarised by one authority on the House of Lords, a former Clerk of the Parliaments, who has commented that,

> 'In theory, the increase in the importance of subordinate legislation has therefore broadened the capacity of the Lords to obstruct the wishes of the government majority in the Commons. But conflict between the Houses on this subject has been exceptional, the reason being that the Lords have used their powers with circumspection.'

Since the House of Lords Act, 1999, removing all but 92 of the hereditary peers from the House of Lords, the Lords have become much more assertive, and more willing to reject secondary legislation. The same authority has argued that, 'the dam has been breached,' and that it seems 'no longer true to say that the Lords do not use their powers on delegated legislation'.[5]

The fundamental reason why the Lords did not, until 1999 at any rate, use their statutory powers to the full, was because they felt bound by a convention, the

---

[4] G M Trevelyan, *Grey of Fallodon* (London, Longmans Green, 1937) 194–5.

[5] Sir Michael Wheeler-Booth, 'The House of Lords' in *Griffith and Ryle on Parliament: Functions, Practice and Procedure* by R Blackburn and A Kennon with M Wheeler-Booth (2nd edn, London, Sweet and Maxwell, 2003) 730–31. Sir Michael's exposition gives an authoritative picture of the Lords as it was until 2003.

so-called Salisbury convention, named after the Conservative leader of the Lords in 1945, Lord Cranborne, grandson of the third Lord Salisbury, Prime Minister at the end of the nineteenth century (Lord Cranborne was himself to become Lord Salisbury on the death of his father in 1947). In the nineteenth century, Lord Salisbury had argued that the role of the Lords was to ensure that the Commons had a mandate for its legislation. Where there was such a mandate, then, by implication, the Lords should not use its powers. In 1945 this doctrine was adapted by the Conservatives in the Lords who were faced, for the first time since the 1911 Parliament Act, with a majority government of the Left. In the Lords debate on the King's Speech in 1945 Lord Cranborne declared:

> 'Whatever our personal views, we should frankly recognize that these [i.e. the government's] proposals were put before the country at the recent General Election and the people of this country, with full knowledge of these proposals, returned the Labour Party to power. The Government may, therefore, I think, fairly claim that they have a mandate to introduce these proposals. I believe it would be constitutionally wrong, when the country has so recently expressed its view, for this House to oppose proposals which have been definitely put before the electorate'.[6]

In 1964 he was to reflect on the position as it had been during the period of the 1945–51 Labour government:

> 'Our broad guiding rule [was] that what had been on the Labour Party programme at the preceding general election should be regarded as having been approved by the British people. Therefore, we passed all the nationalization bills, although we cordially disliked them, on the second reading and did our best to improve them and make them more workable on Committee stage. When, however, measures were introduced which had not been in the Labour Party manifesto at the preceding election, we reserved full liberty of action'.[7]

Although the meaning of the Salisbury convention is perfectly clear, its interpretation in practice can often be uncertain. It seems to mean that, at the very least, the Lords should never reject a bill foreshadowed in the government's manifesto on second or third reading. But, did it mean more than this? What about wrecking amendments? And how could a wrecking amendment be defined? To what extent could the Lords delay consideration of a government bill? And, what about a bill emanating from a minority government—would different considerations then apply? It was in part because of these difficulties of interpretation that in 2006 Parliament established a Joint Committee on Conventions composed of MPs and peers to consider how the Salisbury convention had evolved in the sixty-one years of its existence. The Committee concluded that the convention meant that a manifesto bill should be given a second reading, that it should not be subjected to wrecking amendments and that it should be passed and returned to the Commons so that MPs had the opportunity in reasonable time to consider Lords amendments (para 99). It did not, however, attempt to define 'wrecking amendment',

---

⁶ House of Lords Debates, 16 August 1945, vol 137, col 47.
⁷ House of Lords Debates, 4 November, 1964, vol 261, col 66.

'manifesto bill' nor 'reasonable time', and recognised that this meant that any House of Lords resolution setting out the terms of the convention would inevitably be 'flexible and unenforceable' (pp 76–7). Nevertheless, the Joint Committee expected that 'it will be as possible to deal pragmatically with any problems which may arise in the future as it has been in the past' (para 113). The convention, the Joint Committee believed, should be renamed the Government Bill Convention (para 115). In addition, the Joint Committee believed there was a convention 'that the House of Lords should not regularly reject statutory instruments, but that in exceptional circumstances it may be expected to do so'. It gave examples of what these 'exceptional circumstances' might be, but did not recommend defining them further (paras 227, 229).[8]

After 1945 the Lords had accepted the Salisbury convention for essentially political reasons. They appreciated that their mistake in 1911 had been not only constitutional but also political. From the constitutional point of view the peers who rejected the Lloyd George budget in 1909 had perhaps a stronger case than historians have been willing to recognize. The budget was far from being a measure concerned merely with finance. It also contained wide-ranging proposals for redistributive taxation, and was an example of what was called in the jargon of the day 'tacking' that is, adding non-financial elements on to a finance bill in order to circumvent the veto of the Lords. The Speaker of the Commons at the time of the Parliament Act, James Lowther, declared in his memoirs that he would not have given the Lloyd George budget his certificate as a money bill. 'The celebrated Finance bill of 1909', he wrote, 'which was the immediate cause of the Parliament Act, would not have come under the provisions of Clause 1, section 2 of the Parliament Act, as a 'Money Bill', for it contained a number of provisions which were not within the definition of the clause and section'.[9] Since 1911, only around half of the annual budgets have been classified as money bills. Nevertheless, the Lords were foolish to reject the Lloyd George budget, not so much because they were acting 'unconstitutionally', whatever that might have meant in the circumstances of the time, but because it showed that they had failed to appreciate the significance and the political reality of the great Liberal election victory of 1906, a victory which meant that practices which might once have been tolerable were no longer so. The Lords had certainly learnt that lesson by 1945, and fully appreciated that a non-elected chamber was in no position to defy the verdict of the voters.

Thus, the powers of the House of Lords are limited not only by statute but also by convention; and peers were willing to accept the self-denying ordinance of the Salisbury convention precisely because they appreciated, as their predecessors in 1909 had not, that, being unelected, they lacked democratic legitimacy. This of course leaves open the question of whether the convention would still be observed in an elected upper house whose members *could* claim to enjoy some degree of democratic legitimacy.

---

[8] Joint Committee on Conventions, *Conventions of the UK Parliament*, HL 265 and HC 1212, 2006.
[9] Lord Ullswater, *A Speaker's Commentary* (London, Edward Arnold, 1925) vol II, 103.

IV

The Liberal government in 1911 and the Labour government in 1949 were eager to reform the **powers** of the Lords; they were far less eager to reform its **composition**. The reason is clear. The Liberals, between 1905 and 1914, were implementing, largely under the impact of Lloyd George and Winston Churchill, a radical programme of social reform, a programme continued by the Attlee government after 1945. They were anxious, therefore, to secure the speedy translation of ministerial wishes into law. A government of the Left could not afford delays caused by opposition in the upper house. To rationalise the composition of the upper house, however, would make delay more likely, since a more legitimate upper house would, so the Left believed, also be a more assertive upper house. Therefore the Asquith and Attlee governments concentrated on restricting the powers of the Lords rather than reforming its composition.

Admittedly, the preamble to the 1911 Parliament Act declared that the Act was but a prelude to reform of the composition of the upper house, declaring that it was

> 'intended to substitute for the House of Lords as it at present exists, a Second Chamber constituted on a popular instead of hereditary basis, but such a substitution cannot immediately be brought into operation'.

This preamble had no legal force, but was an expression of the intentions of the government. There must be some doubt, however, as to how far it really reflected the intentions of the government. The majority of Liberals in the Cabinet and the overwhelming majority of back-bench Liberal MPs wanted simply a measure which, by removing the obstacle of the House of Lords, would allow a reforming government to implement its programme. They saw the Parliament Act as a final solution to the problem, not as an interim measure. It seems that the preamble was inserted largely 'to appease Sir Edward Grey' who was so deeply concerned about the dangers of 'single-chamber government'.[10] Having largely destroyed the power of a hereditary chamber to resist progressive legislation, the Liberals were hardly likely to construct a second chamber more legitimate because more democratically based, which would be in a stronger position to wreck their legislation. Lord Carrington, President of the Board of Agriculture in the Liberal government, wrote in his diary in 1911 'We have won, and the battle is firmly over. I firmly believe the House of Lords **as it exists** is safe for another 80 years. There is no real interest in the country with regard to the Reform of the Upper House'[11] [my emphasis]. That was a perceptive verdict. One historian has concluded that 'The passing of the Parliament Act in 1911 represented the triumph of the Liberal view that a Cabinet-controlled House of Commons should prevail. The Unionist

---

[10] G H L Le May, *The Victorian Constitution* (London, Duckworth, 1979) 214.

[11] Quoted in C Ballinger, *An Analysis of the Reform of the House of Lords, 1911–2000* (Oxford D Phil Thesis, 2006) 98. This thesis is an indispensable source for any serious analysis of the House of Lords.

[ie Conservative] view of a bicameral legislature was finally defeated'.[12] It is doubtful, therefore, whether current attempts to reform the composition of the House of Lords designed to make it more legitimate, can fairly be characterised, as one commentator has done, as 'Mr. Asquith's Unfinished Business'.[13]

V

But, although the pledge in the preamble to the 1911 Parliament Act to create a chamber on a 'popular' rather than a 'hereditary' basis has not been fulfilled, there have been major changes in the composition of the Lords since 1911. The most important has been the introduction of life peers under the Life Peerages Act of 1958. This Act also admitted women for the first time to membership of the House. The prime purpose of the Act was to reinvigorate the Lords by enabling more Labour peers to be created. In 1955, in the wholly hereditary house, there were just 55 Labour peers, as compared with 507 Conservatives, 238 Independents and 42 Liberals; at the same time Labour supporters were unwilling to accept hereditary peerages, and many were opposed to the whole concept of a hereditary peerage. With the official opposition so badly represented in the Lords, there was some danger that, as Bagehot had once predicted, the Lords would die, not through 'assassination, but atrophy'.[14]

One important consequence of the Life Peerages Act was the admission into the Lords not only of party politicians but also of experts from all walks of life who were able to make important contributions to the work of the upper house. That, as we shall see, has enabled the Lords to discover a new and valuable role for itself.

Nevertheless, successive creations of life peerages did not seriously undermine the predominance of the hereditary element in the Lords; and in the mid-1990s around two-thirds of the members were still hereditary peers. Since the vast majority of hereditary peers were Conservatives, there always remained a permanent Conservative overall majority in the Lords, whatever the composition of the government of the day. This imbalance was found offensive by many. A permanent one-party legislative chamber, many argued, was as indefensible as a permanent one-party state.

The Parliament Acts, then, ensured that the House of Lords could not act as a constitutional check upon a determined government. The Life Peerages Act, while modifying the composition of the Lords, did little to undermine what seemed to many an archaic second chamber, two-thirds of whose members sat by hereditary right while the other third owed their places to appointment and could be seen as

---

[12] J Ridley, 'The Unionist Opposition and the House of Lords, 1906–1910' (1991) *Parliamentary History,* 253.

[13] I McLean, 'Mr. Asquith's Unfinished Business' (1999) *Political Quarterly.* In 2007 I heard a Liberal Democrat MP at a meeting in the House of Commons on House of Lords reform solemnly apologise for the fact that the Liberals had not fulfilled their pledge to democratize the composition of the Lords. Perhaps his apology was unnecessary. For the pledge was never intended to have been taken seriously.

[14] W Bagehot, 'The English Constitution', *Collected Works,* V, 287.

the beneficiaries of party political patronage. Nevertheless, until recently it seemed that the preservation of an archaic House of Lords was in the interests of both parties. The Conservatives did not feel sufficiently threatened by governments of the Left to seek a stronger second chamber, while Labour was fearful that any reform of composition might strengthen the upper house.

It is for this reason that neither the Asquith nor the Attlee governments made serious attempts to reform the composition of the Lords, while Harold Wilson's complex attempt to reform composition in the 1960s fell victim to back-bench opposition and had to be withdrawn in committee. Following the defeat of the Wilson proposal, the issue of Lords reform disappeared for a time from the political agenda. The next Labour government of 1974–9 found itself constrained by the lack of a working majority, and was in no position to implement further reform of the Lords.

In 1997, however, the Labour Party fought the general election with a manifesto, *New Labour: Because Britain Deserves Better*, proposing a two-phase reform of the Lords. The first phase of this reform, achieved in the House of Lords Act of 1999, had provided for the removal of all but 92 of the hereditary peers from the upper house. The Labour Party had originally sought to remove all of the hereditary peers from the Lords. But it had found that this would lead to political difficulties. The Conservatives in the Lords would have been likely to resist it and the government would then have had to use the Parliament Act. This would have used a great deal of parliamentary time and prolonged unwelcome controversy. The government, therefore, agreed to a compromise suggested by Lord Cranborne, the Conservative leader in the Lords, and grandson of the author of the Salisbury convention, that 92 of the hereditary peers should remain, in order to secure Conservative acquiescence in the removal of the vast majority of the hereditary peers. An amendment to retain the 92 peers was then successfully moved by Lord Weatherill, a cross-bench peer and former Speaker of the Commons.

The Conservative motive in seeking the retention of the 92 hereditary peers was to ensure that the second stage of reform was actually achieved, and that the Lords did not remain a wholly appointed chamber. Many Conservatives felt that Labour could not be trusted to proceed with the second stage of reform, but would remain content with an all-appointed House. If, however, 92 hereditary peers were retained, Labour would be much more likely to proceed with the second stage of reform, since Labour MPs were so bitterly opposed to any hereditary element remaining. In the debate on the Weatherill amendment Lord Irvine, the Lord Chancellor, made a statement committing the government to retaining the 92 hereditary peers until the second stage had taken place, declaring that:

'The amendment reflects a compromise negotiated between Privy Councillors on Privy Council terms and binding in honour on all those who have come to give it their assent. . . . The 10% [i.e. of hereditary peers] would only go when stage two has taken place. So it is a guarantee that it will take place'.[15]

[15] House of Lords Debates, vol 599, col 207, 30 March 1999.

The 92 hereditary peers who were to remain in the Lords were to be selected in the following manner:

2 would be hereditary appointed royal office-holders, who would remain ex officio members—the Earl Marshal and the Lord Great Chamberlain.

15 would be elected by the whole House as office holders, either Deputy Speakers or Committee Chairmen.

The remaining 75 would be elected by the electoral colleges of their hereditary colleagues from their own groups.

> 42 Conservative
> 2 Labour
> 2 Liberal Democrat
> 28 cross-benchers

When an elected hereditary peer died, the vacancy would be filled from the relevant electoral college, and the totality of hereditary peers would thus remain in existence as an electoral college.

It is a paradox that the only elected peers in the upper house are the hereditary peers elected by their fellows.

The House of Lords Act, 1999, transformed the upper house. Before the 1958 Act the only way of becoming a member of the House of Lords, apart from becoming a law lord or a bishop or archbishop of the Church of England, was to acquire or inherit a peerage. Membership of the Lords meant becoming a member of a hereditary aristocracy. Since 1983, however, no new hereditary peerages have been created,[16] and it is unlikely that any will be created in the future outside the royal family. Thus membership of the House of Lords is now acquired primarily through patronage. At the beginning of the twentieth century the Lords was primarily a hereditary and aristocratic institution, but, by the end of the century it had become a predominantly nominated body, comprising both party politicians and also experts. The name of the chamber was the same, but its role and function had become quite different.

The House of Lords Act, 1999, has had four major inter-related consequences. The first was that it meant that no single party or group would enjoy an overall majority in the upper house. This had been one of the Labour Party's aims. Its 1997 election manifesto had declared that, 'No one political party should seek a majority in the House of Lords'. The 1999 Act deprived the Conservatives of their overall majority in the Lords. At the time of writing, Labour is now, for the first time in its history, the largest single party in the Lords. The Conservatives, hitherto dominant, are no longer even the second largest group, that position being occupied by the crossbenchers. It seems rapidly to have become an accepted convention that in future no single party should ever again enjoy an overall majority in the House of Lords. The government of the day, therefore, whether Labour or Conservative, will

---

[16] With the exception of the Earl of Wessex, a son of the Queen.

have to persuade the Lords by argument; it will not be able, like Conservative governments in the past, to take the assent of the Lords for granted. In practice, it is the cross-benchers and the Liberal Democrats who often find themselves in a pivotal position. The Blair government had to work hard to win their support, and also on occasion the support of its own back-benchers, in order to carry its legislation. The House of Lords is, therefore, permanently hung. Paradoxically, it could only come to be controlled by the government were there to be a coalition government in the House of Commons in which the Liberal Democrats participated. In such a situation, the Liberal Democrats in the Lords would be tethered to the government, and there would be congruent majorities in both Commons and Lords. In that situation, the government would dominate both houses.

The second consequence of the reform is that, apart from the remaining hereditary peers, all other peers now owe their position to appointment. The Lords has become a predominantly appointed house. In addition, the appointments procedure has been reformed. The Prime Minister is no longer able to nominate cross-bench peers and peers from other parties. He is able to nominate only members of his own party for working peerages, together with a very small number of cross-bench peerages for 'a limited number of distinguished public servants on retirement' such as the Cabinet Secretary or Private Secretary to the Queen. In January 2005, Tony Blair in a written ministerial statement indicated that he had 'decided that the number of appointments covered under this arrangement will not exceed ten in any one Parliament'. The Prime Minister, in addition, retains other patronage powers. It is he who decides how many peers are to be created at any given time, and what the balance between the parties is to be. But nominations from the other political parties now come from their respective party leaders and the Prime Minister's role is confined to that of transmitting the names to the Queen. Before names are sent to the Queen, they are scrutinised to ensure propriety by a new non-statutory and independent Appointments Commission, established in 2000.

This Commission also has the task of nominating cross-bench working peers to the House of Lords, a power which was formerly held by the Prime Minister. To broaden the base from which cross-bench peers were chosen, the Commission decided to ask the public to make nominations for peerages, or to self-nominate. It received, apparently, 3,166 such nominations initially, and recommended in its first batch in 2001, 15 candidates for life peerages.[17] There had been some talk in the media, which the Commission had not encouraged, of the new peers being 'peoples peers', members of the general public who might have something to contribute to the upper house. But both the first list and also subsequent lists consisted largely of nominations of 'the great and the good', people who might well have been nominated under the old system.

The third consequence of the House of Lords Act of 1999 has been that the peers now conceive of themselves as more legitimate than their pre-1999 predecessors.

---

[17] M Wheeler-Booth, 'The House of Lords' in Blackburn and Kennon (eds) *Parliament: Functions, Practice and Procedures*, 667.

Before 1999, hereditary peers, comprising around two-thirds of the membership, were hesitant about pressing any disagreement with the government since they were in the Lords solely through accident of birth. The House of Lords, however, is no longer a largely prescriptive House, but one in which every member has been specifically chosen, either through nomination—the life peers, or through election—the 92 hereditary peers. The peers, therefore, can argue that they constitute a more legitimate house than they did before 1999. In addition, a vote to oppose government legislation cannot be carried by one party alone, as was the case when the Conservatives had dominated the Lords. There have, therefore, been more government defeats in the post-1999 period than before, and around 40% of these defeats have been accepted by the government, which has not sought to overturn them in the Commons. This new assertiveness of the Lords had been predicted by Lady Jay, Leader of the Lords at the time of the reform, in 1999, when she declared that the House

'will be able to speak with more authority . . . A decision by the House not to support a proposal from the Government will carry more weight because it will have to include supporters from a range of political and independent opinions. So the Executive will be better held to account'.[18]

The fourth consequence of the House of Lords Act has been that, precisely because the Lords see themselves as more legitimate, the Salisbury convention has come under challenge. Lord Strathclyde, the Conservative leader in the Lords, has argued that 'in the wake of the new composition of the House, some of the implications of this convention need to be reviewed', since 'the Labour party has unilaterally overthrown the conditions and circumstances that gave it birth'.[19] The Liberal Democrats have gone even further. Their predecessor party, the Liberals, were not a party to the convention when it was first enunciated in 1945, and nor were the cross-benchers. It has therefore been suggested that 'the Salisbury convention is perhaps more a code of behaviour for the Conservative Party when in opposition in the Lords than a convention of the House'.[20] The Liberal Democrats now claim that, while the convention might have been appropriate when the Lords were permanently dominated by one party, since that condition no longer exists it should be replaced by a new convention more appropriate to modern times. 'The Salisbury convention', Lord McNally, the leader of the Liberal Democrats in the Lords, argued in a debate in the Lords on 26 January 2005,

'was designed to protect the non-Conservative government from being blocked by a built-in hereditary-based majority in the Lords. It was not designed to provide more power for what the late Lord Hailsham rightly warned was an elective dictatorship in another place against legitimate check and balance by this second Chamber'.[21]

---

[18] House of Lords Debates, 8 December 1999, vol 607, col 1262.
[19] Lord Strathclyde, *New Frontiers for Reform* (London, Centre for Policy Studies, 2001) 26.
[20] R Rogers and R Walters, *How Parliament Works* (5th edn, Harlow, Pearson, 2004) 222.
[21] House of Lords Debates, 26 January 2005, vol 668, col 371.

In a later debate he declared 'I do not believe that a convention drawn up 60 years ago on relations between a wholly hereditary Conservative-dominated House and a Labour Government who had 48% of the vote should apply in the same way to the position in which we find ourselves today'.[22] He has described the 'traditional plea to the Salisbury convention' as 'the last refuge of legislative scoundrels'.[23] The government, by contrast, argued that the Salisbury Convention should still be observed. In its view, the rationale of the Salisbury Convention lay in the House of Lords being non-elected and not merely in its being a chamber permanently dominated by one party. Implicit in this view, perhaps, is the admission that, were the Lords to become wholly or partially elected, then new conventions would have to be developed in order to ensure the primacy of the Commons.

VI

The second stage of Labour's promised reform, the creation of a 'more democratic and representative' House of Lords has not yet been achieved. It is not easy to discern clearly the contours of an elected upper house in Britain. Reform of composition involves confronting the very fundamental problem of finding an alternative basis of representation for the upper house, other than representation on the basis of individuals, the basis for representation in the House of Commons.

In 1999 a collection of essays on second chambers, entitled *Senates*, was published. In the introduction to the essays the editors declared that second chambers are 'essentially contested institutions'.[24] By this they meant that few democracies were content with their second chambers, and that many were engaged 'in an apparently incessant dialogue about how they should be reformed'. Amongst the range of democracies they studied, Germany appeared to them 'to be almost unique in having no campaign that seeks to reform the upper house'. Germany, however, is no longer 'almost unique', and there has arisen in recent years a vigorous campaign to reform the *Bundesrat*, the German upper house, which, so it is argued, has served to block necessary labour market and social security reforms. One of the key proposals of the Grand Coalition, led by Angela Merkel, which took office in Germany in 2005, was to reform the *Bundesrat* as part of a wider reform of the German federal system.

The reason why so many countries are unhappy with their second chambers is that there is a problem of a very fundamental kind in creating a second chamber in a modern democracy, especially in a non-federal state. A second chamber needs to be based upon an alternative principle of representation to that embodied in the first chamber. But what is that principle to be? How can the same electorate be represented in two different ways in two different chambers? The first chamber, to

---

[22]   House of Lords Debates, 17 May 2005, vol 672, col 20.
[23]   Cited in P Cowley, 'Parliament', in A Seldon (ed) *Blair's Britain* (Cambridge, CUP, 2003) 32–3.
[24]   S C Patterson and A Mughan (eds) *Senates: Bicameralism in the Contemporary World* (Columbus, Ohio State University Press, 1999) 338.

which of course a government in a parliamentary state is responsible, represents the principle of individual representation. What alternative principle should the second chamber represent? In the nineteenth century, in a pre-democratic age, it was not too difficult to find such a principle. Many second chambers, including the House of Lords, exemplified the principle of giving special representation to hereditary right or to the landed interest. But such a rationale is of course quite unacceptable today.

The problem seems easier to resolve in a federal state than in a unitary state since an alternative principle of representation in a federal state immediately suggests itself—the representation of territory. One obvious answer to the conundrum of discovering an alternative principle of representation to the representation of individuals is to represent territory in the second chamber. That is the principle adopted in federal states such as the United States and Australia, both of which have directly elected Senates representing the sub-national units, the states; and also in states such as Spain which, while not being federal, have devolved bodies covering the whole country.

Some would like the upper house in Britain to follow the same logic, precisely because Britain is now, after devolution, an asymmetric, quasi-federal state. Lord Richard, a Labour peer and former Leader of the House of Lords, proposed a federal-type solution of the problem of the second chamber in a book that he wrote with Damien Welfare, entitled *Unfinished Business*.[25] He proposed that two-thirds of the members of an upper house of 450 members should be directly elected by a regional list system of proportional representation, the system used for elections to the European Parliament. The remaining one-third would be crossbenchers appointed for life by the Appointments Commission. Richard and Welfare argued that this would strengthen regional feeling, so giving England a greater stake in the devolution settlement. Reform of the Lords could, so they believe, play its part in holding the United Kingdom together in the face of centrifugal pressures threatening to pull it apart. A directly elected second chamber, so they argue, 'could be the missing piece of the constitutional jigsaw, serving as the pinnacle of the structure and a focus of unity'.[26]

Proposals of this kind raise two questions. The first is whether the lessons of federal or quasi-federal states such as Spain are applicable to Britain. The second is whether there is any real analogy between Britain, where only 15% of the population live under devolved bodies, and federal or quasi federal states, where there is an intermediate layer of government—either states or provinces, as in a federal state, or regional units created by devolution—covering the whole population of the country.

The prime lesson to be drawn from even a cursory glance at second chambers in federal states is that they recognize less the interests of territory than the interests of the political parties which are strong in a particular territory. In Australia,

[25] I Richard and D Welfare, *Unfinished Business: Reforming the House of Lords* (Vintage, London, 1999).

[26] Ibid, 172.

for example, the Senate represents less the interests of the Australian states than of the state parties. A Senator from New South Wales sees herself less as a representative of New South Wales than as a representative of the Liberal or Labor parties in Australia, and votes, in general, in accordance with the party whip. In almost every democratic legislature party rather than territory predominates. An outcome of this kind had been foreseen by one of Australia's founding fathers, Alfred Deakin, in the debates on federation at the end of the nineteenth century. 'The people', he predicted, 'will divide themselves into two parties. The instant Federation is accomplished the two Houses will be elected on that basis. State rights and state interests . . . will never be mentioned'. That proved a prescient prediction. In 1995, Wayne Goss, the Prime Minister of Queensland, declared that 'none of us any longer pretend that the Senate continues to perform its political and constitutional function on behalf of the States. In fact there have been many cases in which the Senate has actively worked against the interests of the States'. A political scientist, David Hamer, tested this hypothesis, and concluded.

'By any measure of public performance—amendments to Government bills, initiation of private members' bills, motions, questions to Ministers, there is no evidence that Senators have been any more diligent in protecting State interests (real or supposed) than have the [members of the House of] Representatives: if anything they have been slightly less diligent'.[27]

When the Senate in Australia is controlled by the opposition it acts as a forum for the opposition. That was what occurred in 1975 when the Labor government introduced two appropriation bills into the Senate, which was controlled by the opposition Liberal party. The Senate voted that the bills not be further proceeded with until the government agreed 'to submit itself to the judgment of the people', exactly the same claim that the House of Lords had made in 1909 when it refused to pass Lloyd George's 'People's Budget'. In Australia, the only way in which a disagreement between the two houses can be resolved is through a double dissolution. Thus, the Senate can do what the House of Lords succeeded in doing when it rejected the 1909 budget; it can force a dissolution. The Prime Minister, Gough Whitlam, refused to dissolve, however, and was in due course dismissed by the Governor-General, precipitating a constitutional crisis whose effects continue to resonate to this day.

The crisis of 1975 was of course a unique event, but, more recently, the Senate has been controlled by minor parties who use their leverage in order to secure amendments to the annual budget. Fears have been expressed that the Australian budget process is becoming 'Americanised'. The former Prime Minister of Australia, Malcolm Fraser, has argued that the Senate 'is running the risk of making Australia ungovernable . . . [by] turning the annual Budget process into a series of bargains and trade-offs similar to those which occur in the United States'.[28]

---

[27] Cited in M Russell, *Reforming the House of Lords; Lessons from Overseas* (Oxford, OUP, 2000) 210–11.

[28] Quoted in J Uhr, 'Generating Divided Government: The Australian Senate', in *Senates*, 100.

Government in the United States carries the risk of gridlock when the Presidency and Congress are controlled by different parties. Government in Australia is at risk of gridlock when the House of Representatives and the Senate are controlled by different parties.

The Australian example, however, is not the only relevant one for the working of an upper house in a federal or quasi-federal state. It is in fact unique in providing for no remedy other than a double dissolution in the case of disputes between the two houses. In most other countries the constitution lays down provisions by which the lower house can overcome opposition in the upper house. The Australian example **is** typical, however, of upper houses in that its Senate provides a home for a second set of professional politicians, differing in hardly any respects from those sitting in the House of Representatives. It does little to provide effective territorial representation. It would not be easy in Britain to ensure that a reformed upper house did in fact represent the nations and regions of the country, rather than merely replicating the party battle in the House of Commons. Many criticize the Commons because it is dominated by professional politicians, politicians who have made a career out of politics, and have little outside experience or understanding of the problems faced by those they claim to represent. That feature might well be replicated in a reformed upper house; the constraints of party discipline might even be stronger in a chamber elected by a regional list system of proportional representation in constituencies much larger than those of the House of Commons, in which personal contact between voter and member would inevitably be minimal, than it is under first-past-the-post elections for the House of Commons. The likelihood, perhaps, is also that some at least of the candidates for the new upper house would have failed to secure nomination for a House of Commons constituency. Such people would be less effective at scrutinising legislation than most of the regular attenders in the Lords, and less effective than many MPs. Certainly there seems little public demand for an upper house composed primarily of professional politicians of the same type as those who sit in the Commons.

The second question that arises from a consideration of the federal model is whether there is any real analogy between a federal or quasi-federal state in which an intermediate body representing territorial units lies between central government and the localities, and Britain where devolution is confined to the non-English parts of the country, while England, comprising 85% of the UK population, has no intermediate body at all. Regional feeling is very weak in England, even in the north-east where, in November 2004, the proposal for a directly regional assembly was decisively defeated by a 4 to 1 majority. There is no sign at present that England wishes to move further in a regionalist direction. There is, admittedly, a regional framework of government in England—government regional offices, staffed with civil servants, regional development organisations which are appointed bodies, and, in a number of regions, regional chambers, non-statutory bodies of local authority leaders and representatives of the private and voluntary sectors, designed to scrutinize the regional development organisations. But there are no directly elected bodies at regional level. Thus regional institutions in England lack the democratic legitimacy of the Scottish Parliament or the National Assembly of Wales. In England the regions are ghosts. It is difficult to believe that regional list elections to a reformed upper house would be able to change this very much. Certainly, elections to the European Parliament using this system have done little, if anything, to stimulate regional feeling. It is in fact doubtful if many electors would be able to name their MEP. The same would probably be true of members of a reformed upper house elected on regional lists.

Because there are no English regional institutions in any way equivalent to the Scottish Parliament, a directly elected upper house based on territory would introduce the West Lothian question into that house. It would be asked why Scottish elected peers should be able to vote on English laws when English peers could not vote on Scottish laws on domestic matters, since these had been devolved to the Scottish Parliament. A territorial upper house, therefore, far from helping to hold the United Kingdom together, could give added momentum to the centrifugal forces seeking to pull it apart.

VII

It is not easy, then, to discover an alternative principle of representation from that embodied in the House of Commons. The current composition of the House of Lords, however, enables it to evade the conundrum of finding an alternative principle of representation from that used for electing the lower house. It acts, to some extent at least, as a chamber of experts, and, because it lacks democratic legitimacy, it cannot pretend that it is in any way representative, and so cannot mount an effective challenge to the lower house. From this point of view, the very lack of democratic legitimacy of the House of Lords may be a positive advantage in helping to secure effective government.

In 1975, a former Conservative Leader of the House of Lords, Lord Windlesham, wrote that 'the House of Lords should not attempt to rival the Commons. Whenever it has done so in the past it has failed, and usually made itself look ridiculous in the process'. In Lord Windlesham's view, the role of the Lords, following the introduction of expert life peers into the upper house, was quite different. 'In any well-tuned parliamentary system', he argued,

> 'there is a need and a place for a third element besides efficient government and the operation of representative democracy. This third element is the bringing to bear of informed or expert public opinion . . . It is now one of the principal roles of the Lords to provide a forum in which informed public opinion can take shape and be made known'.

Therefore,

> 'In assessing the influence of the House of Lords it is worth distinguishing the influence that comes from the ability to delay legislation from the influence that comes from special knowledge or the representation of interests'.[29]

---

[29] Lord Windlesham, *Politics in Practice* (London, Cape, 1975) 137, 142.

This important role identified by Lord Windlesham, although it still retains its significance, has perhaps been diluted in recent years by the appointment of non-experts, professional politicians, not only ex-Cabinet ministers, but Members of Parliament who have been defeated in their constituencies, and, on occasion, long-serving party workers and candidates who have never succeeded in being elected to the Commons at all. These are the kinds of people whom, it might be said, are more suited to the Commons than the Lords. They are also the kinds of people who would probably become members of the upper house were the upper house to be elected. To this extent, therefore, as the expert element in the House of Lords has come to be diluted, the arguments against an elected upper house have come to be weakened.

Nevertheless, the House of Lords does perform effective work which only an upper house can perform, not only in the revision of legislation, but also, and perhaps even more important, in its Select Committee work.

The Select Committee work of the House of Lords had been largely in abeyance from 1911 to 1972. But the failure of Harold Wilson's attempt to reform the Lords in the 1960s caused some frustration amongst the peers, particularly the life peers. They felt that their expertise was not being effectively used and that the Commons would neither allow any real reform of the Lords giving the upper house more authority, nor give the Lords any really useful work to do. However, Britain's entry into the European Community in 1973 enabled the peers to develop a new role for themselves, scrutinizing European legislation by means of a new Select Committee on the European Communities. So effectively did the peers undertake this work that, by 1977, a Committee established by the Hansard Society for Parliamentary Government, found itself

'struck by the relevance and businesslike nature of the results of the Lords' work in this field, and think it significant that the Commons, who represent the people of this country, have taken in contrast to the Lords, a largely inward-looking and conservative attitude where the opposite was required'.

And, in 1982, a Report of a Study Group of the Commonwealth Parliamentary Association on 'The Role of Second Chambers', concluded that the Lords offered

'the only really deep analysis of the issues that is available to the parliamentary representatives of the ten countries in the Community . . . The Lords reports are far more informative and comprehensive than those produced by the Commons committee on European legislation'.

The Study Group attributed this superiority to the greater specialist knowledge of peers and the comparative absence of partisanship in the House of Lords.[30]

The Lords had been far less divided over whether Britain should join the Community than the Commons, approving membership by 451 votes to 58 in

---

[30] Both reports are cited in C Grantham and C M Hodgson, 'The House of Lords—Structural Changes—the Use of Committees', in P Norton (ed) *Parliament in the 1980s* (Oxford, Blackwell, 1985). This chapter contains an excellent brief account of the working of the House of Lords Select Committee in its early days.

October 1971. In consequence, the process of scrutiny was not bedevilled, as it was in the Commons in the early days of membership, and perhaps still is, by the issue of whether British membership was or was not 'a good thing'; and, although a broad partisan balance on the Select Committee is maintained, membership is determined more by specialised knowledge than by party political considerations. Because of the system of nominating to life peerages men and women of eminence, the Lords contains experts in almost every field of European Union activity, whether the subject-matter be agriculture, law or economics. Since much European legislation is of a highly technical kind, it benefits from having technically qualified legislators to appraise it. There are certainly few political gains to be derived from the scrutiny of European legislation, a task liable to prove both lengthy and time-consuming. The scrutiny provided in the House of Lords European Union Select Committee, as it has been now renamed, has proved to be perhaps the most effective in the European Union, precisely perhaps because the Lords is not an elected chamber.

The House of Lords has also established other Select Committees which enable the expertise of its members to be effectively deployed, such as the Science and Technology Select Committee, the Delegated Powers and Deregulation Committee and the Select Committee on the Constitution. The Select Committees of the Lords, unlike those of the Commons, are not departmentally-related, and are thus able to consider matters which fall across departmental boundaries. In doing so, they make an important contribution in helping to secure joined-up government. The skilled experts who serve on these committees would be unlikely to seek membership of an elected chamber. In this aspect of its work the House of Lords has become a forum for informed public debate, for example amongst the scientific community in relation to major policy issues over a longer time horizon than that with which governments usually concern themselves. With the apparent demise of the Royal Commission, the need for work of this sort is now particularly great. Select Committees of the Lords, therefore, have now become an important part of the work of the upper house.

The problem remains, of course, that the upper house, however valuable the work that it does, lacks the legitimacy necessary in a democratic age. The task then is to secure a more legitimate upper house which yet continues to carry out the functions of the present upper house. The danger is, however, that a more legitimate upper house might use its powers so as to cause gridlock in government. As Lady Jay predicted, the post-1999 House of Lords, feeling itself to be more legitimate than the pre-1999 House, has used its power much more than its predecessor did. The members of a wholly or largely elected upper house might well say that they are more legitimate than their largely appointed predecessor. Therefore, so they might argue, they are entitled to use powers which their predecessors believed had fallen into desuetude—powers such as the rejection of government bills and the rejection of subordinate legislation. The Salisbury convention, which is already being questioned, might well not survive an elected house.

Both the government and a cross-party bench of MPs have, however, argued against this conclusion, that a wholly or largely elected upper house would inevitably acquire greater powers. In evidence to the Joint Committee on Conventions, the government insisted that 'The subordinate position of a second chamber appears . . . to be independent of its composition, and does not depend on the second chamber being wholly (or partially) appointed'.[31] The government, in its response to the report of the Joint Committee, claimed that 'The question of composition of the House of Lords does not dictate its role. Function does not follow form. The questions of powers and composition certainly impact on each other, but are in fact separate'. Evidence for this view, the government believed, could be obtained from international comparisons:

'There is a range of models of second chambers across the world, each constituted differently with varying degrees of power. There is no consistent correlation between the nature of a chamber's composition and its degree of power relative to the primary chamber. It does not follow, for example, that directly elected chambers necessarily have more power than appointed chambers, or that because their members have democratic legitimacy, they have a greater say over legislation . . .'[32]

To support its argument the government cited, in paragraph 14 of its response, the upper houses of the Czech republic, Japan and Poland which 'all have wholly directly elected second chambers, which may be thought to correlate with extensive powers, yet in each case the primary chamber is able to override second chamber amendments'. The democratically elected upper houses in the Czech Republic and Poland, however, are comparatively new, both being post-Communist creations, and they remain in a somewhat unsettled state. With regard to Japan, the election to the upper house in 2007 yielded a majority hostile to the Prime Minister. The Prime Minister was then pressed to resign, because, so it was argued, he had lost popular confidence; and he eventually did in fact resign.

The argument that an upper house with greater legitimacy would not necessarily acquire greater powers was, however, supported by a cross-bench party group of MPs, in their report, 'Reforming the House of Lords—Breaking the Deadlock', published in 2005. The primacy of the House of Commons, they argued, rested not on the fact that the Commons was elected while the Lords was not, but on the confidence convention, the convention, fundamental to the British system of government, that the government was responsible to the House of Commons and not to the upper house.

This argument, however, is not very strong. The confidence convention existed long before the first Parliament Act of 1911. At that time, the Lords wrongly perceived themselves to enjoy legitimacy. That is why they sought to use their powers and why the Parliament Act was necessary. Had the confidence convention been sufficient to secure legitimacy, the Parliament Act would not have been necessary at all. Even so, it took two general elections in 1910 before the first Parliament Act

---

[31] HL 265-II, HC 1212-II, para 14.
[32] Cm 6997, 2006, paras 12, 13.

could be passed. It was, of course, much easier to overcome the unelected Lords in 1911 and 1949 than it would be to overcome an elected chamber, since the unelected chamber lacked democratic legitimacy.

An elected upper house, especially if it is elected by proportional representation, would certainly be likely to conceive of itself as more legitimate than the current House of Lords. In evidence to the Joint Committee on Conventions, Paul Hayter, the Clerk of the Parliaments, declared: 'It can be argued that the greater the proportion of elected members the stronger the mandate. If the Lords were elected by a proportional system they might even claim a superior mandate'.[33] An upper house elected by proportional representation might claim that it was more representative of the people than a lower house elected by the first-past-the-post system with its distorted majorities. For example, in 2005, the Labour government was returned with a comfortable working majority on just 36% of the vote. Assuming that the election for the upper house had been held at the same time and that the votes had been similar to those of the lower house, there would have been no overall majority for any party in the upper house. The upper house could then say that, in rejecting government legislation, it was better reflecting the will of the people than was the lower house in passing it.

Were the upper house to be elected at a different time from the lower house, it might be even more likely to assert itself because it would claim that its mandate was more recent than that of the lower house. Suppose, for example, that there had been elections for an upper house in the autumn of 2007 when the Conservative Party was ahead in the polls, and that the Conservatives proved to be the largest party in the upper house. The Conservatives might argue that while Labour perhaps enjoyed a mandate in 2005, that mandate had now evaporated. By 2007 the view of the people had changed, and it was the Conservatives who now enjoyed a mandate from the people. The government had lost its legitimacy, therefore, and the Conservatives would use the mandate that the people had given them systematically to undermine and destroy government legislation. They might well clamour for the resignation of the Prime Minister, as occurred in Japan, where, in effect, the government had become responsible to the upper house as well as the lower, since an election to the upper house affected the fate of the government.

In his evidence to the Joint Committee on Conventions, the Clerk of the House of Commons, Sir Roger Sands, suggested that the primacy of the House of Commons rested upon three factors. They were: 'its predominant authority in respect of matters of expenditure and taxation, re-asserted regularly during the history of Parliament' and given legal form by the provision in the 1911 Parliament Act that the Lords would lose its power over money bills; the ability of the Commons to override the Lords on non-money bills as provided by the Parliament Acts; 'and, underpinning both of these, the superior authority properly

---

[33] HL 265-II, HC 1212-II, p 84, para 33.

accorded to a chamber whose members are elected by and represent the will of the nation's people over a chamber whose members are not so elected'.[34]

In questioning by the Committee, Sir Roger accepted that the 1911 Parliament Act flowed from the fact that the Commons was elected while the Lords was not. It would seem to follow, therefore, that if this essential relationship were to be altered, then the Parliament Acts would not necessarily survive to define the powers of an elected upper house. Sir Roger accepted that, in these circumstances, 'the Parliament Act would have to be reconsidered'[35]

The preamble to the 1911 Parliament Act certainly implied that, with an elected upper house, its powers would have to be reconsidered. After declaring that 'it is intended to substitute for the House of Lords as it at present exists a Second Chamber constituted on a popular instead of a hereditary basis', the next paragraph continued, '**And whereas provision will require hereafter to be made by Parliament in a measure effecting such substitution for limiting and defining the powers of the new Second Chamber …**' (emphasis added). The implication is that the Parliament Act was to apply only to an unelected house and that new thoughts would be needed were the upper house to be elected.

Concluding a comparative study of upper houses, one authority argues that an effective second chamber would depend upon:

'a distinct membership from the House of Commons; moderate to strong powers to challenge government; and sufficient legitimacy to retain the support of the public, in order to use these powers as appropriate'.[36]

The House of Lords, as it was before 1911, enjoyed the first two of these advantages; its composition was distinct from that of the House of Commons, and its powers were statutorily unlimited. Yet, because it was not perceived as legitimate, when it sought to use its powers it caused a political crisis which led to its powers being severely restricted by statute. The Canadian Senate is a wholly appointed body with wide powers on paper, since the lower house has no means of overriding it. Yet, because it has no democratic legitimacy, it is unable to use its powers.

There can be little doubt, therefore, that in the modern world, the powers of an upper house depend primarily upon its democratic legitimacy. An elected upper house will undoubtedly mean a more legitimate upper house. Even if this does not threaten the primacy of the House of Commons it will prove a more formidable body than the current House of Lords, and a thorn in the side of the government's legislative programme. An elected upper house will therefore mean a stronger upper house, and this might well require reconsideration of the Parliament Acts and a new statutory definition of the powers of the upper house. Perhaps hitherto accepted conventions such as the Salisbury convention would have to be codified and put into statutory form. The Clerk to the Commons told the Joint Committee

---

[34] Ibid, at 100, para 5.
[35] Ibid.
[36] M Russell, *Reforming the House of Lords*, above n 27, 259.

on Conventions that 'it is likely to be difficult to ensure that any definition of the convention [i.e. the Salisbury convention] now would survive a significant change in the composition of the Lords'.[37] There would probably have to be some new and stronger statutory procedure for the resolution of disputes between the two houses.

The Joint Committee accepted this argument and concluded in its report.

'If the Lords acquired an electoral mandate, then in our view their role as a revising chamber, and their relationship with the Commons, would inevitably be called into question. . . . Given the weight of evidence on this point, should any firm proposals come forward to change the composition of the House of Lords, the conventions between the Houses would have to be examined again'.[38] (Emphasis in original).

It is possible that a conventional understanding of the relationship between the two houses would no longer be sufficient. Governments might be unwilling any longer to take the risk that a fractious upper house might make the last year of a government's existence a nullity by rejecting legislation; or, alternatively, that the upper house might come to reject secondary legislation as a matter of course. Therefore, a new statutory definition of the powers of the upper house would have to be enacted. This would presumably involve reducing the powers of the upper house rather than increasing them.

The discussion on conventions in chapter 2 implies that any new conventions would be the outcome, less of calm constitutional reflection, than of an essentially political struggle between two chambers, each claiming democratic legitimacy. The outcome would depend upon political vicissitudes and the state of public opinion.

The government of the day would, no doubt, seek a tighter statutory restriction upon the powers of the upper house, something which the upper house would no doubt resist. The Labour Party's 2005 election manifesto proposed that the delaying power be reduced so that most bills would pass through the Lords in no more than 60 sitting days. But, if the powers of the upper house were to be further restricted, it would become less likely that people of ability would be willing to stand for it. It is often suggested that it is difficult to secure good candidates for local government since local authorities have been denuded of many of their powers. The danger is that the same syndrome might affect the upper house. The more the powers of the Lords are restricted, the more difficult it would be to secure people of ability to stand for election. What person of merit would wish to stand for election to a toothless chamber? It is therefore inconsistent to seek to rationalise and legitimize the composition of the Lords while at the same time reducing its powers.

It is sometimes suggested that members of the new upper house be restricted to just one term, or that they should not be allowed to stand afterwards for election to the Commons until a certain length of time has elapsed after they cease to be

---

[37] HL 265-II; HC 1212-II, para 34.
[38] HL 265-I; HC 1212-I, para 61.

members of the upper house. This provision would, so it is suggested, prevent membership of the upper house from being used as a springboard for election to the Commons—as perhaps membership of the European Parliament is. But this too might mean that ambitious and effective candidates would be deterred from standing for the reformed upper house.

If the elected upper house had fewer powers than the House of Lords, or even perhaps if it had the same powers, there would be a danger that few would bother to vote in elections to it. This danger, which bedevils local authority and European Parliament elections, must be a very real one. Elections for the Mayor of London and the London authority yielded, in 2000 and 2004, a turnout of just 34%, and in 2008 a turnout of 45%, even though the mayoral election attracted candidates with a high public profile; and the functions of local authorities are rather clearer than those of the new upper house would be. Elections to the upper house would, in addition, be unlikely to attract candidates with a high public profile; such people would probably still prefer to enter the Commons in the hope of becoming ministers.

If the electoral system for the new house were to be based on Westminster constituencies, there would be some danger of members of the upper house competing with MPs in representing their constituencies, and MPs could not be expected to welcome such competition. It would be difficult for two representatives to represent the same constituency on a nearly equal basis. If, however, the electoral system were to be based on a regional party list system of proportional representation, as with the European elections, it would be difficult for independent-minded candidates to secure election. Nomination for a high position on a regional list by one of the major parties would be a near-guarantee of election. Thus, the electoral process would turn into a species of nomination. An open list system, whereby there was some choice of candidate, might not prove much more effective since few of the candidates in large regional constituencies would be known to the voters, and so it would be difficult for voters to choose between them on the basis of genuine knowledge.

The vote in the House of Commons in March 2007 undoubtedly created a new political climate in favour of a 'popular' upper house. But an upper house elected on a low turnout and peopled with anonymous nonentities whose only qualification is long party service would be likely to devalue democracy rather than improve it.

Whatever the theoretical imperfections of the Lords, few criticize it for what it does or the way it carries out its tasks. Admittedly, survey evidence has shown that the public favours a directly elected chamber. The members of the Wakeham Royal Commission on the House of Lords, which reported in 2000, were told by many witnesses that the Lords should be elected.. The witnesses were then asked whether they favoured an upper house which replicated the Commons with its confrontational politics and whipped majorities. They of course did not. They wanted an upper house without party politicians which could continue to undertake the valuable work currently done by the House of Lords. Yet, in every modern elected upper house, elections are organised by political parties and run by professional politicians.

To achieve a 'popular' upper house will tax to the full the ingenuity of reformers. For this reason, the present 'temporary' state of the House of Lords may remain for longer than many imagine. What is certain is that an elected upper house, should it ever come about, would have two fundamental consequences. It would make the upper house more rather than less powerful; and it would, as a result, make Britain more difficult to govern.

7

The Referendum

UNTIL 1975, WHEN Britain held her first and, so far, only national referendum, the British constitution knew nothing of the people. The sovereignty of Parliament was seen as being incompatible with that of the people. Democracy in Britain was understood as being exclusively representative democracy. The referendum of 1975 on the issue of whether Britain should remain in the European Community, which she had joined in 1973, was preceded by a good deal of principled argument as to whether it would or would not be 'constitutional' for a sovereign Parliament to agree to hold a referendum. Yet, the referendum was adopted, not for reasons of high-flown constitutional principle, but to contain a damaging internal argument within the Labour Party. Even so, the abstract arguments deployed in the 1970s now seem, in retrospect, somewhat quaint. If Parliament is sovereign, if Parliament can do anything it chooses, then surely it can, if it so wishes, choose to hold a referendum. What Parliament cannot do, according to one version at least of the doctrine of parliamentary sovereignty, is to legally bind itself, either to hold a referendum on any particular issue or to accept the outcome of a referendum. Parliament can always, if it so chooses, ignore the outcome, however politically unwise that might be. The referendum in Britain, so it may seem, can be only advisory, not legally binding.

Although the referendum on the European Community in 1975 was seen by the government as a unique issue and as setting no precedent, it has been the precursor to further referendums, albeit at sub-national rather than national level. These have been on devolution to Scotland, Wales and Northern Ireland, and the establishment of a Greater London Authority and a directly elected mayor. There have also been a number of purely local referendums on a wide range of subjects, but most notably septennial referendums in 'dry' counties in Wales on the Sunday opening of public houses, and, in local authorities, on whether to adopt a directly elected mayor system. There can be little doubt, therefore, that the referendum has now become part of the British constitution. There is, however, considerable disagreement over its role. Under what circumstances is it appropriate or proper for a government to hold a referendum? Are there any issues on which governments should normally be **required** to hold referendums? Some democracies with codified constitutions answer these questions by providing both for the circumstances under which referendums may legitimately be held, and also for the occasions when governments are required to hold them. In a country with an uncodified constitution, however, it is not possible to derive definitive answers to these questions. All that one can do is to rely on precedent, on the sometimes messy lessons of the past.

Although Britain is unusual amongst democracies in lacking a codified constitution, the adoption of the referendum puts her in line with almost every other democracy. Most democracies employ the referendum. Amongst countries which have been continuously democratic since the 1940s, only Germany, India, Israel, Japan and the United States have not used referendums at national level. Only these countries are 'pure' representative democracies. But, in the United States, 'pure' representative democracy is heavily qualified since many of the individual states and their local governments employ the referendum frequently, and all of the states, with the sole exception of Delaware, require a referendum to alter their constitutions.

Yet most democracies use referendums only very infrequently. Switzerland, which has on average around one national referendum a year, is far from being typical. It is in fact very much the exception. Switzerland has held around half of all of the national referendums that have ever been held.[1] Australia and Italy are the only other democracies to have used referendums at national level at all frequently. No other democracy has held more than 45 nationwide referendums.

The experience of other democracies shows that, contrary to what many in Britain feared in the 1970s, the referendum is not addictive, leading inevitably to the subversion of parliamentary government. The holding of a single referendum does not make it likely that a country will follow Switzerland in referring a large range of issues to the people. The norm for referendums is not Switzerland but rather countries such as Austria or Norway which hold them very infrequently.

The referendum serves not to **replace** the machinery of representative government, but only to **supplement** it. The machinery of representative government remains, but certain issues, either before or after they are scrutinised by the legislature, are put to the people for their approval. A measure still requires scrutiny by the legislature before it can become law. But, where there is provision for the referendum, the measure undergoes an extra measure of scrutiny before it reaches the statute book. The dichotomy between 'representative' and 'direct' democracy is, therefore, a highly misleading one. Use of instruments of 'direct' democracy is intended not as an alternative to the mechanisms of the representative system, but as a complement to them. Referendums, it has been said, are 'intricately intertwined with the institutions and agents of representative democracy'.[2] That is true even of Switzerland, the supposed home of 'direct democracy'.

---

[1] See D Butler and A Ranney (eds) *Referendums Around the World* (Washington, American Enterprise Institute, 1994).

[2] M Mendlessohn and A Parkin, 'Introduction: Referendum Democracy' in Mendlessohn and Parkin, *Referendum Democracy: Citizens, Elites and Deliberation in Referendum Campaigns* (Houndmills, Palgrave, 2001) 4.

Seen in this light, the people, acting through referendum, take on the function of a third chamber of the legislature, in addition to the lower and upper houses; and, as with an upper house, the effect of a referendum must, as a matter of logic, be conservative in the sense that the people can only veto legislation, but not initiate it. Thus, legislation, if it is to reach the statute book, needs to surmount three hurdles not two—the lower house, the upper house and the people. The referendum, then, is, as a matter of logic, a conservative weapon. It is hardly surprising that it has been more strongly supported by those opposed to change than by radicals and social democrats. At the end of the nineteenth century, the anthropologist, Sir Henry Maine, argued that Britain's progress had depended entirely on popular opinion being kept at bay. If the public had had its way, Maine believed, there would have been 'no reformation of religion, no change of dynasty, no toleration of Dissent, not even an accurate calendar. The threshing machine, the power loom, the spinning jenny and possibly the steam engine would have been prohibited'.[3] Maine's fears are sometimes echoed on the Left today, and some on the Left use arguments against the referendum which would not have been out of place had they been used by conservatives against the Great Reform Act of 1832, such as that the issues are too complex for the public to understand and that, in any case, there is no pressing popular demand for public participation.

The power of the referendum can be seen not only by evaluating the referendums which have in fact been held, but also by the policies which might have been implemented in the absence of a referendum commitment. There is a good example of this from recent British experience. Tony Blair, Prime Minister from 1997 to 2007, was an advocate of Britain entering the euro zone. Yet he was unable to implement this policy, in part because he had promised to put the issue to the people. Every single opinion poll taken during his premiership showed that the majority were hostile to entry. Without the referendum, therefore, Britain might well now be part of the euro zone.

Democracies employ referendums primarily to resolve three different kinds of issue. They are used, first, to resolve constitutional issues. Referendums are often used when new constitutions are drawn up, as in France in 1958, the year of the launch of the Fifth Republic, or for major changes in the rules such as a change in the electoral system, as in New Zealand in 1993. In some countries—Australia, Denmark and Ireland, for example—amendments to the constitution require approval in a referendum before they can be put into effect. The argument for such a provision is that fundamental changes should not be implemented without the consent of the people.

Secondly, referendums are used to resolve territorial issues according to the principle of self-determination. A referendum was held, for example, in Greenland in 1979, on the issue of whether it wanted home rule within Denmark, and Quebec in 1980 on whether it should become independent from Canada. In the United Kingdom, the 1973 border poll asked voters in Northern Ireland whether they

---

[3] Sir Henry Maine, *Popular Government* (4th edn, London, John Murray, 1890) 88.

wished to remain within the United Kingdom or to join with the Republic of Ireland; and the 1998 Belfast Agreement confirmed the provision in the Northern Ireland Constitution Act of 1973 that Northern Ireland shall not cease to be a part of the United Kingdom without the consent of the people of Northern Ireland expressed in a border poll. It is also generally accepted that a referendum would be required before Scotland could become independent. Issues of this kind involve deep problems of nationality and allegiance. Political parties, based as they are primarily on socio-economic cleavages, are often divided in their approach to them; and, like other constitutional changes, territorial changes are often in practice irreversible. Both constitutional and territorial issues go beyond the mandate that legislators are given at a general election, in that they involve altering the framework of the political system within which policies are decided.

Thirdly, referendums have been held on what might be called 'moral' issues such as divorce or the prohibition of alcohol. These issues also often cut across the normal divisions of party politics, setting politicians from within the same political camp against each other; and, although they may arouse deep feelings amongst many voters, they are generally not the prime issues on which general elections are decided. In Britain referendums have been held in Wales in 1961, 1968, 1975 and 1982 on the Sunday opening of licensed premises. There have, however, been hardly any calls for national referendums in Britain on such 'moral' issues.

II

Britain's one national referendum was held in 1975 when voters were asked, 'Do you think that the United Kingdom should stay in the European Community (the Common Market)?' On a 65% turnout, the outcome was that around 65% of those voting answered 'Yes', with the remaining 35% answering 'No'.

All other referendums in Britain have been sub-national. The 1975 referendum had been preceded in 1973 by the border poll in Northern Ireland, designed to discover whether the people of Northern Ireland wished to remain in the United Kingdom. The value of this poll was much diminished since the parties representing the Nationalist minority advised their supporters to boycott the poll. Nevertheless, on a 58% turnout the outcome was that over 98% of those voting cast their votes for Northern Ireland to remain part of the United Kingdom.

> 591,820 for Northern Ireland to remain part of United Kingdom.
> 6,463 for Northern Ireland to be joined with the Republic of Ireland.

The border poll is the only referendum to have been held under a Conservative government. All other referendums so far have been held under Labour governments, but were first proposed by the Party in opposition, not in office.

In 1979 referendums were held in Scotland and Wales as to whether the Scotland and Wales Acts of 1978 should be implemented. The results were as follows:

Should the Scotland Act, 1978, be implemented? Turnout 63%.

52% Yes.
48% No.

Although a majority of those voting favoured implementation of the Scotland Act, this majority was insufficient since Parliament had laid down the additional requirement that 40% of the registered electorate, in addition to a majority of those voting, would have to vote 'Yes'. In the referendum, however, only 33% of the registered electorate voted 'Yes', and the Scotland Act was accordingly repealed in 1979.

Should the Wales Act, 1978, be implemented? Turnout 58%.

20% Yes.
80% No.

The Wales Act was repealed in 1979.

When, after eighteen years in opposition, the Labour Party returned to power in 1997, it proceeded once again to seek to implement devolution. This time, however, the government decided to hold referendums **before** introducing legislation into Parliament rather than **after** it had been passed by Parliament; and in Scotland, voters were asked, in addition to whether they wanted a Parliament, whether they wished it to have a limited taxing power, the power to vary income tax by threepence in the pound.

The outcome of the 1997 devolution referendums was as follows:

Scotland

61% turnout

Establishment of Scottish Parliament	Yes 74%	No 26%
Limited taxing powers	Yes 64%	No 36%

Wales

50% turnout

Establishment of Welsh Assembly	Yes 50.3% No 49.7%

The Scotland bill and a Government of Wales bill were, accordingly, introduced into Parliament and reached the statute book in 1998.

In 1998 a referendum was held in Northern Ireland, in which voters were asked to endorse the Belfast Agreement, providing for a partnership system of devolution in the province, together with a North-South Council to develop cooperation between Northern Ireland and the Republic of Ireland, and a British/Irish Council to encourage cooperation between Britain, Ireland, the various devolved bodies and the Crown dependencies, the Isle of Man and the Channel Islands. On an 80% turnout, 71% of those voting endorsed the Belfast Agreement, while 29% rejected it. On the same day, 95% of those voting in the Irish Republic endorsed the Agreement.

Referendums have also been held in two regions of England. The first, in 1998, asked voters in Greater London whether they favoured proposals for a Greater

London Authority comprising a directly elected mayor and assembly. The outcome was that, on a 34% turnout, 72% voted 'Yes' while 28% voted 'No'. A Greater London Authority bill was therefore introduced into Parliament, reaching the statute book in 1999.

Finally, in 2004, a referendum was held in the north-east on whether the region wanted a directly elected assembly. On a 48% turnout, the proposal was heavily defeated, with just 22% voting 'Yes', and 78% voting 'no'.

In addition to the referendums that have actually been held, various Acts of Parliament require referendums to be held in certain circumstances. The Northern Ireland Act of 1998 had provided that Northern Ireland cannot cease to be a part of the United Kingdom without the consent of a majority of those voting in a referendum. By the provisions of the Regional Assemblies (Preparation) Act of 2003, a directly elected regional assembly in England cannot be established without the consent of a majority in the region concerned in a referendum; and by the provisions of the Government of Wales Act of 2006, the National Assembly of Wales shall not be granted primary legislative powers without the consent of a majority of the voters in Wales in a referendum.

Between 2000 and 2007 any local authority which wished to be governed by a directly elected mayor was required, under the provisions of the Local Government Act of that year, to secure the consent of a majority of the voters in the particular local authority area in a referendum; but this requirement was removed by the Local Government and Public Involvement in Health Act of 2007. A local authority may, if it so chooses, hold a referendum before instituting a directly elected mayor, but it is no longer required to do so.

As well as referendums actually held, and statutorily required, referendums have been promised before two major policy changes will be legislated. The first, that Britain will not join the euro zone without a referendum was made by Tony Blair in 1996, before becoming Prime Minister, and is supported by all three parties; the second, that the electoral system for elections to the House of Commons will not be changed without a referendum was also made by Tony Blair before becoming Prime Minister. It was reiterated in the Labour Party election manifesto of 2005, which declared that 'A referendum remains the right way to agree to any change for Westminster'.

A referendum was also promised by Tony Blair in 2005 as part of the ratification process of the European constitution or constitutional treaty. This treaty was, however, declared defunct after having been rejected by the French and Dutch in their national referendums, and a new amending treaty, the treaty of Lisbon, was agreed in its place. Critics claimed that the Lisbon treaty replicated the bulk of the constitution, but the government of Gordon Brown, who succeeded Blair as Prime Minister in 2007, argued that there were significant differences between the two documents and that the referendum promise no longer applied.

The various referendums so far held, statutorily required and promised, are listed in the table below.

THE REFERENDUM IN BRITAIN.

A. REFERENDUMS HELD.

1. **1973. Northern Ireland Border poll. 59% turnout.**

   591,820 for Northern Ireland to remain part of United Kingdom.
   6,463 for Northern Ireland to be joined with the Republic of Ireland.

2. **1975. Referendum on EEC membership. (The only nationwide referendum so far held.)**

   'Do you think that the United Kingdom should stay in the European Community (the Common Market)?' 65% turnout

   65% Yes
   35% No

3. **1979. Should the Scotland Act, 1978 be implemented? Turnout 63%**

   52% Yes (33% of electorate)
   48% No

4. **1979. Should the Wales Act, 1978 be implemented? Turnout 58%**

   20% Yes
   80% No

5. **1997. 61% turnout.**

Establishment of Scottish Parliament	**Yes 74%**	**No 26%**
Limited taxing powers	**Yes 64%**	**No 36%**

6. **1997. 50% turnout.**

   Establishment of Welsh Assembly Yes 50.3% No 49.7%.

7. **London. 34% turnout**

   72% Yes to government proposals for Greater London Authority with a directly elected mayor and council.
   28% No

7. **1998. Northern Ireland. Belfast Agreement. 80% turnout.**

   Yes 71%
   No 29%

8. **2004. Regional Assembly in North-East. 48% turnout.**

   Yes 22%.
   No 78%

B. REFERENDUMS STATUTORILY REQUIRED:

1. Before Northern Ireland ceases to be part of the United Kingdom.
2. Before any regional assembly can be established in England.
3. Before primary legislative powers can be granted to the National Assembly of Wales.

C. REFERENDUMS PROMISED:

1. On the euro.
2. On electoral reform.
3. On the European constitution.

III

Referendums have been held in Britain in widely differing political circumstances. The 1975 referendum on the European Community was called to reconcile opposing factions in the Labour Party. During the referendum campaign, all three major parties supported continued British membership of the Community. Those favouring a 'No' vote, included a minority of the Cabinet, led by unpopular Left-wingers such as Michael Foot and Tony Benn, Enoch Powell from the Ulster Unionist benches, Rev. Ian Paisley from the Democratic Unionist Party, and the National Front, precursor of the BNP, all of whom were widely perceived as extremists. An expert on opinion surveys, who conducted polls for the 'Yes' campaign, commented that 'One strong card in our hands now is that the major public figures advocating EEC membership are relatively popular, while those advocating leaving the EEC are relatively unpopular'; a private poll conducted for the Britain in Europe campaign showed that in a list of the twenty best-known politicians, the thirteen pro-Marketeers each attracted a high 'respect and like' rating, while the anti-Marketeers in general received negative rating, with maximum dislike being aroused by Tony Benn, Ian Paisley and Enoch Powell.[4] Thus, it is possible that the large 'yes' majority was less a vote of confidence in the European Community than a vote against the unpopular extremists who were campaigning against it.

The outcome of the 1975 referendum was fortunate for the government. A 'No' result would have led to a convulsion in British politics. Two popular senior Cabinet ministers—Roy Jenkins and Shirley Williams—had indicated that they would resign, and Shirley Williams declared that she would leave politics entirely. The government would have been forced to the humiliating expedient of preparing legislation to take Britain out of the European Community, even though it had argued strongly during the referendum in favour of membership. The government would have had to prepare legislation for a cause to which the majority were opposed.

It was fortunate, also, that the referendum produced a similar outcome in England and Scotland, with both countries returning large 'Yes' majorities. The SNP campaigned in Scotland for a 'No' vote, hoping, no doubt, to boost its support by declaring that Westminster was keeping Scotland in the European community against the wishes of the Scottish people. The SNP was in fact the only major party in Scotland to campaign for a 'No' vote. A 'Yes' vote in England, combined with a 'No' vote in Scotland could have posed serious problems for the legitimacy of the British government in Scotland, and might well have boosted support for Scottish separatism.

The 1975 referendum achieved the main political aim of its supporters, for the time being at least, by maintaining the unity of the Labour Party. But the cross-

[4] Bogdanor, *The People and the Party System*, 46.

party alliances during the campaign amongst the 'Yes' camp played some part, surely, in persuading members of the right wing of the Labour Party that they might have more in common with the Liberals than with some of their party colleagues on the Left. From this point of view, the referendum campaign can be seen as a prelude to the later split in the Labour Party, in 1981, and the formation of the breakaway SDP (Social Democratic Party). On the other hand, if the Labour government had been more successful politically, and had won the 1979 general election, the breakaway would probably not have occurred. Therefore, the referendum offered the Labour Party a chance to maintain its unity, a chance which it did not take.

The referendum also succeeded in resolving, for the time being at least, the question of Britain's relationship with Europe. It legitimised entry into the Community. The holding of the referendum can be justified, not only from the point of view of party politics, to hold the Labour Party together, but also in wider terms, as an essential means of securing legitimacy for Britain's continued membership of the Community. Entry into the European Community was, surely, one of a small number of issues which could not be legitimised by Parliament alone, but needed, also, a positive vote of the people, a popular and democratic mandate. One of Harold Wilson's advisers was later to comment that 'Edward Heath had in 1972 taken the British political establishment into Europe. Harold Wilson and James Callaghan now brought in a majority of the British people'.[5] One journalist declared that 'The Common Market issue is settled. By their unambiguous vote—the most overwhelming expression of popular will, certainly since 1931 . . . Secession is now politically inconceivable in this generation'.[6] That judgment proved, of course, to be an exaggeration. The losing side was not fully committed to accepting the outcome. Admittedly, when the result was declared, Tony Benn said

> 'I have just been in receipt of a very big message from the British people. I read it loud and clear . . . By an overwhelming majority the British people have voted to stay in and I am sure that everybody would want to accept that. That has been the principle of all us who have advocated the Referendum'.[7]

By 1981, however, the Labour Party Conference, under Benn's guidance, had committed the party to withdrawal from the European Community without a further referendum, and that was the policy outlined in Labour's 1983 election manifesto. Today, the issue of Britain's membership of the European Union and the terms of that membership still remain open. Thus, the referendum could not provide a final solution to the question of Britain's relations with Europe. That, however, is not an argument against the referendum. It is not as if there is any alternative institutional mechanism which can provide a final solution to complex and difficult issues of nationality and allegiance. Finality, as Disraeli once noted, is not the language of politics.

[5] B Donoghue, *The Heat of the Kitchen* (London, Politico's, 2004) 180.
[6] D Watt, Financial Times, 7 June 1975, cited in Bogdanor, *The People and the Party System*, 42.
[7] Butler and Kitzinger, *The 1975 Referendum*, 273.

The 1975 referendum could be regarded as, on the whole, a success. But, it was successful, in large part, for fortuitous reasons which would not necessarily be repeated in future referendums.

The 1975 referendum was regarded as a unique and unrepeatable event. The preface to the 1975 White Paper, *Referendum on UK Membership of the European Community*, declared 'The referendum is to be held because of the *unique* nature of the issue'.[8] After the referendum, a Conservative backbencher asked the Prime Minister, Harold Wilson 'Will he keep to his determination not to repeat the constitutional experiment of the Referendum?' The Prime Minister replied, 'I certainly give the Right Honourable member . . . the assurance he seeks'.[9]

A junior minister had explained before the referendum why the European issue was unique.

'I have made it absolutely clear that in my view and that of the Government, the constitutional significance of our membership of the EEC is of a quite different order from any other issue. It is not just that it is more important; it is of a different order. There is, and there can be, no issue that is on all fours with it. That is why we say that this issue is the sole exception to the principle that we normally operate through parliamentary democracy'.[10]

The weakness of this argument had been exposed by Roy Jenkins, who had resigned in 1972 from Labour's Shadow Cabinet, because he was opposed in principle to the referendum. He rejected the claim that the European referendum would be unique:

'Who can possibly say that? Once the principle of the referendum has been introduced into British politics it will not rest with one party to put a convenient limit to its use'.[11]

Within just 18 months of the European Community referendum, the Labour government found itself committed, as a result of back-bench pressure, to concede referendums on devolution to Scotland and Wales. What the referendum of 1975 had done was to create a new method of validating laws.

In introducing the Scotland and Wales bill into Parliament in 1976, the Prime Minister, James Callaghan, declared that the government had not yet made up its mind whether or not to hold a referendum. But his hand was forced by an amendment put forward by a Welsh back-bench opponent of devolution, Leo Abse, MP for Pontypool, inviting MPs not to approve the Second Reading of the bill unless a referendum clause was added to it. This amendment attracted 80 signatures and the government, fearing defeat by its own back-benchers, decided to put forward its own referendum amendment.

This concession, however, was not sufficient to secure the passage of the Scotland and Wales bill. The government failed in March 1977 in its attempt to

---

[8] Cmnd 5925, 1975, 2. Emphasis added.
[9] House of Commons Debates, Vol 893, col 37, 9 June 1975.
[10] House of Commons Debates, vol 881, cols 1742–3, 22 November 1974.
[11] *The Times*, 11 April 1972, cited in Bogdanor, *The People and the Party System*, 48.

guillotine it, and was forced to abandon it. The devolution legislation was then reintroduced in the 1977–78 session in the form of two bills, one for Scotland and one for Wales. But, on 25 January 1978—Burns night—George Cunningham, an expatriate Scot who was Labour MP for Islington South and Finsbury—introduced an amendment which required an Order for repeal of the Scotland Act to be laid before Parliament unless 40% of the *electorate*—as well as a majority of those voting—supported it in the referendum. The argument for this proposal was, according to Cunningham, that many MPs were sceptical of the value of devolution, but were prepared to support it if they could be convinced that there was an overwhelming demand for it. The 40% requirement was a method of testing whether such a demand existed. If turnout were high—80%—then a 50% 'yes' vote would meet the requirement; with a 70% turnout, there would need to be a 57% 'Yes' vote; and with a 60% turnout, a 67% 'yes' vote would be needed. Although opposed by the government, the Cunningham amendment was passed by the Commons, and became part of the Scotland and Wales Acts, which were given the Royal Assent in 1978. The referendums were to be held in March 1979.

Despite the hurdle of the Cunningham amendment, the government could feel reasonably confident that devolution would win popular approval. In Wales, opinion surveys showed that voters were fairly evenly divided over the merits of devolution, while in Scotland, there seemed a large majority in favour of it. The main criticism in Scotland seemed to be that the legislation was too timid, yielding too few powers to the proposed Scottish Assembly, rather than that it was unwanted by the people of Scotland. But, during the 'winter of discontent' in early 1979, the series of public sector strikes which paralysed the economy, opinion began to move against devolution, partly no doubt because the issue was associated with a government that was becoming increasingly unpopular.

In Wales, devolution was defeated by a four to one majority. This was despite the fact that the Wales Act had been supported by three of the four political parties in Wales—Labour, the Liberals and Plaid Cymru—parties which had gained 76% of the Welsh vote in the previous general election held in October 1974, and were to receive 66% of the Welsh vote in the 1979 general election—and opposed only by the Conservatives who had received just 24% of the Welsh vote in October 1974, and were to receive 32% in the 1979 general election. The outcome, therefore, showed the fallacy of the mandate theory according to which a vote for a political party in a general election is also an endorsement of the main planks of its programme. The effect of the referendum was to ensure that a major constitutional change, opposed by a large majority of the Welsh electorate, was not implemented against the wishes of that electorate.

In Scotland, there was a 'Yes' majority, but a majority—33%—falling far short of the 40% hurdle. The SNP argued that, since the referendum had yielded a 'Yes' majority, the government should proceed to implement devolution. The 40% rule, they claimed, lacked legitimacy, since there had been no similar rule in the previous referendum, in 1975, on the European Community. The government could not afford to neglect pressures from the SNP. At the time the devolution referendums were held, the Callaghan government was in a minority in the Commons, dependent for its majority on the support of nationalist MPs. To have any chance of victory in the general election, due no later than October 1979, the government desperately needed time to recover from its unpopularity. The Callaghan government, it appears, made soundings amongst its back-benchers to discover whether there was support for implementing devolution, or, at the very least, for maintaining the Scotland Act on the statute book. But it found that English Labour back-benchers, never particularly well-disposed to Scottish devolution, would not support such a course. The SNP, accordingly, withdrew its support from the government; and in a vote of confidence on 28 March 1979—four weeks after the referendums—the government was defeated by one vote, the first government to be defeated on a confidence vote in the Commons since the first Labour government—also a minority government—in 1924. In the ensuing general election on 3 May 1979, the Conservatives, under Margaret Thatcher, won an overall majority of 43. They were to remain in power for eighteen years.

When Labour returned to power under Tony Blair in 1997, it was once again committed to devolution. But Blair was well aware of the difficulties of getting such a complex measure through a House of Commons in which, after all, the majority of MPs represented English constituencies and saw no advantage for their constituents in devolution for Scotland and Wales. It was for this reason that Blair had insisted that referendums be held in Scotland and Wales, and that these be held **before** legislation was introduced into Parliament, rather than **after** it was on the statute book, as in 1979. By doing this, he succeeded in disarming English critics of devolution, since it would be difficult for them to oppose a measure which had already been endorsed by voters in Scotland and Wales. As a result of the positive outcome of the referendums, the devolution legislation was able to reach the statute book without too much difficulty.

Both in 1979 and in 1997, the government was criticised for restricting the referendums to voters registered in Scotland and Wales. Devolution, critics argued, affected England as much as Scotland and Wales, and it could disadvantage England if powerful pressures from the devolved bodies were to lead to funds being attracted to Scotland and Wales at the expense of England. Devolution, it was claimed, altered the constitution as a whole, and not merely the method of governing Scotland and Wales. It would affect the rights as well as the material interests of English voters and taxpayers.

This criticism, however, failed to grasp the political purpose of devolution. It was intended to meet Scottish and Welsh grievances, and, in so doing, to hold the United Kingdom together. In strict logic, no doubt, English voters had as much right to vote on devolution as the Scots and Welsh. But the whole purpose of devolution would be frustrated if, in a national referendum, it were to be supported by the Scots and Welsh, but defeated thanks to an English majority against it. The Commons, therefore, which contains a majority of English MPs, may be conceived of as waiving the rights of their English constituents to a vote in the interests of good relations between the different parts of the United Kingdom. The future of the kingdom would appear to rest on the English continuing to exercise self-restraint, and not using the power which they undoubtedly possess to overrule the wishes of the minority nations. Therefore, although no doubt the English had a theoretical right to vote in the referendum, that was a right which, in the interest of preserving the unity of the United Kingdom, it would be prudent for them not to exercise.

The devolution referendums of 1979 were the only ones, with the exception of the referendum on devolution in the north-east in 2004, to fail to endorse the policy of the government of the day. But, by contrast with the 1979 referendums, the defeat in 2004 had few political consequences for the government, which was able to drop its programme of devolution to the English regions without much damage to its reputation. But, on both occasions voters may have been using the referendum as an opportunity to punish the government—in 1979 for the 'winter of discontent', and in 2004 for being somewhat remote. Instead of answering the question, 'Do you want devolution?' they were perhaps answering another question, 'Do you want the government to continue in office?' That of course is always a danger with a referendum. It may even take on the character of a vote of confidence in the government, as it did in 1979. When that happens, it comes to be used as an instrument of recall, to oust an unpopular government before it has reached the end of its term.

All of the referendums that have been held, with the exception of the referendum on Scottish devolution in 1979, and that on Welsh devolution in 1997, have produced clear and indisputable outcomes, thereby fulfilling the first requirement for a successful referendum. There could, in the case of all the referendums except that held in Scotland in 1979, be little doubt as to the message which the people were seeking to transmit to the government, and no quarrel with the outcome.

The referendums on the European Community and on devolution in 1979 were held largely because the governing party was divided on the merits of the issue. The referendum was brought into play because it seemed that major constitutional issues could not be resolved through the normal working of the party system. On 'moral' issues such as capital punishment or abortion where governments in the 1960s and 1970s often found themselves divided, they found the answer in the device of a free vote in the Commons. On constitutional issues, the answer was the referendum, a free vote in the country.

But the issue of legitimacy also arises. There are some issues of such fundamental importance that a parliamentary verdict is by itself insufficient to ensure legitimacy. Issues of territorial allegiance are likely to fall into this class. Many would argue that the return of an SNP majority to the Scottish Parliament or to Westminster ought not to be sufficient as a mandate for the break-up of the United Kingdom; the opinion of the Scottish people ought also to be sought through a referendum. The same type of argument would apply to a major change in the political system such as a change in the electoral system, a change which could easily be adopted for purely partisan purposes. In these cases, a referendum is needed to help secure legitimacy.

The referendum, then, is used to supplement the defects of representative democracy, not to replace them. Its future is largely bound up with the future of the mass party as it has developed in Britain since the nineteenth century. As Dicey, the first advocate of the referendum in Britain, noticed in 1915. 'It is certain that no man who is really satisfied with the working of our party system will ever look with favour on an institution which aims at correcting the vices of party government'.[12] The authority of political parties is much less than it was, and traditional tribal allegiances seem in process of dissolution. Therefore, the referendum is likely to remain a potent weapon in British politics.

IV

There can be little doubt, then, that the referendum is now very much part of the British constitution. But its place is uncertain, since there is no consensus on when referendums should be held, nor under what conditions they should be held. The suggestion that they should be held only on 'constitutional' issues is not particularly helpful in a country without a codified constitution. It may seem at first sight as if the lack of a codified constitution means that the precise role of the referendum must remain undefined. In a country without a codified constitution, it is difficult for there to be legal rules requiring a government to hold a referendum on a certain issue. An elastic constitution seems to imply an elastic use of the referendum. The implication is disquieting. It means that use of the referendum is, to some extent at least, at the discretion of the government of the day, although a government can of course be pushed into a referendum through the pressure of public opinion or recalcitrant back-benchers. But this gives rise to a paradox. If use of the referendum lies at the discretion of the government, how can it also constitutionally control the government? Part of the purpose of the referendum, after all, is to limit the power of government by requiring it to secure the support of the people before it can ensure that particular measures reach the statute book. It was first advocated in Britain by Dicey in 1890 to ensure that Irish Home Rule could not be implemented for so long as the British people were against it. Dicey believed, probably correctly, that the people were opposed to Home Rule, even though Parliament supported it. Later in the twentieth century the referendum was advocated by those who sought to make change more difficult on such matters as tariff reform between the wars and, in the 1970s, entry into the European Community. It was intended to be used, as Lord Beaverbrook, the newspaper magnate and an ardent advocate of tariff reform, suggested in 1930, 'not as a spear ... but as a shield'.[13] It was an instrument by means of which the electorate could check Parliament and government. The electorate would have the right to veto what Parliament had decided, or might decide.

---

[12]   A V Dicey, 'Introduction' in *Law of the Constitution* (8th edn, London, Macmillan, 1915) c.
[13]   Cited in K Middlemas and J Barnes, *Baldwin* (London, Weidenfeld and Nicolson, 1969) 571.

Yet, if use of the referendum is at the discretion of government, then, far from limiting the power of government, it could come to augment it, as it did in France during the early years of de Gaulle's Fifth Republic. The 1975 referendum was held not because the then government sincerely sought to discover the view of the British people on the European Community but to overcome opposition in the governing party. Similarly, the devolution referendums were held not because governments sought to discover the views of the Scots and the Welsh as to how they wanted to be governed, but to overcome the opposition of back-benchers from the governing party. Under these circumstances, the referendum becomes both a tactical weapon and a plebiscitary device. In the 1970s, Labour MPs who were opposed to devolution happily voted for the legislation, planning to campaign against devolution in the referendum which would occur after the legislation had been placed on the statute book. In that way, they could oppose devolution without endangering the future of their government. Malcolm Rifkind, one of the few Conservative supporters of devolution, thought that this was 'a unique constitutional matter that this Parliament is likely to put on the statute book a bill in which it does not believe'.[14] Enoch Powell, an Ulster Unionist back-bench opponent of devolution, was even more scathing. In a speech at Bexhill on 25 November 1977, he declared that it was:

> 'an event without precedent in the long history of Parliament . . . that members openly and publicly declaring themselves opposed to the legislation and bringing forward in debate what seemed to them cogent reasons why it must prove disastrous, voted nevertheless for the legislation and for a guillotine, with the express intention that after the minimum of debate the Bill should be submitted to a referendum of the electorate, in which they would hope and strive to secure its rejection'[15]

The referendum seemed to have become, in the words of one authority, 'the Pontius Pilate' of British politics.[16]

It would, however, be premature to regard the referendum wholly as a tactical device, to be used at the discretion of the government of the day. Decided upon largely for tactical reasons by politicians, precedents have now developed which it would be difficult for any future government to ignore. It would be wrong, therefore, to conclude that use of the referendum lies **wholly** within the discretion of governments.

The devolution referendums of the 1970s were certainly not originally intended by the government, but forced upon it by the opposition of back-benchers. Without the concession of the referendum there would have been no chance of getting the devolution legislation through Parliament. The concession of a referendum in 1975 had established a precedent, and it was now ruled that a referendum amendment could be introduced on an already published bill. It had previously been held that such a procedure was unconstitutional. The nineteenth

---

[14] House of Commons Debates, vol 994, col 595, 15 February 1978.

[15] Cited in V Bogdanor, *Devolution in the United Kingdom* (Oxford, OUP, 1999) 185.

[16] S E Finer (ed) *Adversary Politics and Electoral Reform* (London, Anthony Wigram, 1975) 18.

edition of Erskine May, the parliamentarian's bible, published in 1976, had declared that 'Amendments to a bill proposing that . . . the provisions of a bill should be subject to a referendum have been ruled out of order as proposing changes in legislative procedure which would be contrary to constitutional practice'.[17] The committee chair, however, declared that he would admit a motion providing for a referendum amendment to the Scotland and Wales bill, since the European Community referendum of 1975 had created a precedent—a graphic illustration of how the British constitution can be altered by the discretionary decision of a committee chair. The 1975 referendum had not itself been introduced as an amendment to an already published bill. Nevertheless, the ruling of 1976 means that it is open to backbenchers to attach a referendum clause to any bill which they believe should be referred to the people. This increases the power of backbenchers, not that of the government.

Nor should the role of public opinion be ignored. Public pressures were at least partly responsible for the commitment to the 1975 referendum and to the commitment made by all of the major parties in the 1990s to a referendum on the euro. It was strong enough to make Tony Blair feel, in 2005, that he had to promise a referendum on the proposed European constitution, though not, it appears, strong enough to pressure Gordon Brown to hold a referendum on the successor to the defunct constitution, the Lisbon treaty. It is of course possible that Gordon Brown may pay an electoral price for refusing to call a referendum on this treaty.

But the most important limitation to the discretion of the government in calling a referendum is that there have grown up a series of persuasive precedents as to the circumstances in which referendums should be called. These precedents perhaps give rise to a doctrine or even perhaps to a convention of the constitution.

The issues on which referendums have been held—the border poll in Northern Ireland, Europe, devolution—have been issues of territorial politics where, so it seemed, the party system did not work very effectively in resolving them. Issues such as the constitutional position of Northern Ireland, Europe and devolution may be regarded as fundamental. They were all connected, in practice, if not in theory, with issues of sovereignty, with the scope of Parliament's power. Should Parliament continue to rule Northern Ireland? Should Parliament subordinate itself to a superior law-making authority—the European Community? Should Parliament devolve power to Scotland and Wales? All these matters seemed to require validation from the people if they were to be seen as legitimate.

The 1973 border poll, and the commitment in the Northern Ireland Constitution Act of 1973, reiterated in the Belfast Agreement, would seem to indicate that a referendum should be held in the area concerned before any part of the kingdom is allowed to secede. That is a precedent that is likely to be applied to Scotland should the SNP win a majority of the parliamentary seats in Scotland in a general election or in a Scottish Parliament election.

---

[17] Sir David Lidderdale (ed) *Erskine May's Treatise on the Law, Privileges, Proceedings and Usage of Parliament* (19th edn, London, Butterworth and Co, 1976) 523.

The examples of the European Community referendum of 1975 and the referendum in London of 1998, seeking approval for the first directly elected mayor in British history, as well as the promises to hold a referendum before entering the eurozone or changing the electoral system for elections to the House of Commons, would seem to show that a referendum is required when a wholly novel constitutional arrangement is being proposed.

The examples of the devolution referendums in Scotland, Wales and Northern Ireland, as well as the referendum on regional devolution in the north east in 2004, would seem to show that a referendum needs to be held before there is any significant devolution of powers away from Westminster.

The referendum has so far been used not on bills which make changes, however radical, in the laws, but for legislative proposals which provide for **an alteration in the machinery by which the law is made.** There is a strong rationale for this requirement. It lies deep in liberal thought and was well stated by John Locke in his *Second Treatise of Government* (para 141): 'The Legislative cannot transfer the power of making laws to any other hands. For it being but a delegated power from the People, they who have it cannot pass it to others'. Voters, it might be said, entrust MPs as agents with legislative powers, but they give them no authority to transfer those powers, to make radical alterations in the machinery by which laws are to be made. Such authority, it may be suggested, can be obtained only through a specific mandate, that is, a referendum. The referendum, therefore, could be argued to be in accordance with, rather than in opposition to, basic principles of liberal constitutionalism. To this extent, the referendum is not simply an instrument at the discretion of government, but a potent weapon in British politics which can commit the political elite even perhaps against its wishes.

Locke's doctrine would also seem to imply that a referendum is required, not only when power is devolved 'downwards', but also when there is a substantial transfer of powers 'upwards' from Parliament to the European Union. However, there has not been a referendum on any of the five amending treaties to the Treaty of Rome—the Single European Act of 1986, which involved a very wide transfer of powers, the Maastricht Treaty of 1992, the Amsterdam Treaty of 1997, the Nice Treaty of 2000, nor the Lisbon Treaty of 2007. The promise of a referendum on the European constitution but not on the Lisbon Treaty could perhaps be defended on the grounds that the former was a wholly new constitution for the European Union, while the Lisbon Treaty was a mere amending treaty like the Single European Act and the succeeding amending treaties. Significantly, while nine Member States, including Britain, either held referendums or were proposing to do so on the constitution, only Ireland held one on the Lisbon Treaty, and that because she was required by her constitution to do so.

Nevertheless, by analogy with the referendums on devolution, there does seem a strong case in logic for arguing that there should be a referendum before major legislative powers are transferred upwards to the EU as well as downwards to devolved bodies. Were that doctrine to be accepted, it would have made for referendums on the Single European Act and Maastricht, but perhaps not on the

Amsterdam, Nice or Lisbon Treaties, none of which involved major transfers of powers—while the Lisbon Treaty provided for opt-outs for the United Kingdom for many, though not all, of the transfers. There is of course much room for argument as to which transfers of power are 'major' and which are not.

V

As has been seen, the 1979 referendums on the Scotland and Wales Acts are the only ones that have so far been held to ratify legislation already passed by Parliament, the referendum provision being therefore included in the clauses and schedules of the Scotland and Wales Acts of 1978. It therefore provided for the possibility of overriding a decision made by Parliament. The 1975 referendum, by contrast, was on the question of whether an Act, the European Communities Act, which had been on the statute book for three years, since 1972, should in effect be repealed. It sought to confirm or deny an arrangement already in existence. All of the other referendums were pre-legislative. They required, therefore, separate bills providing for referendums to be held. Clearly, separate legislation will always be needed if a referendum is to be held prior to legislation, although with a post-legislative referendum as in 1979, provision for the referendum can be provided for in the legislation itself.

It would, however, be possible to provide permanent legislative provision for the holding of referendums through a generic Referendum Act, as discussed by an independent Commission on the Conduct of Referendums in 1996.[18] The Commission regarded such an option as 'particularly attractive if referendums were to become a frequent event, or if it were proposed to hold a series of referendums' (para 59). This would save parliamentary time, since primary legislation would not be needed for every single referendum. Instead, there would be 'a consistent statutory framework for referendums comparable to that which the Representation of the People Act provides for the conduct of elections' (para 61). But, of course, MPs might then object that they were not given sufficient opportunity to debate the specific issues involved in particular referendums. Perhaps the referendum is not yet sufficiently established in British constitutional doctrine to make this option workable at the present time.

In countries with codified constitutions, the outcome of a referendum generally binds both parliament and government. In Britain, however, with an uncodified constitution, the position is much less clear. Although neither Parliament nor government can be legally bound, the government could agree in advance that it would respect the result, while a clear majority on a reasonably high turnout would leave Parliament with little option in practice other than to endorse the decision of the people. Shortly before the European Community referendum in

---

[18] Commission on the Conduct of Referendums: Constitution Unit and Electoral Reform Society (1996) 31. The author was a member of this Commission.

1975, Edward Short, then Leader of the House of Commons, insisted to the House that 'This referendum is wholly consistent with parliamentary sovereignty. The Government will be bound by its result, but Parliament, of course, cannot be bound'. He then added, 'Although one would not expect honourable members to go against the wishes of the people, they will remain free to do so'.[19] That was an accurate statement of the constitutional position only on the assumption that Short meant that the government would be morally bound. It could not be legally bound. For, in the purely formal sense, it was still the case that the British constitution knew nothing of the people.

It is worth asking, however, whether the authority of the people can be recognised under our constitution, which amounts to asking whether a referendum result could be mandatory rather than advisory, or whether the people must be held to have irretrievably delegated the authority to legislate to their elected representatives in the House of Commons. In 1653 Oliver Cromwell's Instrument of Government declared that legislative power resided in the person of the Lord Protector 'and the people'. Such a doctrine, however, does not seem to have survived the fall of Cromwell. At the beginning of the twentieth century, a leading constitutional theorist, Sir Frederick Pollock, remarked that an identical resolution passed by the electors of every constituency would have no legal force and no court would pay any attention to it.[20] Can a similar claim be made concerning the referendum? Clearly, no court would take any notice of a claim that Parliament had legislated on some issue without calling a referendum; nor would it take any notice of a claim that Parliament was ignoring a referendum result.[21] In form, therefore, the legal doctrine of the sovereignty of Parliament seems so far to have been preserved, just as it was preserved in the European Communities Act providing for Britain's entry into the European Community, in the devolution legislation, and in the Human Rights Act. In substance, however, as with these other measures, the sovereignty of Parliament is not what it was before 1975.

There seems no reason in principle, despite the doctrine of the sovereignty of Parliament, why a referendum result should not be mandatory in the sense that legislation passed by Parliament would automatically come into effect if there were a vote in favour, and automatically be rejected if there were a vote against. There is indeed a precedent, which may well not be binding, for a mandatory referendum—that is a referendum which, with a 'no' result would not come back to Parliament at all. When, in February 1977, the Callaghan government produced its referendum amendment to the Scotland and Wales bill, New Clause 40, this clause did originally provide for a mandatory referendum. The clause originally declared that 'If the decisions in the referendum are that no effect is to be given to the provisions of this Act, this Act . . . shall not take effect'.[22] Conversely, were the

---

[19] House of Commons Debates, vol 888, col 293, 11 March 1975.

[20] F Pollock, *A First Book of Jurisprudence* (5th edn, London, Macmillan 1923) 274.

[21] Unless it were to be accepted that Parliament could entrench legislation by requiring a referendum before it could be amended or repealed.

[22] House of Commons Debates, vol 926, cols 275ff, 15 February 1977.

referendum outcome to be favourable, the government would have been under a legal duty to bring forward a commencement order so that the devolved bodies could be established. Parliament would, of course, have the purely theoretical right to reject the commencement order. The government, however, changed its view during the course of the debate, and provided that the referendum be advisory and not mandatory. Nevertheless, it seems that it might be perfectly possible to frame a referendum provision by which legislation was **required** to come into effect with a 'Yes' vote, and required to be repealed with a 'No' vote; in other words, a mandatory referendum.

The 1979 referendums on the Scotland and Wales Acts are the only referendums on which a qualified majority of the electorate—40% in each case—as well as a majority of those voting, has been necessary to secure implementation. In all of the other referendums, Parliament seemed to be declaring that a simple majority of those voting would be sufficient.

These various precedents give rise to two major constitutional issues. The first is whether referendums should be held before legislation is introduced into Parliament, as with the devolution referendums in 1997, or, by contrast, after legislation has been passed by Parliament, as with the devolution referendums of 1979. The second is whether there should be a threshold requirement. This requirement could be either a minimum percentage of the electorate voting as well as a 'yes' majority as in 1979; or a minimum turnout. In Poland, for example, the outcome of a referendum is invalid unless at least 50% of the registered electorate turns out to vote. These two constitutional issues are, in part, as will be seen, inter-related.

In the Scotland and Wales Acts of 1978 the referendum requirement was incorporated into the legislation as a condition of its coming into operation. If, as in fact happened, the necessary 40% of the registered electorate was not achieved, the legislation obliged the government to lay a repeal order before Parliament. But Parliament was not obliged to pass this repeal order. The government could have asked MPs to reject it. The Callaghan government tried to do precisely this, in the case of Scotland where, after all, a majority had voted for devolution. According to Callaghan's predecessor as Prime Minister, Harold Wilson, in his memoir of the period:

> 'There had been some hope in the Cabinet that having laid the repeal order, their own supporters would vote the other way and keep devolution alive. But strenuous inquiries by the Government Whips revealed that some forty or so Government back benchers would join the Conservatives in killing devolution'.[23]

There would, nevertheless, appear to be a strong argument for holding a referendum before legislation is introduced into Parliament as with the devolution referendums of 1997. If there were to be a 'No' vote as occurred in Wales in 1979 and also, in effect, in Scotland, Parliament would save a great deal of its time. It would know that there was no great public demand for the legislation in question. Were

---

[23] H Wilson, *Final Term* (London, Weidenfeld and Nicolson/Michael Joseph, 1979) 213fn.

there to be a 'Yes' vote, on the other hand, Parliament could act as a kind of Grand Committee and concentrate on improving the legislation rather than party point-scoring. A 'Yes' vote would, admittedly, pre-empt, in practice, if not in law, Parliament's power to reject the legislation. But it would signal to Parliament that the people wanted its role to be that of a Grand Committee not an adversarial assembly. With a post-legislative referendum, by contrast, opponents of a measure have a positive incentive to use parliamentary procedures not to seek improvements to legislation since the better the legislation, the more attractive it will prove in a referendum.

With a post-legislative referendum, it might prove more difficult to dissociate the issue in question from the position of the government. A 'No' vote would appear as the rejection of a major piece of legislation in a government's programme, and the government may find it difficult, in such circumstances, to survive; and electors may be encouraged to vote 'No' as in 1979 not because they dislike the measure but because they dislike the government. With a pre-legislative referendum, by contrast, it is easier for a government to claim that it is carrying out a consultative exercise, as with the 2004 referendum on devolution in the north-east. The government might still be damaged by a 'No' vote, but the damage perhaps will not be quite so great.

The second constitutional issue is whether there should be a threshold, either in the form of a minimum turnout level or a minimum percentage of the registered electorate, for a referendum verdict to be successful. There are strong arguments against requiring such a threshold. It is very difficult to be precise on what constitutes a sufficient turnout or a sufficient majority. Suppose there were a 50% turnout threshold, and the outcome of a referendum was that 49% of the electorate voted 'Yes' and 10% 'No'. Then it would probably be reasonable to implement the measure concerned. If, on the other hand, the result were to be 25% 'Yes', and 22% 'No', it would probably be reasonable not to proceed. Despite the low, 34% turnout, in the referendum on the London mayor and assembly in 1998, the government, quite reasonably, took the view that, with a 72% 'yes' vote, the measure should be implemented.

Similar considerations hold when the threshold is in the form of a minimum percentage of the registered electorate being required to vote 'Yes'. In Denmark in 1939, there was a referendum on the abolition of the upper house, proposed by the government. 92% of those voting supported this measure. But, because turnout was low, this was less than 45% of the electorate—the then requirement in Denmark for constitutional change—it has since been lowered to 40%. Since the 45% requirement was mandatory, the government could not proceed with the change, even though over 9 out of 10 of those voting had supported it.

It would also seem that a threshold requirement in the form of a proportion of the registered electorate is likely to depress turnout. That is because a 'No' voter might believe that an abstention was equivalent to a 'No' vote, and that she need not, therefore, bother to turn up at the polls. Simply by staying at home, she would in effect be voting 'No'. An extraneous factor such as the weather on polling day may influence the result. Suppose that in the Scottish devolution referendum of 1979, turnout had been 80%, and the outcome had been 41% 'yes' and 39% 'No', but one-quarter of the abstainers had abstained in the belief that abstention was the same as voting 'No'. The true strength of the 'Nos' would be not 39% but 44%. A threshold, therefore, may confuse voters and produce an outcome which does not reflect their true intentions.

There is, however, a strong case for using a threshold in Northern Ireland where a simple majority, if composed largely of Unionists, will not be sufficient to yield legitimacy. Instead, a majority of those in both communities would be required. It is, however, difficult to ascertain the view of each community through a ballot other than by asking voters to label themselves 'Unionist' or 'Nationalist'. Therefore, a qualified majority large enough to ensure at least a substantial proportion, if not a majority, of the minority community, as well as of the majority community, would be needed. Where there is to be a threshold in a referendum, it should be in the form of a specific percentage of votes cast, rather than a percentage of the eligible electorate.

In other cases, however, it seems more in accordance with the constitution as it has developed to allow the government and Parliament to make the final decision after a referendum, using its own judgment where there is a narrow majority on a low turnout. The government and Parliament decided, no doubt rightly, not to allow Scottish devolution to go ahead in 1979 despite the small positive majority for it—33%–31%—far below the 40% threshold which Parliament had set. On a figure of 39% to 31%, however, the government would almost certainly have proposed to allow devolution to go ahead. It is, however, difficult to specify in advance the precise margin or size of turnout which would justify the government and Parliament in rejecting a referendum result. That is a matter perhaps best left to the discretion and judgment of MPs.

If the referendum is used before legislation is introduced into Parliament, its consultative nature becomes clear. It is then reasonable to suggest that, in difficult cases, it is for the government and Parliament to interpret the result of the consultation, although, of course, if the outcome is clear-cut and the turnout is large, they will have no choice. But there might be a stronger case for a turnout requirement in **local** referendums. The average turnout in local elections is under 40%, and there is some danger of vociferous local minorities imposing their policies on the apathetic majority, who do not bother to vote. It might be reasonable perhaps to require a turnout of, say, 40% for the outcome in local referendums to be accepted as valid.

VI

Early advocates of the referendum, such as Dicey, saw it as a weapon of entrenchment. One possible way of entrenching legislation might be to suggest that any future amendment or repeal of a particular bill should require a referendum. It would be natural to apply such a provision to legislation of fundamental constitutional importance such as devolution or the Human Rights Act. It might, for example, have been suggested that the devolved bodies in Scotland, Wales and Northern Ireland, which were established after referendums, could not be repealed without a referendum. Upon one interpretation of parliamentary sovereignty, this could not be done, since Parliament could simply ignore the referendum requirement and abolish the devolved bodies without any recourse to the people. The decision of one Parliament cannot, it might be argued, bind a later Parliament. Nothing can prevent later legislation from repealing earlier legislation. But it could be argued that the referendum requirement could be made a condition of a bill purporting to abolish a devolved body receiving the Royal Assent. The referendum requirement would then **redefine** what was to count as valid legislation on a particular topic. The Parliament Acts of 1911 and 1949 had redefined what was to count as valid legislation, by providing that a money bill could be passed without the consent of the House of Lords, and that a non-money bill could be passed without the consent of the House of Lords, provided that the same bill had been passed by the House of Commons in two successive sessions. From this perspective, the referendum requirement would be doing nothing more than laying down further rules for what was to count as valid legislation. There seems, therefore, no reason in principle why such a requirement should not be possible. This issue is further discussed in chapter 11.

If the referendum could be entrenched in this way, a step would have been taken towards removing it from the control of the political class. The referendum on a matter such as, for example, devolution, would have become legally obligatory, and not a matter for the discretion of the political class—although there may well already be circumstances in which use of the referendum has become *politically* obligatory. That would be an important change. So far, however, the referendum has been used only when the political class finds itself unable to resolve a problem; it is used primarily as a convenience for the political class, to avoid a party split or a backbench revolt. It is used primarily as a weapon to defuse political or parliamentary conflict. Far from subverting parliamentary government, therefore, the referendum may well have helped it work more smoothly.

But, precisely because it lies in the hands of the political class whether and when to use it, the referendum, although a valuable part of the new British constitution, is unlikely to be used very frequently; and when it is used it is likely to be as a tactical weapon. The referendum can be useful as a means of ascertaining opinion on fundamental issues, but it cannot of itself help to resolve the crisis of participation which has so preoccupied governments of all political colours in recent years. To achieve that something much more radical is needed. The central weakness of the referendum as a democratic instrument is precisely that it remains under the control of the political class. It is the political leaders, whether in government or opposition, who decide to commit their parties to holding a referendum. The people, although they can put pressure upon the political class, cannot, in Britain, as they can in Italy and Switzerland, *require* a referendum to be called. It is, therefore, somewhat misleading to speak of 'direct democracy' when the use of the referendum is controlled by political elites.[24] The key question, however, which we shall try to answer in chapter 12, is whether it can be taken out of the control of the political class. The referendum is now part of the new constitution. But it is a weapon for the political class, not the people. To make it a genuinely popular weapon would be to go beyond the new constitution.

[24] Mendlessohn and Parkin, *Referendum Democracy*, above n 2 at 4.

8

The New Government of London

I

SHELLEY DESCRIBED LONDON in one of his poems as 'that great sea, whose ebb and flow at once is deaf and loud, and onshore vomits its wrecks and still howls for more'. More people live in London than in either Scotland or Wales—around 7.5 million as compared to just over five million and three million respectively—yet there has been far less political controversy over the government of London than over the government of Scotland and Wales. It is not difficult to see why this should be so. In Scotland, one main motive, no doubt the predominant motive, for devolution was pressure from the Scottish nationalist party, the SNP, and a fear that if concessions were not made to the demand for Scottish autonomy, Scotland would secede, and Labour would lose an important part of its electoral heartland. There have been no similar pressures in London. There has been no London nationalist party threatening secession.

Scotland and Wales are clearly defined geographical national entities. London is not. The history of attempts to reform government in London has been bedevilled by arguments about what precisely is to count as 'London', what areas are to be included in it. Until 1963, London, from the administrative point of view, meant inner London, the area of the London County Council. In 1963, however, the Conservative government, by means of the London Government Act, established a new authority, the Greater London Council, which comprised, in addition to the old LCC area, nearly the whole of Middlesex and the suburban portions of Surrey, Kent, Essex and Hertfordshire. Some argued that even this enlarged area was not large enough since so many people commuted regularly into London from the South East region. But an authority comprising both London and the South East region would include around a quarter of the population of Britain. Therefore, the problem of what area is to comprise 'London' seemed to have been resolved, for the time being at least, by the definition of Greater London drawn up in the 1960s, an area roughly, though not wholly, coterminous with the area enclosed by the M25 motorway.

Even so, there is a much greater degree of social and political conflict within London than within Scotland, and this makes it more difficult to create a civic consciousness in London as strong as that in Scotland. London is a divided city politically. It is divided by social and ideological issues. Scotland no doubt is also divided. But the divisions within Scotland did not inhibit the formation of a genuine Scottish civic consciousness united around the demand for devolution. In the late nineteenth century, central government, in dealing with both Scotland and Wales, 'was mindful of a nationalist rhetoric which depicted Whitehall as a quasi-colonial occupier of the Celtic nations. By contrast, those living in the nation's administrative centre did not naturally think of Whitehall and Westminster as alien powers'. Londoners, admittedly, often complain of subsidising the rest of the country. But their complaints have never quite carried the punch of the SNP slogan of the 1970s, "It's Scotland's oil". 'Whatever the state of relations between Whitehall and County Hall, the language of London politics never contained the metaphors of occupation, even colonialism, to be found in nationalist debate'.[1] In addition, there is conflict in London both between the inner city and the suburbs, and also, as we shall see, between the interests of London as a whole and those of the boroughs. It is in fact the power of the boroughs which serves to differentiate London from other capital cities, and makes the problem of governing London so intractable.

In London, therefore, pressure for reform was much less strong than in Scotland and Wales, and such pressure as there was derived primarily from administrative considerations. The desire for change in London government has generally stemmed from the belief that a new system of government would produce better public services. That was what the early Fabians, Sidney Webb and H.G. Wells, thought when at the turn of the last century they sought regional government for London. They wanted the main public utilities—gas, electricity and water—as well as services such as transport, health and education—to be run by a unified metropolitan authority. This proposal, however, frightened those on the Right who feared municipal socialism and higher rates; there was also a fear that metropolitan government would be more remote from the ordinary ratepayer than smaller units of local government. Reform of London government, therefore, has always tended to be explicitly partisan. The Left has generally sought a strong city-wide layer of government, while the Right has tended to champion the rights of the boroughs, and in particular the outer, suburban boroughs.

In the post-1945 era the hopes for metropolitan government put forward by Fabians such as Webb and Wells were undermined, paradoxically, by a government of the Left, Clement Attlee's Labour government. The Attlee government nationalised the public utilities and established, contrary to the wishes of Herbert Morrison, leader of the London County Council from 1934 to 1940 and a prominent minister in the government, a centralised National Health Service, rather than a service accountable to local authorities. There was little prospect of the Attlee government decentralizing public services to local communities. Therefore, any London-wide authority would have to gain its powers not from central

---

[1] J Davis, 'The Government of London' in D Tanner, C Williams, W P Griffith and A Edwards (eds), *Debating Nationhood and Governance in Britain, 1885–1939* (Manchester, MUP, 2006) 213. This chapter gives an excellent brief account of the historical background to the problems of London government.

government, but from lower-level authorities i.e. the boroughs. This increased the tension between a London-wide authority and the boroughs.

Because the political pressures in London have been far less than those in Scotland and Wales, no government has seriously considered devolving extensive powers to a London-wide body, even though London has 150% of the population of Scotland and over twice the population of Wales. Because London is far more dominant within Britain than many other capital cities, a powerful government in London would compete with the national government. Australia, Canada and the United States have established capitals away from their dominant cities— Canberra rather than Sydney, Ottawa rather than Toronto, and Washington rather than New York—as did Germany, which had its capital city in Bonn until reunification. The most obvious comparison lies with Paris which contains nearly 10 million people out of a total French population of around 57 million. In both Britain and France governments have been frightened of creating a strong city government for the capital lest it threaten their own dominance. The position of mayor of Paris was not created until the late 1970s, and it was established then in the hope of mollifying Jacques Chirac after he had been dismissed from the premiership in 1976 by President Giscard d'Estaing. Chirac, however, proceeded to use the position of mayor of Paris to build a political base for himself; he founded a new party—'the Rassemblement pour la Republique'—and this enabled him to mount a challenge for the presidency. It is understandable if ministers in Britain are wary of creating a similar base for a political rival.

British governments, therefore, have no wish to create in London an authority which can compete with the centre. Both Lord Salisbury, the Conservative Prime Minister at the end of the nineteenth century, and Margaret Thatcher, the Conservative Prime Minister during the 1980s, felt threatened by what they saw as municipal socialism in the capital. Labour Prime Ministers also, in recent years at least, have felt uneasy at the thought of dealing with a powerful London authority; their relations with the first mayor, Ken Livingstone, were by no means always friendly, even though the formal powers of the mayor are very limited, and hardly compare with those of the mayor of Paris.

Constitutional reform in London, therefore, was bound to be more limited than devolution in Scotland and Wales. But reforming the government of London also involved problems different in kind from devolution or, indeed, from reforming the capital cities of other countries, because of the existence of the boroughs, each of which is itself a local authority, and because of social and economic tensions within London.

It has proved extremely difficult to discover a stable structure for government in London. Since the early 1960s, London has had no fewer than four different systems of government. The rapidity of change in the structure of government in London contrasts markedly with stability in the first half of the twentieth century. Until 1965, the basic structure of London government remained that put in place by legislation at the end of the nineteenth century. Before that time, London was without any city-wide system of government at all. It had been excluded from the

1835 Municipal Corporations Act, which had created directly elected borough councils for the larger towns. In the nineteenth century, the square mile of the city was in the hands of the City Corporation, while the rest of London was governed by a conglomeration of local parishes and assorted boards. But the Local Government Act of 1888, which provided for the creation of county councils and county boroughs in England and Wales, also provided for a London County Council—the LCC. The LCC did not, however, cover the area of today's Greater London Authority—the GLA—but only the area covered today by the inner London boroughs; and unlike the other county councils it was given powers over housing. The first elections for the new LCC in 1889 were won by the Left, by a group calling itself the Progressives, comprising Liberals and Fabian socialists. Some idea of the status of the Council can be gained from the fact that its first Chairman was the former Liberal Prime Minister, Lord Rosebery, while another of its prominent members was the Fabian, Sidney Webb. The LCC became a kind of laboratory for the testing of Fabian ideas at local level. The key policy of the Progressive majority was to take public utilities into municipal ownership, and to use revenue from the rates to improve social conditions.

The victory of the Progressives and the dominance of Fabian ideas in the new LCC frightened conservatives in much the same way as the ideas of Ken Livingstone a hundred years later were to frighten them; and proposals to abolish the LCC were launched as early as 1895, just six years after it had come into existence. In 1899, the Conservatives passed a new Local Government Act providing for the creation of 28 borough councils in London which would, so they hoped, counterbalance and dilute the radicalism of the LCC. One consequence of the 1899 Act, however, was the growth of conflict between the borough councils, particularly the more prosperous ones, and the LCC. Nevertheless, the LCC survived. In 1907 it came under the control of the Conservatives who in London called themselves Municipal Reformers; but in 1934 Labour won control for the first time under the leadership of Herbert Morrison, who had been a member of the Cabinet during the last five months of Ramsay MacDonald's second Labour government in 1931, but had lost his seat in the general election of that year. Morrison was to regain his seat in the Commons in 1935, but he continued as leader of the LCC until once again becoming a minister in 1940. Morrison's leadership of the LCC helped to establish the council as a highly effective authority willing to undertake policy initiatives even when they met with the disapproval of central government, such as the building of a new Waterloo bridge in 1937. The LCC gained a high reputation also for its work in education and in providing health facilities, including hospitals, before the establishment of the National Health Service in 1948.

By the 1960s, however, it had come to be felt that the boundaries of the LCC were no longer congruent with the facts of social geography. Many of those who worked in London commuted from the suburbs. They had as much of an interest in the policies followed in inner London as those who lived there, and yet they had no voice in helping to determine these policies, nor did they contribute towards

London rates. In 1960 a Royal Commission on the Government of Greater London under the chairmanship of Sir Edwin Herbert recommended the creation of a Greater London Authority to include the area of the outer as well as the inner London boroughs. This was accepted by the Conservative government, and in 1963 the London Government Act provided for the replacement of the LCC by a Greater London Council—GLC—and 32 London borough councils, to include outer as well as inner London. Herbert Morrison, by then Lord Morrison of Lambeth, was bitterly opposed to the destruction of what he regarded as his own child, and fought the measure with great vigour in the Lords, arguing that it was a political ramp designed to weaken Labour's hold on London. Although the inclusion of the suburbs was bound to help the Conservatives, Labour was nevertheless able to win the first elections to the GLC held in 1964. But Labour lost control in 1967, and the GLC then swung on a fairly regular basis between the parties, tending to be controlled by the party which was in opposition at Westminster.

Tensions between the government and the GLC became intense in 1981, two years after the election of Margaret Thatcher's Conservatives to power at Westminster. In that year Labour once again gained control of the GLC and immediately deposed the leader under whom it had fought the election, Andrew McIntosh, replacing him with Ken Livingstone from the left-wing of the party. Livingstone, so the Conservatives argued, sought to use the GLC as a laboratory for municipal socialism and also to make himself a spokesman for causes which had nothing to do with London government such as those of the nationalists in Ireland and the Palestine Liberation Organisation in the Middle East. Livingstone, the Conservatives believed, saw himself as leading an alternative national government in London, not a local authority.

The Conservatives entered the 1983 general election with a pledge to abolish the GLC, and in 1985 Parliament passed a Local Government Act fulfilling this pledge. The various functions of the GLC were distributed partly to the borough councils, but primarily to various nominated bodies and quangos. From 1986 to 2000 when a new London authority was created, London was unique amongst the large cities of the world in having no city-wide authority at all

Labour had been opposed to the abolition of the GLC and, when the Party finally returned to government in 1997, it promised to remedy what it regarded as a democratic deficit by creating a new structure of government for London, with a mayor and assembly. Labour proposed a directly elected mayor and a scrutinizing Assembly. The opposition parties put forward different and contrasting proposals. The Liberal Democrats rejected the idea of a directly elected mayor, but proposed devolution for London, treating the capital explicitly as an English region. The Liberal Democrats, therefore, wanted an assembly but not a mayor. The Conservatives, on the other hand, wanted a mayor but not an assembly; or rather they wanted an assembly composed of the leaders of the various London borough councils. Curiously enough, Ken Livingstone, the first mayor of London, had come to agree with this view by 2005, since experience had led him to believe that the assembly was an unnecessary layer of government. The Labour government's view, however, was that the role of the boroughs was to consider what was best for the boroughs. The role of the mayor and the assembly, by contrast, would be to consider what was best for London as a whole; and what was best for London as a whole might not be the same as a mere aggregation of what was best for the various boroughs. This new government of London, unlike the GLC would, according to the 1997 Labour manifesto 'not duplicate the work of the boroughs but take responsibility for London-wide issues . . . economic regeneration, planning, policing, transport and environmental protection'.

The Labour government proposed putting its proposals to Londoners in the form of a referendum. The Conservatives argued that there were two separate issues—whether Londoners wanted a mayor, and whether they wanted an assembly—and that the referendum should recognize this by posing two questions. The government, however, sidestepped this argument by posing just a single question in the referendum of May 1998: 'Are you in favour of the Government's proposal for a Greater London Authority with a directly elected mayor and council?' There was a four to one 'Yes' majority but on a turnout of only 34%. In the first elections in the year 2000, 34% voted in the mayoral election and just 31% in the assembly election. The low turnout for the referendum and for the election was remarkable since many had argued that the absence of a directly elected authority was a constitutional monstrosity which was deeply felt by most Londoners, and that the proposal for a directly elected mayor would raise turnout. The low turnout, however, seemed to show that most Londoners were quite uninterested in the constitutional arrangements for the government of the capital city. It could admittedly be argued that the reason why so few went to the polls in the referendum was that the campaign seemed so very one-sided. Few argued for a 'No' vote and the arguments against the new proposals were only weakly presented; it always seemed fairly certain that the proposals would be endorsed. Therefore, so it was suggested, many believed that there was no real point in voting. Whatever the reason, and however low the turnout, the fact that the Greater London Authority had been set up following a referendum meant that it would be much more difficult to abolish than it had been to abolish the LCC or the GLC. It might only be possible to abolish it after a further referendum. From this point of view, therefore, the referendum may be seen as a means of entrenching the new arrangements for the government of London so that the capital would enjoy more stability in the future than it had done in the past.

II

The new structure of government for London has four novel and fundamental features.

The first is that the executive authority in Greater London was to be not a council but a directly elected mayor—the first directly elected mayor in British history. The argument for a directly elected mayor was that it would give excitement and visibility to the government of London. Traditional council leaders have on the whole been party figures, more visible and also more accountable to their party colleagues than to the general public. Local party leaders were seen as people more suited perhaps to a bygone era of tribal politics than to an era when tribal politics was in decline and political allegiances had become more fluid. The idea of a directly elected mayor implied perhaps a move towards a more American-style politics that would be about individuals rather than parties with ideologies and history. The hope was that the mayor of London would be able to engage with the public more effectively because he would enjoy a direct mandate from the public. It would be difficult to deny that the first mayor of London, Ken Livingstone, was able to do just that.

In addition to the mayor, there was to be a small Greater London Assembly comprising 25 members. This Assembly would have a merely scrutinizing role, rather like that of a parliamentary Select Committee. It would have no power to reject the policies of the mayor, and could only amend or reject the budget by a 2/3 majority. This arrangement was very different from the traditional model of British local government in which the council leader was responsible to the council. The mayor, however, being directly elected should not, so it was argued, be responsible to the assembly in the way that a Cabinet was responsible in a parliamentary system, or a council leader in a traditional local authority system.

This argument, however, as we shall see later in chapter 10, was not to be applied to directly elected mayors outside London, where it was the full council which was to set the budget and the local authority's policy framework; although here too in the case of a conflict between the mayor and the council, a two thirds majority of the council would be needed to overthrow a budget or policy decision by the mayor. It could be argued, however, that the mayors outside London were being super-imposed upon pre-existing local authority structures and that the legislation for providing mayors outside London had to respect these structures to some extent. In London, by contrast, there was no pre-existing local authority, but a totally new form of authority was being created. This, so it was argued, made it possible to draw out the full implications and logic of a directly elected head of a local authority. Were the assembly to be given a real power of veto, then, so it was argued, there would be the danger of a regression to the old council model where power resided with the leader of the largest party group. At the very least, there would be two competing sources of authority—the mayor and the leader of the largest group in the Assembly; and, since the Assembly, unlike other English local authorities, was to be elected by proportional representation, it was unlikely that any single party would gain an overall majority. The outcome, therefore, instead of a clear line of responsibility, could easily be endless bargaining leading to gridlock, so nullifying the whole raison d'etre of a directly elected mayor—that of strong, rapid and efficient executive action.

The consequence, nevertheless, of the new structure is that the Mayor of London has much greater autonomy than the leader of any other local authority, whether that leader is a traditional group leader or directly elected mayor. The

Assembly, while it can scrutinize the mayor's policies, has no power to check him, and is somewhat disconnected from the decision-making process. The mayor is not accountable to the Assembly. This, Ken Livingstone has argued, has enabled him to be more effective at policy delivery. It would, he believed, have been impossible for him to implement such measures as the congestion charge or the reconstruction of the system of bus transport, had he been required to secure a majority on every issue in the Assembly.

The second innovation was that neither the mayor nor the assembly would be elected by the first-past-the-post system. The mayor was to be elected by a system called the supplementary vote, allowing for the expression of a second preference. This system presents the voter with two columns on the ballot paper. The columns are labelled 'first choice' and 'second choice', and the voter puts an 'X' in each column, unless she does not wish to vote for a second choice candidate. Then, if no single candidate gains an overall majority, the candidate with the fewest votes is eliminated and second preferences taken into account. 'The mayor's authority', declared the Lord Chancellor, Lord Irvine, 'will be enhanced by the fact that he will enjoy a broader base of support than might be achieved by first-past-the-post alone'.[2] The Assembly was to be elected by the additional member method of proportional representation, a method based on the German electoral system, and also used to elect the Scottish Parliament and the National Assembly of Wales.

The Greater London Assembly was the first local government body in England since the nineteenth century to be elected by proportional representation, and the first experiment with proportional representation in England since the abolition of the English university seats in 1950. This was bound to involve some degree of confusion for Londoners. It meant that Londoners would be subject to four different electoral systems—first-past-the-post for parliamentary elections, the regional list for European elections, the supplementary vote and the additional member system. The London elections were not accompanied by the concentrated electoral campaign that had preceded the Scottish and Welsh devolution elections in 1999 and the single transferable vote elections in Northern Ireland in the 1970s. Perhaps, therefore, the introduction of new and untried electoral systems was partly responsible for the low turnout in the first elections for the mayor and assembly.

The third innovation was one not intended by the government. The first mayor, elected in 2000, turned out to be not a party candidate, but an independent, Ken Livingstone, who stood against candidates from the three main parties, and defeated them. Livingstone had been the Labour leader of the old GLC from 1981 until its abolition in 1986; and in 1987 he had been elected Labour MP for Brent East. He had, however, been rejected in the year 2000 as the Labour Party's candidate for mayor in favour of the former Health Secretary, Frank Dobson. Livingstone claimed that the peculiarly structured electoral college set up by the

---

[2] Lecture to the Constitution Unit on 'The Government's Programme of Constitutional Reform', 8 December 1998.

Labour Party to choose its candidate had been rigged against him. He decided therefore to stand as an independent and duly won the election. Livingstone's victory has been characterised as 'one of the most substantial blows struck against the conventional party system in post-war British politics'.[3] By the time of the second contest in 2004, however, Labour which had expelled Livingstone for standing against a Labour Party candidate in 2000, had come to terms with him, largely because the party had come to believe that Livingstone was likely to win the mayoral election whether he stood as a Labour Party candidate or as an independent. Nevertheless, an important precedent had been created, that an independent could, in a major local election, defeat three party candidates who were backed by their party machines; and although chosen as the Labour Party candidate for mayor in 2004, Livingstone would certainly not have been the first choice of most Labour ministers for the candidacy. He remained a very independent figure within the Labour Party hierarchy. His Conservative successor, Boris Johnson, elected in 2008, was, similarly, a distinctively independent figure in the Conservative Party.

The fourth and final innovation was that the new authority represented a new model of government. It was not simply a re-creation of the GLC, since it had hardly any executive powers. It had no statutory powers, for example, over health, education or housing and it was specifically prohibited from providing these services or spending any money on them. It was indeed forbidden to spend money on any service that was being provided by a borough council or any other public body. Its main statutory powers were to lie in the area of economic development and transport—it has powers, which it has used, to impose a congestion charge— London being the first major conurbation in the world to introduce such a charge—and powers over the buses and the London underground system. Yet, even its powers over the underground system were emasculated since the government, just before Livingstone was elected mayor for the first time, took statutory power to implement a public-private partnership arrangement for the underground, which meant that operational control would rest with private companies. Livingstone, on the other hand, favoured raising funds through the issuing of bonds so that running of the underground would remain within the public sector. Livingstone took the government to court, claiming that his mandate to implement a transport policy for London had been undermined by the public-private partnership policy. The court, however, ruled in favour of the government. Livingstone, however, could argue that his transport strategy had been nullified by the government before he had even begun his first term.

In addition to having few executive powers, the mayor lacks independent sources of revenue. Around 75%–80% of his revenue comes from central government, and around 15% from a precept upon the boroughs. Council tax, the only tax that can be set by local authority representatives, accounts for just under 4% of London's total tax take. The remainder derives from charges and fees such as the

---

[3] J Curtice, B Seyd and K Thomson, 'Devolution to the Centre: Lessons from London's First Mayoral Elections,' Centre for Research into Elections and Social Trends, Working paper, No 90, September 2001, 33. This paper presents an excellent overview of the psephological issues.

congestion charge. It is perhaps odd that a mayor representing the capital city, and one of the largest cities in the world, has no independent sources of taxation. 'London', the *Evening Standard* declared on 5 July 1999, 'is to have the only elected Mayor in the world without a single proper tax to his or her name (New York has six)'. In addition, the fact that the mayor's revenue is in the form of a precept upon the London boroughs means that the true charge of London government is hidden from the council tax payer.

The Greater London Authority was established not as a metropolitan authority for London with executive powers, but as a 'strategic' regional authority, responsible not primarily for the delivery of public services, but for setting a strategy for London. The idea of a regional strategic authority is a wholly new one in British political experience, and it is still by no means clear how it will operate.

The new authority is in many ways a hybrid, and, so critics would argue, a rather uneasy hybrid. It bears some resemblance both to a traditional local authority and to a regional government, but it lacks the executive powers either of the National Assembly of Wales or of the stillborn regional assemblies in England. The argument for this hybrid system was, in the words of Lord Whitty, a junior minister in the Department of the Environment, Transport and the Regions that 'London is unique. It is neither regional nor local in the same sense as the rest of the country. The metropolis requires . . . and will get . . . special treatment . . . The new greater London authority will be a new type of government, tailored specifically to London's needs'.[4] It is a new type of authority without precedent in British experience. It involves a leap of faith. It has not been tested elsewhere in Britain.

III

We have already seen that one reason for the difficulty of deciding upon a new structure for the government of London was the fear of those in central government that too powerful an authority in the capital would threaten their power. That fear is felt by all governments faced with deciding upon a structure of government for a large capital city. But there is, as we have noticed, a further crucial difficulty that applies only to London and not to other capitals. It is that London comprises not just a capital city, but also 32 powerful boroughs, together with the City Corporation, each with its own local authority, and three of which—Hackney, Lewisham and Newham—have their own directly elected mayors as provided for under the 2000 Local Government Act.

The existence of powerful boroughs makes the problem of government in London different in kind from those in other capital cities. For this reason, it is facile to compare the problems of government in London with the problems of government in New York, Paris or Berlin. These cities do not have boroughs as powerful as the London boroughs. It is true that New York has its five boroughs—

---

[4] House of Lords Debates, vol 595, cols 345–46, 30 November 1998.

Brooklyn, the Bronx, Manhattan, Queen's and Staten Island. Yet few New Yorkers have strong loyalties to these boroughs. They see themselves as New Yorkers first and inhabitants of the Bronx second. The boroughs of New York are, in the words of one authority, 'relatively weak units of government . . . pale shadows of their London counterparts: although there are only five of them, the budget of, say, Brooklyn, is far smaller than, say, Lambeth'[5]; and the New York boroughs have far weaker powers than their London counterparts. The boroughs in New York do not deliver services nor do they have their own taxing powers. In London, by contrast, many Londoners, particularly in the outer suburbs, may see themselves more as residents of Barnet, Hillingdon, Richmond, etc. and only secondarily as Londoners. Those living in Bexley and Bromley may regard themselves as belonging to Kent, while those living in Croydon and Sutton may regard themselves as belonging to Surrey. Some would argue that, politically, there is no such entity as London at all. London, they would suggest, is no more than a collection of boroughs or even villages linked together. It has been suggested indeed that London is nothing more than 'a kind of no-man's land . . . a series of linked villages with its centre as more a sort of national territory [lacking] a true local identity'.[6] On this view, London could manage perfectly well without a London-wide authority at all, as in fact it did from 1986 to 2000, the very period of London's dynamic economic growth. The low turnout for the referendum on London and for mayoral elections in London would seem to show that fewer Londoners are interested in a London-wide authority than is often suggested. Perhaps Londoners feel sufficiently well represented by their boroughs and do not need London-wide representation at all. There is perhaps no inherent necessity for a London-wide system of government. It would be perfectly consistent to argue that borough government was sufficient, and that voters would find the boroughs more accountable than the mayor and assembly. It is, after all, easier for the voters to contact their local borough town halls when they have a problem than the inevitably more remote mayor and assembly.

In fact, however, perhaps as a result of the creation of the mayor, the feeling of belonging to London may be rather stronger than the above considerations would suggest. An Ipsos-MORI poll published on 7 April 2004, and entitled, 'Tired of London (Governance?): Londoners' Views Explained', discovered that no fewer than 81% of Londoners were able to name Ken Livingstone as London's mayor, 'a very high percentage given a diverse and mobile population', and a great contrast to the GLC which was able to engage a high degree of public interest only when it was fighting to avoid abolition. The assembly, 'in contrast suffers from under-exposure to the public. It is virtually invisible'. 58% of the London sample declared that they did not know what it did. Significantly, more people—65%—identified with the mayor, than with the London boroughs—48%—or, more surprisingly, with England—57%. Perhaps, therefore, the establishment of directly elected

---

[5] T Travers, *The Politics of London: Governing an Ungovernable City* (Houndmills, Palgrave/Macmillan, 2004) 176.

[6] L J Sharpe, quoted in B Pimlott and N Rao, *Governing London* (Oxford, OUP, 2002) 44.

mayors in other large cities might weaken the salience of the West Lothian Question. By enabling the public to identify with their city, it could lessen the feeling of alienation which is partly based on the view that Scotland has more political clout than areas of England. 'For Londoners', the report concluded, 'the city is a much stronger determinant of identity than any other local regional or national boundary. . . . Given this sense of cohesion and pride there is a ready-made base of support for a London-wide government structure'.

The fact, however, that the loyalty of Londoners may be primarily to their mayor rather than to their borough councils nevertheless causes other problems for the government of London, since the mayor has few powers over the boroughs. The Greater London Authority is in no sense a superior authority to the boroughs. It has hardly any powers to compel, overrule or override the boroughs. It is not an upper-tier authority and the boroughs are not lower-tier authorities. The difference between them lies in their sphere of operation; the boroughs are statutory authorities for their particular areas, while the London authority is expected to take a London-wide view. But, lacking strong executive powers and lacking its own tax base, it is not clear how the mayor can actually implement his London-wide view. His powers are limited mainly to those of persuasion and publicity and these may not be sufficient. The mayor is required, for example, to produce a London-wide plan. But the power of producing the formal Unitary Development Plans, the power to determine whether to allow an extension to a house, a garage or a block of new offices, lies not with the mayor but with the boroughs. The mayor can refuse borough planning applications, but the borough concerned then has the right of appeal to the Secretary of State. Planning powers for London are thus divided between the mayor, the boroughs and central government. The powers of the mayor, therefore, are primarily negative, in vetoing decisions made by the boroughs. What, under these circumstances, can the power to plan for London as a whole actually mean? A major development such as a new office building may need planning permission from the boroughs, the mayor and the Secretary of State. That is not likely to prove a good recipe for effective or positive government. Writing in the *Evening Standard* on 21 February 2006, Ken Livingstone urged, 'Give me the means to help London flourish', 'I can', he went on to say

> 'direct the refusal of a planning application of strategic importance, but I can't direct agreement. Local interest can completely block something with real London-wide consequences, most obviously the need for housing. I firmly believe that local boroughs should remain the mainstay for planning decisions in London, but not at the expense of Nimbyism [Not in my back yard]. Too many good applications for new homes are being turned down—already more than 40% of all applications, the highest in the country'.

The mayor sought from central government powers to direct the boroughs to meet London-wide strategic targets, and the government, as we shall see, responded in the 2006 London Government Act.

Transport is the main area in which the mayor has statutory powers. It would be impossible otherwise for the mayor to develop a bus priority strategy with main routes cutting across London were one borough able to opt out so that the bus priority strategy went to one side of the borough and then resumed on the other side. For such matters the mayor is accountable, not of course to the assembly, but to the electors of London. But, in other areas of policy, his primary role is as a setter of strategies. These strategies, however, rely upon central government and upon the boroughs for their implementation.

The mayor, then, cannot be checked by the assembly, which is primarily a scrutinizing and consultative body rather than a legislative one. The real check on the mayor is exercised by the boroughs. The danger is that the mayor comes to be squeezed between the government and the boroughs so that it becomes impossible for him to implement London-wide policies. The outcome would then be the balkanization of London. The mayor of London, when compared with his counterparts in Paris or New York, presides over a weak government. In New York, following the terrorist attack on 9/11, the mayor, Rudolph Giuliani, appeared as the ruler of the city. He did not have to seek approval from other layers of government—whether the federal government or the boroughs—before implementing his city-wide strategy to deal with terrorism. He had control of the police, fire services, hospitals, housing and the personal social services of New York, while 70% of New York's local expenditure was funded out of local taxation. Giuliani was perceived as one of the most powerful politicians in the United States, and his success in New York led to him becoming a candidate for the presidency. In London, by contrast, following the terrorist attack of July 2005, the great bulk of action taken in response was undertaken by central government.

The mayor of London is responsible for only around 10% of public expenditure in London. The Scottish Parliament, by contrast, is responsible for around 65% of public expenditure in Scotland. Central government remains responsible for spending on the National Health Service in London, further and higher education in London, and housing and social security in London. The boroughs are responsible for spending on schools and on local planning. It was only a slight exaggeration for the Conservative spokesman on London, Richard Ottaway, to argue that 'such are the Secretary of State's powers that, whoever is nominally elected as the first mayor of London, the real first mayor of London will be the right honourable Member for Hull East' [John Prescott the Cabinet minister responsible at the time for local government and the environment] 'He will make the decisions; he has the power. If that is freedom for London, it is freedom in a straitjacket'.[7]

But, although the mayor has comparatively few powers and responsibilities, many may assume that he is responsible for the government of London as a whole rather than for just a minuscule part of it, precisely because he is the only directly elected person with a seeming overall responsibility for the government of London. Apparently, Londoners frequently ask the mayor—what are you doing about crime, homelessness etc? These questions, however, while they might be appropriately directed to a mayor of New York, have little relevance to the mayor

---

[7] House of Commons Debates, vol 322, col 811, 15 December 1998.

of London. All that the mayor can do is to seek to persuade others—central government or the boroughs—to take action; and he has neither the financial nor the executive leverage to make his persuasion effective. The mayor, then, is not, as most American mayors are, primarily a policy-maker or strategist; he is, instead, primarily a spokesperson for London, a cheerleader. He can get his way only by using techniques of persuasion and publicity, techniques of which the first two mayors, Ken Livingstone and Boris Johnson, were masters. Through his political skills, Livingstone was able to broker a number of deals with central government on such matters as the establishment of London's successful bid to stage the 2012 Olympics and the commitment to build Crossrail; in addition he gained permission from the Treasury to borrow £2.9 billion to improve the light rail and underground network in East London. Livingstone was thus able to punch above his weight.

Nevertheless, the considerable disparity between perceptions of the role of the mayor and the realities of his power cannot be in the interests of effective government. In addition, few voters are aware of how the powers over government in London are distributed. It must be a very small percentage of voters who can pinpoint with some accuracy the powers held by central government, by the Government Offices for London, by the mayor, the boroughs, by London-wide quangos such as the London Housing Board and the various health and cultural bodies. Such lack of clarity in the division of functions hardly makes for either effective or for accountable government. The report in 2006 of the Commission on London Governance, set up by the Greater London Assembly and the Association of London Government's leaders committee, representatives of both the Greater London Authority and the boroughs, concluded:

> 'An over-arching theme running through this report is that Londoners should have more say in the way their city is run. One of the current barriers to this is the extreme complexity of London's governance arrangements, which involve not only the GLA and the boroughs but many other agencies and organizations. This complexity, we conclude, undermines attempts by citizens to engage with service providers and shape services. The price of this lack of local engagement can be failure of efforts to reform services, poor performance and low public satisfaction. Inadequate accountability therefore has practical and economic as well as democratic implications, leaving Londoners deprived as both citizens and users of public services.[8]

It might be suggested that there was little point in establishing a new and complex system of government with a directly elected mayor, but then providing him with insufficient powers to make his role effective. The problem was that Labour was in two minds whether it really wanted an effective mayor in the capital, one who might be able to challenge central government. Paradoxically, it is the very size and importance of London which serves to ensure its political weakness.

Labour had sought to square the circle by establishing a 'strategic' London authority, a body which would not enjoy the statutory powers to challenge either

---

[8] Commission on London Governance, *A New Settlement for London*, GLA 2006, 6.

the centre or the London boroughs. But the very concept of a 'strategic' authority is somewhat vague. In 1978, Sir Frank Marshall, leader of Leeds City Council, had been commissioned by the GLC to inquire into the future of government in greater London. The GLC was also seen as a 'strategic' authority, although it had more service delivery powers than the mayor was to enjoy. In his report, Sir Frank had concluded that

> 'The concept of a strategic role was a new one in 1965 when the GLC was created . . . It could thus be adopted as a convenient but undefined description by an authority seeking a role in life but dispossessed of the powerful operational functions which had vitalized its ancestors'.[9]

How can a mayor implement his 'strategic' decisions when he lacks power or leverage over the boroughs? Services such as local planning and education and training are essential, surely, to any strategy for London, and yet the mayor has no powers over them. To make the strategic role, effective, therefore, it would be necessary to rebalance functions, so that the powers of the mayor can become more commensurate with perceptions of his role in the government of London.

In the London Government Act of 2006, the Labour government addressed some of these problems, giving the mayor significant new powers. Perhaps the most important lay in the field of planning. In future, the mayor would be able to direct changes in borough programmes for local development plans so as to ensure that they were in conformity with the overall London plan. He would be given the discretion to determine planning applications of strategic importance. The responsibilities of the London Housing Board would be transferred to the mayor. He would be given responsibility to prepare a London Housing Strategy and a Housing Investment Plan for London. He would also become chair of a new London Skills and Employment Board, and would be responsible for producing an Adult Skills Strategy for London; and he would have the responsibility for producing a strategy to tackle health inequalities in London. Apart from the new planning powers, however, the mayor still lacks the powers to secure the implementation of his strategies over the recalcitrant boroughs.

The 2006 Act, while it does something to improve the government of London, does little to reduce its complexity and lack of accountability. Policy for regeneration, for example, still remains split between four different layers of government—central government, various quangos, the London Development Agency, appointed by and accountable to the mayor, and the boroughs. The mayor still remains responsible for spending only around 10% of London's expenditure; the rest is the responsibility of the boroughs, central government, the Government Offices for London and various quangos. Expenditure on the National Health Service, higher and further education, the arts, housing and social security in London are still determined by central government; expenditure on social care, local transport and local planning are still determined by the boroughs. In

[9] The Marshall Inquiry on Greater London: Report to the GLC by Sir Frank Marshall, QC, GLC 1978, 8.

addition, lacking his own tax base, the mayor has little freedom to determine how the money is spent. Transport for London, for example, the executive board carrying out the mayor's transport policy, is financed almost wholly by a grant from central government, a grant which could, no doubt, be curtailed were ministers to disapprove of the mayor's transport policies. The precept on the London boroughs' council tax accounts for less than 15% of the GLA's gross income, and this means that a small percentage increase in GLA expenditure has a disproportionate impact on Londoners' council tax bills. The Scottish Parliament, by contrast, enjoys full freedom within the law to determine how its block grant is spent.

The Ipsos-MORI survey referred to above on p 207 concluded that, despite the high public profile of the mayor, and 'despite the Mayor's vocal calls for increases in the GLA precept to fund new initiatives, minimal association is made between the Mayor and tax increases by a public short on understanding of public sector finance. When asked who is most responsible for tax rises in the capital, Londoners say first that central government is most culpable. However, and second in line for blame, local councils are twice as likely to get the blame for these rises as the Mayor'. It would, however, be wrong to blame the public for being 'short on understanding of public sector finance'. The arrangements are so complex and opaque that only someone who has studied them for some considerable time could be expected to understand them. Such arrangements do not make for good government.

The 2006 Act makes clear that, as with devolution to Scotland and Wales, the reform of London government is a process and not an event. Further reform is necessary if London-wide strategies are to remain more than paper solutions. We have seen that, when the 1999 London Government bill was being discussed in Parliament, the Conservatives proposed that, in place of the assembly, there should be a forum or senate composed of representatives of the London boroughs. Ken Livingstone has now come to support that idea. The objection is that the boroughs represent just a borough-wide sphere of operation, whereas the assembly can take a London-wide view. In fact, however, the assembly does not find it easy even to scrutinise these policies. Those who were political supporters of the mayor were co-opted on to the various executive boards which carry out the mayor's policies. They were hardly in a good position to scrutinise them when they were in part responsible for implementing them. Livingstone's main political opponents, on the other hand, the Conservatives, found that they did not become recipients of the mayor's patronage. But, in the assembly, instead of taking on a scrutinising role, they acted as a parliamentary opposition. Thus, in practice, the assembly acts as an adversarial standing committee or public bill committee rather than a select committee. All too often, the London-wide vision was forgotten amidst the interplay of adversarial politics. But perhaps such a unified London-wide vision is in any case unattainable since the city is so deeply divided both socially and ideologically.

It may be argued that there is little point in establishing a London-wide authority and giving it only very weak powers. The logic of creating a London-wide system of government requires, first, some devolution of powers from central government, and second, some power for the mayor to over-ride the boroughs. It would probably be far too radical to allow the mayor, together with a majority of the boroughs to over-ride the rest, but perhaps a qualified majority of the boroughs—two-thirds, for example,—should be given the power to over-ride the recalcitrant minority.

Given that the London assembly has found it difficult to articulate a London-wide view or to establish itself powerfully in the minds of many Londoners, it might be sensible to replace it, as the Conservatives argued when the London Government bill was introduced, and as Ken Livingstone now argues, with a London Senate, comprising representatives of the boroughs. The mayor might then be given the power to override recalcitrant boroughs when he has the agreement of two-thirds of the boroughs represented in the Senate.

What is clear is that the London Government Act of 1999 marked, not a final solution to the perhaps insoluble problem of how London should be governed, but a further stage in the search for one. It would be over-optimistic to believe that this process has reached its conclusion. Meanwhile, as one authority on London government has concluded, 'Londoners continue to survive despite their government rather than because of it'.[10]

---

[10] Travers, *The Politics of London*, above n 5, 210.

9

Towards a Written Constitution?

I

THE ERA OF radical constitutional reform since 1997 naturally raises the question of whether it is not time that Britain followed almost every other democracy by enacting a constitution. Since these reforms have caused so much of the constitution to be codified, there seems little reason in principle why the whole of it should not now be codified in one single overarching document. If, as we have argued, one consequence of devolution is to turn Britain into a quasi-federal state, then perhaps Britain should emulate federations by enacting a constitution. If there is, as seems possible, further reform of the House of Lords creating a directly elected upper house, this will, almost certainly, require a statutory redefinition of the powers of the House of Lords vis-à-vis the Commons. It will no longer be possible to rely upon hitherto generally accepted conventions when both chambers can put forward a claim to democratic legitimacy. That, too, will appear as a step towards a fully codified constitution. A constitution might, then, consolidate the constitutional reforms achieved since 1997.

The argument in chapter 1 was that one of the main reasons why we have not already codified our constitution was that our main, perhaps our only constitutional principle, was the sovereignty of parliament. If, however, the principle of parliamentary sovereignty is no longer our dominant principle, then at least that obstacle to the introduction of an enacted constitution has disappeared. It seems that, in a pragmatic and unplanned way, we have come to the recognition that there are certain 'constitutional' statutes, that there may be higher laws which lie beyond the power of Westminster to alter. Therefore, it may be argued, we are now in a position to consider what our constitutional principles ought to be, and then to enact a constitution based upon them. The second main reason why we have not produced an enacted constitution is that we have never enjoyed, as most other democracies have, a constitutional moment, a clear beginning, arising from colonial independence, or the introduction of a new regime, when it would be natural to write down the main principles by which we wished to be governed. Perhaps, however, the spate of constitutional reforms since 1997 amount to a constitutional moment, a new beginning, a discontinuity that greatly strengthens the case for a codified constitution.

It may seem, then, that the two main reasons why Britain should not have an enacted constitution—the conceptual and the historical—have less weight now, at the beginning of the twenty-first century, than they have had in the past. In addition, a constitution, some might argue, could help to reaffirm the notion of Britishness against the centrifugal challenges of devolution and multiculturalism, just as the constitution of the United States has helped to produce a common notion of American-ness in a multi-ethnic society The Green Paper, *The Governance of Britain*, Cm 7170, published by Gordon Brown's government in 2007, emphasised the 'need to ensure that Britain remains a cohesive society, confident in its shared identity' and the need 'to provide a clear articulation of British values', values 'which have not just to be shared but also accepted' (paras 125, 212 and 195). Britain, it was suggested in the Green Paper, 'needs to articulate better a shared understanding of what it means to be British and what it means to live in the United Kingdom' (para 7). The conclusion is that 'This might in time lead to a concordat between the executive and Parliament or a written constitution' (para 212). There is an implication that Britain may now be near a constitutional moment, and that an enacted constitution might help to resolve the question of what it is to be British in the twenty-first century. In a statement to the Commons, however, Gordon Brown insisted that, because a written constitution 'would represent a fundamental and historic shift in our constitutional arrangements', it would be 'right to involve the public in a sustained debate' on whether there were a case for it. Such fundamental change 'should happen only when there is a settled consensus on whether to proceed'.[1]

It is, after all, odd that Britain remains without a codified constitution. This oddity is not always appreciated. One would be surprised if one joined a golf or cricket club and asked to see the rules, to be told that the rules are not, in fact, gathered together all in one place; and, indeed, some of them are not even written down. If you want to find them, you will have to look at decisions made by the committee of the club over many years, as well as rules laid down a long time ago. In addition, of course, there are various conventions, many of which are not written down at all; these are tacit understandings, although it is true that many members of the club do not fully understand them. But, you will come to understand them as you become a long-serving member of the club. It is, in addition, always worth remembering that, if you have to ask what the rules are, that is a sure sign that you do not really belong. Such a response would hardly be regarded as satisfactory to a new member, wondering what is happening to his subscription. Is it any better as a response to someone asking to see the British constitution?

Dicey wrote in *The Law of the Constitution* that a British writer on the constitution 'has good reason to envy professors who belong to countries such as France ... or the United States, endowed with constitutions on which the terms are to be found in printed documents, known to all citizens and accessible to every man who is able to read'.[2] But there would be considerable difficulties in preparing a codified constitution for Britain. These difficulties are of two kinds. There is, **first**,

---

[1] House of Commons Debates, vol 462, cols 819–20, 3 July 2007.
[2] A V Dicey, *An Introduction to the Law of the Constitution*, (10th edn, London, Macmillan, 1959) 4.

the difficulty of deciding what should be included, the problem of **scope**, and that includes the problem of whether **conventions** should be included in the constitution; and, if so, which ones; and **second**, the problem of who is to have the **authority** to draw up, ratify and amend a codified constitution; and then what legal authority the enacted constitution should have. Each of these problems will be considered in turn.

II

The first and most obvious question to be answered relates to scope. What precisely ought to be included in a British constitution? K C Wheare, in his book *Modern Constitutions*, first published in 1951, suggested that in a unitary state, 'the Constitution needs to provide no more than the structure, in general terms, of the legislative, the executive and the judiciary; the nature in broad outline of their mutual relations; and the nature of their relations to the community itself'.[3] Such an approach may have appeared suitable in the 1950s, but most new democracies would think that a constitution drawn up in the twenty-first century should contain much more than a mere organisation chart of government. Most modern constitutions contain, in addition, articles defining citizenship and the territorial application of the constitution, together with articles defining the various territorial levels of government and their respective competencies. For Britain it would be particularly important to define the powers of the devolved bodies and their relationship to Westminster. Most modern constitutions also contain a declaration or bill of rights. Beyond that, however, there is a striking diversity amongst modern enacted constitutions. Many contain a preamble in the form of a 'mission statement' of values, but some do not. Some states add social and economic rights to the standard list of rights, while others do not. There is, therefore, some agreement on a staple core that ought to be in all constitutions, but little agreement on what should be contained beyond that agreed core.

The problem of scope, of what is to be included in a constitution, is bound to prove far more difficult to resolve in Britain than in other democracies with enacted constitutions. This difficulty arises precisely because most constitutions have been drawn up and adopted when a people wished to make a new beginning. Most constitution-makers, therefore, have not faced the difficulty that the British constitution-maker would face, of needing to select from a huge inheritance of existing laws, customs and conventions. The American Founding Fathers, for example, were enacting a constitution *de novo*, so as to replace a confederal entity with a federal one. The Indian constitution of 1950 signified the coming of national independence. Germany in 1949 and France in 1958 enacted new constitutions to mark the beginning of new regimes. Britain, by contrast, would be seeking to enact a constitution that encapsulated and summarised the working of

---

[3] K C Wheare, *Modern Constitutions*, [1951] (2nd edn, Oxford, OUP, 1966) 34.

an already fully functioning regime. But any regime with an uncodified constitution has of necessity been undergoing a perpetual process of adaptation and change.

'There is one reason', declared Sidney Low in 1904,

'why the English (sic) method of government is so hard to describe. Any account of it must be like the picture of a living person. If you want to see exactly how the original appears, you do not refer to a photograph taken twenty or thirty years ago. The features may be the same, but their expression, their proposition, and their whole character have changed. In the interval between one examination of our public polity and another, the formal part may not have greatly altered, but the conventional, the organic, the working portion has been modified in all sorts of ways. The structural elements, it is true, exhibit a wonderful superficial permanence. The Crown, the two Houses of Parliament, the Council of Ministers, [i.e. the Cabinet], the Electorate, the Judicature, and the mutual relations of these various powers and authorities, are the material of all the historians and jurists. There is the same machine, or at least a machine which is painted to look the same'.[4]

To enact a British constitution, therefore, would be to seek to capture the essence of a tradition that was in the process of being altered while it was being described. The problem for the British constitution-maker is that of deciding which elements of a fully functioning system of government ought to be selected as being of such special significance that they should be included in the constitution whilst the system of government is itself changing, and perhaps changing at a particularly rapid rate.

The problem of scope, therefore, of deciding what ought to be included in the constitution, is likely to prove an extraordinarily complex one. The first question to be answered is whether the constitution should contain, as for example the American constitution does, a preamble or 'mission statement' laying out British values. Until recently it would have been generally thought that there was no need for such a statement, indeed that it would be, in a sense, un-British. The British, it could be argued, were uncomfortable with statements of values which they saw as little more than ineffective sermons. Significantly, perhaps, when the students were asked in the seminars referred to on p 10 whether they thought that the British constitution should contain a preamble, they were unanimous in agreeing that it should not. But the Brown government has suggested that there may be some value in such a statement after all. It is currently consulting on a British Statement of Values, (not a statement of British values, which are probably not so very different from French values, Irish values, or Norwegian values, and has little relevance to constitutional matters). The purpose of this exercise is to assist with answering two questions. The first is:

How to hold together Britain, as a multinational state, with asymmetrical devolution?

---

[4] S Low, *The Governance of England* (London, T Fisher Unwin, 1904) 5.

The second is:

How to hold together Britain, as an explicitly multicultural and multidenominational society, rather than a homogeneous, white and Protestant society? This second question is thought to be a particular problem for a society in which, as the London suicide bombings in 2005 seem to show, there is a small but significant section of the population which, despite having been educated in British schools, sympathises with terrorism.

The case, therefore, for a preamble or 'mission statement' of values would, have to be examined carefully in the light of changed conditions at the beginning of the twenty-first century.

Coming to the body of the constitution itself, there are many further questions to be answered in regard to scope. The first modern constitution, that of the United States, enacted in 1789, divides itself into sections according to governmental functions in terms of a classical view of the separation of powers—legislature, executive, judiciary. This constitution was of course drawn up in an age before the development of mass political parties. Experience of dictatorship in the twentieth century has shown, however, that a system seemingly based upon the separation of powers is perfectly compatible with dictatorship if a totalitarian party succeeds in controlling all of the organs of government. In the Soviet Union, the Communist Party controlled the executive, legislature and judiciary; while, in Germany, between 1933 and 1945, a similar control was exercised by the Nazi party. The principle of the separation of powers, then, while a necessary, is not a sufficient condition for democracy. There must also be a competitive struggle by opposing political parties for the popular vote. Yet, neither parties nor elections are mentioned in the United States constitution, nor in many other modern constitutions. Where they are mentioned it is often only in a very general and almost perfunctory manner. The German constitution of 1949 is one of the few that seeks to regulate the activities of political parties. Article 21 gives the Federal Constitutional Court the power to declare unconstitutional any party which by reason of its aims or the behaviour of its adherents, may 'seek to impair or abolish the free democratic order or to endanger the existence of the Federal Republic of Germany'. This provision has been used by the Federal Constitutional Court to ban extremist parties, both on the radical left and the radical right.

Free and fair elections, like a competitive party system, are fundamental to democracy. Yet, again, hardly any constitutions specify in precise detail what electoral system is to be used in choosing the legislature. Those constitutions which do mention the electoral system mostly content themselves with a simple declaration that the system should be 'proportional'. The Irish constitution of 1937 is a notable exception in that it provides in Article 16:2:5 that the Dail be elected by a specific proportional system, the single transferable vote method.

Some might argue that the referendum also ought to be mentioned in the constitution, and that the constitution should state the circumstances in which referendums can be held, and what rules should regulate them. Yet, in Britain, there is no consensus on the answers to these questions.

Differences in how the constitutions of different democracies treat such matters reflect, no doubt, differences in historical experience, but they show that, beyond a basic minimum core, there is often no clear boundary between what is and what is not constitutional. There might be some disagreement, for example, on whether a British constitution should regulate the role of the political parties by including within it the main features of the Political Parties, Elections and Referendums Act, 2000; on whether the parties should be required to be democratic in their organisation, and on whether they should be required to be open and accountable in their financial arrangements. There might also be disagreement on whether the electoral system should be included in the constitution; and, if so, whether only the electoral system for Westminster should be included, or the various electoral systems used for the devolved bodies and for local authorities as well. The difficulty is, of course, that the question of the right electoral system, whether for Westminster or for local authorities, is now very much a matter of political contention. It is perfectly possible that the current systems will be altered in the years to come—local authorities in Scotland have recently switched from first-past-the-post to the single transferable vote method of proportional representation, and Welsh local authorities may also come to be elected by this method; and it is not totally inconceivable that the electoral system for the Commons itself will be changed in the foreseeable future.

The issue of the electoral system raises a further problem. Tony Blair promised that there would be no change in the electoral system for the House of Commons without a referendum; and, in a research paper published in 2007, the House of Commons Library claims that there is a 'constitutional convention that changes to the electoral system should be agreed as far as possible on an all-party basis'. It then goes on to declare in the next sentence, somewhat confusingly, that 'This convention is not universally observed'.[5] Is this supposed convention part of the constitution? Should the constitution provide that a change in the electoral system for the Commons requires a referendum? Clearly, a statute altering the electoral system that was not put to the people would not be invalidated by the courts. Some might argue, however, that there is now fairly widespread agreement amongst the political class that a change in the electoral system for the Commons should require a referendum so as to avoid governments manipulating the electoral system for political advantage.

The drafters of a British constitution would have to consider, then, whether the constitution should mention the electoral system at all; and also, whether there should be a provision that changes to the electoral system should require all-party agreement and/or a referendum. It would be difficult to reach a widely acceptable verdict.

---

[5] House of Commons Library: Standard Note: *Speaker's Conference*, SN/PC/4426, 12 September 2007, 1.

There are, however, further problems with regard to scope. Decisions would have to be made as to how asymmetrical devolution should be treated. There would be some disagreement over whether the role of separate nationalities within the United Kingdom should be recognised in the constitution, and whether they should be given constitutional protection. There would have to be agreement also on the procedure to be followed should one part of the United Kingdom, eg Scotland, seek to secede from it.

Part of the difficulty of deciding whether such matters should appear in the constitution, and, if so, in what form, is the difficulty of distinguishing between the constitution as it is and as we might think it ought to be. We might wish it were the case that, constitutionally, a change in the electoral system in Britain requires a referendum; but does such a provision reflect the working of the constitution as it actually is? What is clear is that the question of scope, of what should be included in the constitution would not be an easy one to resolve. The question of how it might be resolved will be considered later in this chapter.

III

A further reason why the problem of scope is so difficult is that so much of our system of government depends upon conventions whose content and scope are at times unclear. The problem of identifying conventions, and deciding which, if any, should be included in the constitution, is at least as difficult as the problem of scope. The problem of identifying conventions is particularly great in Britain as compared, for example, with Israel, another democracy contemplating producing a codified constitution, since Britain, unlike Israel, founded in 1948, is an old democracy, with a huge accretion of conventions, some of which are difficult to distinguish from traditional practices or mere usages. With a country seeking to draw up a constitution *de novo*, as, for example, Germany in 1949, the problem of course does not exist.

One authority has argued that, by their very nature, it is impossible to identify conventions with any degree of precision. 'It is . . . very difficult to draw the line between an obligatory and a non-obligatory practice. The characteristic of conventions, namely that they supplement the laws which are enforced by the courts would seem to preclude their precise definition'.[6] If this were true, however, then it would be difficult for the constitution to contain a precise statement of, for example, the powers of the Queen. In fact, however, conventions in some areas have been crystallised in recent years in the form, for example, of written codes of practice for civil servants, ministers and MPs. It seems implausible to suggest, therefore, that conventions are inherently incapable of being identified and stated. The courts have sometimes recognised the existence of conventions. In a case in 1982, *Reference re Amendment of the Constitution of Canada*, the Canadian

---

[6] E C S Wade 'Introduction' to 10th edition of Dicey's *Law of the Constitution*, clv.

Supreme Court went even further. It not only recognised a convention, but proceeded, for the first time in a common law jurisdiction, to adjudicate a dispute as to whether a practice—that of securing provincial consent to constitutional amendments affecting the powers of the provinces—amounted to a convention or was merely a usage.[7] There seems no inherent reason therefore why conventions should not be clearly defined, and no reason in principle why some at least should not be included in a codified constitution. But there are, nevertheless, many problems involved.

The first problem is to decide whether conventions should be included in the constitution at all. If they were not, the outcome would be, in the words of one authority, a constitution which would be 'a bare framework, compounded of statute law and the royal prerogative and presiding with a suppositious dignity over the real world of flesh and blood', a solution characterised as one of 'voluntary schizophrenia'.[8] A constitution which identified the Queen as part of the legislative process, but did not state the convention that the Queen normally assents to legislation passed by the House of Commons and the House of Lords, would be a rather odd document. Ideally, then, a constitution should spell out actual practice, and this must mean taking into account constitutional conventions. Were the Queen to refuse to assent to legislation, we should certainly say that this refusal was unconstitutional. It seems, therefore, that some conventions at least should be included in the constitution.

The second problem is to identify what the conventions actually are. This is not always easy to do. It is not always easy to distinguish conventions from mere customs or regularities of behaviour, which could at any time change without any political consequences. It has, for example, become customary for the Prime Minister to call on the Queen at Buckingham Palace on Tuesdays when both are in London, and for the Prime Minister to live at 10 Downing Street; but no one would regard these matters as conventions of the constitution. Similarly, many of the practices of Parliament, such as the role of Black Rod in summoning MPs to the House of Lords to hear the Queen's Speech, have been in existence for a long time and seem to have become almost sacrosanct, but they could nevertheless be altered without there being any obvious untoward political consequences. They are part of what Bagehot called the 'dignified' part of the constitution. To alter such customs, therefore, would not seem to involve any breach of convention.

Identifying a convention also involves distinguishing a genuinely normative rule from one which depends upon political vicissitudes or particular political conditions which may be passing away. Until 1960, for example, it was generally thought to be a convention that the Foreign Secretary should sit in the House of Commons. When, in 1955, Anthony Eden sought to make Lord Salisbury his

---

[7] (1982) 125 DLR (3d) 1. See P W Hogg, *Constitutional Law of Canada* (5th edn, Scarborough, Ontario, Thomson/Carswell, 2006) 1–26.

[8] S A de Smith, *The New Commonwealth and its Constitutions* (London, Stevens, 1964) 78. Chapter 3 of this book contains an excellent account of the arguments for and against incorporating conventions into a constitution.

Foreign Secretary, he was dissuaded from doing so by this supposed convention. In 1960, however, when Harold Macmillan appointed Lord Home Foreign Secretary, and in 1979, when Margaret Thatcher appointed Lord Carrington Foreign Secretary, hardly anyone accused them of a breach of convention, and the few who did were ignored.

Until 1932, it was generally believed that the convention of collective responsibility required all Cabinet ministers to avoid public disagreement on matters of government policy, and the breach of the convention in that year was explained away as being necessitated by the unusual circumstances of a coalition government. In 1975, however, the experiment was repeated by a single-party government, the Labour government of Harold Wilson, and then again in 1977 by the Callaghan government on the issue of direct elections to the European Parliament. At that time, the leader of the Opposition, Margaret Thatcher, asked Callaghan whether the convention of collective responsibility still applied to his government, only to receive the reply. 'I certainly think that the doctrine should apply, except in cases where I announce that it does not'.[9]

A more complex example had arisen in 1909, when the House of Lords rejected Lloyd George's 'People's Budget' precipitating a constitutional crisis whose outcome was the 1911 Parliament Act imposing, for the first time, statutory limitations upon the powers of the House of Lords. The rejection of the budget is generally held to have been unconstitutional, since it broke the convention that the non-elected house should not interfere with money bills. The peers, however, argued that the 1909 budget was far more than a money bill, since it had, attached to it, wide ranging measures of redistributive taxation. The budget was, in the view of the peers, an example of 'tacking', that is, adding on to the budget, matters which were not purely financial in content. This argument did not in the event prevail. The Liberal government went to the country twice on the issue, in January and December 1910, and although it lost its overall majority, it was able to continue in government with the support of the Labour Party and the Irish nationalists. The Liberals then passed the Parliament Act statutorily depriving the Lords of all legislative power over money bills.

Suppose, however, that, in the general election of January 1910, the Conservatives had been able to defeat the Liberals and form a government. Then, presumably, the Parliament Act would not have been passed, and the argument of the peers would have been vindicated. It would have been said that the convention that the House of Lords should not reject a money bill had not in fact been broken, since the 1909 budget was far more than a money bill; the convention, it would have been said, applied only to measures which were purely financial in nature; or, alternatively, it might have been said that what was thought to have been a convention was not in reality a convention at all. It is perhaps worth noting that the definition of a money bill in the 1911 Parliament Act is highly restrictive, and applies only to a bill which involves the 'imposition, repeal, remission, alteration or regulation of taxation'. As

---

[9] House of Commons Debates, vol 933, col 552, 16 June 1977.

we noted in chapter 6, the Speaker at the time, James Lowther, later declared in his memoirs that the Lloyd George Budget would not have been regarded by him as a money bill.

Whether, therefore, a particular practice is regarded as a convention, may depend, in part at least, upon political vicissitudes. What may seem at one time an unshakeable convention can change when the political concatenation of forces changes. How, then, is one to distinguish between those conventional rules which are permanent from those which depend upon the political balance of power? Can one in fact draw such a distinction at all—or is there no real difference between the constitutional limits on power and the political limits? One authority has argued that conventions are no more than mere inductive generalizations, 'an expression and ex post facto legitimation of practices rather than principles . . . They reflect observed regularities of behaviour'.[10]

Yet a convention is not merely something **regarded** as obligatory, but something which **is** obligatory. It is not always easy to distinguish the two, however, and sometimes, as in some of the examples discussed above, it may not become clear for some years. It is not, therefore, always easy to distinguish between what we might believe to be a convention and what we might believe *ought to be* a convention. One authority has suggested that conventions are part of the 'critical morality'[11] of the constitution. If that is so then a historical or sociological investigation would not succeed in discovering what they are; for to say that a convention exists is to make a normative statement rather than a complex statement about a matter of fact.

Once we have identified conventions, a further difficulty arises—precisely which conventions should be included in the constitution. It would, declares Jennings, be 'a singular constitutional law which mentions the Cabinet because it is referred to in the Ministers of the Crown Act, 1937, but cannot say what it does . . . It is a 'constitutional' law which says very little about the constitution'.[12] Should the constitution enact the Sewel convention, that Parliament does not 'normally legislate with regard to devolved matters in Scotland without the consent of the Scottish Parliament'?[13] Should the precise powers of the House of Lords be specified? What are these powers? In law, the answer is clear. The Lords have powers only over non-money bills, which they can delay for just one session, and over a bill to prolong the life of Parliament on which they retain an absolute veto. They also have absolute power to reject secondary legislation, since the Parliament Acts apply only to primary legislation. Few, however, would accept as a sensible statement of the constitutional position that the Lords enjoy an absolute power to

---

[10] D Feldman, 'One, none or several? Perspectives on the UK's constitution(s)' (2005) *Cambridge Law Journal*, 334.

[11] G Marshall, *Constitutional Conventions* (Oxford, OUP, 1984) 210. This book offers a penetrating analysis of problems arising from the existence of constitutional conventions in the UK.

[12] I Jennings, *The Law and the Constitution* (5th edn, London, University of London Press, 1959) 70–1.

[13] House of Lords Debates, vol 592, col 791, 21 July 1998.

reject secondary legislation. The powers of the House of Lords are limited not only by statute but by convention.

Another example might be whether there is now a convention that a government needs the support of Parliament for military action. It is perfectly possible for a single instance, in this case the House of Commons vote on the Iraq war on 18 March 2003, to create a precedent. During the debate, Jack Straw, the Foreign Secretary, declared that it was 'constitutionally proper in a modern democracy' for the government to seek 'explicit support of the House of Commons for military action', even though it had never done so before.[14] This vote may have created a precedent. In evidence to the House of Lords Select Committee on the Constitution in 2007, Jack Straw, as Lord Chancellor and Secretary of State for Justice, spoke of a 'fundamental principle that decisions about going to war have to be made ultimately by the elected chamber',[15] and in the Governance of Britain Green Paper in 2007, it was made a specific proposal, with certain exceptions, eg for nuclear response.

Defining a convention and distinguishing it from a practice or a mere usage, therefore, are by no means simple, and some conventions are so very general that it is difficult to interpret their meaning with any real degree of precision. It may be objected that the same is often true of statutory rules. But these can be interpreted by the courts; there is no similar umpire for conventions. Where the interpretation of a convention is unclear its resolution will often depend upon political developments. Use of the personal prerogatives by the head of state, for example, has been greatly limited by the development of a two party system, which has meant that the Queen has not been called upon to use her discretion as to whom to appoint Prime Minister, nor whether to accept a prime ministerial request for a dissolution. The answer, when there are only two parties, is generally obvious. But that could change were there to be a hung parliament when the answers would no longer be obvious; while, if the Commons came to be elected by proportional representation, every parliament would probably be hung since no government has achieved 50% of the vote since 1935. Such a change could significantly alter the role of the Queen, although the extent of the likely alteration in the role of the Queen should not be exaggerated.[16]

An enacted constitution which codifies conventions might seem to entail a considerable juridification of constitutional arrangements. What in the past was essentially political might now become a matter of constitutional law. It would in theory be for the courts to decide how conventions should be interpreted. They would no longer be dependent upon political vicissitudes but might become justiciable. But this change raises very large problems. Could the courts really decide, for example, what the principle of ministerial responsibility entailed? Would they be asked to lay down precise rules as to what information ministers

---

[14] House of Commons Debates, vol 401, col 900, 18 March 2003.

[15] Minutes of Evidence, 23 October 2007, Q 26.

[16] See also Bogdanor, *Multi-Party Politics and the Constitution* (Cambridge, CUP, 1983).

ought to disclose to Parliament, and the circumstances under which ministers ought to resign following administrative fault? If so, the courts would come to play a far more central role in the political process than they have ever performed hitherto. The courts, however, faced with such questions, would almost certainly resist being brought into the political process, and would probably adopt the 'political questions' doctrine that the United States Supreme Court has often, though not invariably, adopted when faced with issues concerning the doctrine of the separation of powers.

Conventions can be of very different types. Some may be quite fundamental, such as, for example, the convention that the government must resign following defeat in a confidence motion in the House of Commons; the interpretation of other conventions, for example the convention of individual ministerial responsibility, although perhaps equally fundamental, may evolve over time and their interpretation may be more opaque; other conventions, for example the convention that members of the royal family do not make speeches which have party political implications, may be less fundamental and indicate what is merely inadvisable.[17] How do we decide which conventions should be included in the constitution and which of those should be justiciable?

An attempt has been made to answer these difficult questions with respect to the Australian constitution. In 1985, an appointed committee, confusingly called a Convention, composed of delegates from the Commonwealth and State governments, representing all of the major parties, sought to identify the conventions of the Australian constitution. Its report set out a list of 34 conventions, governing such matters as the relationship between the Prime Minister, the Governor-General as the Queen's representative, and the House of Representatives.[18]

In a paper submitted to the Australian Constitutional Convention, Cheryl Saunders and Ewart Smith distinguished between conventions of different kinds: 'Some conventions might appropriately be included in a written constitution, subject to enforcement in the courts; others might be included in the constitution as non-justiciable declarations of principle; others might be articulated outside the constitution by way of an informal agreement on the content of which is understood'.[19] Unfortunately, however, they give no indication of which conventions belong to which category. Perhaps the reason for this is that it is difficult, if not impossible, to know a priori, whether a convention is justiciable or not. The answer will occur only after the judicial process has occurred, since the existence

---

[17] A Heard in *Canadian Constitutional Conventions: The Marriage of Law and Politics* (Toronto, OUP, 1991) 141, draws a threefold distinction of this kind between conventions.

[18] Details of these conventions can be found in the appendices to an article by C Sampford and D Wood 'Codification of Constitutional Conventions in Australia' (1987) *Public Law* 239–40. See also Sampford 'Recognise and Declare'. An Australian Experiment in Certifying Constitutional Conventions' (1989) *Oxford Journal of Legal Studies*, 369–417; and H V Evatt, *The King and his Dominion Governors* (Oxford, OUP, 1936). Dr Evatt, later a leader of the Australian Labor Party, was the first to suggest that the conventions should be incorporated into the Australian constitution.

[19] *Identifying Conventions Associated with the Commonwealth Constitution* (Australian Constitutional Convention, Standing Committee 'D', vol 2, 1982) 1, cited in Heard, *Canadian Constitutional Conventions*, 151.

or supposed existence of the convention will be part of the argument of one of the parties to the litigation.

Nevertheless, it is clear that not all conventions would be likely to prove both suitable for enactment and also justiciable. It would, admittedly, be possible to enact a convention but expressly exclude it from enforcement by action in the courts. Yet, although it is not easy to separate what is political from what is constitutional/legal, it is certainly possible to do so as the experience of other jurisdictions has shown.

At this point, however, a critic might ask, if some at least of the conventions are to be non-justiciable, what is the precise point of enacting them? The answer can only be that enactment might help to bring clarity into what is often a confused area, and therefore offer some assistance in the resolution of constitutional crises. Nevertheless, the enactment of a constitution could well lead to a threefold division amongst hitherto conventional rules—rules which are enacted and justiciable, rules which are enacted but non-justiciable, and rules which are not enacted, but which might nevertheless be authoritatively stated. In the case, however, of a rule that had been enacted but was declared non-justiciable, one wonders what authority a court would have for pronouncing upon it, and what force a judgment would have, since such a judgment would have no legal consequences.

One should not exaggerate the extent to which enacting a convention would bring clarity. The convention would have to be stated in very general terms and its interpretation might still remain a matter of some controversy. Even more fundamentally, enacting a constitution would not remove the fundamental difficulty that deciding what is to count as a convention is, as the example of the Salisbury convention shows, by no means a purely intellectual or juristic activity, but an essentially political one. Where there is dispute about whether a particular practice amounts to a convention, and about precisely what it prescribes, this dispute may well be a political as much as a purely intellectual dispute. Similarly, a dispute about the 'real meaning' of the commerce clause or the equal protection clause in the United States constitution is not primarily one about the meaning of the words; nor will such a dispute be one over a matter of fact, over whether political actors do actually feel obliged; it will be a dispute about whether they *ought* to feel obliged. It will be a dispute about what terms such as 'equal protection' **ought** to mean as much as one about what they do **in fact** mean. Similarly, a dispute about whether the Salisbury convention holds or not is more than a merely intellectual dispute, but in part a dispute about the proper locus of political power. There may thus be no wholly satisfactory way of determining who is 'right' in such disputes, since the answer may depend upon the balance of political power, and upon political vicissitudes and the state of public opinion.[20] In Britain, it will often be the case that where conventions are concerned, the limits of the constitution tend to coincide with the limits of political power. Living as we do during a period of some

---

[20] See, on this point, G C Moodie, 'The Monarch and the Selection of a Prime Minister: A Re-Examination of the Crisis of 1931' (1957) *Political Studies*, 18–19.

constitutional ferment, it has become particularly difficult to predict the outcome of what is an essentially political struggle, and difficult, therefore, to discover a satisfactory solution to the problem of enacting, for example, the powers of the Lords in a constitution.

IV

The problem of determining how we are to decide which conventions should be included and how they are to be formulated leads to the final and even more fundamental problem. Who is to have the authority to draw up, ratify and amend the constitution? A constitutional document, it might be suggested, cannot be drawn up in the same way as an ordinary legislative measure. Yet the report of the Australian Constitutional Convention—see page 226 above—valuable as it is, raises the question of what authority such a statement by a committee, however eminent, should enjoy. In order for it to carry legitimacy, presumably all-party representation on a constitutional assembly would be required, as was the case in Australia. Suppose, however, that there was not unanimous agreement on what the convention is, but rather some disagreement as with, for example, the Salisbury convention. Would such disagreement prevent it from being regarded as a convention? Would the representatives of one political party, however small, be able to exercise a veto—or could the issue be decided by majority or qualified majority vote? Some conventions in the Australian report were in fact decided by majority vote. How would conventions come to be altered—by unanimity, by majority vote, or by qualified majority? The answer is by no means clear. It would seem that the Australian Convention may have succeeded, therefore, in creating a rule of recognition for conventions, but not a rule of change. There would be some danger of creating 'an almost unique degree of inflexibility limited to indeterminacy and ineffectiveness, born of non-justiciability'.[21]

An assembly of the 'great and the good' is by no means the only institutional method by which proposals for a constitution might be drawn up. In Britain, some have proposed that a directly elected Convention be established. Sir Menzies Campbell, when leader of the Liberal Democrats, proposed that half of the membership of such a Convention should be chosen by random lot.[22] Others have suggested that it should be wholly elected. But since few people find constitutional issues matters of pressing concern, turnout for the election to the Convention might be low, and, in consequence, it would lack legitimacy.

An alternative suggestion is a representative but non-elected constitutional Convention analogous to that which met in Scotland from 1989 to 1995.[23] This

[21] Sampford, 'Recognise and Declare' above n 18, 403. The reference to the rule of recognition is of course derived from H L A Hart, *The Concept of Law* (Oxford, Clarendon Press, 1961).

[22] Sir M Campbell, 'A Rescue Plan for Politics', *Guardian*, 6 September 2007.

[23] See V Bogdanor, *Devolution in the United Kingdom* (Oxford, OUP, 1999) 196–98 and K Wright, *The People Say Yes: The Making of Scotland's Parliament* (Edinburgh, Argyll Publishing 1997). The Rev Kenyon Wright was Chair of the Convention.

Convention, however, was established to consider just one, fairly specific, issue, namely devolution; and it was composed only of supporters of devolution, since the Conservatives and the SNP refused to take part. Scotland is a more cohesive civic society than England, and it may be easier to achieve a consensus there, particularly on issues concerning Scottish nationality. A constitutional Convention in the United Kingdom as a whole would have to deal with a much wider range of issues, and it would be far more difficult than it was in Scotland to secure accurate representation of the various streams of opinion. If all parties agreed to be represented on it, the Convention might just replicate the party dogfight at Westminster; while if any of the opposition parties refused to be represented on it, as happened in Scotland, the Convention would be seen as unrepresentative, and perhaps as a mere instrument of the government in power.

Some might argue that a popular Convention, however chosen, would be the wrong instrument to present proposals for an enacted constitution, since few members of the public have formulated precise proposals on this topic. Yet experience of the British Columbia Citizens Assembly on Electoral Reform, discussed in chapter 12, seems to show that it is all too easy to under-estimate the potential of ordinary people to play their part in resolving complex constitutional problems. Guidance could, however, be provided by 'the great and the good' in the form of a Royal Commission. Members of the Commission would be experts nominated by the government, although no doubt the government would seek the approval of the main opposition parties for the nominees. The great advantage of such a Commission is that it would be a learning exercise. It would take written and oral evidence in different parts of the United Kingdom, and its oral evidence sessions would no doubt be televised, and would receive considerable publicity in the local as well as the national media. That attention would raise the profile of issues connected with democracy and might encourage people to think about them. Between 1969 and 1973, the Royal (Kilbrandon) Commission on the Constitution, which dealt primarily with devolution, held evidence sessions in different parts of the country, and this served to raise the profile of the devolution issue very considerably.

Once a constitution had been drawn up, a procedure would need to be found for ratification. The preamble to the United States constitution begins 'We the people', the implication being that the people of the United States have given themselves a constitution. The people, however, were not directly consulted either in the choice of Founding Fathers or in the ratification of the constitution, both of which were undertaken by elected representatives. Similarly, the preamble to the German constitution of 1949 declares that 'The German people have adopted, by virtue of their constituent power, this Basic Law', though that Law too was ratified by elected representatives rather than directly by the people. In some countries, however, France, for example, the constitution has been directly ratified by the people. It would be natural to suggest that a British constitution be put to the people for ratification. Parliament would then have signalled in the clearest possible way that in future it would no longer be sovereign, for it would then be bound by a constitution which had been enacted not only by itself but also by the people, from whom it would derive both its powers and also the limitations upon its powers.[24]

Should amendment of the constitution also be subject to referendum, or should Parliament alone be able to amend it; and, if Parliament has the sole power of amendment, should it be able to amend the constitution in the same manner as it amends other legislation, or should some special procedure, such as explicit repeal, a qualified majority or a referendum be required. It would be possible to give the House of Lords an absolute veto over a bill amending the constitution, similar to that which the Lords enjoy over a bill prolonging the life of a parliament. That provision provides a precedent for other legislation enjoying a special constitutional status. Whatever the solution reached, most would surely agree that the constitution ought not to be treated as if it were just an ordinary statute. The prime purpose of enacting a constitution is to provide for some form of 'higher' law, provisions more difficult to alter than those of the ordinary law. A constitution, therefore, would finally register and give legal effect to the proposition that Parliament had abdicated its sovereignty.[25]

V

The difficulties involved in drawing up a codified constitution are, therefore, formidable. But there is no reason to believe that they are insuperable. There is no reason to believe that it would not be possible to produce a codified constitution which would put Britain in line with almost every other democracy. There is no reason why this should not be feasible, no reason at all why, almost alone amongst democracies, Britain should be unable to enact a constitution. What is difficult to dispute is that the enactment of a constitution would be, to some extent at least, a normative and a political exercise as well as an intellectual one; and that it would be difficult to separate our judgment of what the constitution in fact *is* from our judgment of what it *ought* to be. The selection of what is to go into the constitution would involve normative choices. It can be argued that it is time that we as a country began to make these choices. We cannot be said to know what our constitution actually is, much less to understand it, until we have proceeded to enact it.

There are, therefore, powerful intellectual arguments for a codified constitution, arguments which it is difficult, in principle, to resist. Nevertheless, it is doubtful whether the present is the most appropriate time to produce one. The main reason for this is that there is a sense of incompleteness about the constitutional reforms since 1997, an uncertainty about their final direction. Constitutional reform has been a process rather than an event, and so far it is an incomplete process.

---

[24] Compare O Hood Phillips, *Reform of the Constitution* (London, Chatto and Windus/Charles Knight, 1970) 156.

[25] I owe this point to Professor Anthony Bradley. But he is not responsible for the use that I have made of it.

We have in fact been doing something unique in the democratic world. We have been transforming an uncodified constitution into a codified one, but in a piece-meal and ad hoc way. This is so for two reasons. The first is that there is no real political will to do anything more, constitutional reform being a distinctly sub-sidiary interest both for the people and for most politicians. The second reason is that there is no consensus on what the final end point should be. There is no consensus, for example, on how 'the English question' should be resolved, nor even on whether a solution is possible or necessary. There is no consensus on the future of the upper house. There is no consensus on the future role of local government. There is no consensus on the role of the referendum; and, perhaps most important of all, there is no consensus on the right electoral system for the House of Commons. As a result, the reforms since 1997 do not amount to a new constitu-tional settlement; and, at the time of writing, such a settlement appears elusive. Constitutional reform, then, has by no means reached its end-point. Until that end-point has been achieved, there seems little point in drafting or enacting a constitution.

Part III

Beyond the New Constitution

10

A New Localism?

LOCALISM HAS BECOME one of the catchwords of the age. The major political parties all proclaim their belief in it. Indeed, they argue not just for localism, but for 'a new localism', devolution not just to local government, but also to the people—double devolution. Real localism, on this view, involves giving to the people themselves the right to make decisions on local matters. Such a programme would have radical consequences for the new British constitution. So far, however, little has been done to secure this grandiose aim, and the place of local government in the British constitution remains far from clear. There are, in fact, strong obstacles to a genuine policy of decentralisation and they are as much cultural as constitutional or political. They do not derive only from central government, from ministers and civil servants; for the centralising instinct has corresponded, on the whole, with popular attitudes. Decentralisation would involve considerable costs as well as benefits and it is by no means clear whether the people are prepared to accept them.

There is, at the outset, a problem in fitting local government into any coherent account of the British constitution. Under the old British constitution, it could have no guaranteed role, no constitutional status at all. Local government, so it seemed, was just as much subject to the doctrine of the sovereignty of Parliament as any other public institution. It is true that the origins of local government lie far back into the past; local authorities existed before Parliament was created; and the House of Commons was indeed originally composed of representatives from boroughs and shires. Local authorities certainly came into existence before the doctrine of the sovereignty of Parliament was fully developed. Nevertheless, every local authority is now a statutory creation of Parliament. Local government, therefore, has no independent constitutional status and it would appear that if a government were to seek, through Parliament, to abolish local government by statute, it could legally do so. Such a statute would not be declared unlawful by the courts. So it would seem difficult to entrench local government as part of the constitution. It seems to have no independent constitutional status.

From another point of view, however, it could be argued that local government is and has always been very much part of the British constitution. Until the devolved bodies were set up in the 1990s, and, with the exception of the Northern

Ireland Parliament which sat from 1921 to 1972, local authorities were the only representative elected institutions in the country apart from Parliament. They were also the only bodies outside Parliament with the right to levy a tax—the business and domestic rates until 1989, then, for a brief interlude, the ill-fated community charge, the so-called poll tax, and now its replacement, the council tax. Local authorities, therefore, are a fundamental part of the machinery of representative democracy in Britain. It follows, some would argue, that they are also part of the constitution. Even though a government might lawfully, through Parliament, abolish local government entirely or emasculate its powers, few would regard such an action as constitutionally acceptable. The implication is that there are, despite the doctrine of the sovereignty of Parliament, constitutional limitations upon the power of Parliament with respect to local authorities. These, however, are limitations not of statute but of convention. In the words of an official report on local government, the sovereignty of Parliament is 'underpinned by a corpus of custom and convention as to the manner in which that sovereignty should be exercised'.[1] In the broader sense of the term 'constitutional', therefore, in which it can be held to refer to the conditions under which political authority in a democracy ought to be exercised, local government is most certainly a part of the constitution. The implication is that if it is to enjoy a political authority independent of government and of Parliament, it must have an assured constitutional status.

The need for local government to enjoy an assured constitutional status was recognised by the Blair government when, in 1998, it ratified the Charter of Local Self-Government of the Council of Europe. This Charter had been drawn up by the Council in 1985 and was regarded by it as an analogue to the European Convention on Human Rights. The Convention on Human Rights defines the rights of the individual, while the Charter defines the rights of local communities and of their elected representatives. The Charter had been signed by all of the member states of the Council of Europe, except for the Irish Republic, which did not sign until 2002, and Britain, even though the provisions of the Charter had been watered down to make it more acceptable to Margaret Thatcher's government, which was highly unsympathetic to the whole project.

The Charter, unlike the Convention on Human Rights, is in no way binding upon those member states of the Council of Europe which choose to ratify it, and there is no European court to interpret its provisions. It is an international treaty and does no more than lay down principles and standards for local democracy. It provides, therefore, no more than a symbolic commitment to the values of local self-government, but there is an expectation that governments will adhere to the principles that they have accepted in the Charter, and they are required to provide information to the Council of Europe showing how they have complied with it.

---

[1] Report of the Committee of Inquiry into the Conduct of Local Authority Business, Cmnd 9797, 1986, para 3.4.

The articles of the Charter lay out the principles required to develop democratic local authorities with, 'a wide degree of autonomy with regard to their responsibilities, the ways and means by which those responsibilities are exercised and the resources required for their fulfilment'.

Perhaps the two most important articles are Article 2 which states:

'The principle of local self-government shall be recognised in domestic legislation, and where practicable in the constitution'.

And Article 3 which states:

'Local self-government denotes the right and the ability of local authorities, within the limits of the law, to regulate and manage a substantial share of public affairs under their own responsibility and in the interests of the local population'.

Article 4 of the Charter provides for the principle of subsidiarity in stating that 'Public responsibilities shall generally be exercised, in preference, by those authorities which are closest to the citizen' and that 'Powers given to local authorities should normally be full and exclusive'. Article 9 declares that local authorities should be given the freedom to determine expenditure priorities and to raise adequate resources.

It is, however, doubtful whether ratification of the Charter in 1998 has led to any real improvement in the status of local government. There are strong obstacles to be faced before there is a genuine acceptance either by national political elites or by the people as a whole of 'the principle of local self-government'. These obstacles are not just constitutional, but also political and cultural. The constitutional subordination of local government to Parliament is underpinned by its striking political weakness and by cultural attitudes which favour centralisation. It has been persuasively argued that, despite the Charter, 'the cumulative impact of twentieth-century developments has resulted in a disintegration of the constitutional tradition of local government'.[2] The principle of local self-government has become, so it seems, attenuated.

II

Despite much rhetoric about the values of localism and decentralisation, there are few indications of any great popular support for local government in Britain. Turnout in local government elections is generally between 30% and 40%—the lowest by far in Western Europe. In Ireland, turnout in local elections is around 62%, in Germany it is 72% and in Sweden 88%.[3] Turnout is lowest in inner city wards and amongst the less well-off—precisely those social groups who, so it may

[2] M Loughlin, 'The Demise of Local Government', in V Bogdanor (ed) *The British Constitution in the Twentieth Century* (Oxford, OUP, 2003) 521.

[3] See, for comparative figures of turnout in local government elections, J A Chandler, *Explaining Local Government in Britain: Local Government in Britain since 1800* (Manchester, MUP, 2007) 321. This book provides an excellent account of the history of local government and of its current problems.

be argued, need the vote the most. It is difficult to explain low turnout by a lack of interest in local issues, since survey evidence shows that 67% of 18 to 24 year olds, the generational group least likely to vote, say that they are in fact interested in local issues. Survey evidence further seems to indicate that people 'want to be involved and have their say, but the structure and culture of politics alienates and deters them'.[4] But, in addition, of those who do vote, the vast majority support the same party locally as they do in national elections. One political scientist has characterised local elections as 'second-order' elections by contrast with national elections which are 'first-order' elections. Voting behaviour at second-order elections is primarily determined by the political situation at national level, and, in particular, by the popularity of the government of the day.[5] Voters generally make a judgment not so much on the effectiveness of their local council as upon the effectiveness of the national government. It is for this reason that, when an incumbent administration has been in office for some time, there will be a swing against it in local government. In 1979, when the Conservatives were elected to power in the aftermath of a highly unpopular Labour government, they controlled 244 local authorities in Britain, while Labour controlled 109. By 1996, one year before the end of the long period of Conservative rule, they controlled just 14 councils, while Labour controlled 207. After the 2008 local elections, by which time the Labour government, first elected in 1997, had also become unpopular, Labour controlled just 48 local authorities while the Conservatives controlled 215.[6]

Voters, then, generally treat local elections, not as a means of deciding upon local issues, but as a plebiscite on the record of the government of the day. That is also how the results are presented in the national media. Local elections are interpreted as indicating the likely fate of the government at the next general election, not as a judgment on local matters or the performance of particular local councils. National, not local, politicians are asked to comment on the outcome. That is not a new development. As long ago as 1948, Lord Woolton, the Chairman of the Conservative Party, in his opening address to a Party local government conference, exhorted Conservatives to secure election to local authorities, saying:

> 'In April and May 1949, we shall have a miniature general election in the country. In every local authority in the country—county, district, borough—there is a prospect of seeing the efficiency of our party machine and testing the steadfastness in the faith of our members. Later on there will be a Parliamentary Election, and I want to make these elections next spring into a battle ground for the big (*sic*) contest'.[7]

It is partly because local government seems to be so little valued, and because so many local authorities do not represent areas with secure natural identities, that

---

[4] *Communities in Control: Real People, Real Power*, Cm 7427, 2008, para 1.34.

[5] K Reif (ed) *Ten European Elections* (Aldershot, Gower, 1985) 8.

[6] C Rallings and M Thrasher, 'The Demise of New Labour? The British 'Mid-Term' Elections of 2008', (2008) *The Forum*, Article 7, 2.

[7] Quoted in K Young, 'Party Politics in Local Government: An Historical Perspective' in Research Vol IV: *Aspects of Local Democracy: Committee of Inquiry into the Conduct of Local Authority Business*, Cmnd 9801, 1986, 100–1.

national governments of both political parties have been able to take powers away from them with so little protest. In consequence, Britain has become a profoundly centralised society, and any government which genuinely seeks to restore localism will face formidable obstacles in doing so. Centralisation is not only a matter of institutional dominance, but of cultural preconceptions. The rhetoric may be decentralist, but the practice remains largely centralist. Whether the new constitution comes to embrace decentralisation, therefore, will depend upon whether there is the popular and the political will to counter the deep-seated cultural trends which have legitimised centralisation. At present, it may be argued, the voters have logic on their side in treating local elections as miniature general elections. If central government effectively makes the crucial decisions for local authorities, including decisions as to how much local authorities are allowed to raise in council tax and how much they are allowed to spend, then the only purpose of a local vote can be to send a message to central government. But why is local government so little valued in Britain?

Local government, if it is to be effective, needs to rest upon a well-defined sense of locality. The fundamental problem confronting advocates of localism, however, is that of recreating a sense of locality in what has become a rootless society. During the twentieth century, the sense of locality has been undermined by geographical and social mobility, and by continual structural reorganisations which have had the effect of creating local authorities remote from the public and which the public find difficult to identify with. This does not mean, of course, that the vast majority of the population is in continual movement. Even at the beginning of the twenty-first century only a minority of the population move very far during their lifetime from where they were born. But it is increasingly the energetic and ambitious minority, the socially mobile, which tends also to be geographically mobile. These are precisely the people who might be expected to assume leadership positions in local government. With the expansion of higher education—it is currently a government aim that 50% of young people should go to university—increasing numbers of the ambitious and energetic will leave their local roots behind them. The kind of locally rooted society celebrated by novelists such as Arnold Bennett will have gone, never to return.

During the twentieth century the sense of locality was radically undermined by developments in transport, and, in particular, by the development of the motor car, which tended to obliterate the distinction between town and country. The suburban commuter came to replace the local craftsman, working in the town, but living in the suburbs or the countryside. Work-place and service centre came to be divorced from home, which became a retreat to be enjoyed in the evenings and the weekend. A locality was no longer a natural resting-place which one remained rooted to throughout one's life, but rather a place for arrival and departure. One was, as it were, always in transit.

The problem of preserving a sense of locality against strong countervailing trends is not of course peculiar to Britain, but is common to most, if not all, industrialised societies. Whether these trends can be resisted depends in large part upon political arrangements, and, in particular, whether there are strong inter-connections between local and national politics. Territorial politics in Britain, however, has been characterised by a sharp separation between local and national political roles, with the local being strictly subordinate to the national. There is of course a link in that many MPs are former councillors. Over the past hundred years, there has been a steady rise in the percentage of MPs with local government experience. In 1911, for example, if Ireland is excluded, 29% of MPs had local gov-ernment experience, while in 2006, the figure was 54%. But there has been a steady decline in the number of MPs who **remain** councillors once they have been elected to the House of Commons. In 1889, shortly after the first elections to the new county councils, 87 MPs (and 131 peers) were also councillors, and remained councillors. In 2006, by contrast, just 18 MPs were councillors. Of these, 16 had first been elected in 2005, and could be expected to leave their local council in due course. The other two, who had first been elected in 2001, were a husband and wife team, Peter and Iris Robinson, who represented constituencies in Northern Ireland. It seems safe to conclude, therefore, that 'In recent decades almost all newly elected MPs who were councillors have either immediately resigned from their local authority or simply have not stood again when eligible for re-election as councillors'.[8] One important reason for this trend is that it is rare for someone to be elected as an MP for the constituency in which he or she had been a councillor. John Major, the first Prime Minister to have been a councillor since Clement Attlee, had been a member of Lambeth council. As a Conservative he would have had little chance of being elected in Lambeth, but he eventually secured adoption for the safe Conservative constituency of Huntingdon. Similarly, a Labour coun-cillor in Henley or a Conservative councillor in Tower Hamlets would have hardly any chance of being returned as a local MP. They would have to seek their fortunes elsewhere. 'In a system where parliamentary representatives have no necessary relationship to their electoral districts, a Shropshire lad may still write Shropshire poems, but to be political he must necessarily become a Westminster City lad'.[9] It is of course the first-past-the-post electoral system and its natural concomitant, the safe seat, which makes for this disconnection between local and national poli-tics. So, despite the direct and intimate relationship which is held to exist between MPs and their constituencies under the single-member constituency system, it remains true that, as one authority noted in 1975, the links between MPs and their localities

'are far more tenuous in Britain than in many other countries. Relatively few members are people with roots—formed by birth, upbringing or professional experience—in the area they represent. The carpet-bagger climbing the ladder of party success is an all too common phenomenon in British politics. . . . Indeed, there are grounds for believing that local political vitality is sapped in Britain by reason of the sharp division between national

---

[8] Chandler, *Explaining Local Government*, above n 3, 235–6, 242.
[9] B Barber, 'Participation and Swiss Democracy', *Government and Opposition* (Winter 1988) 42–3.

and local political life: the former does not draw strength from the latter, and neither does the latter gain any real voice in national affairs'.[10]

The first-past-the-post electoral system makes constituency representation very much a carpet-bagger's charter. The consequence is that 'By the twenty-first century, for an ambitious politician, local government service may be a stepping-stone to power, but it is rarely a central interest as distinct from a means to an end.'[11] Most members of Parliament are rootless, and perhaps that is one reason why Britain itself has become so geographically rootless a society.

Over the past 150 years there have been only three politicians who have defied this trend and built national careers on their success in local government. The first was Joseph Chamberlain, the radical mayor of Birmingham from 1873 to 1876, when he became MP for a Birmingham constituency. In 1880 he was appointed a member of the Cabinet in Gladstone's second ministry, but in 1886 he broke with the Liberal Party because of his opposition to Gladstone's policy of Irish Home Rule, joining Lord Salisbury's Unionist Cabinet in 1895 as Colonial Secretary, a position which he retained until he resigned once again in 1903. Chamberlain was, for much of the period between 1876 and 1903, a leading figure in national politics. The strength of his national position was based in part on the solidity of his local political base. When he broke with the Liberals in 1886, he could survive as a Liberal Unionist against official Liberal opposition primarily because of this local base. When he swung to support the Conservatives, Birmingham swung with him, and remained solidly Conservative until 1945, except for the years 1929 to 1931.

The second politician to have built his career upon success in local government was Herbert Morrison, who became mayor of Hackney in 1920. He was first elected to the London County Council in 1922, and became the first Labour leader of the London County Council in 1934. These local government positions helped him to acquire the administrative and leadership skills which he needed for his Cabinet posts as Home Secretary in the wartime coalition and Leader of the House of Commons in the post-war Labour government. But, when Morrison stood for the leadership of the Labour Party in 1935, he was defeated by Attlee, and one of the reasons for his defeat was that he would not agree to relinquish his local government position were he to be elected Labour leader. He was seen in fact as too much of a London local government man by many MPs from the provinces and by many of the trade union MPs. His leadership position in local government was seen as a handicap, not as an advantage.

The third politician to have built his reputation through service in local government was Ken Livingstone, leader of the Greater London Council from 1981 until its abolition in 1986. But, elected as MP for Brent East in 1987, Livingstone made less impact in the Commons than he had in the GLC. He was not invited to

---

[10] N Johnson, 'Adversary Politics and Electoral Reform—Need We Be Afraid?' in S E Finer (ed) *Adversary Politics and Electoral Reform* (London, Anthony Wigram, 1975) 81.

[11] Chandler, *Explaining Local Government*, above n 3, 237.

become a member of the Blair government elected in 1997, and stepped down from Westminster at the general election of 2001.

The successes of Chamberlain, Morrison and Livingstone owed more to their personal qualities, their political skills, their flair for publicity and their ability to build a power base for themselves, than to the offices they held. Other mayors of Birmingham, leaders of the LCC or GLC failed to emulate their success, which was achieved despite the system rather than because of it. Chamberlain, Morrison and Livingstone are very much the exception to the rule that central and local politics in Britain remain in separate spheres, with little interaction between them. This sharp separation of national and local spheres contrasts strikingly with politics on the Continent and in the United States, where success at local or provincial level provides both a springboard for national advancement and also an opportunity for a national leader to gain executive experience. In the United States, presidents such as Carter, Clinton and George W. Bush had been state governors, not members of Congress. In Germany, every Chancellor between Kiesinger in 1966 and Angela Merkel in 2006 was the leader of a provincial government, not a member of the Bundestag. In France, many leading politicians, including ministers, have been mayors of the constituency which they represent in the National Assembly, and they retain their position as mayor even after being elected to the national legislature. As Interior minister in Jacques Chirac's government, for example, Nicolas Sarkozy insisted upon remaining President of the General Council of Hauts de Seine. In 2008, no fewer than 282 out of the 577 deputies in the National Assembly were mayors, and 380, including the 282 mayors, remained members of a municipal council. Other deputies remained members of other local authorities. There were, in 2008, just 68 deputies in the National Assembly who held no local government position at all. The interconnection between local and national politics in the United States, Germany and France helps to ensure that leading national politicians have already proved themselves by their achievements at executive level in local or regional politics. Few British political leaders have this sort of executive experience; and, when they have, as Herbert Morrison discovered, it is not necessarily seen as an advantage. It is because there is so sharp a disconnection between local and central government in Britain, and because the local sphere is seen as distinctly subordinate to the national, that local government is so little valued, by ministers and officials and by the public.

III

Local government has had to meet the challenge of a decline in the sense of locality, a decline accentuated by successive reorganisations. The reorganisation of local government has been largely determined by the interests of central government, not by the needs of localities themselves. Local authorities were seen as a vested interest. It was ministers who decided what sort of local government structure they wanted, not local authorities nor the people who would be affected by reform. In 1957 a Royal Commission, chaired by Sir Edwin Herbert, was established to consider the future shape of local government in London. This Commission did not contain a single member with any experience of local government. A precedent was set that radical changes in local government could be proposed and then implemented 'without allowing the local authorities affected to take any part in the formulation of the terms of reference of the inquiry preceding change, or in the process following the inquiry but preceding Ministerial decision'.[12] In 1966 another Royal Commission was set up, chaired by Lord Redcliffe-Maud, to consider the future of local government in England. By contrast with the Royal Commission on London government, this did contain representatives from local authorities, both members and officers. But the local government representatives were all from the larger authorities, the counties and the county boroughs. There were no representatives from the smaller, rural and urban districts, the non-county boroughs nor the parishes, whose interests were bound to be affected by reform. The reason for there being no such representatives might well have been that the government had already decided that these small authorities should be swept away. What cannot be doubted is that the composition of the Royal Commission on Local Government in England tended to predispose it towards the conclusion that the smaller units should be eliminated. 'Members were likely', one commentator has suggested, 'to accept the basic premiss that local government was based on too many small and unequal units and needed restructuring into fewer larger authorities'.[13] The remedies for the ills of local government were to be devised for it primarily by ministers. Local government was no longer part of the 'political constitution'.[14] The process was carried even further in the Local Government Act of 1985, when Margaret Thatcher's government abolished the Greater London Council and the metropolitan county councils. The powers of these authorities were not, in the main, transferred to other local authorities, but to non-elected bodies, quangos, or to Whitehall. The 1985 Act was more than a mere reorganisation, but involved the unilateral abolition of an elected tier of local government, without consultation either with the local authorities concerned or with the people by means of referendum. It raised constitutional issues of great magnitude, and set a dangerous precedent for any future administration which sought to abolish an elected layer of local government of whose policies it disapproved.

The two Royal Commissions—on local government in London and on local government in England—were part of an ongoing process of local government reorganisation which consumed much energy in the post-war years. The standard criticism of local authorities by central elites in the 1950s and 1960s was that there were too many of them, that they were too small, and therefore inefficient. That

[12] L J Sharpe, ' "Reforming" the Grass Roots: An Alternative Analysis' in D Butler and A H Halsey (eds) *Policy and Politics: Essays in Honour of Norman Chester* (Houndmills, Macmillan, 1978) 103.

[13] Chandler, *Explaining Local Government*, above n 3, 197.

[14] K Young, 'The Party and English Local Government', in A Seldon and S Ball (eds) *The Conservative Century: The Conservative Party since 1900* (Oxford, OUP, 1994) 443.

diagnosis was in tune with the modernising ethos of the period, which believed that larger institutions were likely to be more efficient than smaller ones. The spirit of the age was that of managerialism, an ideology whose other manifestations lay in the Industrial Reorganisation Corporation, which encouraged government-sponsored mergers to improve the efficiency of British industry, the view that the main advantage of the European Community lay in the large markets which they made available for British exports, the view that the civil service should follow the practices of private business, and the view that large, federal departments of government of the kind that were to be set up by Edward Heath in 1970, would improve the efficiency of central government. So far as local government was concerned, the ethos of managerialism was given authoritative recognition in 1969 when the Royal Commission on Local Government in England came to issue its report.

The leitmotif of the report was that a smaller number of larger local authorities would prove more effective than the existing system and that this restructuring would make decentralisation possible. Larger and more efficient local authorities would, in the words of Lord Redcliffe-Maud, increase 'the power of defiance by the local community of the central government'.[15] The Redcliffe-Maud Commission even went so far as to hint that a reformed local government system might be empowered to take over some at least of the functions of the National Health Service.[16] Yet the case for larger local authorities was also stressed, with suspicious unanimity, by the departments of central government themselves. The Department of Education and Science, for example, proposed a minimum size of half a million for an education authority, as well as the 'creation of a small number of really big authorities covering the main concentrations—such as the Birmingham, Manchester and Tyneside areas—to act as pace-setters in the educational field'.[17] This proposal was not, however, based upon any rigorous interpretation of the evidence, nor on any comparative analysis which might have disproved it, since there were many smaller educational authorities in Continental countries, and it would be difficult to argue that the standard of education in these countries had suffered as a result. In Britain, a number of quite small local education authorities had proved highly innovative. Chesterfield, for example, had been the first local authority to raise the school-leaving age to 16, while Cambridge had been the first to introduce a school dental service.

What was striking about the Royal Commission report was that it took so little notice of the research which it had itself commissioned. This research seemed to disprove the argument that size led to efficiency. The Royal Commission's Research Study No 1, for example, after an exhaustive analysis of three local authorities—Oxford, Oxfordshire and East Sussex—declared that:

---

[15] Oral Evidence to the Royal Commission on Local Government in England, 27 February 1967, HMSO 1967, para 509.

[16] Report of the Royal Commission in Local Government in England, Cmnd 4040, 1969, 92–4.

[17] Written Evidence of the Department of Education and Science to the Royal Commission on Local Government in England, HMSO 1967, 15.

'The most striking conclusion to emerge from this discussion is in fact negative: it is not the case that the largest authority is able to effect a consistently greater degree of specialization than the smallest'. (p 293)

And, in paragraph 266 of his Memorandum of Dissent to the Report of the Royal Commission, Derek Senior commented:

'Research Study No. 4's exhaustive analysis of twenty-seven performance indices in relation to fifteen measurable characteristics of local authorities produced only one significant finding that held good for both counties and county boroughs and that was the unexpected one that large education authorities do not exploit their potential advantage of being able to afford a higher proportion of specialist advisers'.

One cynical commentator, a Labour back-bench MP John Mackintosh, felt that the unanimous agreement on the part of central departments that local government units should be larger was precisely because larger authorities would be **less** able to defy central government than smaller ones.

'At a recent conference on local government reform, a senior civil servant was pressed as to why department after department recommended 30 to 40 local authorities in England ... Eventually, after much pressure, he put down his notes. 'Don't you see that 30 to 40 is the number of local authority officials you can conveniently get together in one room at the Ministry and then knock their heads together.' (*The Times*, 12th December, 1969)

Lord Redcliffe-Maud's view that a smaller number of large local authorities would encourage decentralisation was, to say the least, implausible; and, far from leading to the devolution of power, local government reform proved but a further stage on the path to centralisation, since it severed local authorities from their local roots. The Director of Research for the Commission, L J Sharpe, declared in 1989 that the research 'convinced me that it would be probably better to leave the whole local government system alone'.[18]

The Conservative government of Edward Heath, elected in 1970, although it departed from the precepts of the Redcliffe-Maud Commission in a number of respects, did, nevertheless, accept the case for larger authorities, primarily at district council level. Nevertheless, the 1972 Local Government Act, steered through Parliament by Peter Walker, the Secretary for the Environment in the Heath government, was a brave attempt to modernize local government so that it could meet the challenge of the age of the motor car; and, despite the various alterations that have been made to it, the 1972 Act still remains the basis of the local government system in England.

The Act removed the all-purpose county boroughs, and reduced the number of county councils in England and Wales to 47, with a lower tier of district councils; in the conurbations, it established 6 metropolitan county councils and 36 district councils. The central theme of the reform was to unite town and country. For this purpose most of the all-purpose county boroughs were merged into their historic

---

[18] 'The Redcliffe-Maud Royal Commission Twenty Years On' *Contemporary Record* (Summer 1989) 35.

counties or into newly created counties. Some of the new district councils created by the Act joined together competing town centres, creating new authorities with strange and artificial names. The district council of North Hertfordshire, for example, combined together the very different towns of Letchworth, Baldock, Hitchin and Royston, which had worked together happily as separate authorities, but found combination in a new district council difficult. The same was true of Hertford and Bishops Stortford, artificially put together into the new district of East Hertfordshire. This pattern was repeated in most parts of England outside the metropolitan areas where a district population of at least 100,000 was the preferred template.

In fact, the average population of the lower tier of local government in England, the district council, is, at around 139,300, by far the highest in Western Europe. The next largest is Ireland where the average population size is around 93,000, followed by the Netherlands with 49,000, Portugal with 32,349 and Sweden with 29,200. In Germany, the average population of a *gemeinde* is just 9,000 while the average size of a French *commune* is 1,500.[19] There is no reason to believe that the larger local authorities in Britain are more efficient than their Continental counterparts.

Britain now has both the largest average size of local authority in Western Europe and the lowest turnout. These two facts may well be interconnected. In seeking to adapt local government to the age of the motor car, ministers had created a structure of local government that was no longer very local. A national survey of community attitudes undertaken for the Redcliffe-Maud Commission had 'found that people thought of their local community as a quite small area—a village or small town and, if they lived in a larger town, as a ward or group of streets'.[20] Certainly voters found it more difficult to identify with the new authorities, particularly the new, artificial counties, Avon, Cleveland and Humberside, which were to be dismantled in the 1990s, or new district councils with new names that reflected no identifiable locality at all. The reorganisation, therefore, caused, as the White Paper of 2008, *Communities in Control*, noticed, a 'disconnect between the place people say they live in, and the name of the local authority which delivers their services and collects their council tax. So for example a resident of Malmesbury or Pewsey, in Wiltshire is unlikely to say they live in Kennet, even if that is the name of the council which collects their tax every year'.[21] In larger authorities it was more difficult for councillors to be aware for themselves of conditions on the ground, and therefore more discretion would inevitably be left to officers. This trend had been foreseen by the Urban District Councils Association as early as 1942, in evidence submitted to an inquiry on the proper shape of local government after the war. 'The urban district councillor', it suggested,

---

[19] See the table in Chandler, *Explaining Local Government*, above n 3, 321.
[20] Lord Redcliffe-Maud and B Wood, *English Local Government Reformed* (Oxford, OUP, 1974) 38–9.
[21] *Communities in Control*, Cm 7427, para 4.25.

'lives among the people he is trying to serve and has a fairly intimate knowledge of the matters the council is dealing with. He is not entirely dependent upon officers' reports. His knowledge is first hand. Also he can gather local opinion. On the other hand a county councillor is often discussing matters arising in regard to areas distant from his own and of which he cannot have the same knowledge as the man on the spot'.[22]

It would be difficult to find a more succinct or prescient summary of the main weakness of the structure of local government introduced in the 1970s. For, even if the new system of local government had been more efficient—and that itself is very arguable—this efficiency would have been purchased at the expense of the democratic values of local self-government which formed the fundamental justification for having a system of local authorities at all. Both the Redcliffe-Maud report and the Heath government saw local government primarily as a means to an end (the delivery of services) rather than as an institution which represented local communities. Many have reacted against this instrumental and technocratic approach, and opinion has in some quarters swung back to the idea that local government units should be based on a sense of local community identity. This would imply much smaller units of local government. The idea was well expressed by Lady Blatch, the Conservative local government spokesman in the House of Lords in a debate on local government in 1991,

'We believe that the best local government is local government which is built on communities and which reflects people's sense of identity with the place they live. Local authorities based on real communities will be stronger local authorities better able to voice local views and respond to local needs and circumstances.'[23]

But neither Conservative nor Labour governments have been prepared to follow the practical implications of such statements, and the local government system is still based upon the principles laid down in the Redcliffe-Maud report and the 1972 Act.

The creation of large authorities did not even end the conflict between town and country. Instead, this conflict took place within the authority itself, and once proud county boroughs such as Bristol and Reading increasingly resented their subordination to the counties. It was largely for this reason that, in the 1990s, provision was made for a further reorganisation and the recreation of some of the county boroughs as unitary authorities. Finally, the hope that the new structure of local government would lead to a significant devolution of powers was also frustrated. The very Local Government Act of 1972 which provided for reorganisation also removed the personal health services and water supply from the purview of local authorities; while, during the 1980s and 1990s, under the Conservative governments of Margaret Thatcher and John Major, so many powers were taken from local government that, in the view of two authors who had worked with Major at No. 10, 'It looked for a time as if local authorities might be cut right back to

---

[22] Chandler, *Explaining Local Government*, above n 3, 234.
[23] House of Lords Debates, vol 532, col 712, 18 November 1991.

rubbish collection and street lights—the kind of services they could reasonably be expected to provide out of money they could raise themselves'.[24] In addition, it appears that Margaret Thatcher's Chancellor, Nigel Lawson, seriously considered abolishing local taxation so that all local authority services would have been funded from central government, a course which, in the view of three observers, 'would have involved the abolition of local government worth the name'.[25]

There was, however, one major and almost certainly unintended consequence of the 1972 Local Government Act, which was to strengthen the grip of tightly organised party politics upon local government. Because the Act created larger local authorities and larger local government wards, it heralded the demise of the independent councillor. Independents were no longer able so easily to canvass the large wards created by the reorganisation. Wards containing more than around 2,500 electors are probably too large for an independent to canvass. To canvass larger wards requires the help of the party machine. In the 1970 county council elections, the last before the 1972 Act, there were only four counties with wards averaging more than 3,000 electors where the majority of councillors were without party labels; conversely there were only four counties with wards averaging fewer than 2,000 electors where the majority of councillors **did** have a party label. In most of the new county authorities, the ratio of councillors to electors was around 1 to 5,000, while in some it was 1 to 10,000 or even more. Before reorganisation, independents held a majority in 13 English counties and were the largest single group in 5 others. By 1977, they controlled just 4 county councils.[26]

The demise of the independent in local government was, admittedly, by no means an unmixed evil. In many areas dominated by independents, local elections had been uncontested and the unopposed candidate had been chosen by the local 'establishment'. In the early years of Cheshire County Council, for example, a councillor once selected 'had a very good chance of representing his division, frequently unopposed until either his retirement or death'. One ward did not have a contested election from the time of the creation of the Council in 1888 until 1922.[27] A student of local government, 'observed in 1970 an arrangement of Welsh farmers to decide among themselves who would be nominated for their local community council. On one occasion an unwise English settler got herself nominated separately from the local arrangement and occasioned an election, which she lost'.[28] In the 1960s, around half of the county council members and up to three-quarters of rural district councillors in England were elected unopposed. In Devon, in the last county council elections before reorganisation, in 1970, every candidate was an independent but there were contested elections in just 16 of the 75

[24] S Hogg and J Hill, *Too Close to Call: Power and Politics—John Major in No. 10* (London, Warner, 1995) 58.

[25] D Butler, A Adonis and T Travers, *Failure in British Government: The Politics of the Poll Tax* (Oxford, OUP, 1994) 296.

[26] W Grant, *Independent Local Politics in England and Wales* (Farnborough, Saxon House, 1977) 2.

[27] J M Lee, *Social Leaders and Public Persons: A Study of County Government in Cheshire since 1888* (Oxford, OUP, 1963) 59.

[28] Chandler, *Explaining Local Government*, above n 3, 239–40.

divisions.[29] It would be wrong, therefore, to idealise the independent councillor. Nevertheless, a local authority dominated by independents might well be in a stronger position to represent the local community and resist the depredations of central government than a local authority dominated by party political councillors.

Of course, party politics in local government is by no means a recent development. Political parties contested local elections well before the county councils were created in 1888. What is more recent is not the contesting of local elections by political parties but the tight party political management of council business.[30] The one does not necessarily imply the other. Studies of various Labour authorities in the north of England before reorganisation, show that very different managerial styles prevailed, with tight political management of council business being mainly confined to the larger, more urban, authorities.[31] In Glossop during the 1950s, neither the Conservative nor the Liberal councillors held party meetings. The Labour councillors did hold such meetings, but, nevertheless, often voted in different ways. There seemed no sign of a party whip.[32] In the rural district council of Newcastle-under-Lyme, the Labour councillors did not meet as a group at all until the 1960s.[33] The most tightly controlled local authority of all was the London County Council under the rule of Herbert Morrison and his successors from 1934. Clement Attlee apparently regarded the LCC under Labour as 'the nearest thing to a totalitarian state in Western Europe', while Hugh Gaitskell saw as one cause of Labour's election defeat in 1959 the autocratic behaviour of some Labour councils.[34]

The 1972 Local Government Act not only created larger local government wards and larger local authorities, but, by merging county boroughs into historic or newly created counties, it had the effect of bringing the urban style of party politics into the countryside.[35] Before 1972, nearly every large town had a party political local government. But, in a number of rural counties, even where councillors wore party labels, the party whip was not rigidly applied, and local interests often overrode party doctrine. At a time, for example, when the policy of the Conservative Party at national level was broadly opposed to comprehensive education, a number of rural local authorities established comprehensive schools as community schools in suitable areas where the sparseness of population meant that no genuine choice of secondary school was, in practice, possible. Conversely, many Labour local authorities in urban areas were rather sceptical of comprehensive education which they thought might damage the chances of bright working-class children. In addition, chairmanships in a number of rural authorities were decided not so much on party affiliation as on knowledge and expertise.

[29] Redcliffe-Maud and Wood, *Local Government Reformed*, above n 20, 63.
[30] K Young, 'Aspects of Local Government', Vol IV of the Report of the Committee of Inquiry into Local Authority Business, Cmnd 9800, 1986, 104–5.
[31] J G Bulpitt, *Party Politics in English Local Government* (London, Longman, 1967).
[32] A H Birch, *Small Town Politics: A Study of Political Life in Glossop* (Oxford, OUP, 1959) 119.
[33] F Bealey, J Blondel and W P McCann, *Constituency Politics: A Study of Newcastle-under-Lyme* (London, Faber and Faber 1965) 339.
[34] K Young, 'Aspects of Local Government', above n 30, 103.
[35] M Steed, 'The New Style of Local Politics' (1973) *New Society*, 5 April, 11–13.

In Oxfordshire, for example, a not untypical rural county, the large Conservative majority, regularly appointed, before the reorganisation of 1973, a Labour councillor as chairman of the important education committee, on the grounds that he was the best person for the job because of his interest in education. That became impossible after reorganisation when the party whip came to be applied more rigorously. So, although the 1972 Local Government Act did not initiate a trend towards tighter party politics in local government, it had the effect of accelerating it. Given the trend towards intra-party dissidence at Westminster over the past thirty years, local councils are probably now under tighter party control than are MPs in the House of Commons. That is a paradox, since the years since 1970s have seen a decline in party identification and fall in party membership, with many local party organisations having become nearly empty shells in consequence. Parties have become weaker amongst voters but stronger in local government.

The strengthening of party politics in local government has also had the effect of undermining the connection between 'social leaders' and 'public persons', the connection between status in local society and membership of the local council.[36] During the early part of the twentieth century, councillors had often been 'social leaders', men of status through ownership of land or success in local business, the professions or the trade unions. This status gave them the qualifications to become 'public persons'. They had an independent prestige which did not need to be validated by membership of an elected authority. On the contrary, they were lending their prestige to the authority by standing for election. Local councillors, particularly in rural areas, were part of an oligarchic establishment based largely on the landed interest; so, until 1906, were ministers and MPs. Later, it was those who were successful in business and the professions who achieved dominant positions both in local government and at Westminster. So there was a culture of shared assumptions which made deep-seated conflict unlikely; and local councillors enjoyed a prestige and strength which could be used in defence of their localities. That is no longer the case. Council membership has now become almost entirely disconnected from social or professional success, and of course from the ownership of land. Someone on the ladder of promotion in business or the professions is unlikely to be able to find the time to stand for the local council, and will find it difficult to secure leave from work duties. The time required to master local council work tends to exclude the ambitious and the upwardly mobile. In addition, ambitious people in business or the professions are now far more likely to be required to travel extensively and to be geographically mobile. They are more likely to be rootless than rooted in their local communities. The idea of a job for life rooted in the area in which one was born has virtually disappeared, and this has further weakened the sense of locality, of rootedness. In consequence there seems no longer to be a local leadership or a local government class. Elected members therefore derive their authority less from their standing in local communities—it

---

[36] This is the terminology of J M Lee, whose history of Cheshire County Council until 1963 is highly illuminating: *Social Leaders and Public Persons: A Study of County Government in Cheshire since 1888* (Oxford, Clarendon Press, 1963).

is doubtful if many voters are able to name their local councillors—than from their position in a political party. It is the favour of their political party that they need, not that of their local community. So, while in the past a role in local government tended to be seen as an extension of a local community role, with party affiliation being secondary, today, by contrast, local office derives not from a community leadership role but from a connection with a political party. Councillors, instead of bringing their status as local leaders to the council, acquire status by becoming members of a local council. They have become less community leaders than public persons. They have become part of the political class. They have become, for most intents and purposes, emissaries of their political parties, and, in consequence, independent-minded people are deterred from seeking election to local authorities. Partly as a consequence, the vast majority of those who vote in local elections decide their vote on national not local issues, and vote in the same way as they would vote in national elections. That is one main reason why local elections have become plebiscites on the government of the day rather than on the performance of local councils.

The reorganisation of local government embodied in the 1972 Act never secured popular acceptance. There was pressure to reform it by creating unitary authorities almost as soon as it had been passed. In 1985, the six metropolitan county councils were abolished, while, in 1992, a further Local Government Act provided for reorganisation to create new unitary councils. During the 1990s, distinct urban areas were enabled to opt out of the new authorities created by the 1972 Act, so in effect recreating the old county boroughs; and after 2000, the government proposed to create large unitary authorities in the counties. In consequence, rural, small-town and suburban England increasingly finds itself without any truly recognisable local government, but is instead faced with large and remote authorities. Nevertheless, most of England, as well as almost all of Scotland and Wales, now has unitary local authorities.

The unpopularity of the 1972 Act was partly a consequence of the runaway inflation of the 1970s which would have made life difficult for local authorities, however they had been organised. It would have made life particularly difficult for smaller authorities, and that is perhaps the best defence for the creation of large authorities in 1972. Nevertheless, a system more rooted in popular sentiment would have been better able to withstand many of the attacks made upon it. When local government came under threat from the centre during the long years of economic crisis following 1974, it was unable to mobilise public support in its defence. Far from defending local councillors as bastions of local democracy, many seemed to regard them as just another layer of professional politicians and bureaucrats. They were seen not as representatives of 'us' but of 'them'. They were part of an alienated superstructure. The appeal of Ken Livingstone, leader of the Greater London Council from 1981 until its abolition in 1986 was in part precisely because he was regarded as an independent-minded figure who would be as willing to challenge the leaders of his own party, Labour, as he would the Conservatives, and he was perceived by voters, even by those who had little time for his Left-wing views, as being genuinely concerned with the interests of Londoners rather than with political advancement or remaining in good standing with his party. For this reason the campaign against the abolition of the GLC struck a genuine popular chord. It was an illustration of what might have been had there been equally independent-minded figures in charge of local government elsewhere. But in the rest of the country local government found itself friendless and unloved, lacking the popular support which would have enabled it to resist the assault from the centre.

IV

We have seen that trends in society have been working in the twentieth century to weaken localism, and that the reorganisation of local government, far from counteracting these trends, has actually helped to accelerate them. But, trends in post-war politics have also been distinctly unhelpful to those who sought to preserve localist values. The development of the welfare state has been a powerful factor encouraging the centralization of government. A fundamental principle of the welfare state is that the distribution of benefits and burdens should depend not upon geography but upon need. That objective was difficult to achieve with a service which remained under local authority control. Before 1939, much of the health service was in the hands of local government. But local health services were something of a patchwork, their effectiveness depending upon the party composition, the efficiency and, above all, the wealth of individual local authorities. Doctors' salaries also varied depending upon the wealth of the local authority in which they worked. Sir George Godber, a former Chief Medical Officer at the Department of Health and Social Security, who had been involved in the early planning of the National Health Service, observed that

> 'Anyone familiar with the pattern of development of local authority health services before 1948, despite the fact that they were then limited and at relatively low cost, knows well that the wealth of an authority has a direct bearing on the quality of the service provided. . . . A county like Surrey, for instance, was able to recruit doctors for its public health services in the 1930s much more easily than a country borough like, say, Bootle, for the simple reason that it offered £600 a year as compared with £500 a year, which was the minimum negotiated rate'.[37]

When the post-war Attlee government came to consider how best to organize a health service, there was a Cabinet battle between Herbert Morrison, the former leader of the London County Council, and Aneurin Bevan, the Minister of Health. Morrison wanted health to be, like education, a local authority service. 'It would be disastrous', he argued in Cabinet in October 1945, 'if we allowed local government to languish by whittling away its most constructive and interesting functions

---

[37] Sir G Godber, 'Regional Devolution and the National Health Service' in E Craven (ed) *Regional Devolution and Social Policy* (Houndmills, Macmillan 1975) 77.

and we must not blind our eyes to the fact that to deprive the local authorities of public health responsibilities would be a very serious thing from this point of view'.[38] Bevan, however, saw local control as incompatible with the idea of a **national** health service, largely because he wanted to avoid the anomalies which had characterised the pre-war health system. In addition, local authorities lacked a sufficiently strong financial base to sustain a health service; and the doctors might well have refused to join a service run by local authorities, for fear that they would become, like teachers, mere salaried local government employees and their professional status would suffer. It was in fact only by a narrow majority that the British Medical Association eventually agreed to participate in the health service at all. Bevan nationalised the local authority hospitals in order to develop what he hoped would prove a uniform system of health care for Britain. It would be the minister, and not the local authorities, who would be politically responsible for the health service.

The Attlee government further weakened local government by nationalizing public utilities such as gas, electricity and transport, which had been run in part by local authorities before the war; although, in compensation the welfare functions of local government—education, housing and the social services as well as land use planning—expanded greatly during the post-war years. Nevertheless, it can be argued that the decline or even the demise of local government began not with the Heath, Wilson, Callaghan or Thatcher governments—the usual candidates suggested—but far earlier with the Attlee government, Britain's first majority Labour government, a government dedicated to creating a welfare state, in which anomalies resulting from geography were to be overcome through a truly national welfare policy. Admittedly, neither the Attlee government nor its successors has succeeded in achieving territorial equality through policies of centralisation. There remain considerable divergences in service provision between different parts of the country. It is often used as an argument against centralisation that centralised management of, for example, the National Health Service has not succeeded in eliminating territorial disparities. But that is a fallacious argument, since territorial disparities are seen as reasons for criticism, not for celebration. Most people resent the postcode lottery, rather than applauding it; and only central government is in a position to remove territorial disparities. It would not be easy to remove such disparities in a service that was run by local authorities. In the twentieth century, the principle that citizens in different parts of the country had an equal right to the nation's resources came to displace concerns about the representation of place. Perhaps, devolution, if it is a success, will help to restore the primacy of the representation of place. Perhaps it will stimulate a demand for diversity so that the postcode lottery becomes the postcode preference. It is too early to tell.

In the 1970s a further factor accelerated the decline of local government, as voters became anxious about the quality of local authority services, and especially

---

[38] Chandler, *Explaining Local Government*, above n 3, 169.

education. This anxiety brought ministers into the detailed management of these services, something that, until then, they had sought to avoid. Until 1945 Britain could be characterised as a 'dual state' in which ministers concentrated primarily upon matters of 'high politics', foreign policy, defence and economic management, while leaving 'low politics', matters such as education, housing and transport to local authorities. So, while Parliament enjoyed sovereign powers over local authorities, these powers were in practice rarely used, since local authorities dealt with matters which MPs on the whole regarded as having little importance for them. But, in the post-war world, with the development of the welfare state, the 'dual state' broke down, as issues concerning education, housing and the social services moved to the forefront of the political debate.[39] During the 1970s and 1980s, as the post-war consensus began to break down under the impact of economic crisis, so also did the culture of shared assumptions between local government and the centre; while in the 1980s, in reaction to Margaret Thatcher's government, a number of urban authorities were captured by the Left wing of the Labour Party which used local government to experiment with a form of municipal socialism that was bound to prove unacceptable to a Conservative administration. The background of consensus which had helped to sustain good relations between local authorities and central government had broken down, and the dual state collapsed.

Pressure from the voters contributed to this collapse. In the 1970s, it was, in particular, education which became a focus for popular concern as parents began to complain about the quality of education that their children were receiving in local authority schools. These parents were not mollified by being told that they should complain to their local councillor or the Chief Education Officer of their authority. They argued instead that the quality of education was an issue of national significance, that politicians constantly promised in their election manifestoes to maintain and improve educational standards, and that, therefore, central government was responsible for the quality of education in the schools. They refused, therefore, to allow politicians at Westminster to disclaim responsibility for education. Politicians, for their part, came to believe that complaints about education could cost them votes in a general election. If they continued to respect local government autonomy, therefore, they would be accepting responsibility without enjoying the power that went with that responsibility. If, then, governments were to be held responsible for the quality of local authority education, it would be only natural for them to seek the power which could enable them to exercise that responsibility effectively. It was for reasons of this sort that James Callaghan, as Prime Minister, launched in 1976 a 'Great Debate' on education, calling for higher standards in schools, and insisting that school standards were a responsibility of central government. He demanded, in particular, that government be allowed to enter what had hitherto been regarded as the 'secret garden' of the curriculum,

---

[39] The theory of the 'dual state' is brilliantly outlined in J G Bulpitt, *Territory and Power in the United Kingdom* (Manchester, MUP, 1983).

something which, so he believed, could no longer be left to the uncoordinated wishes of teachers or local authorities. The debate launched by Callaghan culminated in 1988 in the Education Reform Act of Kenneth Baker, Education Secretary in Margaret Thatcher's government. This Act provided for a national core curriculum in the schools, national monitoring of standards in schools and the nationalization of the polytechnic sector of higher education, hitherto the responsibility of local education authorities. It is said that an education minister in the dying Soviet Union congratulated Baker on the degree of centralisation that he had achieved. The centralisation of the education service continued under the governments of John Major and Tony Blair, with the development of national funding formulas for schools. In addition, the Blair government implemented a wide-ranging programme of city academies to counter the weaknesses of the comprehensive system and to deal with the problem of failing schools. These academies are no longer under the aegis of a local authority, and responsibility for them lies directly with ministers at the head of a Whitehall department. Governments, however, have centralised the education service not primarily because of a desire to secure more power for themselves, nor because of a fundamental disdain for local authorities, but as a response to perceived inadequacies of a major public service, inadequacies which had led to public disquiet. Education, although it had been in large part the responsibility of local authorities, is not a local service, but a national one, since questions of educational performance and achievement are of national significance. In the post-war years, therefore, governments had been compelled to take an interest in the performance of local education authorities; and, when that performance had been held to be inadequate, it was almost inevitable that they would take a greater degree of control over the education service. Since the 1970s, therefore, governments have been engaged in the process of acquiring the power to match their responsibilities. Nevertheless, the net effect was that, by the end of the twentieth century, the public services that were most important to voters—health, education and the police—were, in effect, no longer under local control.

During the 1970s, economic pressures accelerated the trend towards centralisation. Hard-pressed by inflation, governments came to believe that local authorities were profligate in their expenditure and needed to be controlled, by cutting grants to local authorities. But local councils, instead of cutting expenditure, could maintain it by raising the rates. The domestic rate combined with the business rate allowed some authorities, for example some London boroughs, and, in the late 1980s, Hertfordshire and Surrey, to finance virtually all of their expenditure from local sources. The level of the rates lay outside government control, and was regarded by the Treasury, in particular, as a loophole in the system of public expenditure control.

During the 1980s, central government stopped this loophole. There was a major constitutional change in the methods by which governments sought to control local expenditure. Previously, governments had sought to control the global total of local government expenditure by varying the amount of grant which they paid to local authorities, that is by varying the amount derived from central taxation. But, in the 1980s, central government sought to determine how much **individual** local authorities should spend, and how much local revenue derived from **local** taxation, they should be allowed to raise. The Local Government Finance Act of 1982 first established expenditure targets for individual local authorities, and central government began to develop indicators, called standard spending assessments, by means of which it could decide how much each local authority ought to be spending. The implication was that it was no longer for the local authority itself to decide what its pattern of expenditure ought to be and how much it should be spending, but rather a matter for central government.

The Local Government Finance Act of 1982 began the process by which central government decided how much each local authority should be **spending**. The Rates Act of 1984 began the process by which central government came to decide how much each local authority should be **raising** from its own revenue, by empowering the Secretary of State to 'cap' the rates, that is impose maximum rate levels upon local authorities. This principle of capping was continued during the brief period of the poll tax, and then with the council tax which replaced it. The Labour government replaced universal capping with selective capping of those local authorities which, so it believed, had overspent. In recent years, government has threatened to cap local authorities which allow council tax increases of over 5%. The effect of this is to constrain the decisions made by local authorities concerning the appropriate level of council tax and also local expenditure. Capping breaches the principle, which lies at the heart of an effective system of local self-government, that it is for the individual local authority to decide how much it wishes to raise locally, and that central control should be exercised solely through varying the level of central grant. But as central government came to increase its responsibilities, so the pattern of local authority finance came to reflect this increased responsibility. So, although, in theory, local authorities remained responsible for important public services, the pattern of public finance legitimised central intervention. At present, local authorities are responsible for around 25% of public expenditure, but raise only 4% of tax revenue. They raise on average around 20% of their expenditure from council tax. The rest derives primarily from central government grants and from the proceeds of the uniform business rate which is set and collected by central government and then distributed to local authorities on a formula basis.[40] Thus, most of the money that tax payers contribute goes to Whitehall, and is then redistributed back to local authorities by central government; and the amount raised by local authorities varies according to no discernible principle. In 2001, for example, St Albans raised 50% of its revenue from council tax, East Staffordshire 40%, Somerset 30% and Newham just 11%. As a result, although local government is accountable to its voters for the decisions

---

[40] At the time of writing, a Business Rate Supplements bill is being considered by Parliament, giving local authorities the power to raise a supplementary business rate to fund economic development projects. The mayor of London is proposing to use the London-wide supplement to help pay for Crossrail.

which it makes on local spending, it lacks any real control over its revenue base, except at the margin. Most voters, therefore, find it difficult to see any clear relationship between the amount they contribute to local government in the form of the council tax, and the services which they receive.

A 'new localism' would have to begin by reforming local government finance, since current arrangements sustain a centralist rather than a localist approach. When the bulk of local government revenue is raised from the centre, it is natural for local authorities to look to the centre rather than to their own voters for guidance. Instead of having to carefully balance out local needs and local taxation, local authorities find themselves pressing the centre for more money. They become one of the numerous interest groups pressing the centre for cash. They are put in the position of being perpetual grumblers. It is almost always the case that services could be improved if more money were provided by central government; the demand for better services is, after all, nearly infinite. This puts a premium on buck-passing between local authorities and the government of the day. Local authorities can always argue that local services would be better if only central government provided them with more grant. The government, however, can reply that local services would be better if local authorities were more efficient, and that rises in council tax to pay for better services are wasteful. The local voter has no means of evaluating these claims, for the system of local government finance establishes a regime of perverse incentives and serves to undermine the spirit of local patriotism which a good system of local government finance ought to sustain. There has, however, been little incentive to reform local government finance since the ill-fated experiment of the community charge or 'poll tax' in 1989 which led to widespread popular protest and had to be withdrawn just a year after its introduction in England and Wales.

The Conservative administrations of Margaret Thatcher and John Major, which ruled Britain from 1979 to 1997, saw local government through the prism of market economics. Market criteria were, it was held, of universal applicability, and these criteria conflicted with the idea of diversity which lay at the heart of the defence of local government. The local voter was seen as a consumer whose main concern was with the efficient delivery of public services. The programme of public service reform initiated by the governments of Margaret Thatcher and John Major had a broadly centralist dynamic. It implied centrally-imposed targets and the monitoring of performance of local authorities by central government. The assumption was that there is an agreed agenda of reform, one shared by local authorities and central government, and that the task of local authorities was to help implement this agreed agenda.

Under Tony Blair there was much talk of a new partnership between central and local government, but this was seen as a partnership whose terms were set primarily by the centre. It was a partnership whose purpose was to help secure the objectives of the centre. One partnership mechanism introduced by the Blair government was the local area agreement, which seems at first sight a localist development. These agreements are intended to join up all local services—not only those run by local authorities, but also health and the police. Local authorities are to lead the process of joining-up. Area agreements, however, tend to be implemented by officers rather than elected councillors, and the purpose of joining-up is to achieve outcomes decided upon by the centre. Local area agreements, therefore, are primarily managerial in nature, and reflect central government's view that local authorities are service deliverers rather than part of a vibrant democratic system. The flavour is well conveyed in a White Paper from the Department of Transport, *Local Government and the Regions*, published in 2001, which declared that 'Councils will make their most effective contribution if, alongside central government, they take responsibility for key national priorities and instigate corrective action when standards are not met'.[41]

The role of local authorities, therefore, was to be a partner in the delivery of national programmes. The public services, services such as education, housing and the social services are, governments have insisted, national services. They must be available to all on the basis of equity. Therefore they should be subject to national standards. Local government was to be judged according to whether it was, or was not, an effective delivery mechanism. Yet, local authorities, like Parliament, are directly elected. They may well be controlled by opposition parties; and, when a government has been in power for a long period, as with the Conservatives between 1979 and 1997, or Labour by 2009, that is very likely to be the case. The opposition parties may well not share the diagnosis of central government as to what is wrong with the public services and how they ought to be improved. They may well have developed a different diagnosis, and have come to favour alternative methods of improving public services.

For the public services are inherently political, and political in at least two senses. First, because they compete with each other for scarce public resources; and secondly because those belonging to different political parties legitimately disagree about relative aims and priorities. There is not just one set of agreed aims, but a multiplicity of conflicting aims. This disagreement is not one that can be resolved by an appeal to the higher authority of experts, since it reflects a difference of values and not of techniques. In a democracy, therefore, some institutional method must be found to resolve such disagreement, and this institutional method will express the choices made by a society as to how its political relationships ought to be shaped. Were local authorities to accept a 'partnership' role in which they accepted the diagnosis of ills in the public services and the remedies for these ills proposed by central government in their entirety, they would be in danger of becoming mere instruments or agents for the implementation of central government policies. Then, there would hardly be any case for elected local authorities at all, let alone a 'new localism'. We would have reached a post-ideological age, an age that would signify not just the end of history, but also the end of politics. Politics would have come to be transformed into technocracy, a

---

[41] *Strong Local Leadership-Quality Public Services*, Department for Transport, Local Government and the Regions, Cm 5237, para 3.6.

debate about means rather than about ends. The institutions of democracy would remain, but much of its spirit would have died.

The notion of a local community had, then, been severely attenuated by local government reorganisation in the 1970s and it was to be further attenuated by individualism and the market philosophy of the 1980s and 1990s. Individualism was an ethic which encouraged fluidity—geographical and social mobility— rather than the rootedness needed for a strong system of local government. The new individualism thus accentuated the trends devitalising local government, and it did not seem hyperbole to write, in a book on the history of the constitution in the twentieth century, of 'the demise of local government'.[42]

V

The Labour government, elected in 1997, had, however, been committed to reversing the long trend towards centralisation and to re-establishing the role of local government in the constitution. Accepting the Charter of Local Self-Government was intended to symbolise this aim. Its effect, in the absence of a constitution constraining the centre, has been little more than symbolic. For the problems attending a revival of localism are deep-seated. The demise of local gov-ernment cannot be attributed solely to malign politicians at the centre. Any attempt to revive local democracy must tackle the root cause of its decline, which lies in the replacement of local democracy by a very rigid form of local party gov-ernment, the replacement of local authorities which represented communities by larger and unwieldy units, and the concomitant rise of a professional political class in local government, a class apart. Perhaps, in an ideal world, the Labour govern-ment might have sought to move towards the continental pattern in which very small basic units of local government were combined with a regional tier; and it did seek, albeit unsuccessfully, to achieve a regional tier of government in England. But there was, as that attempt showed, little appetite for regional reform, and lit-tle appetite also for a further large-scale reorganisation of local government. The Labour government, therefore, had to accept the fundamentals of the existing structure, fundamentals which had been laid down in the 1970s.

The main thrust of Labour thinking on local government reform was to strengthen leadership at local level. The Local Government Act, 2000 required local authorities to replace the committee system, dominant in local government since the Municipal Corporations Act of 1835, by either a cabinet or a mayoral sys-tem. Under the committee system, the whole council was both the legislature and the executive. Each councillor was, in theory, equal to every other councillor, and was a member both of the legislature and of the executive. In practice, however, with the development of party politics in local government, the key decisions were

---

[42] The title of M Loughlin's chapter in Bogdanor, *The British Constitution in the Twentieth Century,* above n 2.

taken by party groups, and it was the majority group rather than the full council that normally selected the chairs of the various committees and the leader of the council. The mayor was a purely ceremonial figure, and the leader of the majority group who became the leader of the council was the dominant political figure. The committee system thus obscured the political reality of who held power in the local council. The key decisions were taken, not in committee, still less in full council, but 'upstairs' in meetings of party groups. This made local government less accountable and meant that the decision-making process was opaque to most voters, few of whom were able to name the leader of their local council.

The government believed that a more visible focus of executive leadership would encourage more transparent and accountable local government. The Local Government Act, 2000 required all local authorities to adopt constitutions providing for either a directly elected mayor or a cabinet system, where the leader would be elected by the council, and the cabinet would either be appointed by the leader or elected by the council. The leader would serve a four-year fixed term. In 2006, a White Paper proposed that there might be directly elected council leaders.[43]

Local authorities which adopted the mayor option would, by contrast with the system in London, where the mayor ruled alone as a single executive authority, be required to choose a cabinet, comprising between two and nine members, from the elected members of the council; and it would be the full council which would decide upon the budget and the annual plans of the major services run by the council. One authority, Stoke-on-Trent, chose a variant on this model, by which, instead of an elected mayor and cabinet, there would be an elected mayor and council manager, appointed by and responsible to the local authority as a whole. The principle behind this form of executive was to secure a clear separation between policy development by the elected mayor and implementation of policy by the council manager. Stoke, however, abandoned this model in 2008. Under either mayoral regime, the mayor would be directly elected, like the London mayor, by the supplementary vote system. If, however, an authority wanted to choose the mayoral option, it would first have to secure the approval of local electors in a referendum.

The premiss of the reform was that a cabinet system or a directly elected mayor would, by formally recognising the role of the majority party and its leader, bring the structure of local government more in accord with the realities of modern party politics. In addition, by dividing powers between the executive and backbenchers, it was hoped that the new arrangements would yield better scrutiny, with back-bench councillors becoming the equivalent of members of Select Committees in the House of Commons. Under the old dispensation, many councillors felt that the only meaningful position was that of committee chair, but, under the new arrangements, councillors who were not members of the executive would have the important duty of scrutinising the cabinet and the mayor. So, while formally councillors might appear to be in a weaker position, it was hoped

---

[43] *Strong and Prosperous Communities*, Cm 6939-I, 2006, ch 3.

that in practice their influence would be greater. The government suggested, in regulations drawn up for guidance to local councils that, if decision makers were to be held to account, this 'will require a change in the way members have traditionally questioned decisions. Although this is a matter for political parties to consider . . . The Secretary of State believes whipping is incompatible with overview and scrutiny and recommends that whipping should not take place.'[44]

The government no doubt hoped that many local authorities would seek the directly elected mayor option. A directly elected mayor would be beholden, not to her party group, but to local electors. A mayoral system might thus help to break the hold of tribal politics upon local government. With an electoral mandate behind her, a mayor could mobilise public opinion and speak for local electors in a way in which the traditional council leader could not. A survey undertaken in 2004 showed that 57% could name their elected mayor from a prompt list, compared to 25% who could name their council leader. Name recognition rose to 73% for mayors in the north east.[45] Therefore, so it was hoped, a directly elected mayor would be able to provide a clear focus of accountability for voters, personalizing local government and making it more exciting. The traditional local authority leader was a local councillor, elected in a particular ward, and chosen for the leadership position by her party from which she derives her power. A mayor, by contrast, would be directly elected by voters from the local authority as a whole, and not just one particular ward, and so would derive her powers directly from the voters. She would be likely to hold a much higher public profile than the traditional council leader. The mayor would hold power for a fixed term of four years; many local authorities, by contrast, hold annual elections, and, as compared with such authorities, the mayor would be able to provide a more stable administration and better long-term planning. In addition, there are, in an increasing number of local authorities, hung administrations, with no single party enjoying an overall majority on the council. A directly elected mayor could evade the need for the tactical coalitions which are frequently needed to operate hung councils successfully. Directly elected mayors, so it was hoped, could make a new localism possible. They would provide more visible and accountable leadership; they, rather than central government, would be held accountable for the performance of the local authority. Ministers, so it was argued, would be more likely to devolve where such clear lines of accountability emerged.

The government, however, faced the problem that, while survey evidence seemed to indicate that there was some popular support for the idea, most councillors seemed to be opposed to it, fearing no doubt that their own powers would be undermined. A MORI poll in 1998 in five major English cities outside London had found between 60% and 70% support for the directly elected mayor option. But only 2% of local councils supported it. Between the year 2000, when the Local

---

[44] Department of Communities and Local Government, 'New Council Constitutions: Guidance to English Authorities', 2006, para 3.44

[45] A Randle, *Mayors in mid-term: lessons from the eighteen months of directly-elected mayors* (New Local Government Network, 2004).

Government Act was passed, and 2008, just 22 councils decided to hold referendums, and the last of these was held in 2002. Fearing such an outcome, the
government provided for an alternative mechanism, the initiative. This was a
constitutional innovation, an innovation with very radical possibilities. It allowed
voters themselves to secure a referendum on a directly elected mayor. Any 5% of
registered local electors in a local authority area could, by signing a petition,
require the authority to hold a referendum. This device, so it seemed, would be a
way of overcoming the opposition of the local authority establishment to the
introduction of directly elected mayors. In addition, the Secretary of State could,
under certain circumstances, require a local authority to hold a referendum. This
power has been used only once, in Southwark, but the proposal for a directly
elected mayor was defeated.

The survey evidence and other indicators of public opinion which seemed to
show considerable popular support for directly elected mayors proved misleading.
Most local authorities adopted the safe course of choosing the cabinet model.
Between 2000 and 2008, there were just 33 local referendums, including those trig-
gered by initiatives, and they were successful in only 11 local authorities outside
London. Despite the seeming enthusiasm of the public for the mayor option
expressed in opinion surveys, turnout in the referendums was generally low, even
where all-postal ballots were held. In only one local authority area was turnout
over 42%. The lowest turnout was in Ealing where it was 10%. Sedgefield, Tony
Blair's constituency, rejected the mayor option in a postal ballot on a 33% turnout.
In some cases, the outcome laid itself open to ridicule. Hartlepool, for example,
elected as mayor the local football team's mascot, H'Angus the Monkey, while
Middlesborough elected a police superintendent who was under suspension by his
force. There were, admittedly, signs that, as in London, the mayor option was succeeding in breaking down the tribalism of party politics. Of the 11 directly elected
mayors outside London, 4 were independents. Nevertheless, the reform has clearly
not succeeded to the extent that the government hoped. The government, therefore, in the 2007 Local Government and Public Involvement in Health Act,
removed the referendum requirement. Any council which wanted to introduce
this model could now do so without a referendum. The initiative was maintained,
but the government declared that it would consult on reducing the 5% trigger.[46]
These reforms may not be sufficient to remove the political obstacles that lie in the
way of the introduction of more directly elected mayors—public apathy and the
hostility of entrenched local councillors. It has therefore been suggested that the
government either requires all urban authorities—unitary councils and metropolitan districts—to hold a mayoral referendum on the same date, so providing for a
national day of debate on local government and galvanising interest in the topic;
or that the government should abandon the referendum requirement entirely, and
legislate for mayors in urban authorities.[47] For central government to impose

---

[46] It also removed the mayor and council manager model, adopted solely by Stoke-on-Trent, from
the statute book.

[47] M Kenny and G Lodge, 'Mayors rule' (2008) *Public Policy Research*, March–May.

mayors on local authorities would contradict the ethos of the reform of local government executive structures, that it should be for a local authority itself to decide what structure it favours. That, however, was how directly elected mayors were introduced in Germany and Italy; and it may be that, paradoxically, central government intervention is required to bring about true localism.

It was widely thought that the government particularly wanted the great conurbations outside London to adopt the directly elected mayor option. There is some evidence that a directly elected mayor could help to create a sense of identity that would otherwise be absent in a large local authority. A political leader who was not tied too closely to a political party and who was seen as 'Mr' or 'Ms' Newcastle, Liverpool, Manchester, etc. could help to regenerate that sense of civic pride which is otherwise sadly absent in major cities. If that happened, then, by stimulating local patriotism, the mayoral option could help defuse the sense of resentment in England which lies behind the 'West Lothian Question'. Chapter 4 showed that there is no logical answer to the West Lothian Question under a system of asymmetrical devolution. Nevertheless, perhaps the West Lothian Question is more of a political than a constitutional question. Behind it lies a sense of English resentment at the seeming inequities of the devolution settlement. There is a Scottish Parliament which acts as a powerful voice for Scotland, but there is no similar institution which can speak for England. At present, resentment is merely simmering, but it could easily become more intense, especially if the government comes to be dependent upon Scottish votes at Westminster. But chapter 8 showed that the London mayor has stimulated a sense of belonging to London, a sense of 'Londonness' which is now stronger than the sense of Englishness. In other words, the introduction of the London mayor has led to the growth of London patriotism. It is possible, then, that the introduction of mayors into the great conurbations outside London, such as Birmingham, Liverpool, Manchester and Newcastle, could similarly regenerate a sense of civic patriotism in those cities. There would then be political leaders who could speak, not of course for England as a whole, but for some of the great English cities whose interests may have been ignored because they are unable, as Scotland is, to generate a powerful nationalist party. If that happened, then the introduction of mayors could reduce the sense of English alienation which lies behind the West Lothian Question, providing a political if not a constitutional answer to the Question.

Most local authorities, however, have chosen the safer option of a cabinet system. Such a system makes the governance of a local authority more transparent by bringing the machinery of party government into public view rather than hiding it through the fiction that the whole council can act as an executive body. In doing so, however, the cabinet system merely emphasises the dominance of party politics in local government, and this has weakened local government. If local government is to become a real part of the constitution, that dominance must be reduced.

VI

One way of loosening the grip of party upon local government would be to reform the electoral system for local councils, from first-past-the-post to the single transferable vote system of proportional representation. It is the first-past-the-post system that helps to entrench a rigid form of tribal politics in local government. Under this electoral system, many local government wards are permanently safe for one party, while a swing against a party nationally generally means that the local councillors representing that party are defeated in local elections. In single-member wards, there is no way in which the elector can distinguish between effective and less effective councillors. This means that effective councillors are doomed to defeat along with the less effective solely because the party to which they belong is unpopular at national level; and because so many wards are safe, many local elections are uncontested, and so electors find themselves disfranchised. In the year 2007, for example, in 30 out of the 312 English councils holding elections—nearly 10% of the total—at least one fifth of the wards were uncontested. In Wales in 2008, 102 councillors in 8% of the seats on Welsh local authorities were returned unopposed.

In many other local authorities there may seem little point in voting, since the outcome, under first-past-the-post, is a pre-ordained clean sweep, with one party gaining nearly all the seats on the council even though its vote does not approach anywhere near to 100%. Such clean sweeps are much more likely to occur in local government than in elections to the House of Commons. The only parliamentary clean sweep in the twentieth century occurred in 1931, when the Conservative-dominated National Government, with around 2/3 of the vote, won 554 of the 615 constituencies, and the opposition had too few seats to be able to scrutinise the government effectively. But clean sweeps occur quite regularly in local government. In 2007, for example, in East Hertfordshire, the Conservatives gained 47% of the vote, but won 84% of the seats on the council; Labour with 11% of the vote won no seats at all, though the Liberal Democrats and Independents, each with 8% of the vote, did secure representation. Six wards, all with Conservative candidates, were uncontested. In Tunbridge Wells in 2007, the Conservatives won all the seats on 58% of the vote, the remaining 42% of the voters remaining entirely unrepresented. In Leicester, by contrast, it was the Labour Party which benefited in 2007, gaining 70% of the seats on just 39% of the vote. The Liberal Democrats won more votes than the Conservatives but gained fewer seats. In Bolsover, too, Labour was the beneficiary in 2007, gaining 75% of the seats on 50% of the vote. The Conservatives did not put up any candidates at all, and so their supporters were in effect disfranchised.

Such outcomes cannot be good for democracy. To be effective, local administrations, like all governments, need a lively opposition to keep them on their toes and scrutinise what they are doing. One-party dominance, by contrast, means that there is no way to check the dominance of the party machine. A permanent one-party local authority seems almost as offensive as a permanent one-party state.

In national elections the 'wrong' side wins very infrequently. In the 26 general elections in the twentieth century, just three—the elections of 1929, 1951 and February 1974—resulted in the party with the most votes winning fewer seats than its main opponent. In two of these cases—1929 and February 1974—the outcome was a minority government which was unable to survive for a full parliamentary term. Such perverse outcomes, however, occur, year after year, in local government elections. In 2007, for example, the party with the most votes failed to win the most seats in 15 out of the 312 English local authorities. In 2008, there was a particularly flagrant example in Cardiff, where the Liberal Democrats, third in the popular vote, gained more seats than Labour and the Conservatives combined, and therefore led the council. The consequence of such distortions is that, year after year, voters are not given the result for which they have asked.

The distortions of the system are by no means random. The clean sweep tends to benefit the largest party, the Conservatives in rural areas, Labour in the inner cities. The system thus exaggerates social and geographical divisions, making England appear more divided than in fact it is, by depriving the Labour minority in the countryside and the Tory minority in the conurbations of their political voice. The Labour Party is sometimes accused of being insufficiently sensitive to the needs of rural areas. If that is so, it is hardly surprising since the Party has so few councillors in rural areas, while the Conservatives for a similar reason tend to be insufficiently aware of the problems of the inner cities.

The first-past-the-post system is currently used for local government elections only in England and Wales. In Northern Ireland the single transferable vote system of proportional representation has been used since 1973, while, in Scotland, the Parliament provided for this system of proportional representation to be adopted in local government elections from 2007. The National Assembly of Wales is currently considering whether to adopt this system, recommended by the Richard Commission on devolution in Wales which reported in 2004. Scotland, where the single transferable vote method of proportional representation was used for the first time in 2007, offers a striking contrast to England in the working of local government elections. In 2003, Labour had won 71 of the 79 seats in Glasgow on just 48% of the vote, and had won Edinburgh despite winning less than 28% of the vote, while in Renfrewshire the SNP had won control of the council despite being outpolled by Labour. No such anomalies occurred in 2007, and there were no uncontested seats at all, as compared with 61 in 2003. 74% of first preference votes helped to elect a councillor, as compared to 52% of votes in 2003, and there was a 9.5% increase in valid votes cast. Councils hitherto thought to be no-go areas for particular parties were opened up. Labour won representation in Newton Mearns, while the Conservatives won seats in the safe Labour area of Ravenscraig. The local elections in Scotland, therefore, helped to produce much more genuinely representative local government than local government elections in England. But, in addition, the single transferable vote offers voters a choice of candidate from within their favoured party. Under this system, in place of the 'X' which the voter places by her favoured candidate in the first-past-the-post system in single-member wards, there are multi-member wards and the voter casts her vote preferentially, '1', '2', '3' etc. The single transferable vote system thus combines a primary and an election, and it is a primary in which every voter takes part simply by casting her vote. There is no need for a separate primary election in which fewer are likely to participate, with participation in primaries frequently being restricted to party members. The single transferable vote system enables voters to vote across parties if they so wish, and to discriminate amongst members of their favoured party. A Labour voter might thus choose between various Labour candidates on the basis of who had been, or might prove, the more effective councillor. It thus enables a much more discriminating choice to be made between candidates. The first-past-the-post system reflects the old world of tribal politics where voters divided themselves into two camps—Labour and Conservative—and rarely switched allegiances. In today's more sophisticated world, by contrast, voters naturally seek wider choices. The single transferable vote system of proportional representation, a preferential system, would allow such wider choices to be reflected in local government.[48]

It is perhaps not for the government to decide upon the best system for each local authority area, but for local voters themselves. Under the Local Government Act, 2000, 5% of registered electors in every local authority area were given the power to secure a referendum on whether their authority should have a directly elected mayor. It would be natural to follow this precedent by allowing 5% of the registered electorate similarly to secure a referendum on the local voting system. Were voters to choose to alter the electoral system, they would be able to secure a more representative system of local government; and it is possible that, when every vote counts and there are no longer safe wards, turnout rates will start to rise, and voters will take local government more seriously again. A change in the electoral system seems an essential precondition of making local government a more effective part of the constitution.

The 2000 Local Government Act created an important constitutional precedent in providing for use of the initiative at local level. This, for the first time, gave voters the power to override the wishes of their local council, and to repair what they may see as a sin of omission on the part of their local authority by refusing to hold a referendum on the mayor option. There is also provision for voters to require a referendum on the abolition of grammar schools in their authority, although so far only one such referendum has been held, in Ripon. The initiative, we have argued, could be used to secure a referendum on a reform of the voting system in local government. But there seems no reason why it should be confined to such issues. It may be argued that, if the voters are to be entrusted with deciding the voting system for their local authority, they might also be entrusted with decisions about, for example, the shape and size of their local authority budget and the

---

[48] For further details of the working of this system, see, for example, V Bogdanor, *Power and the People*, (London, Gollancz, 1997).

level of the council tax, the organisation of education in their local authority, and a host of other issues. A wider use of the initiative would be a real example of 'double devolution', that is devolution not merely from central government to local authorities, but from local authorities to the people. It would be a radical constitutional change, but perhaps one which could genuinely stimulate interest and participation in local affairs.

VII

In 1894, following the Local Government Act establishing elected parish councils, an Act which almost completed the great Victorian enterprise of establishing a representative system of local government in Britain, a Continental lawyer, Josef Redlich, observed that

> 'England has created for herself 'Self Government' in the true sense of the word . . . that is to say, the right of her people to legislate, to deliberate and to administer through councils or parliaments elected on the basis of popular suffrage . . . And this is the root of the incomparable strength and health of the English body politic'.[49]

During the twentieth century Britain moved far away from that inspiring vision. By 2007 one authority could insist that 'Local government is no longer, in any meaningful sense, a part of the British constitution.'[50] It remains to be seen whether the twenty-first century will succeed in reversing that trend, so that local government becomes, once again, part of the constitution.

The demise of local government has not been without its political costs. Local government has the potential to be closer to the citizen and more responsive to her needs than national government. It is easier for the citizen to contact local councillors and officials than to get in touch with her MP or with officials in Whitehall, civil servants protected from the citizen by distance and by time.

Local government is predominantly government by lay people rather than by professional politicians; and government by many more people than can hope to find themselves returned to Parliament. There are at the present time just 646 MPs, but around 22,000 local councillors. Local government is in essence, as Redlich noticed, a form of self-government, and self-government must be a vital element in any well-functioning democracy, a school for participation and training in the arts of politics. It is possible, however, that self-government may not be compatible with a tightly organised system of party politics, especially party politics of a tribal kind such as has dominated British politics during the post-war years.

A strong system of local government can act as a powerful check upon the power of the centre. Strong democratic local institutions allow reforms to be adopted and evaluated at local level before being adopted on a national scale, when

---

[49] J Redlich and F W Hirst, *The History of Local Government in England*, [1903] (London, Macmillan, 1958) 221.

[50] A King, 'The Ghost of Local Government', in *The British Constitution* (Oxford, OUP, 2007) 177.

they cannot be withdrawn without massive consequences, both administrative and political. For innovations to be successful there needs to be honest feedback on progress. Centralised decision-making and the uniform application of best practice are unlikely to achieve this. Local experimentation, by contrast, is better placed to identify failure before it is implemented on a national scale. Pluralism, therefore, as well as providing for a necessary check on government, is also likely to lead to more efficiency in government. If knowledge derives, as Karl Popper believed, from a process of trial and error, then local government is best placed to ensure that such a process of trial and error actually takes place. Centralised government is essentially the product of an age of rationalism and social engineering, in which it is believed that larger is better. Such social engineering was exemplified by the moves towards comprehensive education in the 1960s, masterminded by Labour's Education Secretary, Anthony Crosland. This reform has been described by one commentator as not 'inherently foolish'. What was wrong

> 'was the scale of the experiment and the absence of honest feedback on progress. . . . The widening gap between the self-congratulation of the educational establishment and the everyday experience of parents propelled educational reform to the top of Britain's political agenda . . . the common-sense belief that central co-ordination and direction are bound to improve performance remains ingrained despite the contrary evidence derived from the failure of planning in both government and business organizations around the globe. In an uncertain, changing world, most decisions are wrong, and success comes not from the inspired visions of exceptional leaders, or prescience achieved through sophisticated analysis, but through small-scale experimentation that rapidly imitates success and acknowledges failure'.

For public sector services, local government offers an excellent institutional framework within which such 'small-scale experimentation' can take place.[51] It has been pointed out that many

> 'central government changes of a substantive or innovative kind, such as the introduction of new standards or methods of service provision, are . . . most frequently generalisations of existing local government practice or responses to demands produced by local authorities' practical experience, rather than ideas originating with government departments'.[52]

Perhaps the strongest argument for local government, and indeed for devolution and decentralisation in general, is that it can, at its best, stimulate a sense of local patriotism which can lead to real improvements in the public services. In a decentralised system of government, each local authority will strive to ensure that its own performance is better than that of its competitors. One local authority may say that, although it receives insufficient funds from central government, it has done wonders with its schools for children with special needs, which are far supe-

---

[51] J Kay, 'The Centralised Road to Mediocrity', *Financial Times*, 27 February 2006.
[52] P Dunleavy, *Urban Political Analysis: The Politics of Collective Consumption* (Houndmills, Macmillan 1980) 105.

rior to those in neighbouring authorities. A neighbouring authority might counter that, although it does not receive sufficient funds from the government, it has done wonders with its nursery schools which are far superior to those of other local authorities. The emphasis is on local pride and achievement, on what has been done, rather than upon grumbling. The hope is that competition will raise standards in the public services.

Conversely, a centralised system institutionalises grumbling. If those who run the National Health Service or the universities declare that their services are effectively run, that they have made major improvements, the government is always likely to respond that, if that is the case, it will shift resources to other services. Anyone in a centralised public service who trumpets success is letting the side down. The emphasis must therefore always be not on successes, but on deficiencies, so that central government can be persuaded to provide more resources. This process must have a demoralizing effect on any organisation. An organisation which can never be seen to be successful, but must always be in the position of pointing out its deficiencies so that it is awarded extra funds, is hardly likely to stimulate that pride in performance which so often produces improvements in service.

At present, however, the place of local government and of the new localism in the new British constitution remains quite uncertain. The programme of constitutional reform initiated in 1997 has so far done little to regenerate local communities. There are, it is clear, strong political and cultural forces underpinning the centralisation of government. There remains a curious state of confusion about the proper place of local government in the new British constitution. In terms of political rhetoric, there is general agreement that Britain suffers from over-centralisation, that power should somehow be returned to the people, and that this process involves a policy of radical decentralisation. In practice, however, little has been done to implement this philosophy, and Britain remains one of the most centralised countries in Europe. Without a codified constitution, local government lacks constitutional protection. Whether local government enjoys powers or not remains dependent upon the discretion of the government of the day. Thus, although the Labour government signed the Charter of Local Self-Government, it is still for ministers to decide whether to reform the system of local government finance, remove capping, or give local government wider powers. They do not do so because they see no electoral advantage in it. The balance of power between central and local government is decided by the centre, which need have no regard to the constitutional principle of local self-government. The hurdles which a policy of genuine decentralisation has to surmount are very high. But these hurdles have been erected not only by central government and by politicians ambitious to extend their power. They have been erected by the people themselves, whose professions of localism are often belied by their actions.

Local government has been defined as 'the government of difference'.[53] The new localism can be effective only if there is a positive demand for diversity, a

---

[53] J Stewart, *The Nature of Local Government* (Houndmills, Macmillan 2000) 1.

greater demand for diversity than seems currently to be present, in England at least. The Blair government may have helped create that demand, perhaps inadvertently, through its policy of devolution. If devolution is seen to work well in Scotland and Wales, it is possible that it will create a demand for diversity within England. It is a paradox, perhaps, that the devolution of power to Scotland and Wales has coincided with the decline of local self-government in England. Whether devolution does in fact stimulate a demand for diversity in England remains still to be seen. A revival of localism must depend upon there being a greater willingness to tolerate local divergences than has been apparent in the post-war period. At first sight the signs are good. In an affluent society there may be more willingness to tolerate variation than in a society where there are many who are struggling to achieve a basic minimum. There is perhaps a greater willingness than there was for voters to become 'active citizens'. Nevertheless, popular demands for 'localism' or greater local control are often combined with criticism of a 'postcode lottery', criticism of the fact that standards are different in different parts of the country. Localism, however, is likely to intensify the postcode lottery. To give local authorities power is to give them the power to diverge from neighbouring authorities. It is to give them the power to improve services. But it is a power that may or may not be used wisely. It is therefore inconsistent both to seek local autonomy and to decry the 'postcode lottery', although with a strong system of local government, the postcode lottery can become the postcode preference. There can be little doubt, however, that popular pressures during the post-war years have served to enhance rather than to counterbalance centralisation, and that it is, in the last resort not the politicians but the people themselves who are to blame for the demise of local government. Any reversal of this trend depends upon a radical change in popular attitudes. As yet there is no sign of any such radical change. Until it does occur the new localism is likely to remain little more than a rhetorical flourish and the new British constitution, like the old, will remain a highly centralised one. Localism, therefore, represents an aspiration of the new British constitution; whether it becomes a reality depends not only on government but on us, the people.

11

The Constitutional State

I

THE CENTRAL THEME of this book is that the constitutional reforms since 1997, together with Britain's membership of the European Union, have served to provide us with a new British constitution. This has been little noticed, partly because the various reforms have been legislated piecemeal, and because they seem without internal coherence. They have been regarded, therefore, as a disparate collection of unrelated measures rather than as a package. In addition, the process is incomplete, and its end-point by no means clear. So it has been difficult to appraise the impact of the various reforms taken together. The reforms have made less impact than they would have done in a country with a codified constitution where they would have been the subject of constitutional amendments and, no doubt, considerable discussion and debate.

Nevertheless, the radicalism of the reforms should not be under-estimated, nor the challenge they offer to traditional assumptions about the constitution. These assumptions, and in particular the principle of the sovereignty of Parliament, have been crucially and, almost certainly, permanently undermined. While, therefore, the outlines of the final settlement, the resting-place, as it were, can at present be only dimly perceived, it is clear that the old guidelines no longer offer a sense of direction.

The new constitution contrasts strikingly with the old in numerous respects. Perhaps the most obvious feature of the new constitution is that it is written down, embodied in statute, while the old constitution was more heavily based on uncertain conventions, tacit understandings or intimations. If one wants to know how Scotland, for example, is governed, one can consult the Scotland Act of 1998; if one wants to know how human rights are protected one consults the Human Rights Act. If one wants to know what government information one is entitled to see, one can look at the Freedom of Information Act of 2000; and so on. Parts of the old constitution, however, were implicit, based on 'understandings' which were not always clear, and its interpretation was pragmatic. During the twilight era of the old constitution, one authority insisted that it was 'no more and no less than what happened'.[1] There were few normative guidelines.

---

[1] J A G Griffith, 'The Political Constitution' (1979) *Modern Law Review*, 19.

In chapter 1 we saw that the old constitution comprised both a process—the evolutionary process, analysed by Bagehot—and a doctrine—the sovereignty of Parliament, analysed by Dicey. Both have now been superceded in the new British constitution.

Bagehot understood the constitution in Burkean terms as adaptive; it evolved without being consciously planned. It was the product not of rational reconstruction but of history. It was a 'historical' constitution, as Dicey was to point out, and one tampered with it at one's peril. It was the product of evolution, not of deliberate design. No one ever planned it. Bagehot saw British institutions as being 'like old houses which have been altered many times, they are full both of conveniences and inconveniences which at first sight would not be imagined. Very often a rash alterer would pull down the very part which makes them habitable, to cure a minor evil or improve a defective outline'.[2] It would certainly be pointless to codify a series of ancient habits and practices, sanctified by time. 'Constitution-making is the necessary misfortune of new nations' Bagehot insisted, 'of nations whom an unsuitable set of institutions compels to break with their past'.[3] The metaphors used to characterise the constitution were often biological—the constitution, it was often said, was both fluid and adaptable. 'We are not concerned', Sidney Low had declared at the beginning of the twentieth century, 'with a solid building to which a room may be added here, or a wing there, but with a living organism in a condition of perpetual growth and change'.[4] Professor Lowell of Harvard added the comment that 'The system was not excogitated by an a priori method . . . It has grown up by a continual series of adaptations . . . In this it is like a living organism.'[5]

The implication of such statements is that the rules of constitutional behaviour are changed not only, or even primarily, by changes in the law, but by changes in convention. It was conventions which were, in the words of Sir Ivor Jennings, 'the flesh which clothes the dry bones of the law'.[6] But, unlike changes in statutes, changes in conventions were made imperceptibly and therefore often hardly noticed. 'An ancient and ever-altering constitution', Bagehot says, 'is like an old man who still wears with attached fondness clothes in the fashion of his youth; what you see of him is the same; what you do not see is wholly altered'.[7] Change thus came about almost imperceptibly and there was none of the obvious discontinuity that occurred in a country with a codified constitution.

The new constitution is quite different. Britain's entry into the European Community in 1973, the introduction of the referendum in 1975, and the spate of constitutional reforms since 1997, have certainly not been imperceptible; nor have

---

[2] *The Collected Works of Walter Bagehot*, vol 7, 312.
[3] 'The English Constitution' in *Collected Works*, vol 5, 204 fn.
[4] S Low, *The Governance of England* (London, T Fisher Unwin, 1904) 2.
[5] Lowell, *The Government of England* (London, Macmillan, 1908) vol 1, 14.
[6] Sir Ivor Jennings, *The Law and the Constitution* (5th edn, London, University of London Press, 1959) 81.
[7] 'The English Constitution' in *Collected Works*, vol 5, 203–4.

they been continuous with Britain's traditional constitutional development. The most striking quality of the new constitution is its startling and radical discontinuity with the old. This is most obvious with the European Communities Act of 1972 providing for Britain's entry into the Communities. This Act provided for the acceptance of a legal order which was superior to that of the Westminster Parliament. It sought ingeniously to reconcile that legal order with the principle of the sovereignty of Parliament. But *Factortame* and later cases showed that the Act, at the very least, bound future parliaments until it was explicitly amended or repealed; and this was something that classical exponents of the doctrine of parliamentary sovereignty such as Dicey had always held to be impossible. The effect of the 1972 Act raises the obvious question, if Parliament could bind itself in this one respect, why could it not also bind itself in others? The European Communities Act, as it has been interpreted by the courts, shows therefore that there can be, not just obligations of honour, moral obligations limiting the power of Parliament, something that had been readily conceded by Dicey, but very real legal obligations limiting its sovereignty so long as Britain remains within the European Union. The Act, therefore, had fundamental implications for the doctrine of parliamentary sovereignty.

Devolution, too, involved a marked break with the evolutionary tradition of reform. It might, admittedly, seem, from one point of view a natural progression from the idea of the union state, that is a state with different provisions for governing each of its various territories. It has always been accepted that the different components of the United Kingdom might need to be governed differently and asymmetrically according to their different needs. It was for this reason that Scotland since 1885 was governed through a Scottish Secretary, later a Secretary of State rather than directly from Whitehall; Wales secured a Secretary of State in 1964; while Northern Ireland has had distinctive political arrangements since it was recognised as a political entity in 1920. These developments allowed for the distinctive voices of the non-English parts of the United Kingdom to be heard in Westminster and Whitehall. It was precisely because Britain was a territorially differentiated union state as opposed to a unitary state that governments were able to react with some flexibility to the challenges posed by the demand for Scottish and Welsh autonomy. Because the government of the United Kingdom had always been, to some extent, asymmetrical, governments could respond to these challenges by conceding devolution to Scotland and Wales without feeling that they had to adopt an overall 'federal' settlement by devolving power to England also, when all the signs were that England did not seek devolution. The idea of the union state thus enabled governments to pursue a policy of asymmetric devolution. From this point of view, therefore, devolution may seem a self-consciously adaptive policy, building on the existing structure of administrative self-government in Scotland and Wales.

But devolution is in reality far from a mere evolutionary change. Britain was, until 1999, with the exception of the brief experiment with devolution in Northern Ireland, a unitary and centralised state, governed from Westminster, and the boundaries and permanence of the United Kingdom were taken for granted. Devolution, as chapter 4 showed, creates fundamentally new constitutional relationships in the United Kingdom, new relationships both between its component parts and also within Parliament itself, within the House of Commons between Members of Parliament representing constituencies in the different parts of the United Kingdom. It introduces for the first time, with the *de minimis* exception of the failed Northern Ireland experiment in devolution from 1921 to 1972, the federal spirit into the British constitution; while the very recognition of the wishes of the Scottish and the Welsh people as a constitutional factor marks a further erosion in the doctrine of the sovereignty of parliament; for the right of the people of Northern Ireland and Scotland to self-determination has been accepted at Westminster. Devolution, therefore, has transformed the United Kingdom from a nation-state to a multinational state; and the devolution legislation constitutes explicit recognition of the claims of the nations comprising the United Kingdom to their autonomy and, should they at any time in the future wish it, national independence. What began as a legislative measure from Westminster, devolving power to Scotland, could come to take on the character of a self-generated Scottish constitution. Certainly, from the point of view of many Scots, including many who do not support the SNP, the authority of the Scottish Parliament rests less on the sovereign legislative power of Westminster than on the consent of the Scottish people themselves. They regard the Scotland Act not as devolution from Westminster, but as the basis for a new contractual relationship with the rest of the United Kingdom.

All this requires a new understanding of the notion of Britishness, something that has particularly exercised Gordon Brown, who succeeded Tony Blair as Prime Minister in 2007. In the past, the concept of Britishness seemed simple. It meant that one belonged to a single British nation. Devolution, however, meant that Britain had become a multinational state, a state comprising a number of nations living together on a contractual or negotiated basis. The union between England, Scotland, Wales and Northern Ireland, seemed now to be subject to continual negotiation and renegotiation, and perhaps even dissolution, while the Britain of the twenty-first century was, by contrast with the white, predominantly Protestant society of the first half of the twentieth century, a multicultural and multidenominational society. This too meant that some renegotiation of traditional norms would be necessary. So it seemed that, in the twenty-first century, the concept of Britishness was no longer something firm and settled, but was becoming the subject of a conversation, a long and difficult conversation, about matters that it was not easy to settle definitively.

The Human Rights Act, like devolution, can be seen from one point of view as also an evolutionary development, although, like devolution, it is in reality a reform of a radical, indeed almost revolutionary kind. From one point of view, admittedly, it might be understood as merely drawing out the logical implications of Britain's accession to the European Convention of Human Rights in 1951 and its acceptance of the right of individual petition in 1966. It seemed illogical that

British citizens could realise their rights only in an international and not a British court. In addition, the Human Rights Act came at the end of a period of enhanced judicial activism. From the 1960s, judges had taken a more active role in reviewing administrative decisions, so that governments were less able to rely upon their discretionary powers in the administrative field. Judges had also become more active in employing traditional common law rights to defend the individual against the executive. Therefore, so it could be argued, the Human Rights Act merely recognised and accepted a seemingly inexorable trend.

To argue in this way, however, is to miss the deeper significance of the Human Rights Act. Before the Act the rights of the individual in Britain were seen in largely 'negative' terms. One had a right to do anything that one was not prohibited from doing; and it was not easy, within this framework, to press the idea that the individual had rights against the state. Rights were **inductively** derived from statutes and the decisions of judges. They were in general residual rather than fundamental, negative rather than positive. Under the Human Rights Act, by contrast, rights are defined in specific and 'positive' terms, and it is intended that they 'trump' the power of the state. Rights are **deductively** derived from principles laid out in the European Convention. It is for the judges to determine the precise scope of these human rights, and they have already shown that they are prepared to adopt an activist stance particularly where the rights of vulnerable and unpopular minorities are concerned. Therefore the Human Rights Act, like the devolution legislation and the European Communities Act, implies a real discontinuity with the past. It cannot be understood within the traditional evolutionary framework of the British constitution.

Two other major constitutional reforms have been discussed in this book—the referendum and the introduction of directly elected mayors to London, and to a few other local authorities. Both are clearly innovations and cannot be understood as part of a process of evolution or adaptation. Admittedly, both had been advocated by reformers for many years, yet there was no precedent for them in British constitutional history. They are discontinuous with the past. They both imply the undermining of hitherto accepted conventions and practices. The referendum undermines the centrality of Parliament in the political process. Directly elected mayors undermine the traditional relationship between the council and the executive in British local government. In addition, both of these innovations strike a powerful blow at the dominance of party in British politics. The referendum makes it possible for electors to reject the policy or legislation of the governing party, thereby imposing a check upon the 'elective dictatorship' in British politics.[8] The institution of directly elected mayors makes it easier for voters to choose a local government executive that is independent of party. In 4 out of the 11 local authorities outside London which have decided to adopt directly elected mayors, independents have been elected; while, in London, Ken Livingstone was first elected as an independent.

---

[8] See parts 1 and 2 of Bogdanor, *The People and the Party System*, for an historical account of how reformers have sought to use the referendum to impose a check upon party government.

All the referendums that have been held so far have been formally advisory. Yet, there can be no doubt that a clear outcome on a high turnout in practice binds both Parliament and both government. Thus, the referendum can in practice be used by the people to bind Parliament.

The Local Government Act, 2000, went even further in providing, for the first time in British history, for the initiative. In any local authority area in England or Wales, 5% of registered electors could require a referendum to be held on the question of whether that authority should have a directly elected mayor. The referendum is an instrument designed to repair Parliament's sins of commission, to prevent Parliament passing laws which the people do not want. The initiative, by contrast, is designed as an instrument to repair Parliament's sins of omission, to ensure that Parliament **does** pass laws which the people want. It has not, however, been seriously proposed for use at national level. In Western Europe only Italy and Switzerland use national initiatives at all frequently. Nevertheless its use at local level, even in the limited way provided for by the 2000 Local Government Act, creates an important precedent. So, although the era of constitutional reform has brought the people into the British constitution in only the most minimal way, precedents have been created with very radical implications for the future. The people, having established a bridgehead, may well seek to expand it so that use of the machinery of direct democracy escapes from the narrow confines within which governments have sought to contain it.

The constitutional reforms of the years since 1997 cannot, then, be understood in evolutionary terms. They represent nothing less than a revolution in our constitutional affairs, a radical discontinuity from what has happened before. Little is heard today of the 'evolutionary', 'historic' or 'adaptable' nature of the British constitution. The British constitution is no longer an 'historic' constitution; much of it is now based upon deliberate design. It has been refashioned in a highly self-conscious and deliberate way. Further, it may be argued that the European Communities Act, the Human Rights Act and the devolution legislation have the character of fundamental law, something that is of course anathema to Dicey's conception of the constitution. What must clearly be evident is that the evolutionary constitution, the constitution of Burke and Bagehot, is dead and can never be revived. Bagehot, at least, might not have been surprised. He insisted that his analysis was not timeless, but depended for its validity upon the configuration of British society, and, in particular, upon Britain remaining a deferential society, one in which there was a high degree of trust in Parliament and in political leaders. Since that deferential society has passed away it is hardly surprising that the constitution which was dependent upon it is also passing away. Traditional constitutional *forms* are now found to be no longer congruent with modern social *forces*. In addition, these traditional forms are being subverted by an ideological force, a force that is becoming powerful in many western democracies, and is exemplified in the European Convention of Human Rights. That ideological force is liberal constitutionalism.

II

The central, perhaps the only, principle of the old constitution was Dicey's doctrine of the sovereignty of Parliament, and one reason why it was so difficult to pin down so much of the old constitution was that there seemed little point in seeking to establish competing principles. But with the raft of constitutional legislation since 1997, combined with Britain's entry into the European Community in 1973, the principle of parliamentary sovereignty seems to have been severely qualified, in substance if not in form.

It has been argued in this book that the Human Rights Act lies at the heart of the new constitution. It used to be thought that the principle of parliamentary sovereignty posed an insuperable barrier to the better protection of human rights, since Parliament would be unable to entrench them. Whatever one parliament did could be undone by another. Perhaps, however, the era of constitutional reform has shown that parliamentary sovereignty need not be so strong a barrier to the protection of human rights as was previously imagined; and, in particular, that it need not necessarily prevent legislation from being entrenched.

There are, it appears, two methods by which, even within the principle of parliamentary sovereignty, legislation may be entrenched. The first is through the development of a new common law doctrine, that there is a class of constitutional statutes which cannot be repealed by implication, but only through the express and specific terms of an Act of Parliament. The second is through redefining Parliament by, for example, imposing a requirement for a qualified majority or a referendum for certain types of legislation. These two methods will be examined in turn.

There is a standard common law doctrine known as implied repeal, which means that later statutes 'trump' earlier ones. This doctrine, it used to be thought, makes it impossible for Parliament to entrench legislation. Were this doctrine to hold with regard to all statutes, then legislation passed after 1972 which conflicted with the European Communities Act would 'trump' that Act. But, as we have seen, the effect of the Act is to bind future parliaments. It might then be asked why, if Parliament can be so bound with respect to one particular statute, it cannot also be bound with respect to other statutes; and, as we saw in chapter 3, the Human Rights Act cannot be impliedly repealed. Perhaps the devolution legislation is also entrenched in this way.

In a landmark case, *Thoburn v Sunderland City Council*,[9] Lord Justice Laws, in giving judgment, declared that there was, in English law, a category of 'constitutional' statutes. These included Magna Carta, the Bill of Rights, the Reform Acts of 1832, 1867 and 1884, the European Communities Act, the devolution legislation and the Human Rights Act. He defined a 'constitutional' statute as one 'which conditions the legal relationship between citizen and state in some general,

[9] [2002] EWHC 195 (Admin), [2003] QB 151.

overarching manner', or which 'enlarges or diminishes the scope of what we now regard as fundamental constitutional rights'. A similar view, that there were certain 'constitutional' statutes, a form of higher law, was taken by the parliamentary Joint Committee on the Draft Civil Contingencies bill in 2003. This Committee proposed that certain Acts be made exempt from ministerial powers to amend and repeal legislation in emergencies. It compiled a list of 21 such statutes, dating back to Magna Carta, which, in its view, comprised 'the statutory patchwork of the British constitution'.[10]

This notion of a 'constitutional' statute implies a radical challenge to traditional interpretations of the British constitution. That is because, if Parliament is sovereign, there can be no such thing as a 'constitutional' statute. Under the doctrine of parliamentary sovereignty Parliament can make or unmake any law, and there is no difference in this regard between a law affecting human rights and one affecting, for example, municipal drainage. The notion of a 'constitutional' statute, by contrast, implies that there is a hierarchy of statutes. Part of the point of enacting a constitution is to protect certain fundamental matters, including human rights, against the powers of a transitory majority. But perhaps this same protection can be achieved in a country without a codified constitution.

Lord Justice Laws in the *Thoburn* case argued that the constitutional statutes which he had defined could not be repealed, merely by implication, but required express repeal. The doctrine of implied repeal, Lord Justice Laws insisted, being a common law doctrine, the scope of its application could be determined by the judges. He was not arguing that a special procedure was needed for amending or repealing such legislation. Nevertheless, his argument does imply that constitutional statutes should be more difficult to amend or repeal than non-constitutional statutes, and certainly that they should be protected from accidental or inadvertent amendment or repeal. Human rights, it may be argued, are so fundamental that they should not be overridden by ambiguous words. Parliament must be required to face the full implications of overriding such rights. If this view is correct, then some limited degree of entrenchment and of the protection of rights can be secured without formally jettisoning the principle of parliamentary sovereignty. There are at least two things that Parliament cannot do, namely impliedly repeal the European Communities Act and the Human Rights Act. There is no inherent reason why there should not be others.

The second method of entrenching statutes without abandoning the doctrine of parliamentary sovereignty is by redefining the sovereign authority, by redefining Parliament. The Parliament Acts of 1911 and 1949 had this effect, redefining Parliament so that, for money bills, it now consists of the House of Commons and the Queen, while for non-money bills it now consists of the House of Commons, the House of Lords and the Queen, with the role of the House of Lords being restricted to that of a merely delaying power. The Parliament Acts redefined

[10] Joint Committee on the Draft Civil Contingencies bill, *Draft Civil Contingencies Bill*, HL 184, HC 1074, 2002–3, 53.

Parliament so that all legislation, with the single exception of a bill to lengthen the life of a Parliament, could be passed without the consent of the House of Lords. This of course made it easier for the government to secure its legislation. The interesting question is whether it would be possible to redefine parliament by making it more difficult for a government to secure its legislation. Such a redefinition could be achieved either by requiring a qualified majority, say 2/3 of MPs, to carry legislation, or by requiring a referendum.

Britain has, as yet, no experience of redefining Parliament so as to make it more difficult for a government to secure its legislation, either through special parliamentary majorities or through referendums. There is, of course, experience of the referendum, although so far, as chapter 7 showed, the referendum has been used on an ad hoc basis, and every referendum so far held has been advisory. But there is a precedent dating from 1978 which seems to show that Parliament has the power to provide for a **mandatory** referendum, a referendum which would bind Parliament. The important ruling made by the chairman of committees in 1978 that such a provision was possible may well constitute a valid precedent—see p 191. The referendum has not, however, been used as a genuinely constitutional instrument in that Parliament has not been asked to pass a generic Referendum Act requiring that certain specified categories of legislation be put to the people before being placed on the statute book. Were that ever to happen then the Referendum Act too would, no doubt, also be regarded as a 'constitutional' statute, to be amended or repealed only by the explicit wish of Parliament, and not by implication.

Although there is not a Referendum Act, there is, as chapter 7 showed, a powerful precedent, amounting almost to a convention, that legislation on devolution, the transfer 'downwards' of the powers of Parliament, be put to referendum. So far, every bill providing for devolution, with the exception of that providing for 'Stormont' (the Northern Ireland Parliament established by the Government of Ireland Act, 1920) has been put to referendum either before or after its enactment. It now seems established that legislation providing for devolution needs to be put to the people, and it is difficult to imagine any future devolution legislation unaccompanied by a referendum, although, of course, it would not be unlawful for it not to be so accompanied. Further, it would be politically difficult, though not of course unlawful, to abolish any of the devolved bodies against the wishes of a majority of the inhabitants of a particular devolved area, as was done with Stormont in 1972. To this extent, the devolved bodies are entrenched. Some would wish to see a similar precedent established, to the effect that any major amendment to the European Communities Act, any expansion in the powers of the European Union, any major transfer of power 'upwards', should also be put to referendum. So far, however, all governments, whether Conservative or Labour have resisted referendums on European Union treaties.

The referendum serves to entrench certain 'constitutional' provisions by providing that a special procedure involving the consent of the people is necessary to amend or repeal them. It does so by redefining the procedure necessary for legislation to reach the statute book, by redefining the sovereign legislature. It creates, in effect, an extra chamber of parliament comprising in addition to the Queen, the Lords and the Commons, the people. Parliament could go further still by requiring a qualified majority in a referendum, thus raising the hurdle which legislation has to surmount, as it did in 1978 when it required 40% of the registered electorate as well as a majority of the voters to support devolution in Scotland and Wales for the devolution legislation to be placed on the statute book, so imposing an extra hurdle for advocates of devolution in Scotland and Wales to overcome. But, as we argued in chapter 7, if there is to be a threshold, it would be better to provide for it in the form of a specific percentage of the votes need to pass a measure eg 60%, than in the form of a percentage of the electorate.

There are, then, so it appears, two methods by which, even under a sovereign Parliament, legislation of a 'constitutional' kind can be entrenched. The first is by entrenching it against implied repeal. The second is by redefining Parliament so as to make it more difficult for legislation to be passed.

III

But the question also arises of whether the principle of parliamentary sovereignty itself has been eroded in the new constitution. The doctrine of parliamentary sovereignty is in fact far more complex and obscure than it may appear at first sight. Its complexities have been the subject of much theoretical discussion since the time of Hobbes, who first propagated it in its modern form. In the crudest version of the Hobbesian doctrine, the sovereign is a single individual who commands others and whom no one else can command. This doctrine is an easy one to understand, but it is questionable as to whether it has any relevance to systems of parliamentary government. As soon as an institution rather than an individual is designated as the sovereign, problems arise. This is because an institution such as a legislature is a complex rule-governed body. It must first be determined what is to count as Parliament. There must be rules defining the sovereign institution. In Britain the sovereign parliament comprises the Queen, the House of Lords and the House of Commons. Second, there must be rules determining how the three parts of the legislature are to be determined—the monarchy is a hereditary institution, the House of Lords is composed of nominated and elected hereditary peers and bishops, and the House of Commons is composed of elected MPs. Third, there must be rules determining what is to count as a valid enactment. If, for example, the members of the House of Commons, House of Lords, together with the Queen, were all to gather together in Hyde Park and to assent by acclamation to a particular proposal, that would not count as a valid enactment. There must be rules determining both what is to count as correct procedure and also the relationships between the three parts of the legislature. These rules need not of course be written down; and, with regard to the role of the Queen, they are largely unwritten and conventional. Nevertheless, Parliament is sovereign only when it acts in a certain manner prescribed by the rules. These rules may be made subject to change. This means that fourth, and finally, there must be rules determining how, if at all, the existing rules are to be changed. The notion of parliamentary sovereignty, therefore, already has built into it the idea of a rule, an idea which is logically prior to the concept of the sovereign.

Understood in these terms the doctrine of the sovereignty of Parliament amounts to saying that there are certain rules defining Parliament and the way in which it has to act if it is to enact valid legislation. Clearly, one of the crucial rules in Britain, ignoring for the moment complications arising from the European Communities Act of 1972, is—or perhaps was—that Parliament cannot bind itself. But there seems no logical necessity for the existence of this rule. It might seem, at first sight, perfectly possible for Parliament to alter it, if it so wished, and to establish a totally different rule. Dicey thought that this would be impossible; what he meant, so it seems, is that it would be logically impossible, though he sometimes seems to imply that it would be something that, as a matter of fact, would be difficult to achieve, like running a mile in three minutes. The only way, so Dicey believed, that Parliament could divest itself of power was to abdicate. But Dicey failed to notice an inherent ambiguity in the notion of a sovereign Parliament. In one interpretation a sovereign Parliament can do anything except bind itself, since if it binds itself, future parliaments would not be sovereign. On another interpretation, if Parliament can do anything, then it can also bind itself. Dicey adopted the first interpretation, but there is no reason in logic why sovereignty needs to be interpreted in this sense. The second interpretation, that, if Parliament can do anything, it can also bind itself, follows just as much or as little from the idea of a sovereign Parliament as the first. It is a little like the conundrum concerning God's omnipotence. If God is omnipotent, she can do anything; but, if she binds herself, then she has in fact limited her omnipotence in the future. If, however, the second interpretation of parliamentary sovereignty is correct, and Parliament can in fact bind itself, then it would be possible, contrary to what Dicey and many others have thought, for Parliament explicitly to limit its sovereignty without abdicating completely. Many would argue that Parliament has already done this through the European Communities Act. But, is this second interpretation in fact correct?

To this question, no definitive answer can at present be given. There is no theoretical answer to the question, 'which conception of sovereignty is the correct one'? In logic, either of the two interpretations is possible. But the question is not really one of logic, nor perhaps is it an intellectual or theoretical question at all, but a practical one.

Before the European Communities Act, the basic rule of the British legal system, its rule of recognition, was that Parliament was sovereign; in terms of Dicey's interpretation, that it could not bind itself. This perhaps has been gradually changing since the European Communities Act, but there is by no means a consensus that Dicey's interpretation has been explicitly abandoned; nor of course was there any intention of explicitly abandoning the notion of parliamentary sovereignty.

Whether these changes happen or not depends, however, not only on Parliament, but also on the courts and, in the last resort, the people.

Suppose that Parliament were to seek explicitly to limit its sovereignty by establishing a requirement for a qualified referendum for certain sorts of legislation—legislation affecting human rights, for example; and suppose a future Parliament were to seek to override this provision by passing what purported to be an Act of Parliament by a simple majority. It would then be for the courts to determine whether this purported second Act was valid. But, on a matter as important as this it would be difficult for the courts to make such a judgment in a vacuum. They might well wish to take into account the state of public opinion. A new rule of recognition could not simply be imposed by the courts. It would have to be accepted by public opinion as well. Thus, with the question of the rule of recognition, we reach, as it were, the limits of a legal interpretation of the constitution. The question of what the rule of recognition is cannot be merely a legal or theoretical question. It involves complex issues of politics and sociology as well. It also depends upon political developments. If, for example, an admittedly unlikely hypothesis at the present time, the European Union were to develop into a more integrated system, and this were to be accepted by the British people, then, no doubt, the legal system would have to evolve so as to take account of this development and the formal doctrine of parliamentary sovereignty would come to be abandoned. If Scotland were to develop wider powers under devolution, then perhaps the Scotland Act of 1998 would come to be interpreted, not as an example of devolution, but as the basis of a new contractual and negotiated relationship with Scotland; and, once again, the law would be likely to take account of such a development in due course. The law in each case would follow in the wake of political developments. We are at present in a period of transition when a traditional interpretation of parliamentary sovereignty, that Parliament cannot bind itself, is falling into desuetude. But no new doctrine has yet taken its place. Such a new doctrine would have to establish itself, not only in the decisions of the courts, but also in the hearts and minds of the people. At present, however, any answer to the question of which interpretation of parliamentary sovereignty is valid is bound to be speculative. Eventually, no doubt, the courts will make authoritative pronouncements on these issues, basing their pronouncements upon political developments that have already occurred; the law would have come to recognise the realities of politics.

IV

The doctrine of parliamentary sovereignty, then, so it appears, need not prevent the entrenchment of constitutional measures. Nevertheless the doctrine itself remains, in form at least. It remains in the sense that an Act explicitly conflicting with the European Communities Act, the Human Rights Act or the devolution legislation would not be declared unlawful nor would it be likely to be disapplied by the courts. But the doctrine of parliamentary sovereignty clearly means something very different from what it meant before Britain entered the European Community in 1973. It remains in form, but not in substance. In practice, therefore, if not in law, parliamentary sovereignty is no longer the governing principle of the British constitution.

For the principle of parliamentary sovereignty is not merely a legal principle. It also has political implications. To be effective politically the sovereign power must be accompanied by the exercise of real political authority. That was certainly what Dicey thought, which is why he believed that, although Irish Home Rule was in form compatible with the doctrine of parliamentary sovereignty, in practice it was not. The political implication was that the government of the day was omnicompetent, for, of course, the House of Commons is normally controlled by the government of the day, while the House of Lords cannot resist a determined government. It is now clear, however, that the government is no longer omnicompetent and that power and effective authority has been ceded over large areas of policy to the European Union; and, insofar as their domestic policies are concerned, to the devolved bodies of Scotland, Wales and Northern Ireland; and also, in matters of human rights to the judges. It is not easy to imagine circumstances in which the power and authority so ceded can be reclaimed by Parliament. So, while it may be still true in form that Parliament can make or unmake any law, it is no longer true in substance. The powers of Parliament have been severely and probably permanently circumscribed, and powers which were once exercised by Parliament are now exercised by other bodies.

But, in addition, Parliament itself has become more effective in holding the government to account. The reformed House of Lords is a far more professional and assertive body than it was when dominated by the hereditary peers. An elected House of Lords, if it comes about, can be expected to prove even more assertive towards the government of the day. The House of Commons has also become more assertive. Reforms of the House, although much less noticed than reforms to the House of Lords, and more piecemeal in nature, have made that chamber also more effective in holding the government to account. The departmentally-related Select Committees, established in 1979, have grown increasingly confident and professional in their working methods. Tony Blair was the first Prime Minister to appear regularly before a Select Committee, the Liaison Committee, comprising the chairs of some of the departmentally-related committees; and this practice is likely to continue under Prime Ministers from all parties. MPs are far more willing now to vote against their party whip than they were in the 1960s when party cohesion was so near to 100% that there was little point in measuring it. In the first Parliament of Tony Blair's premiership, no fewer than 50% of Labour backbenchers voted against their own government at some time during the Parliament.[11] The stereotype that MPs are mere passive sheep is quite remote from

---

[11] P Cowley, *Revolts and Rebellions; Parliamentary Voting Under Blair* (London, Politico's, 2003) 4, 231. This book provides an excellent scholarly account of the growth in parliamentary dissent in recent years.

the truth, as the votes on such issues as the Iraq war, foundation hospitals, top-up fees in universities and city academies in the second term of Tony Blair's premiership show. These votes revealed a greater degree of back-bench dissent than any parliamentary votes since the repeal of the Corn Laws in 1846. Admittedly, the rebellions made little impact on policy. That was because the dissentient MPs were rebelling against a government which enjoyed an overall majority in the House of Commons of 165, the second largest since the war. But this majority was an artifact of the electoral system, not an indication that the government, which had gained 42% of the vote in the general election of 2001, enjoyed overwhelming support in the country. It is, therefore, the first-past-the-post electoral system, which currently produces comfortable if not landslide majorities for a party on a minority of the popular vote, that condemns parliamentary rebels to impotence.

There is, however, a vital but hardly noticed reform, beginning in the parliamentary year 2006–7, that has greatly strengthened the role of the Commons in the legislative process. In that year, the standing committees were renamed public bill committees, and given the right to take written and oral evidence from officials and experts from outside Parliament. This change allows legislative committees to act in Select Committee or inquisitorial mode, and it is likely to make legislative scrutiny far more effective. All this means that, contrary to public perceptions, the House of Commons, like the Lords, has become a more professional and more assertive body than ever it has been in the past. Governments, even if they enjoy a secure majority in the Commons, can no longer be sure of controlling Parliament as they could in the 1950s and 1960s.

The various constitutional reforms discussed in this book all have the effect of in practice limiting the sovereignty of Parliament, and so limiting the power of government. Governments, therefore, can no longer do what they were accustomed to do before the 1970s. They cannot, for example, legislate freely and with confidence on such matters as agriculture or fisheries; for the bulk of agriculture and fisheries policy is determined by the European Union. They cannot with confidence promulgate legislation on domestic matters in Scotland and Northern Ireland; nor, to a large extent, in Wales; and they do not in practice promulgate legislation against the Human Rights Act, even though legally entitled to do so.

But, although the sovereignty of Parliament has been limited, the institution of Parliament itself has been strengthened. A stronger Parliament imposes further limits upon the power of a previously omnicompetent government. Britain, therefore, is much less of an elective dictatorship than it was thirty years ago. The Diceyan constitution, which emphasised the exercise of real political authority by the government over all matters, persons and things in the United Kingdom, is but a shadow of its former self. Bagehot's constitution is dead, while Dicey's constitution is dying before our eyes.

V

The constitutions of Bagehot and of Dicey, then, are dead or dying. What, is to replace them? What are the main principles of the new constitution?

The constitutional reforms implemented since 1997 have fundamentally altered the balance between the main institutions of government—the legislature, the executive and the judiciary. They have also, albeit in a limited way, strengthened the role of the people against the government. The consequence may be summarised by saying that the idea of the sovereignty of parliament has been replaced by that of the separation of powers, so putting Britain on the path to becoming a genuine constitutional state. The old constitution was based upon the sovereignty of Parliament. The new constitution is based on the idea of a constitutional state based upon a separation of powers. The sovereignty of Parliament is gradually and slowly coming to be replaced by the sovereignty of a constitution.

Traditionally the British constitution has been characterised as one in which there is no separation of powers at all. Indeed, Bagehot saw the idea of the separation of powers as incompatible with the idea of parliamentary government.[12] Instead, so he believed, the British system of government was characterised by a fusion of powers between the executive and the legislature, between the Cabinet and Parliament. Executive and legislative power were, so he thought, concentrated in a single body, the Cabinet, which was 'a committee of the legislative body selected to be the executive body' and 'a combining committee—a *hyphen* which joins, a *buckle* which fastens, the legislative part of the state to the executive part of the state'.[13]

Bagehot's notion of a fusion of powers has attained classic status. This may have prevented its absurdity from being noticed. For the only part of the constitution where there was a genuine fusion of powers was in the committee system in local government, before it was replaced by a cabinet or mayoral model after 2000. Under that system the whole council was both the legislature and the executive. That is precisely not the model of a Cabinet system, where there is a separate executive in the form of the Cabinet. Unless every MP and peer were also to be a minister—which would of course be an absurdity—there must be a separation of powers between the Cabinet and Parliament. The extent of that separation depends upon the extent to which Parliament chooses to assert itself against the government of the day; and that, of course, depends upon political vicissitudes. Bagehot himself contradicts his thesis of the fusion of powers when he writes, in the introduction to the second edition of *The English Constitution* that the majority supporting the government in the House of Commons is not 'a mechanical majority ready to accept everything, but a fair and reasonable one, predisposed to think the Government right, but not ready to find it to be so in the face of the facts

---

[12] Dicey too attacked the doctrine of the separation of powers, but only in what he regarded as its 'exaggerated' form, 'as misapplied by French statesmen of the Revolution'! *Law of the Constitution*, 338.

[13] *The English Constitution* in *Collected Works*, V, 211–12.

and in opposition to whatever might occur'.[14] When presented with unpopular proposals, it would rather desert its own leaders than ensure its own ruin, although in practice wise ministers usually ensure that such unpopular proposals are withdrawn before being introduced on the floor of the House of Commons to face probable defeat. The situation that Bagehot is describing here is not one of either a concentration or a fusion of power.

It makes equally little sense to speak of the Cabinet as a 'committee' of the House of Commons. In Bagehot's day the Prime Minister was chosen by the Queen, not by the House of Commons, and then appointed a Cabinet. In modern times it is in practice the electorate that chooses the Prime Minister. The government is of course responsible to the House of Commons, and, ultimately, to the people at a general election. The government, however, can destroy the body to which it is responsible by dissolving Parliament. Few committees can do that! And it certainly makes little sense to call the Cabinet a committee of the electorate, or to suggest that there is a fusion of power between the Cabinet and the voters. The Cabinet, in fact, has too much independent authority for it to be regarded merely as a 'committee', whether of the legislature, as in Bagehot's day, or the electorate in ours.

There is, then, a partial, though not of course a total, separation of powers between the Cabinet and Parliament, two bodies with quite different functions. Although Parliament is, in legal terms, the lawmaker, in practice it is the Cabinet which has the function of devising policies and making laws, while the primary function of Parliament is to scrutinise legislation emanating from government ministers before it reaches the statute book. But there is also a separation of powers, one that is almost total, within the executive itself, between ministers, entrusted with the making of laws, and civil servants, entrusted with the task of carrying them out, and with advising ministers; while ministers are partisan and subject to dismissal by Parliament and the Prime Minister, civil servants are neutral, not of course between the government and the opposition, but between governments of alternative political colours; they are screened from Parliament by the principle of ministerial responsibility and they enjoy security of tenure. Ministers are temporary, but in Britain the civil service is permanent. Parliament can neither exercise direct executive power itself nor appoint the civil servants whose role it is to implement laws, civil servants being accountable to ministers and not to Parliament. Civil servants, in turn, cannot be part of the political executive nor of the legislature.

The Cabinet, then, is a policy-making policy, Parliament a scrutinising body, and the civil service an advisory and implementing body. The judiciary is a rule-interpreting body whose judgments offer an authoritative statement of the law. Part of the meaning of the concept of judicial independence is that the judges should not be subject to pressures from the other institutions of government—the Cabinet, Parliament or the civil service—whose interests may be affected by their

---

[14] Introduction to the second edition of *The English Constitution* in *Collected Works*, V, 185.

judgments. The executive, in particular, should not interfere with the judiciary. But, equally, the judges should not interfere with proceedings in Parliament.

There has always been, therefore, contrary to what Bagehot believed, at least a partial separation of powers in Britain. It would be difficult to regard any state where such a partial separation did not exist as a constitutional democracy. There was, in 2008, some controversy as to whether the police should be given the power to detain suspected terrorists for up to 42 days without charging them. Were the system of government to be such that the executive had the power to commit anyone to prison at will without charge, that system could hardly be characterised as constitutional. It would in general be absurd for one institution to ape the procedures of another. The executive would hardly be likely to adopt a legislative procedure i.e. public debate, followed by a vote, to make policy; nor would it be sensible for it to adopt a judicial procedure—to hear the case of the two opposing sides, and put the verdict to a jury for resolution. Equally, it would not very sensible for judges to decide disputed cases by using either a legislative or an executive procedure.

The doctrine of the separation of powers is, then, as Montesquieu believed, a doctrine of universal validity. There must be, for any state to be called constitutional, some element of the separation of powers; there must be, at the very least, a partial separation of powers. Some democracies of course will emphasise the doctrine more than others. Comparing different countries, and comparing the British constitution at different points in time, the issue is not whether the doctrine does or does not apply, but rather the extent to which it applies.

In Britain, a central consequence of the era of constitutional reform has been to enhance the separation of powers. Devolution has brought about a territorial separation of powers. But there has also been a strengthened separation of powers within the central institutions of government. Under the old constitution, much of the separation of powers was guaranteed solely by convention. Under the new constitution it is strengthened by statute. There has been, in particular, a strengthening by statute of the institutional barriers between the judiciary and the executive. The Human Rights Act strengthens the position of the judiciary, and the Constitutional Reform Act of 2005 complements the Human Rights Act by explicitly recognising the judiciary as a third branch of government and, through a new appointments procedure for England and Wales, insulating it from the political process and from ministerial interference, so bolstering its independence. It does so in three ways. First, although judges will, under the provisions of the Act, continue to be appointed by the Queen, on the recommendation of the Lord Chancellor, the Lord Chancellor's role becomes almost purely formal, and the selection of most senior judges is now undertaken by the newly-established Judicial Appointments Commission. The Constitutional Reform Act, therefore emphasises the principle of judicial independence by ensuring that judges are not appointed by members of the executive. Second, the Act emphasises that a member of the executive should not sit as a judge as previous Lord Chancellors have done, although, admittedly, with some infrequency in recent years. Third, the Act, by removing the highest court of appeal from the House of Lords, ensures that members of the judiciary should no longer have a legislative role. It was in any case always anomalous that, in Britain, the highest court in the land should be, in form, a committee of the upper house, the House of Lords. The Act thus elevates the judiciary by more firmly separating its role from that of the executive and the legislature.

The separation of powers, therefore, between the judiciary and the other institutions of government, has been emphasised and strengthened by legislation. The separation of powers between government and Parliament has also been intensified. This has been in part the result of legislation, for the House of Lords Act of 1999, removing all but 92 of the hereditary peers from the House of Lords had the consequence, almost certainly unintended, of creating a more assertive and determined second chamber. The main source of parliamentary assertiveness, however, has resulted not so much from legislation as from changes in legislative behaviour in both houses, a consequence in part of the decline in deference that has been so widespread a feature of British society in recent years. Despite rhetoric concerning 'the decline of Parliament', often from some mythical golden age, it can be confidently asserted that never has Parliament been so professional and assertive as it is today.

In consequence of these changes the description of British government as an elective dictatorship is no longer appropriate. Such a description was becoming out of date even when it was first made by Lord Hailsham in the 1970s, since MPs were already becoming more willing to vote against the party line, and judges were already becoming more assertive. The nearest Britain has come to an elective dictatorship in the post-war era was in fact in the two decades after the war, sometimes regarded as a golden age of parliamentary government. Before the 1960s the judges tended to be deferential towards the executive, while before the 1970s there were few large parliamentary rebellions, and the unreformed House of Lords was a somewhat passive, usually sleepy, body. A government with a majority would have no problem in securing its legislation. Today, by contrast, a government, even if it has a comfortable majority, must ask itself a number of questions before considering whether to introduce legislation to Parliament. The first is whether such legislation can be construed to be consistent with European Community law. If it cannot, then it could be disapplied by the courts, as the *Factortame* and later judgments show. Next, the government must consider whether the legislation falls genuinely within the parameters of the quasi-federal system of government created by devolution. If it deals with domestic affairs in Scotland, Wales or Northern Ireland, then, by convention, it lies outwith the government's powers. So, if a government wishes to introduce legislation on some matter such as health or education—National Health Service foundation hospitals for example, or city academies—it must, by convention, restrict its legislation to England.

Assuming that these hurdles have been successfully surmounted, a government must then ask itself whether it can ensure that its legislation will pass the House of Commons. The answer to this question, as votes on such matters as National

Health Service foundation hospitals, top-up fees for universities and 42 days detention show, can no longer be taken for granted. Once legislation has passed the Commons, ministers then have to ask themselves whether they can ensure that it passes the House of Lords. The answer to that question, too, is far less certain than it used to be before 1999. It is almost certain that no single party will ever again enjoy an overall majority in the Lords, and the outcome of votes now depends primarily on the stance taken by the Liberal Democrats and the cross-benchers, the two groups holding the balance of power. The cross-benchers, in particular, are likely to be swayed by the balance of the argument, since they are beyond the reach of any party whip. Therefore, ministers have to win the argument in the House of Lords as well as the Commons. But, even if legislation is likely to pass both houses of Parliament, ministers still cannot be sure that it will proceed safely to the statute book. They also have to ask themselves whether the legislation will survive scrutiny by the judges. The Human Rights Act has, in effect, though not in form, given the judges a new weapon, the power of judicial review of legislation. And, on some laws, admittedly a highly restricted category at present, there is a yet further hurdle that legislation has to surmount—the hurdle of the people. Acceptance of the referendum as a constitutional mechanism makes it more difficult for a government to secure passage of certain 'constitutional' measures. A government seeking to join the eurozone needs the support of the people as well as that of Parliament. The people have become, albeit in a very limited way, part of the law-making element of the constitution.

The era of constitutional reform has emphasised, therefore, the role of the separation of powers in the constitution and given it a wholly new importance. That, perhaps, has been the central theme of the reforms. The change in emphasis has been so great as to amount to a change in quality. Liberty, it may be argued, is power cut into pieces. In Britain, constitutional reform has indeed cut power into pieces, and it is the power of the executive that has been cut into pieces. Parliament, both Commons and Lords, has more power, the judiciary has more power and the people have more power—all at the expense of the executive. The British constitution is now characterised not by the sovereignty of Parliament and a concentration of power at the centre, but by a separation of powers at the centre, and a quasi-federal territorial separation of powers between Parliament and the European Union, on the one hand, and the devolved bodies on the other. Britain is in the process of becoming a constitutional state, one marked by checks and balances between the different organs of government, and a state in which the judiciary now has a crucial role to play in the determination of individual rights and in determining the scope of government action. It is the beginning of the transformation of Britain into a constitutional state that forms the deepest significance of the era of constitutional reform.

But this transformation is only . . . part of its meaning. It has been secured primarily through parliamentary legislation, but it can be conceived of in another light. It can be understood as the British people, through their elected representatives, in effect giving themselves a constitution. The theory of the American constitution is that the people, through their elected representatives in Congress, can maintain a democratic dialogue on how that constitution is interpreted. The question may therefore arise of why it is that in Britain, the people should not, through Parliament, be able to initiate a similar democratic dialogue. Yet, despite the introduction of the referendum into the British constitution, the people are still kept at arm's length from Parliament and government, still expected to play a primarily passive role in political affairs. They are to remain subjects, not active democratic citizens. Twenty years ago, an American commentator said that 'Nowhere in the democratic world is there less sympathy for populist and participatory forms of democracy than England'.[15] That remains the case, even after the era of constitutional reform. Britain may have been transforming herself into a constitutional state. She has not yet begun to transform herself into a popular constitutional state. That task remains to be achieved during the next period of constitutional reform. It is part of the history of the future.

---

[15] B Barber, 'Participation and Swiss Democracy (1988) *Government and Opposition*, Winter, 43.

12

Towards a Popular Constitutional State: Democracy and Participation

I

THE NEW CONSTITUTION, we have suggested, has the effect of cutting power into pieces. It has dispersed power. Yet this dispersal of power has hardly registered with the electorate. The reforms have done little to counteract that widespread disenchantment with politics which characterises modern Britain, as well as many other advanced democracies. Surveys undertaken in 2002, for example, showed that only a minority felt that such reforms as devolution, the removal of hereditary peers from the House of Lords, and freedom of information, had improved the system of government to any marked degree. The vast majority thought that they had made little difference. Even in Scotland, 44% felt that devolution had made little difference; and there is no evidence that trust in the political system in Scotland is any greater than it is in England. Perhaps there was an exaggerated expectation of what constitutional reform could achieve in a very short period of time. Nevertheless, there has been little sign in later surveys of any increase in popular confidence in the British system of government.

Commenting on the evidence of the 2002 survey, those who conducted it concluded that 'Constitutional reform does not appear to have been the right remedy for the recent decline in confidence in government'. It had not succeeded in 'reconnecting' voters with government.[1] Constitutional reform seems to have done little to combat disenchantment with politics. That disenchantment has been marked by a fall in turnout in general elections, a decline in the membership of political parties, and by a weakening in popular identification with political parties. It is true that these phenomena have been noticeable, to a greater or lesser extent, in many other advanced democracies. But the constitutional reform programme was introduced to counteract these trends. It has failed to do so.

In the general election of 2001, in the very midst of the era of constitutional reform, turnout was just 58%, the lowest since women were given the vote in 1918; and in the general election of 2005 it was only marginally higher at 62%. Low turnout amongst young people has been particularly noticeable. In 2005, it was

---

[1] C Bromley, J Curtice and B Seyd, *Has Constitutional Reform 'Reconnected' Voters with their Government?* (London, Constitution Unit, 2002) 3, 5, 7.

around 37% amongst those aged between 18 to 24, and only 33% amongst young women in this age group.

The fall in turnout has been sudden and precipitous. The decline in membership of political parties, by contrast, has been steady since the 1950s, though no less worrying for the health of democracy. In the early 1950s, the Labour Party had a million individual members, the Conservatives around 2,800,000. Labour now has only around 150,000 members, down from nearly 400,000 in 1996, following membership drives by John Smith and Tony Blair. The Conservatives have around 250,000 members, as compared with one and a half million in 1975, when Margaret Thatcher became Conservative leader. They have lost over four out of five of their members in the last 34 years, for 18 of which they were in office. Both parties have lost over half of their members during their years in office. The point may be put in another way. Fifty years ago, around 1 in 11 of the electorate belonged to a political party; today just 1 in 88 do. In addition, voters feel far less attached to political parties than they once did. In 1964, 44% described themselves as identifying 'very strongly' with a political party. In 2001, only 14% did so.[2] A study of Britain's civic culture undertaken fifty years ago, in 1959, concluded that 'The participation role is highly developed. Exposure to politics, interest, involvement and a sense of competence are relatively high . . . there is general system pride as well as satisfaction with specific government performance'.[3] Such a verdict could hardly be delivered today.

Some suggest that disenchantment with politics is part of a wider phenomenon, a loss of community engagement, a decline in what social scientists call social capital, the willingness to form social bonds and networks. Yet survey evidence seems to offer little support for such a view, at least so far as Britain is concerned. It seems to show instead that popular interest in politics is as strong as it has ever been, and that there is a powerful sense of civic obligation in modern Britain. Around 40% of the population belong to a voluntary organisation, while around 3 million 18–24 year olds, the very generation that is least likely to vote, volunteer every year. Although young people are far less likely to vote than the over 50s, a Citizenship Survey undertaken between April and December 2007 showed that those aged between 16 and 24 were more likely than the over 50s to participate in *informal* voluntary activities at least once a month—41% compared with 32%.[4]

The same survey showed that 77% of people in England had given to charity in the four weeks prior to interview.[5] 81% of British adults gave to the tsunami appeal, twice the rate of the United States and two to three times the rate of many European countries. The National Trust and the Royal Society for the Protection of Birds each has more than a million members, over twice as many as the membership of all of the political parties added together. Survey evidence seems to indicate that four out of ten adults belong to at least one type of group. '18 million

---

[2]　P Whiteley, 'The State of Participation in Britain' (2003) *Parliamentary Affairs*, 611.
[3]　G Almond and S Verba, *The Civic Culture* (Princeton, NJ, Princeton University Press, 1963) 315.
[4]　*Communities in Control*, 33.
[5]　*Communities in Control*, Evidence Annex, 28.

adults in Great Britain belong to, 11 million participants participate in, and four million volunteered their time and labour for organisations'.[6] It is not so much, therefore, 'that participation has declined, but rather that it has evolved over time and taken on new forms'.[7] Popular interest in politics remains high, but electors no longer see parties as the best means by which to influence political events. Perhaps they are right. It seems in any case somewhat paradoxical to blame the people if they do not find the political parties attractive. It is all somewhat reminiscent of Bertolt Brecht's quip after the 1953 uprising in East Germany—the government has lost confidence in the people; therefore it must dissolve the people and seek a new people.[8] Why should we not blame the institutions rather than the people? The truth seems to be that, in Britain, the democratic spirit is healthy enough. It is the institutions in which that spirit is reflected that are at fault. The decline of traditional networks of representation is a consequence less of apathy than of disenchantment, and also, of course, of competition from other institutions and activities. It is not so much that there is a generalised disengagement with politics, but 'rather that a vital link that connected citizens to the state and the formal democratic process has been broken'.[9] How, then, can constitutional reform be extended so as to channel this civic spirit and desire for community engagement?

It has become a commonplace to speak of a crisis of democracy in Britain. But these trends—towards lower turnout in elections, lower party membership and falling identification with political parties—are by no means unique to Britain. In almost all democracies turnout has fallen from the higher levels of the 1960s and 1970s: the 2007 presidential election in France, in which turnout was over 80%, was a striking exception to the general trend. In almost all democracies party membership has fallen, as has party identification. The trends discernible in Britain have become common to most advanced democracies, whatever their constitutional structure. They are as common in democracies with enacted constitutions as those without, as common in democracies with electoral systems based on proportional representation as in democracies, such as Britain, whose electoral system is first-past-the-post, as common in federal as in unitary states. It would be implausible to suggest, therefore, that the malaise in politics is caused by a particular institutional set-up. It would also be implausible to argue that constitutional reforms of the kind implemented since 1997 could do much to cure the problems which seems to have afflicted not just Britain but many other democracies as well.

In 2005, in a poll conducted by Gallup International, 79% agreed with the proposition that democracy was the best form of government, but as many as 65% did not believe that their own country was ruled by the will of the people. What is perhaps even more remarkable is that these percentages were highest in advanced

---

[6] L Byrne, MP, 'Powered by Politics: Reforming Politics from the Inside' (2005) *Parliamentary Affairs*, 615.

[7] P Whiteley, quoted in ibid, 614.

[8] See his poem, 'The Solution' in *Bertolt Brecht: Poems 1913–1956* (London, Methuen, 2000) 440.

[9] M Taylor, 'Can Funding Reform Stir the Party Animal?' (2005) *Parliamentary Affairs*, 640.

and stable democracies, such as Britain, Denmark, France, the Netherlands and Sweden. It seems that there is some systemic problem in the structure of modern democracies which is causing disenchantment. There can certainly be little doubt that the reasons for disengagement from politics are deep-seated and pervasive, and that they have not so far been remedied by constitutional reform. We must, therefore, look deeper into the problem of democracy in Britain, at the very basis of our representative system of democracy which dates back to the nineteenth century and grew to fruition in the twentieth century, but whose foundations now look very creaky. Disenchantment with democracy flows from the conflict between a maturing democracy, accustomed to universal suffrage and the political rights that go with it, and the traditional mass party which increasingly serves, not to give effect to popular demands, but to frustrate them.

Mass parties came to fruition in the twentieth century. They have now entered a phase of decline as an ideological space has been opening up for a renewed radical individualism. 'The age of the mass party has passed', one authority has remarked, 'and at least in any foreseeable future, it is unlikely to be recoverable'.[10] The story of the rise and fall of the mass political party is one of the great unwritten books of our time, and the consequences of the decline of the mass party are likely to prove very profound. Our representative system of democracy has been based upon political parties since long before the era of universal suffrage, but in Britain the mass party was in large part the creation of Joseph Chamberlain, the radical mayor of Birmingham in the 1870s. The Birmingham caucus, created by Chamberlain, was the first mass party organisation in Britain. It was extended to national level in 1877 when the National Liberal Federation was established, and Chamberlain's model was adopted, with some variations, by the other parties, the Conservatives, in the 1870s, and also the Labour Party, founded in 1900. The organisation of the Labour Party, based as it was on the mass trade union movement, gave a political voice to the organised working class whose members would otherwise almost certainly have lacked one. The growth of the mass party was, therefore, a necessary response to the expansion of the suffrage and the need to canvass and win the support of a wider electorate than could be achieved by a candidate who lacked the aid of a party machine. The mass party came to replace the party of individual opinion. In Britain mass political parties reached their zenith in the immediate post-war era, a period which lasted until roughly the mid-1970s. During this period, most voters' political views depended on their social class position, and their views seemed to change little during their lifetime. That accounted for the relative stability of electoral politics and the greater degree of attachment to political parties than exists at present. 'Class', one authority suggested, writing in 1967, was 'the basis of British party politics; all else is embellishment and detail'.[11] Party identification was high, and most people believed that it was their civic duty to vote.

---

[10] P Mair, cited in B Rogers, 'From Membership to Management? The Future of Political Parties as Democratic Organisations', in (2005) *Parliamentary Affairs*, 602.

[11] P G J Pulzer, *Political Representation and Elections in Britain* (London, George Allen and Unwin, 1967) 98.

In the immediate post-war era, it seemed that the politics of class was leading the two main parties, whom no fewer than 97% of the voters supported in the general election of 1951, to develop a politics based on two competing ideologies, socialism and anti-socialism. During this era, it was still genuinely possible to believe in a radical transformation of society, away from the capitalist or mixed economy into something qualitatively different. In 1945, after all, the Labour Party had declared in its election manifesto. 'The Labour Party is a Socialist Party and proud of it'. Admittedly, after the experience of the first majority Labour government, which ruled from 1945 to 1951, many in the Party abandoned socialism in practice if not in theory. In 1956, Anthony Crosland published an influential book, *The Future of Socialism*, arguing that socialists should in future rely less upon public ownership, and more on other instruments such as redistributive taxation and comprehensive schools to create a socialist society. But, even in this 'revisionist' form, there was still an assumption that society could be consciously transformed by human will. Socialism, both in its traditional form, and in its more modern, revisionist form, rested upon a sociological proposition, that it was the ideology of the working class, organised in trade unions, and that this social base was a progressive one.

During the last quarter of the twentieth century these assumptions gradually came to be unravelled. In post-war Britain the organised working class was to become a smaller and smaller proportion of the electorate. In 1979, around 13 million belonged to trade unions; today fewer than 8 million do; nor were the sympathies of the working class always progressive. The fundamental problem, however, was that members of the working class sought individual advancement for themselves and their families rather than emancipation as a class. They favoured what Tony Benn in 1971 called, 'the individual escape from class into prosperity, which is the cancer eating into the Western European Social Democratic parties'.[12] So it was that class came, in Ralf Dahrendorf's words, to be 'transformed into individual social mobility'.[13] Gradually the traditional socialist vision faded. The leaders of the Labour Party continued for some time to lead their followers towards the promised land, but the followers were ceasing to follow— they were in fact ceasing to see themselves as followers at all. It is individualism rather than collectivism that has become the letimotif of the modern age, and parties of the left, if they wish to be electable, have been forced to come to terms with it. That, no doubt, was the essential reason for the establishment of Tony Blair's New Labour Party which, symbolically, in 1995 deleted Clause 4 from the Party's constitution, the clause committing it to the public ownership of the means of production, distribution and exchange.

Political scientists are accustomed to distinguish between 'position' politics and 'valence' politics.[14] 'Position' politics is a politics of conflict between fairly stark

---

[12] T Benn, *Office Without Power: Diaries 1968–72* (London, Hutchinson, 1988) 356. Entry for 16 July 1971.

[13] R Dahrendorf, *Reflections on the Revolution in Europe* (London, Chatto and Windus, 1990) 56.

[14] See D Stokes, 'Valence Politics' in D Kavanagh (ed) *Electoral Politics* (Oxford, Clarendon Press, 1992) 141–64.

alternatives, such as the nationalisation of basic industries, the retention or aban-
donment of nuclear weapons and the maintaining or shedding of the colonies.
It was a politics of this type that was prevalent during the early post-war years.
But there has now been a shift from 'position' politics towards 'valence' politics,
where there is a large measure of agreement on fundamental aims—for example
an effective National Health Service and better schools, with disagreement largely
confined to the issue of which party is best placed to achieve these aims. There is a
broad agreement about ends but disagreement about means. Much political argument, therefore, is now about competence rather than ideology. 'In our view,'
argue three leading students of elections in Britain, 'the most important factor
underlying electoral choice is valence—people's judgments of the overall competence of the rival political parties'.[15] There has been, since 1992, broad agreement
that the fundamental framework established by Margaret Thatcher, based on pri-
vatization, a liberal economy and a weakened trade union movement, should be
maintained. The point at issue at general elections since 1992 has been which party
is best able to administer this dispensation effectively. The general election of 1997
was the first since the Labour Party had been formed in which nationalization was
not an issue. We are living, therefore, in a post-ideological and a post-socialist age.

The politics of collectivism which marked the early post-war era has been
replaced by a politics of individual aspiration. The successful politicians of the
modern era have been those who have recognised this new politics and have been
able to accommodate their parties to it—Margaret Thatcher, John Major and
Tony Blair. But the new individualism and the end of the socialist era have served
to undermine, not just the Labour Party, but all mass parties. These parties were
essentially the product of a collectivist age. The demise of collectivism, therefore,
may also herald the demise of the mass party. Political leaders have been adjusting
to these new realities. Both Margaret Thatcher in the 1980s and Tony Blair since
1994 sought to transform their parties so that they became vehicles for their own
personal vision of leadership. There are signs at the time of writing that David
Cameron is seeking to do the same. One element of the appeal both of Margaret
Thatcher and Tony Blair may have been that both were, to an extent, plebiscitary
leaders, leaders who appealed over the heads of their parties directly to the people.
Both Margaret Thatcher and Tony Blair instinctively understood the populist
implications of the decline of the mass party.

There are, then, signs, and not only in Britain, that the mass party, plagued by
falling membership and a weakening sense of party identification, is dying on its
feet. Certainly the grip of the parties upon the electorate is far weaker than it has
ever been. Yet the grip of the parties on the institutions of government remains as
strong as ever; and politics has come to be dominated by the career politician who
has made politics his occupation and has no other professional aim than to remain
in politics. MPs now tend to resemble each other more than those they claim to
represent. Westminster has come to be disconnected from the people; it has

---

[15] H Clarke et al, *Political Choice in Britain* (Oxford, OUP, 2004) 9.

become a home for professional politicians, a house without windows. Local government, too, has come to be dominated by the professional politician, and it is largely for this reason that local government was unable to mobilise the support which would have enabled it to withstand the assaults launched upon it by central government. Local authorities, therefore, have ceased to be vehicles for democratic engagement. Yet, there is an inchoate yearning in Britain for representation by men and women of independent spirit, whose interests are not constrained by the requirements of tightly organised mass parties.

It is hardly surprising, then, that the constitutional reform programme has made so little impact upon political disenchantment, for it has done little to open up a political system dominated by political parties whose roots are no longer as deep as they once were, whose relationship to social interests is far less intimate than it was in the past, and which are not able ideologically to penetrate British society. Parties are no longer the pre-eminent mechanism for the expression of political opinion in Britain. They have become primarily a means by which the voter can choose between competing teams of rulers. The constitutional reforms do little to touch this condition; they do little to meet popular aspirations in a post-socialist and individualist age. They do little, therefore, to meet real popular grievances. Suppose that one were to visualise an average voter living in England. Such a voter does not seek devolution for England in the form either of English regional government or an English Parliament; such a voter might well think that the Human Rights Act is a useful reform, but probably hopes never to have to consult lawyers or to appear in the courts. Were such a voter to ask, 'What difference has constitutional reform actually made to me?' it would be difficult to frame a convincing answer.

The real achievement of constitutional reform is to have redistributed power, but it has redistributed power between elites, not between elites and the people. It has redistributed power 'downwards' to politicians in Edinburgh, Cardiff, Belfast and London, 'sideways' to the life peers in the House of Lords and 'sideways' to the judges interpreting the Human Rights Act. The value of this dispersal of power should not be underestimated. It has made it easier for the power of government to be made subject to constitutional control so that twenty-first century Britain is much less of an elective dictatorship than it was in the 1970s when Lord Hailsham first produced his famous characterisation. But constitutional reform has not redistributed power to the voter. It has not shifted power from the politicians to the people. That is the crucial weakness in the constitutional reform programme, as it has so far been implemented. That is the central reason why it has made so little impact on entrenched attitudes towards the political system. It has not gone far enough in implementing the radical programme of the constitutional reforming liberals of the nineteenth century.

The demise of the mass party raises fundamental problems for democratic government. In the past, political parties were the prime institutions linking the aspirations of voters with the machinery of government. But, if they are no longer the primary vehicles of political engagement, then, inevitably there will be radical changes in the relationship between the people and government. Of course parties will remain, for the foreseeable future, crucial in the formation of governments and in ensuring the periodic accountability of rulers to the people in general elections. But what is to replace mass parties as vehicles of engagement? What shape is the democracy of the twenty-first century likely to take? In a perceptive Fabian pamphlet written as long ago as 1992, entitled *Making Mass Membership Work,* Gordon Brown argued that, 'In the past, people interested in change have joined the Labour Party largely to elect agents of change. Today they want to be agents of change themselves'.[16] He instanced as agents of popular participation such bodies as tenants associations, residents groups, school governing bodies and community groups. There can be little doubt that, in the future polity, such innovations, including various forms of direct democracy, will come increasingly to supplement, though not of course, to replace, the traditional machinery of representative government. There is a need to go beyond the traditional agenda of constitutional reform, to refashion our democracy so that it meets the needs of a new age, an age in which participation has to reach beyond party. We need to move, then, beyond the new constitution.

II

The next stage of constitutional reform, therefore, and a far more difficult stage, must be a redistribution of power, not from one part of the elite to another, amongst those professionally involved in politics and the law, but from politicians to the people. This was heralded in the Green Paper issued by Gordon Brown's government in the summer of 2007, entitled 'The Governance of Britain'. Together with a series of reforms designed to make government more accountable to Parliament, by, for example, rendering the war-making power accountable to Parliament, it contained a short but important section entitled, 'Improving direct democracy'.[17] 'In the past', the Green Paper declared, 'individuals and communities have tended to be seen as passive recipients of services provided by the state. However, in recent years people have demonstrated that they are willing to take a more active role, and that this can help improve services and create stronger communities'. (para 169) The government proposed, therefore, to begin a consultation process on such matters as the introduction of citizens juries and on giving citizens the power to ballot i.e. call for referendums, on local spending decisions. In doing so, the government was moving, however tentatively, into a new area of constitutional reform, the introduction of new elements of direct democracy into the British political system.

These proposals, limited though they are, recognise that the era of pure representative democracy, as it has been understood for much of the twentieth century, is now coming to an end. During the era of pure representative democracy,

---

[16]   Quoted in L Byrne MP, 'Powered by Politics' (2005) *Parliamentary Affairs,* 620.
[17]   Paras 157–79.

the people, though enfranchised, exercised power only on relatively infrequent occasions at general elections. Between general elections, they trusted their elected representatives to act on their behalf. There was some degree of deference towards elected politicians and, in any case, in an era when educational standards were lower than they are now, few voters believed that they had the political competence to make decisions for themselves. In the late 1940s, for example, the level of political knowledge was pitiable. Just 49% could name a single British colony, while, in a sample survey in Greenwich during the 1950 general election, barely half could name the party of their local MP.[18] Voting tended to be tribal and instinctive, based largely on an inherited viewpoint derived from parental attitudes and on social class. That, however, was bound to be a transitional stage. It was bound to take time before universal adult suffrage came to be taken for granted, and its implications for popular enfranchisement fully understood. Universal male suffrage had been introduced in 1918, and universal female suffrage in 1928. It took until the general election of 1950, however, for the principle of one person one vote to be fully implemented, since it was not until the 1948 Representation of the People Act that plural voting was abolished. Universal suffrage, therefore, is still a relatively new phenomenon.

The model of representative democracy—perhaps guided democracy would be a better term—that was acceptable during the first years of universal suffrage is no longer adequate. The exercise of a modicum of power at relatively infrequent general elections is seen as insufficient. Voters wish to exert some influence upon events between elections as well as at them. Deference has largely disappeared, and it is no longer accepted that political decisions should be made only by politicians. Elected politicians, therefore, are no longer accepted as the sole source of power and authority. Few now believe that the system of pure representative democracy is sufficient to enfranchise them, and this feeling of disengagement seems most pronounced amongst the young. It is one of the main reasons why turnout has fallen so precipitously amongst this age-group. In addition, many voters, better educated than those of their parents' generation, find themselves empowered in many other areas of their lives, while the collective organisations which previously ruled their lives, in particular the trade unions, have lost much of their authority. Margaret Thatcher responded to these developments by opening up the economic system, by restricting the powers of the trade unions and by her policy of privatisation. There are now more shareholders in Britain than there are trade unionists. John Major's response was to open up the public services so that their customers were encouraged to expect the same high standards from them as they were from the private sector, and to complain if these standards were not achieved. Targets have been established for most public services—league tables for school achievement and hospital waiting lists, for example. Such reforms have given individuals much greater power over their lives. Yet, in politics, the people are still expected to remain passive and deferential. The political system has not yet responded to the

---

[18] D Kynaston, *Austerity Britain, 1945–51* (London, Bloomsbury 2007) 382.

new individualism. Despite the wave of constitutional reforms since 1997, the political system itself has not been opened up. It is, however, hardly possible to bifurcate human beings, hardly possible to expect someone who is expected to be independent and self-reliant in her economic dealings and in her dealings with the public services not also to demand a more active role in the political system as well. There is a striking contrast between the empowered consumer and the passive citizen. Britain may be on the way to becoming a constitutional state. It has not yet become a popular constitutional state.

III

Constitutional reform, then, has done little to alter the basis of democracy in Britain which is still predicated upon the passivity of the majority. The next stage of reform, however, is likely to redistribute power away from the political professionals to the people. It is likely to emphasise new instruments of participation which open up the party system so that the people are able both to make more decisions for themselves and also more effectively control decisions made by those in government.

Three objections are commonly made to proposals to increase participation. The first, which originates with the Austrian/American economist and political sociologist, Joseph Schumpeter, is that the people are not competent to make political decisions for themselves in a highly complex society and that more effective decisions will be made by experts and political professionals.[19] The second is that most people do not really wish to participate. The crucial objection to socialism, Oscar Wilde once quipped, was that it took up too many evenings. Where mechanisms for participation are present, so it is suggested, they tend to be used by the better educated and the better off, groups which already enjoy considerable political resources and whose voices perhaps are already given excessive weight in the making of public policy. The poor, members of ethnic minorities and the less well educated, tend not to use these mechanisms. But they are precisely the people who need the vote the most so as to redress the social and educational inequalities from which they suffer. To increase opportunities for participation, therefore, has the effect of decreasing rather than increasing political equality, skewing the political system further in favour of those who already enjoy considerable political resources. It would have the effect of increasing the advantages already enjoyed by the well-educated, the well-off and the articulate. The third objection is that, even if participation were desirable and even if it could be shown not to damage the efficiency of decision-making, it is not possible to achieve it in a complex and advanced industrial society. A small Greek city state might well be a suitable arena for participation; but it is not possible to replicate such conditions in large modern societies.

---

[19] J Schumpeter, *Capitalism, Socialism and Democracy* (London, George Allen and Unwin, 1943).

It is worth remarking that these objections, if well-founded, are not objections against participation only, but also, in a sense, objections against the principle of democracy itself. Democracy means, surely, government by the people. The first two objections bear a striking similarity to those made before the Great Reform Act of 1832 against extending the franchise. The people, it was said, were not capable of exercising the vote effectively; and they did not really want to have the vote, being perfectly content to leave decision-making in the hands of those who knew best, and whom they could trust to represent them effectively. Yet, even if such criticisms had been well-founded at the time, they became less so once the franchise had actually been extended and the new voters had become accustomed to the new opportunities available to them. 'As we do not learn to ride or swim, by merely being told how to do it', Mill insists, 'but by doing it, so it is only by practising popular government on a limited scale, that the people will ever learn how to exercise it on a larger'.[20] It might well be that, although the people may have made but limited use of the opportunities now available for participation, they would make a much greater use of them as these opportunities came to be more accepted.

The third objection—that the scale and complexity of modern advanced industrial states makes effective participation impossible—would have had more force before the invention of information technology than it does now. Participation would then have required all those participating to be physically present in a specific arena as with the Greek city state. But the miracle of information technology allows discussion and deliberation to take place without the participants needing to meet together. It may, nevertheless, still be the case that participation can be most effective, at least in its early stages, at the local rather than the national level, where issues are more immediate, and the consequences of decisions more concretely felt. Admittedly, however, participation at local level requires a revival of local feeling and the chances for that do not seem at present to be very propitious.

It probably makes little sense to evaluate the benefits and difficulties of participation in the abstract rather than considering particular institutional embodiments of participation and looking at the advantages and disadvantages of specific instruments. Some instruments under some circumstances will be found to yield benefits, others in other circumstances will not. The test must be a severely empirical one. We may conclude, therefore, by looking briefly at four such instruments for increasing participation—primary elections, the single transferable vote system of proportional representation, the referendum and initiative, and the Citizen's Assembly enabling the people themselves to legislate on particular issues. The first two of these instruments—primary elections and the single transferable vote—enable the citizen to exercise more effective control over whom to elect by opening up the party system; while the referendum and initiative, and the Citizen's Assembly enable the citizen to play a direct part in, to take a share in, the legislative process, which ceases to be the sole prerogative of the professional politician.

[20] J S Mill, *Essays on Politics and Culture*, Gertrude Himmelfarb (ed) (Peter Smith, 1973) 186.

The first instrument to be considered is the device of the primary election. Primary elections increase the degree of choice available to the voter under the first-past-the-post system of election by enabling her to choose between candidates of her favoured party. But in Britain, and indeed in most democracies other than the United States, primary elections are generally restricted to party members. This means that only a small, and, in Britain, a diminishing, proportion of the electorate can take part in choosing the candidate of their favoured party. The primary, therefore, offers only very limited opportunities for participation. But, in 2007, David Cameron, the Conservative leader, instituted an open primary election in London to choose a Conservative candidate for mayor of London which was open to all London voters, regardless of whether they were Conservative party members or not. This open primary was a radical and imaginative extension of the idea of primary elections. Some suggested that a primary of this sort would be open to tactical manipulation by the Conservatives' opponents, who would deliberately choose the Conservative candidate least likely to win. In fact, however, the primary resulted in a victory for Boris Johnson, the most popular of the candidates on offer, and the one most likely to win the election for the Conservatives. This kind of primary election may well constitute a precedent and, if it does, the candidate selection process will be opened up, and a wider range of voters will be encouraged to participate in this selection.

The second instrument—the single transferable vote—involves a change in the electoral system, from first-past-the-post to a specific system of proportional representation. Many had hoped that, through proportional representation, devolution would help to open up and regenerate the political system in Scotland and Wales. Proportional representation has certainly led to fairer representation in Scotland and Wales in that the number of representatives that a party wins in the devolved legislatures is far closer to their share of the vote than is the case with elections to the House of Commons. But, although proportional representation and the prevalence of coalition and minority government have led to new forms of executive government, and also to legislative reform, the hope that it would open up the political system in Scotland and Wales has remained unfulfilled. There is an obvious reason for this. It is to be found in the type of proportional representation that has been adopted for elections to the devolved bodies.

The particular system used, which is based on elections to the lower house in Germany, the Bundestag, combines two elements—a constituency element by means of which candidates are elected by the first-past-the-post system as in elections to the House of Commons, and a list element, to secure proportionality, by means of which candidates are elected through a party list.[21] The party list is a highly rigid one, with the ordering of the candidates being entirely determined by the party organisation rather than by the voter. The voter can do nothing to change the decisions made by the party machine. Anyone chosen for a high

---

[21] A fuller description of this system can be found in Bogdanor, *Power and the People*, 70–2.

position on the party list by one of the major parties is, therefore, virtually sure of election whatever the voters may think of her. The voter is restricted to voting for a party list. She cannot choose between candidates on the list. Thus the electoral system, rather than widening choice for the voter, has served, if anything, to strengthen the position of the political parties. The position of the voter is in fact weaker under such rigid list systems of proportional representation than it is under the first-past-the-post system. Under that system the voter has the opportunity, admittedly a merely theoretical one in a safe constituency, of removing an MP from the House of Commons by voting against her. Under rigid party list systems of proportional representation, by contrast, there is no such opportunity, a high position on the list of a major party virtually guaranteeing election. In the eighteenth century, the electors of Middlesex, the constituency of John Wilkes, declared, in a petition to the government of Lord North, that 'if any power on earth can dictate our choice, and prescribe who shall and who shall not become candidates to represent us in Parliament, we may talk of our rights, and take pride in our freedom, but in fact we have none'.[22] That is the situation which faces the voter under a rigid list system of proportional representation.

Of course, not every system of proportional representation has this characteristic. Proportional representation is not the name of a single electoral system, but a generic term referring to a wide range of different systems with every different political effects. Discussion of different systems of proportional representation is often dismissed as a waste of time, of interest only to obsessives and those with an interest in the esoteric. Yet the differences between the various systems can be of crucial importance in relation to the health of the democratic polity.

The key distinction lies between an electoral system which, by allowing the voter to choose between candidates of the same party, opens up the political party, and a system, such as the rigid list, which takes control away from the voter and gives it to the party machine. There are a number of proportional electoral systems which have the effect, unlike the rigid list system, of widening the range of electoral choice. These proportional systems are known as personalised systems of proportional representation. Of these systems, the only one currently used in Britain is the single transferable vote, at present used for all elections in Northern Ireland, except elections to the House of Commons, and, since 2007, for elections to Scottish local authorities. Under this system, the voter casts her vote preferentially—'1', '2', '3' etc. rather than with an 'X' as in the first-past-the-post system. The voter thus selects not only a party but also a candidate. She is able to distinguish between candidates in terms of their policy differences, and, in so doing, to cast votes across party lines if she wishes. She may, for example, be a Labour supporter but a strong Eurosceptic. She might then rank Labour Party candidates in terms of their Euroscepticism. But, alternatively, if her Euroscepticism is stronger than her Party allegiance, she might rank her preferences across parties. Her first

---

[22] Quoted in P Paterson, *The Selectorate: The Case for Primary Elections in Britain* (MacGibbon and Kee, 1967) 184.

preference might be for the Labour candidate least sympathetic to Europe, her second for a Conservative Eurosceptic, her third for a UKIP candidate. Alternatively, she may decide to use her vote to ensure a better representation of women or ethnic minorities in the House of Commons by using her preferences across party lines for female or ethnic minority candidates.

The single transferable vote system thus combines a general election with a primary election. But this primary election is not one confined to party members, it is one in which every voter automatically takes part simply by the act of voting. Under STV, the primary does not involve holding a separate election at which many fewer will participate than in a general election, but is, instead, conceptually combined with a general election.

We have now identified two institutional instruments which might open up the political system—a reformed system of party primaries and use of the single transferable vote system of proportional representation. The referendum is a third instrument of participation. So far its use has been strictly limited to those questions defined as 'constitutional' by governments, which have often used it as a tactical weapon. The referendum in Britain remains a weapon under the control of the political class, not, as in countries with codified constitutions, an instrument whose use is determined by the constitution.[23] But the referendum can, in principle, yield legislative power to the people. It is possible that the people will in due course be able to wrest it from the political class so that it comes to be used on occasions when the political class may not want it to be used. The initiative is certainly an instrument that can be used against the wishes of the political class. There is already a precedent for its use in local government; and the initiative, too, is an instrument capable of radical extension.

These instruments of direct democracy open up the political system by enabling the people to share legislative power with political leaders. But they by no means exhaust the possibilities of increasing popular engagement with politics. One striking and radical democratic innovation occurred in the Canadian province of British Columbia in 2004. In that year the government of the province established a Citizens Assembly on Electoral Reform by means of which a randomly chosen group of electors was invited to propose a new electoral system for the province. The government of the province promised to put the system decided upon by the Assembly to the people through a referendum. This meant that the Citizens Assembly would not be a mere talking shop. Its deliberations would have a practical result. The Chair of the Assembly emphasised that the Assembly was a huge innovation in democratic participation, declaring that 'Never before in modern history has a democratic government given to unelected 'ordinary' citizens the power to review an important public policy, then seek from all citizens approval of any proposed changes to that policy. The British Columbia Citizens Assembly

---

[23] See V Bogdanor, 'Western Europe' in D Butler and A Ranney (eds) *Referendums Around the World*, (American Enterprise Institute, 1994) 24–97.

on Electoral Reform has had this power and responsibility and, throughout its life, complete independence from government'.[24]

The Assembly was selected randomly to include one man and one woman from each of the 79 electoral districts, together with two Aboriginal members and an independent chair. Every member was paid an honorarium and arrangements were made, where necessary, for child care, so as to ensure that all members could play a full part in the proceedings. The Assembly collected written and oral evidence, holding 50 public hearings over a twelve month period. Its report, 'Making Every Vote Count' proposed the single transferable vote system. This was duly put to referendum, but it failed to achieve the qualified 60% majority which the government declared to be necessary to implement the change. The Assembly nevertheless demonstrated, in the words of one commentator 'how extraordinary ordinary citizens are when given an important task and the resources and independence to do it right. Over the eleven-month course of the Assembly, only one of the 161 members withdrew and attendance was close to perfect—the Assembly members demonstrated a quality of citizenship that inspired us all'.[25] There is to be a second referendum on the electoral system in British Columbia in 2009. In Ontario in 2007, a similarly constituted Citizen's Assembly on Electoral Reform reported and recommended a variant on the German electoral system. This proposal, however, was rejected by the electorate in Ontario, and the referendum, the first in Ontario since 1924, attracted the lowest turnout level ever in the province, 53%.

The experiments in British Columbia and Ontario show that it is perfectly feasible to extend participation in a modern democracy. The principle of selection ensured that the assemblies were representative, with an equal opportunity for all to participate, and so participation need not be geared to the better-off and the better-educated. The experiments show that there is considerable potential for government and decision-making by those who are not professional politicians and who do not belong to the political class. There is, surely, scope for using this principle of selection by lot in Britain, not only in the choice of citizens assemblies, as in British Columbia and Ontario, but perhaps also in local institutions. It would be possible, for example, to experiment with selection by lot in local councils and parish councils by providing for some of the members of these bodies to be chosen in this way. The rotation of those selected by lot on a regular basis would ensure that all citizens enjoyed a reasonable chance to be selected. This method of choosing representatives reflects a fundamental premiss of democracy that 'all citizens have the right to and are capable of taking part in political decisions . . . Citizens can be legislators'.[26]

---

[24] Quoted by G Smith, *Beyond the Ballot—57 democratic innovations from around the world. A report commissioned by POWER: An Independent Inquiry into Britain's Democracy*, 75. This report gives an excellent account of various methods of widening participation.

[25] Smith, ibid, 75–6.

[26] Smith, ibid, 89.

Analysis of these various methods of increasing popular participation shows that Britain, like most other democracies, has hardly begun to utilise the potential of the people. The task of the next phase of constitutional reform, surely, is to utilise that potential, to transform Britain into a popular constitutional state.

IV

Political authority in a democracy is sustained, in the last resort, by ideas, by a public philosophy; and a country's constitutional arrangements are bound to be deeply affected by that public philosophy. During the twentieth century that public philosophy was primarily social democratic. Today it has become liberal again, if not even radical, seeking as it does to secure liberty by cutting power into pieces, the letimotif of the era of constitutional reform. The new constitution is a constitution that limits the power of government, and the idea of limited government is in essence a liberal idea. It may be said indeed to be a central idea of liberalism. The new constitution, although largely implemented by a government calling itself New Labour, exemplifies in essence a philosophy of liberalism. That is a striking paradox, since it is often assumed that the classic age of liberalism lay in the nineteenth century, and that it came to an end with the coming of the First World War. But the constitutional reforms implemented since 1997 resurrect an ideology that has long been regarded as having been superseded.

There is a further paradox about the liberal era. During the classic age of liberalism in government, in the nineteenth century, before the coming of universal suffrage, government in Britain was formally unlimited. Few in the liberal era called for an enacted constitution or for formal limits on the power of government. At a time when the franchise was limited, it was generally believed that governments would be effectively limited by social forces and by the power of educated public opinion. Some liberals rested their hopes on the continuation of a restricted franchise. Others, such as John Stuart Mill, accepted democracy but sought refuge in devices such as the university vote and the single transferable vote method of proportional representation which, so they hoped, would allow educated opinion to continue to make itself felt; local government, so Mill believed, could help to train the newly enfranchised in democratic ways. Bagehot was optimistic for a different reason. He believed that deference was the social force which sustained the constitution, and that so long as Britain remained a deferential society, power would remain with the traditional elites who would continue to use it in a restrained manner. In this way liberty would continue to be protected without the need for formal limits upon government. What both Mill and Bagehot hoped to achieve was to integrate the customs and attitudes of the Whig and Tory ruling classes in the nineteenth century into a wider political culture.

Dicey had shared this point of view. He, too, had believed that the force of educated public opinion would be sufficient to constrain government. But his optimism had been given a rude shock when, in 1885, Gladstone proposed to give

Home Rule to Ireland, a reform which Dicey thought harmful in itself and also one to which most voters were opposed. The crisis over Home Rule seemed to show that a government could implement a fundamental change in the constitution even though the majority disapproved of it. Public opinion, swayed, Dicey believed, by ignoble motives, was pressing governments to expand their powers over society. Dicey particularly condemned the 1905–1915 Liberal government for enacting social legislation which, by providing benefits to the indigent, the irresponsible and the unemployed, undermined individual responsibility and took the country too far in the direction of socialism. To prevent these depredations he believed that it was now necessary to seek formal checks upon government.

The main formal check which Dicey advocated was the referendum. He was in fact the first in Britain to propose it in an article in *The Quarterly Review* in 1890. After 1911, he pressed it with even greater intensity to fill what he regarded as a gap in the constitution. In the eighth edition of his great work, *An Introduction to the Study of the Law of the Constitution*, published in 1915, the last edition which he was personally able to supervise, he wrote a long introduction advocating use of the referendum.[27] It would hardly have occurred to Dicey that the gap in the constitution which he had noticed might be filled more satisfactorily by the judges. Yet, at the beginning of the twenty-first century, it can be seen that it is to the judges that we must look rather than the referendum to secure protection against an overweening executive. It is not perhaps surprising that Dicey was unable to foresee this development. In the liberal era during which Dicey lived, the judges were, partly as a result of his teaching, generally deferential to the executive. It was not until the 1960s that their stance began to change.

Dicey shared with his great opponent over Irish Home Rule, Gladstone, opposition to what the Victorians called 'construction', the idea that government could, through social and economic measures, reconstruct society in accordance with a blueprint. Both Dicey and Gladstone were strong believers in limited government. But, during the early twentieth century, the brand of liberalism which believed in limited government was to be superseded by another brand of liberalism which legitimised an increase in the power of the state. This was the so-called 'New Liberalism', championed by men such as Hobson, Hobhouse and Graham Wallas. The New Liberalism was an attempt to reconcile liberalism and social democracy. It favoured a strong executive so that the machinery of government could be used to improve economic conditions and social welfare. The ideas of the New Liberals were highly influential. Many of their ideas on welfare reform were implemented during the Prime Ministership of H H Asquith between 1908 and 1916, through the influence, in particular, of two of the radical members of the government, Lloyd George, Chancellor of the Exchequer from 1908 to 1915, and Winston Churchill, President of the Board of Trade from 1908 to 1910. The reforms of the

---

[27] In this introduction he deprecated what he regarded as other dangerous constitutional reforms such as proportional representation and female suffrage. See my contribution to the symposium celebrating the centenary of the first publication of *The Law of the Constitution*, V Bogdanor, 'Dicey and Constitutional Reform' (1985) *Public Law*.

New Liberals, and in particular Lloyd George's National Insurance Act of 1911, providing for the introduction of health and unemployment insurance, laid the foundation on which the Attlee government, elected in 1945, built the welfare state.

The term 'New Liberalism', however, was in part a fudge, masking the fact that there might be some incompatibility between liberalism as a creed and social democracy. Much of the legislation that the Asquith Liberal government enacted—such as, for example, the National Insurance Act which demanded compulsory contributions from employer and employee, and the Trade Union Act of 1913, which required trade unionists specifically to contract out if they did not wish to contribute to the political fund used to support the Labour Party—was hardly liberal in the sense of expanding individual freedom of choice; it involved instead an element of compulsion, while some of the motivation for these reforms derived from movements such as the Fabians and the 'National Efficiency' schools whose *raison d'etre* was as much that of improving the efficiency of the state as of liberating the individual. There were some elements in the reforming coalition which were quite explicitly anti-liberal. From our modern perspective, therefore, it can be seen that liberalism and social democracy were in fact diverging after 1906, and that social democracy was coming to supplant liberalism of the traditional sort. Social democracy and liberalism are different and perhaps incompatible philosophies, the one legitimising strong and centralised government, the other favouring limited government and, in modern times, constitutional reform as well which, so most modern liberals believe, is needed if government is to remain within its proper limits.

The period from 1906 to 1979 saw the growth of social democracy, the doctrine that society and the economy could and ought to be transformed by state action so as to improve the condition of the people. During this period, traditional liberalism was a political philosophy in decline. There was no need, so it was believed, for formal limits on the power of the state. A beneficent and public-spirited elite of politicians and civil servants could be trusted to serve the common good; that was a belief which Keynes and Beveridge, both of whom were members of the Liberal Party, shared. The philosophy behind the New Liberalism and behind social democracy, though generally unarticulated, was, therefore, Benthamite. The state existed to achieve the greatest happiness of the greatest number. In that quest notions of fundamental law and natural rights were little more than an outmoded hindrance. Natural rights, Bentham had declared in his pamphlet, *Anarchical Fallacies*, were nonsense, and natural and imprescrictible rights of the kind laid out in the French Declaration of the Rights of Man 'nonsense on stilts'. The state needed to be freed from the quaint shibboleths of the past if it were to be able effectively to serve the public interest, the needs of the people. The people seemed to share this view. With the achievement of universal suffrage in 1918 and 1928, the newly mobilised electorate proved to be less interested in completing the liberal democratic programme of constitutional reform than in improving social and economic conditions. Politics became the politics of the democratic class struggle, and the nineteenth century type of party of which Gladstone's Liberals were a paradigm, the party of opinion, found itself in sharp decline. The liberal programme seemed to have been completed, and the liberal movement played out. The development of the two major parties—the Conservatives and Labour— around the issues of the democratic class conflict, made constitutional issues appear irrelevant. Democracy and the welfare of the people were best secured by tightly organised mass political parties, and so, in Britain, the debate on participation came to an end. The decline of the liberal and radical movement, with its interest in constitutional reform, mirrored developments elsewhere. The first edition of *The International Encyclopedia of the Social Sciences*, published in 1932, had a long entry on the 'Referendum'. The new edition, published in 1968, had no entry on the subject at all.[28]

The year, 1968, however, proved a turning-point, in Britain as in other democracies; it is not accidental that many of those in the vanguard of the constitutional reform movement in Britain, and many of the ministers in the Labour government which implemented the reforms, were deeply influenced by the events of that year. It was in 1968 that the first signs of the unfreezing of political institutions became visible. There is a paradox about the rebels of 1968. The rhetoric of the rebellion was neo-Marxist, and the rebels believed themselves to be developing doctrines from the writings of Marx and his modern disciples such as Herbert Marcuse. In reality, however, they were rediscovering the doctrines of liberal and radical reformers at the beginning of the twentieth century. The main catchword of the rebels was *participation*, and the basic message of the revolt was distrust of the mass party and other mediating institutions, and of all the large bureaucracies that had come to dominate modern representative democracies.

In place of such institutions the rebels favoured direct election, party primaries, party reform, the recall, the initiative—instruments of direct democracy which would, so it was believed, enable the people to hold their leaders genuinely to account. The aim, in the words of one of the rebels of the 1968 revolt, was to secure 'what is seen as a fuller, and more genuine, version of the old democratic ideal'.[29] The rebels of 1968 sought a more participatory democracy, not a more humane collectivism. They owed little to Marx, but a good deal to Rousseau and even more, though most of them were hardly aware of it, to John Stuart Mill. The instruments of direct democracy which they favoured were less part of the armoury of Marxism than of the radical liberalism of the beginning of the twentieth century. They were elements in the programme of those radical liberals who believed that the liberal programme had not been completed by the great constitutional reforms of the nineteenth century, but needed extension so as to bring the people more fully within the pale of the constitution.

Those who favoured this new radical programme saw themselves as being on the Left. They did not, however, belong to the traditional left, the left that had

---

[28] M Steed, 'Participation through Western Democratic Institutions' in G Parry (ed) *Participation in Politics* (Manchester, Manchester University Press, 1972) 96.

[29] A Arblaster, 'Participation, Control and Conflict', in Parry (ed) *Participation in Politics*, 55.

defined itself as state socialist or social democratic. They were helped by the decline of this movement, by the decline of the traditional Left, the decline of socialism. Since 1979, the fundamental idea of socialism, the idea that the state can reconstruct the economy and society so as to improve standards of social welfare, has found itself in retreat. The age of rationalism, the idea that governments can successfully plan for the future, is dead. Tony Blair's invention of New Labour was in part an attempt to provide some sort of ideological accommodation for that retreat. The new constitution, although largely a product of New Labour's constitutional reform programme since 1997, reflects, in part, a movement away from social democracy and a return to older, nineteenth century ideas of liberalism and diversity. From this point of view, 1997 marks not so much the beginning of a new era, but the return of themes from an old era, from the nineteenth century rather than the short twentieth century, the heyday of social democracy, the years between 1906 to 1979. In this sense, then, the constitutional reform programme initiated by New Labour is not new at all, but very old, a regression to the distant past, back far beyond the twentieth century, to the nineteenth, to a philosophy that prized diversity as an end in itself, a philosophy that was highly sceptical of the benefits of 'construction', the idea that the state can engineer social outcomes. Insofar as constitutional reform is concerned, the triumph of New Labour is in reality a belated triumph for the nineteenth century liberal and radical movement.

It is, in the last resort, ideological forces which determine constitutional and political forms.[30] Perhaps the era of constitutional reform since 1997 has brought out a hitherto latent tension between our inherited political forms and a new ideological force, or rather an old ideological force which has come, in nearly every advanced democracy, to be resurrected, namely liberal constitutionalism. It is of course unclear how this tension will eventually be resolved. We are only part of the way towards resolving it—we are, as it were, children of the transition. We have left Egypt but remain some distance from the Promised Land. How the tension is to be resolved, whether it is resolved by transforming a constitutional state into a popular constitutional state, cannot now be predicted. But the attempt to make our constitutional and political forms congruent with ideological forces, with our public philosophy, could prove one of the fundamental issues of our time. The future, of course, remains to be written, and no one can foretell how it will be written. What is certain, however, is that in a democracy it will be written not only by the politicians but by the people. In a democracy, the people are not only characters in the drama but also authors of that drama; it falls to them, therefore, to write the next scene in the play. What this means is that our constitutional future has yet to be written, and that it is the people who will have to write it.

---

[30] This conflict between ideological forces and political forms was the central theme of the liberal political sociologist, M Ostrogorski, in his great work, *Democracy and the Organisation of Political Parties* (1902). See also R Barker and X Howard-Johnston, 'The Politics and Political Ideas of Moisei Ostrogorski', (1975) *Political Studies*, vol XXIII, 415.

Index